ATHEISM FROM THE REFORMATION TO THE ENLIGHTENMENT

ATHEISM FROM THE REFORMATION TO THE ENLIGHTENMENT

Edited by
MICHAEL HUNTER
and
DAVID WOOTTON

CLARENDON PRESS · OXFORD

1992

Oxford University Press, Walton Street, Oxford OX2 6DP
Oxford New York Toronto
Delhi Bombay Calcutta Madras Karachi
Petaling Jaya Singapore Hong Kong Tokyo
Nairobi Dar es Salaam Cape Town
Melbourne Auckland
and associated companies in
Berlin Ibadan

Oxford is a trade mark of Oxford University Press

Published in the United States
by Oxford University Press, New York

British Library Cataloguing in Publication Data
Data available

Library of Congress Cataloging in Publication Data
Atheism from the reformation to the enlightenment / edited by Michael
Hunter and David Wootton
Includes index
1. Atheism—Europe—History.   I. Hunter, Michael Cyril William.
II. Wootton, David, 1952–
BL2765.E85A84   1992   211'.8—dc20   92–3324
ISBN 0–19–822736–1

Typeset by Cambridge Composing (UK) Ltd
Printed and bound in
Great Britain by Biddles Ltd.,
Guildford and King's Lynn

CONTENTS

NOTES ON CONTRIBUTORS

DAVID BERMAN is Senior Lecturer in Philosophy and Fellow of Trinity College, Dublin.

SILVIA BERTI is Ricercatore of Modern History at La Sapienza University, Rome.

NICHOLAS DAVIDSON is Lecturer in History at the University of Leicester.

TULLIO GREGORY is Professor of History of Philosophy at La Sapienza University, Rome, and Director of the Lessico Intelletuale Europeo.

MICHAEL HUNTER is Reader in History at Birkbeck College, University of London.

ALAN CHARLES KORS is Professor of History at the University of Pennsylvania.

RICHARD H. POPKIN is Professor Emeritus at Washington University, St Louis, and Adjunct Professor of History and Philosophy at the University of California, Los Angeles.

NIGEL SMITH is Fellow and Tutor in English at Keble College, Oxford, and Lecturer in English at the University of Oxford.

RICHARD TUCK is Lecturer in History at the University of Cambridge and Fellow of Jesus College, Cambridge.

DAVID WOOTTON holds the Lansdowne Chair of the Humanities at the University of Victoria, British Columbia.

Introduction

MICHAEL HUNTER and DAVID WOOTTON

One of the great differences between our world and that of our ancestors is the relatively limited role that religion plays in modern society, and the extent to which unbelief has come to seem rationally defensible and morally respectable. This may not be the most important transformation that separates our world from the Middle Ages and the early modern period: nobody would deny the overriding significance of the industrial, scientific, and democratic revolutions. But any account of the major transformations that have given rise to the modern world would have to give the advance of atheism, agnosticism, and religious unbelief in general a central place.

This book is concerned with the early history of this process: with those individuals who more or less overtly rejected religious faith in the period from 1520 to 1780. The beginning of our period is marked by the first expressions of fear that unbelief and irreligion were on the rise, in the context of the Reformation and the new attitudes towards religious commitment engendered by that event. Its end sees the sustained and systematic attacks on Christianity mounted by philosophers such as Hume and d'Holbach, building on and adapting the new polemical weapons furnished by the intellectual changes of the seventeenth century and the Enlightenment.

This, one would think, ought to be a classic field of enquiry within the history of ideas. But if one compares the literature on early modern scientific thought, political theory, or theology with that on irreligion, the first thing one is bound to notice is the absence of any sustained tradition of intellectual enquiry into the rise of unbelief. In the past few years a major shift has taken place: a series of important studies have appeared that approach this subject in new and provocative ways. But the authors of these studies have been working in isolation from one another, and little attempt has been made to correlate and compare the different approaches and to make an assessment of their relative strengths and weaknesses.

Our goal in compiling this volume has been to bring together a number of essays, either written specially for the occasion or translated for the first time into English, which cover a wide range as regards chronology, geography, and types of approach. Our aim was to include accounts of a representative range of countries (in fact, we have concentrated on Britain, France, Italy, and The Netherlands); to publish studies spanning the sixteenth century to the eighteenth, though with greater emphasis on the latter part of the period, when heterodox ideas were expressed more openly and in a more sophisticated form; and to exemplify different ways of looking at the subject, ranging from broad surveys or expositions of the ideas of leading irreligious writers to detailed studies—often of more obscure figures—which throw significant light on the networks by which irreligious ideas were disseminated and the milieux in which they were divulged. The variety of approach is reflected by a noticeable disparity of length between different chapters, some giving definitive accounts of novel research, while others represent more concise essays in reinterpretation.

One of the difficulties in approaching this topic is an elusiveness that owes something to the inhibitions imposed on free-thinkers by the attitudes of the orthodox authorities of the day, but something also to the conceptual problems involved in defining exactly what it is that is being studied. We have used the term 'atheism' in our title; this seems to us best to encapsulate the articulate assault on Christianity and, often, on religion in general that is to be found in this period. But we would readily admit that it is neither helpful nor even feasible to attempt to concentrate exclusively on figures who were overtly atheistic according to a modern definition of that term. In part, this is because orthodox contemporaries were prone to conflate with 'atheism' a range of positions that appeared to them to militate towards it, particularly deistic formulations of religious belief that played down the role of revelation and an active personal deity. In addition, the dangers associated with open expression of irreligious sentiments encouraged many to temper their sceptical opinions, at least in public. Such considerations render this a particularly treacherous area of study, while doing nothing to reduce its significance.

Alongside the problems posed by the study of unbelief itself, one must place the difficulty of establishing its relationship to the process of secularization that has taken place since the Reformation.[1] Unbelief is not by any means the only cause of secularization. Thus, attempts by orthodox apologists to establish religion on a secure, rational basis often had an unintended secularizing effect, in that the criteria of rationality could oust the sanction of the supernatural. More important has been the effect of religious pluralism, the separation of Church and State, and the view that religion was essentially a private and personal matter, which often contributed to the secularization of key areas of public life, such as education, even when most individuals retained strong religious commitments. Such secularization would have horrified Luther and Calvin as much as St Carlo Borromeo, though it has now become the norm in most Western democracies. But even if the origins of secularization have been religious as well as irreligious, its advance has slowly made it possible for unbelievers to claim and win the same rights as believers. Nowhere in the West does unbelief remain a crime, though it was not, for example, until the 1961 US Supreme Court decision in *Torcaso* v. *Watkins* that American atheists established the right to hold state office— and along with it, it is presumed, the right to vote, serve on juries, and testify in court—despite the continuing existence of some state laws to the contrary. Moreover, there can be no doubt that the progress and legitimization of unbelief has in turn contributed to the process of secularization. Irreligion

---

[1] For a recent discussion of the beginnings of the process of secularization in England, see C. J. Sommerville, 'The Destruction of Religious Culture in Pre-Industrial England', *Journal of Religious History*, 15 (1988), 76–93. See also Peter Burke, 'Religion and Secularization', in Peter Burke (ed.), *The New Cambridge Modern History*, xiii (Cambridge, 1979), 293–317; and W. J. Bouwsma, 'The Secularization of Society in the Seventeenth Century', in *Proceedings of the Thirteenth International Congress of Historical Sciences* (Moscow, 1970).

has not replaced belief, and may never do so; but it has established itself alongside it everywhere.

Partly because of issues like these, it seemed essential at the outset to survey the state of the field, examining the historiography of the subject and the different views on it that currently exist. David Wootton has undertaken this in the chapter which follows this introduction. In it he evaluates earlier writings on the subject, commenting particularly on the attacks on traditional histories of rationalism mounted in the post-war years by widely influential authors such as Lucien Febvre and P. O. Kristeller. These attacks had a powerful inhibiting effect on the study of irreligion, an effect that still continues. Wootton then looks at the question of definition, considering the origins of the terminology used to describe atheism, its relationship to heterodox opinion that was actually expressed, and the way in which both may have changed in the course of the period. He also deals with the problems caused by the fact that the expression of irreligious views was widely proscribed, encouraging the adoption of subterfuge in this regard. Lastly, he examines the question of periodization. The balance of the coverage of this book itself reflects the fact that the period *c.*1680–1715 was a pivotal one in the emergence of atheism: Wootton shows why this was the case, illustrating the extent to which the growth of explicit formulations of irreligion was a by-product of major shifts in the European sensibility at this time, though it would be wrong to underestimate the extent to which irreligious weapons were available earlier. In the course of laying out the current state of the field on each of these issues, Wootton provides a survey of the relevant literature that should be of value to all those who wish to pursue this important topic for themselves.

We then move to Nicholas Davidson's study of irreligious ideas and their expression in Italy from 1500 to 1700. In the early modern period Italy was proverbial as the home of atheism, as reflected in the views of a succession of commentators from Roger Ascham onwards, and Davidson takes a detailed look at the reasons for this atheistical image. He considers the range of sources for atheistic ideas that existed among the learned, sources derived particularly from classical antiquity, but he also indicates the extent to which scepticism was in evidence at a non-learned level: here, a range of ideas was to be found that may have owed something to the views of Anabaptist and other radical Protestant groups, but that went beyond them in the extent of heterodoxy involved. Thus, apart from commenting on notorious cases of educated infidels like Giulio Cesare Vanini, Davidson also provides examples of irreligion at a more popular level, drawing on the work of Carlo Ginzburg and on his own research into cases which came before the Venetian Inquisition. The result is at once to give a substantial amount of information about the actual expression of irreligious opinion in the period, and to illustrate the interrelationship between educated and popular ideas. In addition, Davidson shows how, in Italy as elsewhere, concern about atheism increased in the latter part of the seventeenth century, linked partly to anxieties about the atheistic implications of the new science, anxieties which had existed since the time of Galileo.

If Italy was notorious for atheism in the sixteenth and early seventeenth centuries, the same was equally true of early seventeenth-century France. Indeed, in the 1620s the Minim friar and Christian apologist Marin Mersenne went so far as to assert that Paris contained 50,000 atheists. It is with Mersenne that Tullio Gregory begins his chapter's reassessment of Pierre Charron's *De la sagesse*. Along with the *Essais* of Michel de Montaigne, this is one of the key texts for understanding the culture of the so-called *libertins érudits* of seventeenth-century France. The context was one in which the disorienting effect of the Wars of Religion, seen first in Montaigne, was cross-fertilized with the impact of the sceptical tradition of antiquity and with a relativism born of the Voyages of Discovery. The result was to lead to the emergence of an ethos attacking custom, undermining the authority of universal consent, and, instead, lionizing reason: this, as Gregory cogently argues, had the effect of undercutting the authority of religion and secularizing morality. Though Charron's work has sometimes been interpreted as a fideist tract, Gregory convincingly refutes this. Only the extent to which the *libertins* advocated external conformity with the mores of the society in which they lived reduced the radical impact of the critique of traditional values that Charron expressed.

In the shift towards a more overt expression of irreligious ideas, an important figure was Thomas Hobbes. Hobbes's actual religious views have been the subject of extensive debate, but there can be no doubt of his long-term significance in this connection, both for the irreligious implications of the materialist philosophy that he so cogently expressed in *Leviathan*, and for his argument in that work that religious authority should be vested in the secular arm. In his chapter Richard Tuck makes an important clarification of Hobbes's thought by illustrating the point at which he moved to an essentially heterodox position. He argues that, in his *De cive*, Hobbes subscribed to the tradition stretching from sixteenth-century Italian humanism to the Enlightenment that allied essentially deistic philosophical attitudes with the advocacy of civil religion. Such ideas could be quite orthodox, as seen in such authors as the Dutch intellectual Hugo Grotius or the Anglican divine Henry Hammond, who combined such a philosophy with the belief that the Church, as an interpreter of revealed truth, should have an authoritative role. If this was Hobbes's early position, it was one that he abandoned in *Leviathan*, where he argued that the civil sovereign rather than the Church had proper authority in religious matters, and effectively denied that Christianity had a special status, treating it as comparable to any other civil religion. Such views made it more feasible than hitherto to mount an open attack on Christianity.

Tuck argues that Hobbes's change of position is to be read in the context of the state of affairs in England in the years following the Civil War, when monarchical authority was toppled and many traditional values were brought in question. Certainly there was much radical questioning of religious doctrines at this time, and some have seen such attitudes as symptomatic of an attack on religion and the dawning of a new, more secular society, a tendency seen particularly in Marxist historians like Christopher Hill. The issue of the relationship between atheism and the religious heterodoxy of the period is addressed by Nigel Smith in his chapter. He points to the danger of accepting conflations of differing positions made by hostile contemporaries, and to the tendency of historians to secularize essentially religious thinkers. On the other hand, he examines the extent to which certain radical figures did pick up ideas which bear some similarity to the arguments against religion expounded in other chapters in this book. Examples are Richard Overton's mortalism; Laurence Clarkson's pantheism, which overlapped with deistic views of the eighteenth century; and William Walwyn's indebtedness to Montaigne and Charron and the sceptical crisis that inspired their ideas. Smith also comments further on the interchange of popular and learned ideas analysed by Davidson, in the context of the wide and ingenious speculation that characterized English thought during the Interregnum.

If the critique of Christianity seen in these works—and, some would say, even in the writings of Vanini, Charron, and Hobbes—may have been incipient rather than actual, by the later years of the seventeenth century much more overt strategies were in evidence. One important and neglected source of anti-Christian ideas is surveyed by Richard Popkin in his chapter on the circulation of Jewish polemics against Christianity at this time. In general, Jews were segregated and their views were forcibly repressed in early modern Europe, but there were exceptions to this, particularly in the relatively freer conditions of The Netherlands. Here, as elsewhere, Christian intellectuals believed that the Last Judgement should be preceded by the conversion of the Jews, and this led to the circulation of Jewish religious polemics, which their enemies believed they should be familiar with so as to be better able to refute them. Such treatises were often written by Jews who knew enough about Christianity to make their assaults on it all the more deadly, and Popkin chronicles the stages by which the writings of authors like Saul Levi Mortera and Isaac Orobio de Castro entered general circulation, first in manuscript and then, by the later eighteenth century, in print. He also points out how arguments taken from such books became 'part of the irreligious arsenal of the Enlightenment', fuelling the attack on orthodox Christianity by authors like Anthony Collins and the Baron d'Holbach.

As Popkin acknowledges, Jewish texts were not the only openly anti-Christian treatises in circulation by the time of the Enlightenment. In addition, during the seventeenth and early eighteenth centuries various anonymous, subversive compilations began to enjoy a clandestine circulation, among them the *Theophrastus redivivus* and the *Traité des trois imposteurs*. Both of these were compendia of overtly anti-Christian sentiments culled from such authors as Vanini, Charron, La Mothe le Vayer, and Hobbes—in other words, the pantheon already encountered in earlier chapters—while the *Traité des trois imposteurs* added a new and more dangerous ingredient, in the form of the ideas of a figure who had himself emerged from the Jewish background surveyed by Popkin, Baruch Spinoza. Silvia Berti's chapter breaks new ground in establishing the links between the text of the *Traité des trois imposteurs* and the works of Spinoza, and in reconstructing the circumstances in which the work was originally composed and published. Berti enables us to understand why the first edition of the *Traité des trois imposteurs* was accompanied by a life of Spinoza. She brings new evidence to bear to suggest that this treatise was composed not by Rousset de Missy in the 1710s, as recently claimed by Margaret Jacob, but at a slightly earlier date by the diplomat Jan Vroesen. In her painstaking demonstration of this, Berti throws important fresh light on the subversive networks that linked freethinkers and provided the materials for an open assault on Christianity in the late seventeenth and early eighteenth centuries. In addition, in her final section she clearly illustrates how Spinoza's ideas fuelled the irreligious tradition, though she argues that in some respects they acquired a cruder, more simplistically materialist edge in the hands of his interpreters than had been the case with his own expression of them.

With Michael Hunter's chapter we return to an actual case of articulate irreligion that ended up in the courts, rather similar to the case of Geoffroy Vallée, with which Wootton's chapter begins, or to some of those dealt with by Davidson. As with Davidson's cases, there is an interesting overlap here between oral and written culture: Aikenhead was a student, and he clearly derived a number of his ideas from books to which he had access, which evidently included the writings of Vanini and Spinoza. But what is interesting about Aikenhead is the ingenuity that he displayed in adapting such views, and Hunter argues that it was this outrageousness which provoked so explosive a reaction in the narrow context of Presbyterian Scotland, leading to Aikenhead's execution. This would make the case interesting in itself, but the unusual detail available renders it peculiarly illuminating in various broader respects: since written texts by Aikenhead have survived, as well as reports of oral outbursts on his part, it is possible to assess the relative significance of the two in fuelling concern about the growth of irreligious tendencies in the period; it is also possible to examine the interrelationship between orthodox anxieties and the actual expression of aggressively irreligious views.

Aikenhead's fate evidently made clear to others the need for circumspection, and this theme is illustrated in David Berman's contribution to this volume, which probes the role of subterfuge in the writings of two notorious English free-thinkers, Charles Blount and John Toland. In this subtle and challenging essay Berman draws both on Blount's and Toland's own statements and on analogues to them to illustrate the purpose and method of literary insinuation as a subversive technique. He asserts the significance of texts that were deliberately written in bad faith and that were intended for an audience capable of reading between the lines. In addition—taking up a theme developed elsewhere in his writings on free-thought—Berman makes illuminating use of the ideas of Freud. He suggests that, through negation, such writers made a deliberate attempt unconsciously to influence their less alert readers: in the words of one of their contemporaries, Sir Richard Blackmore, they were attempting 'the unwary to incline' with their carefully coded subversive messages.

Finally, with Alan Charles Kors's chapter, we reach the high tide of atheism in the French Enlightenment. While other thinkers—such as Denis Diderot—continued earlier, more ambivalent traditions, limiting their public utterances to an extreme form of deism, the Baron d'Holbach and Jacques-André Naigeon explicitly (if anonymously) advocated materialistic atheism. Once again, there is continuity with authors discussed in earlier chapters in the book: the views expounded by these militant atheists owed much to the heterodox traditions of the sixteenth and seventeenth centuries, and particularly to the writings of figures like Hobbes and Toland. Yet at the same time their bold systematization of a directly atheistic position was quite novel. Naigeon and d'Holbach attacked religion more openly than ever as irrational, dysfunctional, and to be deprecated. In its place they advocated a potentially progressive materialism, supremely rational and enlightened, although (as Kors points out) they remained aware of its limitations. If part of their inheritance was the subversive tradition of previous irreligious authors, they also owed much to the ideas of ostensibly orthodox thinkers like Descartes, Locke, and Newton, drawing out implications from the doctrines of naturalism, mechanism, and sensationalism from which others shied away. This is shown by Kors's survey of the reaction to the ideas of d'Holbach and Naigeon by Voltaire and others who were essentially theistic, for all their deistic critiques of orthodox Christianity: the debate exemplifies the bifurcated state of European culture at this time, and the way in which it contained the seeds of the parallel theistic and materialistic lines of thought that have coexisted ever since.

Of necessity, the coverage of a book like this is somewhat selective. We have considered d'Holbach and Naigeon but not Hume or Paine; Charron but not Montaigne; France and Italy but not Spain or Germany. In part, this reflects a deliberate attempt to achieve balance and to draw on the most interesting and suggestive work currently in progress in the field. But, even if we had aspired to completeness of coverage, its achievement would not have been feasible in a single volume. The whole object of this book is to open the field to wider study rather than to imply that its boundaries are already fixed. Our aim is to give a sense of the work that is currently being undertaken, and hence to stimulate wider interest in this crucial and neglected theme in the history of European culture.

At one time it might have seemed as if those involved in the history of atheism were engaged in an impossible quest for unbelievers who refused to be captured by history, if indeed they existed at all. But the work represented here shows that, by various means, their reality *can* be captured. Sometimes such rediscovery involves the reinterpretation of familiar figures along lines that will perforce be controversial, as in the work of Gregory included here or in David Wootton's work on Paolo Sarpi. But it often involves drawing attention to figures who have been largely ignored by historians—figures like the Friulian miller Menocchio, studied by Carlo Ginzburg, or Aikenhead, or Vroesen, to whom Hunter and Berti draw our attention. Increasingly, painstaking research is bringing to life a hidden world of subversive opinion and expression. The multifaceted character of unbelief in the early modern period, and the very varied nature of the sources to be drawn upon, means that there is probably no single 'history of atheism' to be written, any more than there is one cause of early modern unbelief, or any particular form of modern irreligion towards which it should be seen as developing. Rather than a history of unbelief, we offer here a representative sample of fresh reconstructions of it, some conflicting, many complementary. And we celebrate the return to cultivation of an important field of enquiry, for too long left fallow.

New Histories of Atheism

DAVID WOOTTON

La Béatitude des Chrestiens

In February 1574 Geoffroy Vallée, a nobleman from Orléans who had moved to Paris some ten years before, was executed for denying God. His body, and the pamphlet he had written and published, were burnt. Only one copy survived; we can read it alongside the record kept of his interrogation. Vallée had been in trouble for some time. Just over two years before, his family had begun a campaign (eventually successful) to have him declared mentally incompetent. He owed them money. And he had strange values: he was said to be a virgin and to have as many shirts as there were days of the year, sparing no expense to ensure that they were whiter than white. He may have suffered fits. And at one point, incarcerated, he tried to throw himself out of a window.

In May 1573 he found someone to publish the little book, *La Béatitude des chrestiens, ou le fleo de la foy*, which was to bring him to the scaffold. In six paragraphs he attacked in turn Catholicism, Protestantism, Anabaptism, libertinism, and atheism. Libertinism, which doubted revealed religion, but did not deny God's existence, he took to be the best of these. Vallée was angry that people accused him of denying God's existence; but he was hostile to all religions that inculcated fear. He was no heretic arguing for a better understanding of the New Testament: he seems to have had no time for miracles or for revealed truths, and to have had no sense that Christ represented a model to be followed. He thought one should believe only in things of which one could have personal, direct, reliable experience. Modern attempts to categorize his thought have been careless and anachronistic. The texts to which he himself refers are Ecclesiastes (which contains a blunt attack on the idea of life after death) and the first Psalm. From Ecclesiastes he may have learnt not only that there is a God, but that one should wear white and be wary of women. In both he saw an ideal of fraternity contrary to the injustice and violence of the society around him.

Was Vallée mad? His book is coherent; and when he published it he tried hard to get copies out of the country. He seems to have foreseen prosecution. His defence, of course, was that he was not of sound mind. Perhaps Vallée dared to publish because he thought he could never be convicted. Perhaps his family regarded him as mentally incompetent not because he was deranged, but merely because his view of the world was at odds with theirs. The doctors examined him; the judges, after some dispute, convicted him, though some insisted that only a madman would deny the truths of Christianity. Vallée saw his own death as a crucifixion, and cursed his neighbours' vineyards as he went to the scaffold.

Vallée's story epitomizes some of the problems we encounter in studying early modern unbelief. The one surviving copy of his book reminds us of the fragility and paucity of our sources. The notes we have of his interrogations—in which he by turns denied, reneged, explained, and, at the last, confessed he knew not what to say—remind us that there were few unbelievers so foolish as to speak freely; that most were careful to say nothing that an inquisitor could quote against them; and that, as a consequence, there are few who speak to us straightforwardly across the records of the past. His reading of the Bible reminds us that subversive ideas could be found anywhere, but only by those who sought them, and perhaps only by those who had been educated to seek them out. For Vallée did not read only orthodox books: he claimed to have read somewhere, though he would not say where, that Moses was a magician. The question of his mental competence brings home the difficulty we have in assessing the beliefs, convictions, and motives of men and women about whom we know so little. Above all, the few details we do have bring home to us that the history of unbelief is not a history only of abstractions, of arguments, of ideas. Vallée's physical beauty (he was 'bellum Vallensem'), the coat that was torn in two as he tried to escape his first captors, even his neighbours' vines, have a place in his story.

Historians and Unbelief

Vallée found no enduring place in history. Pierre Bayle, whose *Dictionnaire historique et critique* became a handbook for eighteenth-century atheists, thought he deserved one, and used him to illustrate one of his favourite themes, that reason, unchecked, must lead to unbelief.[1] In 1920 the surviving documents in his case were published by Frédéric Lachèvre.[2] In 1922 Henri Busson devoted several pages to him.[3] There has been no significant discussion of him since: this, too, makes his case typical, and the first question that any survey of the recent literature on unbelief must address is why the history of unbelief has for so long been a barren field of enquiry.

If one looks to nineteenth- and early twentieth-century accounts of the advance of unbelief (at least those written by free-thinkers), certain common characteristics are apparent: the history of unbelief is linked to the Renaissance, which encouraged secular learning; to the Reformation, which, in defending the rights of conscience, opened the way to freedom of thought; and to the Scientific Revolution, which encouraged a new spirit of rationalism and, where it did not come into direct conflict with religious modes of thought (as in the case of Galileo), was bound to be corrosive of them. The history of atheism could thus find its place within a wider evolutionary story, where Renaissance and Reforma-

---

[1] *The Dictionary Historical and Critical of Mr Peter Bayle* (5 vols.; London, 1734), v. 440–1.
[2] Frédéric Lachèvre, *Mélanges (Le Libertinage au XVIIᵉ siècle,* viii) (Paris, 1920; repr. Geneva, 1968), 5–59.
[3] Henri Busson, *Le Rationalisme dans la littérature française de la Renaissance,* rev. edn (Paris, 1957), 522–34. Busson's attempt to assimilate Vallée to the 'libertins spirituels' is not, I think, convincing.

tion opened the way to Enlightenment and Industry. In modern rationalism all the main developments of Western intellectual history converged.[4]

Modern scholarship has consistently been at odds with this traditional picture. More and more emphasis has been placed upon the Christian character of Renaissance thought. The Reformation, it is now stressed, did not lead necessarily or naturally to freedom of thought, but for the most part merely established new orthodoxies and new systems of control upon discussion and publication. As for the Scientific Revolution, its greatest achievements were those of Newton, and Newton's theory of gravitation, because it involved the rejection of all purely mechanical explanations of the movements of the heavens, was widely interpreted as evidence for the constant intervention of God in the working of his universe. It might well seem, then, that the explanation for the rise of modern unbelief must be sought in the eighteenth century, and not before.

In 1942 Lucien Febvre mounted the single most important attack upon the naïve history that had been so widely accepted.[5] Febvre's subject was Rabelais, whose anticlerical humour was seen by many critics as embodying rationalism and unbelief. Febvre set out to show that there was no evidence that Rabelais was not a believing Christian, and to argue that what we take for granted as the mental tools upon which unbelievers must rely were simply missing in mid-sixteenth-century France. Febvre believed that, for the most

[4] J. M. Robertson, *A History of Freethought*, 4th rev. edn. (2 vols; London, 1936), surveys 'previous histories' (pp. 12–20), and stresses the perceived need 'to contemplate freethought scientifically as an aspect of mental evolution common to all civilizations' (p. 18).

[5] Translated by Beatrice Gottlieb as Lucien Febvre, *The Problem of Unbelief in the Sixteenth Century: The Religion of Rabelais* (Cambridge, Mass., 1982). For the circumstances under which the book was written, see Natalie Zemon Davis, 'Rabelais among the Censors', *Representations*, 32 (1990), 1–32. For a discussion of Febvre's arguments, and a survey of much of the recent literature on unbelief, see David Wootton, 'Lucien Febvre and the Problem of Early Modern Unbelief', *Journal of Modern History*, 60 (1988), 695–730. A view that is in some respects similar to Febvre's is that of Stephen Greenblatt, 'Invisible Bullets', in his *Shakespearean Negotiations* (Berkeley, Calif., 1988), 21–65, although the interpretation of this already famous essay is a matter of dispute: see S. Greenblatt, *Learning to Curse* (New York, 1990), 165–6.

part, the fundamental doctrines of Christianity were simply taken for granted by our early modern ancestors: a systematic attack upon them would have required the biblical criticism and the experimental science of the nineteenth century; even the materialist dogmatism of the Enlightenment had no roots in the sixteenth century. In the age of Reformation and Counter-Reformation people had little choice but to believe.[6] Accusations of 'atheism' were thrown around by contemporaries, but the term was used recklessly, a fact that has greatly misled literal-minded historians. In truth, there could be no real history of irreligion until one entered the second half of the seventeenth century and began to measure the impact of the Cartesian distinction between mind and body upon the European intellectual community.[7]

Febvre combined immense learning with remarkable polemical vigour, and his authority had a great deal to do with the stagnation in the history of unbelief that can be seen in France over the next forty years. But his outlook triumphed in the English-speaking world as well, even amongst those who had not read him. One cause of this was the widespread rejection of what came to be termed 'Whig history': history which sought to find in the past elements of continuity with the present, to read the past as a precursor of contemporary preoccupations and beliefs.[8] Far from looking for the roots of modern rationalism in the sixteenth century, one should concentrate on understanding the pervasive presence of religion and magic in sixteenth-century life. The very idea of a history of unbelief seemed suspiciously anachronistic.[9]

---

[6] The only available alternative was a return to classical attacks upon Christianity: Lucien Febvre, *Origène et Des Périers* (Paris, 1942).

[7] Lucien Febvre, 'Aux origines de l'esprit moderne: Libertinisme, naturalisme, mécanisme', in his *Au cœur religieux du XVIe siècle* (Paris, 1957), 337–58.

[8] Adrian Wilson and T. G. Ashplant, 'Whig History and Present-Centered History', *Historical Journal*, 31 (1988), 1–16, and T. G. Ashplant and Adrian Wilson, 'Present-Centred History and the Problem of Historical Knowledge', *Historical Journal*, 31 (1988), 253–74.

[9] A few valuable, but scattered, studies did continue to appear, amongst them Giorgio Spini, *Ricerca dei libertini* (Rome, 1950; rev. edn, Florence, 1983); F. E. Manuel, *The Eighteenth Century Confronts the Gods* (Cambridge, Mass., 1959); J. S. Spink, *French Free Thought from Gassendi to Voltaire* (London, 1960); D. C. Allen, *Doubt's Boundless Sea: Skepticism and Faith in the Renaissance* (Baltimore,

Strictures against Whig history were, however, honoured more in the breach than the observance. Historians of science happily explored the birth of the experimental method; historians of political theory tracked down the distant origins of modern democratic theory; meanwhile the history of atheism marked time. In part, this was because of the very progress of secularization. In Italy, where anticlericalism was a continuing political and intellectual force underlying much of the support for the Communist party, the history of unbelief continued to be written almost without interruption, and it is there that, in the last fifteen years, the new history has been most vigorous and sophisticated.[10] Elsewhere, though, the liberal intelligentsia had no need for a hagiography or a martyrology: the persecution faced by early unbelievers was irrelevant to its immediate concerns. The history written in the last forty years has been unconsciously shaped by the fact that its authors have lived in the first societies where freedom of thought has been institutionalized and securely established.

There was, though, a more important reason for the withering-away of the history of unbelief. Largely without being aware of it, more and more historians committed themselves to a new definition of historical evidence.[11] The historian, it was held, must be able to support every claim he or she made by reference to a primary source, a source written by someone in a privileged position to know what was really going on. Applied to intellectual history, the results of this approach were bound to be remarkable. Hobbes, for example, had always been regarded, both by contemporaries and by historians, as a mocker of Christian-

---

1964); Cornelio Fabro, *God in Exile: Modern Atheism* (New York, 1968); John Redwood, *Reason, Ridicule and Religion: The Age of Enlightenment in England* (London, 1976); and more recently, F. E. Manuel, *The Changing of the Gods* (Hanover, 1983).

[10] Two volumes may serve as an introduction to Italian work in this field: Sergio Bertelli (ed.), *Il libertinismo in Europa* (Milan, 1980); Tullio Gregory *et al.* (eds.), *Ricerche su letteratura libertina e letteratura clandestina nel Seicento* (Florence, 1981).

[11] The methodological issues raised by a restrictive definition of evidence are well illustrated by the recent debate on the Ranters: J. C. Davis, 'Fear, Myth and Furore: Reappraising the "Ranters"', *Past and Present*, 129 (1990), 79–103.

ity. But what documentary proof could be offered in support of this interpretation? Accounts of Hobbes's unbelief were bound quickly to give way to a new industry, the study of his theology as carefully outlined in the last half of *Leviathan*.[12]

A further obstacle stood in the way of any study of unbelief. If philosophers like Pomponazzi and Hobbes had been attacked by contemporaries as unbelievers, they themselves had rejected these charges. To take the side of their accusers seemed a morally suspect activity. The traditional view was that one could not libel the dead, and that the historian's job was to make his or her best guess at the truth. Just as one might be convinced that a politician was being economical with the truth without having enough evidence for a court of law, so one might be morally certain that Hobbes was no Christian without having any incontrovertible proof: his tone, the implications of his arguments, his range of interests, the opinions of contemporaries might be evidence enough. The new view was that the historian should see himself or herself as judge and jury, not detective, or prosecuting counsel, or even disinterested observer. In the absence of hard evidence, the case must be dismissed.[13] It was necessary, in effect, to place restrictions upon the type of evidence that the historian would consider such as had previously been peculiar to the criminal law.

These new standards of evidence were given a moral justification: to reject them was to run the risk of condemning the innocent. No one seems to have worried that approaching the question in these terms appeared to involve accepting the assumption that atheism was to be thought of as a crime. No one was prepared to argue that historians should think of themselves as observers incapable of influencing the course of events, rather than as judges burdened by the responsibility

---

[12] But see David Johnston, *The Rhetoric of 'Leviathan'* (Princeton, 1986), and E. Curley, ' "I Durst not Write so Boldly", or How to Read Hobbes' Theological-Political Treatise', in E. Giancotti (ed.), *Hobbes e Spinoza* (Naples, 1990). I am grateful to Professor Curley for showing me a pre-publication copy of this essay.

[13] P. O. Kristeller, 'The Myth of Renaissance Atheism and the French Tradition of Free Thought', *Journal of the History of Philosophy* 6 (1968), 233–43 (here pp. 242–3) (first published in Spanish in 1952).

of punishing the guilty. The real problem was not, I think, that atheism was seen as wicked: it was that hypocrisy and insincerity had come to be regarded as incompatible with intellectual life. Historians lost sight of the fact that wherever persecution and censorship are established, there will be those who practise what Hume termed 'innocent dissimulation'. In an era of freedom of speech dissimulation no longer seemed innocent.

Thus the history of unbelief became, and long remained, intellectually disreputable. In its place appeared new histories of belief, perhaps the most important of which was R. H. Popkin's *History of Scepticism from Erasmus to Descartes*, in which French sceptics who had previously been seen as opponents of Christianity—Montaigne, Charron, Naudé, La Mothe le Vayer—were presented as true believers who had questioned the efficacy of reason, but had turned from the rationalist religion of their scholastic contemporaries to a humanist fideism that seemed in many ways closer to the religion of our own day.[14] Popkin knew that there was nothing novel about his way of reading early modern sceptics: in large part he was following the views of Pierre Bayle, whose *Dictionnaire historique et critique* (1695–7) had sought to defend the reputations of many of those traditionally accused of atheism by insisting that only hard evidence could be taken into account (although Bayle's own approach to this question was less than consistent, and his methodological recommendations may have been partly designed to deflect charges of atheism directed against himself[15]).

[14] (Assen, 1960); rev. and expanded edn., *The History of Scepticism from Erasmus to Spinoza* (Berkeley, Calif., and Los Angeles, 1979). Popkin's book on scepticism should be compared to the classic study of René Pintard, *Le Libertinage érudit dans la première moitié du* XVIIᵉ *siècle* (2 vols; Paris, 1943; rev. edn Geneva, 1983). Amongst recent work on the *libertins érudits*, one may note P. S. Donaldson, 'Gabriel Naudé: Magic and Machiavelli', in his *Machiavelli and Mystery of State* (Cambridge, 1988), 141–85; Lorenzo Bianchi, *Tradizione libertina e critica storica* (Milan, 1988). An important text in the history of scepticism is Francisco Sanches, *That Nothing Is Known* [1581], ed. E. Limbrick and D. F. S. Thomson (Cambridge, 1988).

[15] David Wootton, 'Pierre Bayle: Libertine?', forthcoming in M. A. Stewart (ed.), *Oxford Studies in the History of Philosophy*, 3 (Oxford). If Bayle's methodological principles were deliberately invented to mislead, this would not be the first time such principles had a major effect on historical method: see the discussion of Giovanni Nanni in Anthony Grafton, *Forgers and Critics* (Princeton, NJ, 1990).

Because these charges of anachronism, bias, and indifference to the facts were devastating for traditional histories of unbelief, the first consequence was the withering-away of a whole area of enquiry. Geoffroy Vallée, along with many others, disappeared back into the oblivion from which scholars like Lachèvre and Busson had temporarily rescued him. And yet this development also opened up an important intellectual possibility: what would happen if one tried to rethink the history of unbelief on the assumption that Febvre had been correct? What sort of history would result?

Theological Conflict

Volume 1 of Alan Charles Kors's *Atheism in France, 1650–1729* (volume 2 has yet to appear) looks at the problem of atheism as it was discussed by Christian intellectuals in the pre-Enlightenment period.[16] He shows first of all that theologians insisted that there could be no rational doubt as to God's existence: the Bible, after all, said 'the fool has said in his heart "There is no God."' No sensible person could reach this conclusion using his reason. Yet, because Aristotelian philosophy insisted that objections to every line of argument must be explored, theologians did not hesitate to propound arguments against the standard demonstrations of God's existence. The 'atheist' was thus primarily an invention of orthodox theology: a critical interlocutor, whose task it was to test orthodox reasoning and press for its improvement. There was nothing new about this, but in the second half of the seventeenth century two new factors intervened to transform the balance of the debate between the theologian and the imaginary atheist.

---

[16] Alan Charles Kors, *Atheism in France, 1650–1729* (2 vols.; Princeton, NJ, 1990–). Kors's argument was foreshadowed in '"A First Being, of whom we Have no Proof": The Preamble of Atheism in Early Modern France', in Alan Charles Kors and P. J. Korshin (eds.), *Anticipations of the Enlightenment* (Philadelphia, 1987), 17–68, and in 'Theology and Atheism in Early Modern France', in A. Grafton and A. Blair (eds.), *The Transmission of Culture in Early Modern Europe* (Philadelphia, 1990), 238–75.

One of the key arguments for God's existence had traditionally been the argument from universal consent: if all
nations believed in God, then no rational person could doubt
his existence. But the travel literature of the seventeenth and
early eighteenth centuries produced more and more evidence
of primitive peoples who had no knowledge of a God. Above
all, the prolonged debate between the Jesuits and their
adversaries about the missionary methods to be adopted in
China turned on the question of whether the Confucian élite
in China was atheistical or not: the Jesuits lost ground in this
debate, and it increasingly came to be accepted that atheism
was the dominant ideology in China. In addition, a growing
literature demonstrated the extent of unbelief among ancient
Greek and Roman philosophers. Thus, by the end of the
seventeenth century the argument from universal consent was
in disarray: it was not true that all societies were religious,
nor that all civilized societies were, nor that all great philosophers were.

Secondly, Aristotelians had sought to use the nature of the
universe to demonstrate that there must be a God, arguing
that there must be a first cause and a first mover, and that the
universe was obviously the product of design, not chance. In
the second half of the seventeenth century these arguments
came under systematic attack from Cartesians, who insisted
that nothing one could learn about the material world could
give one knowledge of an immaterial entity. They sought to
deduce God from another immaterial entity: the idea they
had of him in their own minds. This, they said, was an idea
of infinite perfection; but no finite mind could formulate
such an idea. The idea of God must therefore originate with
God himself. This and other Cartesian arguments were met
by the Aristotelians with scorn. Cartesians, they complained,
sought to prove God's existence by assuming that their idea
of him was well founded: but since it was precisely this that
needed to be proved, they were merely arguing in a circle.

Kors gives a magnificent account of the conflict between
Aristotelians and Cartesians, a conflict that was not merely
an argument over ideas, but a struggle for the control of
education in pre-Enlightenment France. He concludes that
the outcome of this debate—conducted in front of a vast new

audience, the readers of such literary journals as Bayle's *Nouvelles de la république des lettres*—was the undermining of all existing philosophical arguments for belief in God. Thus the stage was set for the atheist—initially a theological fiction—to take on a life of his own, to turn the arguments of the theologians against Christian faith, and to lay claim to a positive unbelief. This new atheism appears in the clandestine manuscripts of the early eighteenth century, and is the direct precursor of the atheism of d'Holbach and Naigeon.[17] It is the child of philosophical dispute amongst believers: believers who accused each other of opening the way to unbelief.[18]

It is too soon to reach a final judgement on Kors's achievement. Volume 2 will have to show the impact of theological debate upon eighteenth-century atheists. It will also have to justify Kors's concentration upon French sources. It is true that during the seventeenth century vernacular languages increasingly replaced Latin in intellectual life, and that this to some extent separated intellectuals into distinct linguistic communities; but, to take just two examples, Spinoza's work was widely known in France, and Hobbes was even translated into French. At this point we must concentrate on Kors's strategic decision: to follow Febvre in seeing atheism as a chimera of the theologians, not

---

[17] The classic study of the clandestine manuscripts is I. O. Wade, *The Clandestine Organization and Diffusion of Philosophic Ideas in France from 1700 to 1750* (Princeton, NJ, 1938). Many of the manuscripts studied by Wade have been published recently, including: *Theophrastus redivivus*, ed. Guido Canziani and Gianni Paganini (2 vols; Florence, 1981–2); [Robert Challe], *Les Difficultés sur la religion proposées au père Malebranche*, ed. M. Deloffre and M. Manemencioghu (Oxford, 1982); *Traité des trois imposteurs*, ed. Pierre Rétat (Saint-Étienne, 1973) (Silvia Berti is currently working on an edition to be published by Einaudi); [Nicholas Fréret], *La Lettre de Thrasibule à Leucippe*, ed. S. Landucci (Florence, 1986); the autobiography of Jean Meslier, in *Œuvres complètes de Jean Meslier* ed. J. Deprun, R. Desné, A. Soboul (3 vols; Paris, 1970–2); *L'Âme matérielle*, ed. A. Niderst (Paris, 1969); ' "Essais sur la recherche de la vérité" (manoscritto clandestino)', ed. S. Landucci, *Studi settecenteschi*, 6 (1984), 23–82; *Le Philosophe*, ed. Herbert Dieckmann (St Louis, 1948); Pierre Cuppé, *Le Ciel ouvert à tous les hommes*, ed. P. Cristofolini (Florence, 1981).

[18] A similar approach is that of M. J. Buckley, *At the Origins of Modern Atheism* (New Haven, Conn., 1987), reviewed sympathetically by Alan Charles Kors in *Eighteenth-Century Studies*, 22 (1989), 614–17, and more critically by J. E. Force in 'The Origins of Modern Atheism', *Journal of the History of Ideas*, 50 (1989), 153–62.

a real object existing in the sixteenth and seventeenth centuries. If this strategy is sound, then Kors becomes the first proper historian of philosophical atheism.

Encounters with 'Atheists'

Before we can advance further we need to take stock. Readers are probably already puzzled by the imprecision of my vocabulary: terms like 'unbelief', 'irreligion', 'atheism' have been used as if they were nearly interchangeable. Febvre was looking for a systematic rejection of the principles of revealed religion. Kors is looking for something else: philosophical atheism, arguments against the very existence of God (and is prepared to acknowledge in passing the existence of seventeenth-century deists and of others who did not believe in the Christian revelation). Others have shown an interest in statements and attitudes that show a complete disregard for traditional Christian teaching, recording cases of blasphemy and libertinism.[19] What is the proper object of study? What is the proper terminology to employ? Our answer to these questions will determine how we approach the case of Geoffroy Vallée. Kors, for example, refers to him because Vallée expressed the conventional view that no sensible person could be an atheist. He acknowledges that he was 'antireligious', but sees him as essentially irrelevant to a history of atheism.[20] C. J. Betts pauses to establish that he was no deist.[21] Thus Vallée slips between the cracks of our contemporary categories.

One of the central problems in Febvre's study was that he saw that 'atheism' was a term used in the sixteenth century with what appeared to be reckless abandon, but he failed to see the importance of the history of the word, or to look with any care at the definitions of its meaning given by

[19] This theme, amongst others, is explored in François Berriot, *Athéismes et athéistes au XVIᵉ siècle en France* (2 vols.; Lille, [1977]).

[20] Kors, *Atheism in France*, 26–7.

[21] C. J. Betts *Early Deism in France* (The Hague, 1984), 7–8.

contemporaries.[22] The first thing to recognize is that the modern word is an invention of the sixteenth century. It did exist, of course, in classical Greek, but it is significant that the Middle Ages, which had a sophisticated language for heresy, felt no need of a specialized language for describing unbelief, assimilating beliefs which threatened the Christian faith as a whole (Averroism, for example) to heresies. This is not because there was no unbelief in the Middle Ages. Around 1020, for example, two clergymen in Orléans apparently insisted that the universe had existed from eternity, that heaven and hell were fictions, and that the doctrine of the Trinity was incoherent.[23] This, in the eyes of contemporaries, was impiety, not atheism.

The Reformation saw the rapid construction of a new vocabulary to describe unbelief. Of the terms that came into use then, first in Latin and then in the vernacular languages, some have survived to the present (atheist, deist), others have dropped out of use (Epicurean, a-Christist, Lucianist, libertine). Other words came into use in the late seventeenth and early eighteenth centuries (materialist, free-thinker, pantheist), and still others in the nineteenth (agnostic, fideist).[24]

This mid-sixteenth-century linguistic innovation needs, in the first place, to be explained. Did the religious crisis of the division of Christendom foster unbelief? Did theologians—with Calvin in the forefront—become increasingly impatient of views and attitudes which had long existed?[25] Secondly, we need to study what these new terms meant, avoiding the presumption that they had 'modern' meanings. It was generally agreed in the sixteenth and early seventeenth centuries that an atheist was *either* someone who did not believe in the existence of God *or* someone who held beliefs which made

[22] Wootton, 'Lucien Febvre', 703–7.
[23] Christiane Lauvergnat-Gagnière, *Lucien de Samosata et le lucianisme en France au XVIe siècle: Athéisme et polémique* (Geneva, 1988), 195. See now Susan Reynolds, 'Social Mentalities and the Case of Medieval Scepticism', *Transactions of the Royal Historical Society*, 6th Ser., 1 (1991), 21–41.
[24] A valuable case-study is Jean Delumeau *et al.*, *Croyants et sceptiques au XVIe siècle: Le Dossier des épicuriens* (Strasbourg, 1981).
[25] Calvin's importance is stressed in Perez Zagorin, 'Libertinism, Unbelief and the Dissimulation of Philosophers', in his *Ways of Lying* (Cambridge, Mass., 1990), 289–330.

God's existence irrelevant: someone who did not believe, for example, in the immortality of the soul. This double definition creates (and created) endless confusion: Vallée was described by his contemporaries as an atheist, despite the fact that he himself, relying on a narrow definition of the term, insisted he was not. By the late seventeenth century it was increasingly common to declare that the term should be confined to its more narrow meaning, a process that led to a new stress upon 'deism'.

When theologians said that there were no thoughtful atheists, they were often referring only to the first part of the standard definition of the term: even Averroists accepted that there was a first cause, while denying immortality. Secondly, they were taking advantage of the fact that in every country in Europe avowed unbelief was likely to lead to judicial execution: they could rejoice in atheists' inability to dispute with them. Thirdly, they had on their side the fact that even unbelievers agreed that religion was necessary as social cement: without fear of God amongst the populace at large, social order would collapse (the first to contest this view in print was Pierre Bayle in 1682).[26] Even by their own standards, unbelievers were under an obligation to remain silent: the exceptions were often men, like Vallée, who were prepared to attack the existing social order along with conventional religion. Hume laughed at the way in which theologians were always attacking atheism while at the same time denying its existence: he compared them to knights errant in quest of dragons.[27] This contradictory behaviour needs an explanation, but the conclusion that atheism (at least if broadly defined) existed only in the pages of theology books is not the only possible (or most convincing) one.[28]

[26] David Wootton, 'From Duty to Self-Interest', in Wootton (ed.), *Divine Right and Democracy* (Harmondsworth, 1986), 58–77; D. F. Norton, 'Hume, Atheism and the Autonomy of Morals', in *Hume's Philosophy of Religion: The Sixth James Montgomery Hester Seminar* (Winston-Salem, NC, 1986), 97–144; Christopher Hill, 'From Oaths to Interest', in his *Society and Puritanism in Early Modern England* (London, 1964), 382–419.

[27] David Hume, *An Enquiry Concerning Human Understanding*, ed. L. A. Selby-Bigge, 3rd rev. edn. (Oxford, 1975), 149.

[28] See David Berman, 'The Repressive Denials of Atheism in Britain in the Seventeenth and Eighteenth Centuries', *Proceedings of the Royal Irish Academy*, C 82 (1982), 211–46.

Four factors make it unconvincing: in the first place, evidence of unbelief is to be found in trials and autobiographies. Secondly, the fact that avowed unbelief was punishable by death means that we will never know how many unbelievers there were, but we can be sure that our sources give us information only about an unrepresentative sample. Thirdly, theologians regularly tell us that they have disputed with actual unbelievers.[29] We have a rare report of such a dispute taking place in public, under the shelter of a pretence of anonymity. In a work published in 1709 Casimir Freschot defends Venetians against the charge that their city is full of atheists. But he goes on to report conversations with non-believers in Venice and, most remarkably, a debate that had taken place during carnival time between a Jew, who was known to be an avowed atheist, and a monk, both of whom were wearing masks. The atheist presented his arguments so well that Freschot concluded that the Devil had perhaps never had a more effective apostle. But Freschot was astonished to hear the truths of religion debated in a 'theatre of charlatans' with all the sophistication that one would have expected to find in a university: such discussions must normally have taken place behind closed doors.[30] Finally, much of the intellectual activity of the late sixteenth, seventeenth, and early eighteenth centuries, from Montaigne's 'Apology for Sebond' to Pascal's *Pensées*, Browne's *Religio medici*, and Locke's 'Essay on Miracles', makes no sense at all unless it is recognized that there was a real (and not merely fictional) dialogue between belief and unbelief. Montaigne, Pascal, and Browne expected to be read by 'atheists'. So too, of course, did the innumerable authors of confutations of atheism and unbelief.

This is not to say that these 'atheists' would have denied the very existence of God. What we should study primarily are those arguments that concerned not the existence of God, or his role in nature, but his relevance to human concerns, for these are the arguments that contemporaries felt did most to undermine belief in the Christian God. The alternative

---

[29] Kors himself gives an example: *Atheism in France*, 54.
[30] [C. Freschot], *Nouvelle relation de la ville et république de Venise* (Utrecht, 1709), 425–6.

approach, which looks for the origins of 'deism' or 'atheism' as we now understand those terms, tells us very little about the history of unbelief before the eighteenth century. Even then, it fails to take account of many arguments that were fundamental for those who ceased to believe in Christianity, giving us an unduly narrow picture of the intellectual foundations of unbelief.

This approach, which seeks to avoid the anachronism implicit in a systematic use of modern terminology, is only valid for the study of ideas, not behaviour. Until the late seventeenth century it was generally assumed that there was a close correlation between belief and action (Bayle, following in the steps of the Jansenists, mounted a concerted assault on this view). It was agreed that those who lived evil lives must lack religious faith, just as those who lacked faith would be bound to live evil lives. The term 'atheist' was thus to be applied to people who were in fact believers, because their conduct was held to imply unbelief. Since we do not share this view of the relationship between thought and action, we cannot follow this aspect of early modern usage, for we would end up with a history of unbelief that concerned itself with the aberrant behaviour not of atheists, but of believers.

Let us take an example from the end of our period. In October 1765 Elijah Leach was presented by the jury at the general sessions in Plymouth, Massachusetts: 'On the ninth of June last, the said Elijah, in a lewd, indecent and disorderly manner, did misbehave himself by unbuttoning his breeches and exposing his private members to the open view of divers of his majesties good subjects, both men and women, then and there being present.' Worse was to come: 'the said Elijah . . . on said 29 day of June last past, did in a contemptuous manner, in the hearing of many of his Majesties subjects say and declare "that he did not care a turd for God in Heaven or on the Earth".' Leach pleaded guilty, and was fined 10s. for indecency and 40s. for irreverent speeches.[31]

Was Leach an atheist? Or merely a drunken trouble-maker? The truth is that we will never know. But it will not do to

[31] D. T. Konig (ed.), *Plymouth Court Records* (13 vols.; Wilmington, Del., 1978–81), iii. 219.

assume that none of those who engage in irreverent speech has given serious thought to what he or she wants to say. The trial of Aikenhead, in late seventeenth-century Scotland, started as an investigation of irreverent speech: but Aikenhead's gallows speech shows that he had formulated a systematic hostility to Christianity. As Michael Hunter stresses in Chapter 8 of this book, irreverence could be a most effective way of communicating ideas and convictions, and it is wrong to take only systematic statements of unbelief seriously.

Aikenhead is an example of how we can have reliable knowledge of an unbeliever's views. He and Vallée do not stand alone. Uriel da Costa published a treatise against the immortality of the soul in early seventeenth-century Holland. Every copy was destroyed, but we know of his opinions both from the refutation published by a contemporary and from his own autobiography.[32] In 1582 Noël Journet was burnt in Metz: two manuscripts went up in flames with him. In one he had exposed the inconsistencies in the Bible narrative and dismissed the whole Bible as a fable. How, for example, could Moses have written Deuteronomy when his own death was described therein? How could the Egyptian magicians have turned water into blood when Moses had already transformed all the water in Egypt? In the other he had attacked tithes and taxes and called for political equality. Journet was no atheist (in the modern sense): but he thought that the God of the Christians was a wicked God. He declared that he wanted to establish a new and better religion, comparing himself to Christ. Since he thought that Christ was a mere man, this does not mean that he thought of himself as a true Messiah. He thought that he too could play the role of impostor. We know of his opinions from the documents of his trial and, again, from a contemporary refutation.[33] Earlier still, in 1550, Jacques Gruet was burnt, again in the company of his manuscript, in Geneva. He may

---

[32] *Die Schriften des Uriel da Costa*, ed. Carl Gebhardt (Amersterdam, 1922); U. Acosta, *A Specimen of Human Life* (New York, 1967).

[33] François Berriot, 'Hétérodoxie religieuse et utopie politique dans les "erreurs étranges" de Noël Journet (1582)', *Bulletin de la Société de l'histoire du protestantisme français*, 124 (1978), 236–48.

well have been a true atheist, for he denied that the world had been created.[34]

Such men shared a common scepticism about the reliability of the Bible text (or, in da Costa's case, for he was a convert to Judaism, of the text of the Torah), and a common conviction that one had to make sense of the world without appealing to revealed truth. For most of them the conflict between reason and religion did not end when they recognized the Bible text as incredible, for they went on to question the moral values and social institutions upheld by the Church. Kors ends his book in 1729, with the death of the curate Meslier, who left behind an autobiography in which he defended atheism and communism. But it is only if one insists on atheism as narrowly defined that Meslier stands at the beginning of a series rather than at the end.

Indeed, research is bringing to light more and more trials of 'unbelievers'. Many of these, however, come from the archives of the Inquisition, and in such cases it is a mistake to assume that every accusation is well founded. A good example is the series of trials of atheists that took place in Naples in the 1680s and 1690s and that have been studied by Luciano Osbat.[35] Osbat establishes that the initial accusations were directed against 'atheists' who were closely associated with prominent politicians, and suggests that they had a political purpose. Members of the lower classes who were accused received summary (and harsh) justice. But the most prominent figure against whom the accusations were addressed, de Cristofaro, lingered in prison for six years while the case against him hung fire. At no point did he confess, and in the end he was merely convicted of having 'given grounds for suspicion' that he was an atheist. Are we entitled to conclude that atheism (to be specific, Lucretian atomism) was widespread in late seventeenth-century Naples?[36] Or was this a witch-hunt directed against innocent

[34] Berriot, *Athéismes*, 449–51, 849–67.
[35] Luciano Osbat, *L'Inquisizione a Napoli: Il processo agli ateisti, 1688–1697* (Rome, 1974).
[36] On convictions for suspicion, see J. H. T. Langbein, *Torture and the Law of Proof* (Chicago, 1977), 47–9, who argues that such verdicts were used when the court was persuaded that the accused was guilty. New light on the importance of

men? De Cristofaro's claim that he was never even present at discussions of atomism flies in the face of the testimony of several other witnesses, and his guilt seems much more likely than his innocence. The case against him would not necessarily be stronger if he had confessed and been convicted. Faced with anonymous accusations (for the Inquisition never revealed its sources to suspects) and sometimes subjected to torture, the innocent may often have concluded that confession would secure better treatment than 'obduracy'.

However one interprets the evidence in particular cases, it is clearly wrong to think that unbelief was impossible before 1650.[37] The conflict between Cartesians and scholastics may have made atheism as narrowly defined a concrete intellectual prospect; and if one takes d'Holbach as one's yardstick for modern unbelief, then this is a fact of the greatest significance. It appears less significant if one takes, for example, Hume, who accepted that the 'religious hypothesis' was the best explanation for the ordered nature of the cosmos, but who denied the immortality of the soul or the credibility of a revealed Scripture that required belief in miracles.

Arguments against the immortality of the soul had long been available—Cardano had offered more than fifty in the sixteenth century. Systematic arguments against the credibility of reports of miracles were much newer; but they had an origin quite independent of the disputes between Cartesians and scholastics, in the emergence of modern probability theory after 1660.[38] Above all, the strongest argument against

---

early modern atomism is cast by Pietro Redondi, *Galileo Heretic* (1983; Eng. trans., Princeton, NJ, 1987). For criticism of this book, see Vincenzo Ferrone and Massimo Firpo, 'From Inquisitors to Microhistorians', *Journal of Modern History*, 58 (1986), 485–524, and the exchange between Redondi and Ferrone and Firpo in *Rivista storica italiana*, 97 (1985), 934–68.

[37] See, to take one example, John Edwards, 'Religious Faith and Doubt in Late Medieval Spain', *Past and Present*, 120 (1988), 5–25. Edwards is concerned with the beliefs of *conversos*: pre-Reformation Jewish communities faced problems that Christians rarely encountered before the Reformation. Similar examples can be found, as Edwards points out, in areas divided between Catholicism and Catharism. There is a debate between Edwards and C. J. Sommerville in *Past and Present*, 128 (1990), 152–61.

[38] David Wootton, 'Hume's "Of Miracles": Probability and Irreligion', in M. A. Stewart (ed.), *Studies in the Philosophy of the Scottish Enlightenment* (Oxford, 1990), 191–229.

the Christian conception of an omnipotent, benevolent God
was the presence of evil in the world: in the late seventeenth
century Bayle pushed this argument to its furthest extent,
arguing that natural reason would lead one to Manicheism,
but theologians had long seen it as the central stumbling-
block to faith. Finally, if the second half of the seventeenth
century saw a crisis in the argument for God's existence from
universal consent, an earlier crisis had seemed potentially
devastating. The Renaissance brought home to a new, lay,
educated public the possibility of non-Christian ways of
thinking and non-Christian moral values. Machiavelli was
widely believed to have claimed that pagan religions were
preferable to Christianity, and a practical devotional treatise
of the fifteenth century had addressed unbelief as the first
temptation suffered by the Christian: the temptation not of
atheism, but of a Roman indifference to death and what came
after it.[39]

To concentrate on one set of arguments that threatened
faith at the expense of others is perfectly legitimate, providing
one does not draw the conclusion that this issue is the only
one of importance. Scholastics accused Cartesians of offering
proofs of God's existence so weak that they were bound to
encourage disbelief. But Cartesians insisted that they not
only had better proofs of God's existence than Aristotelians;
they also had the only decisive arguments for the immateriality and immortality of the soul. The debate between Cartesians and scholastics turned as much on the 'old' issue of the
rationality of belief in immortality as on the 'new' one of the
rationality of belief in a God.

Atheists Reading Atheists

Conflict over the credibility of Christianity thus took place
on several fronts at once. The approach of Febvre and Kors

[39] Alberto Tenenti, 'La religione di Machiavelli', in his collection of essays, *Credenze, ideologie, libertinismi* (Bologna, 1978), 175–219; A. Tenenti, *La Vie et la mort à travers l'art du* XVe *siècle* (Paris, 1952), 55.

would imply that this conflict took place within the minds of believing philosophers and theologians. We have seen that, nevertheless, there were unbelievers. Kors himself recognizes a solitary exception to his claim that atheism did not exist until the early eighteenth century: the author of an anonymous mid-seventeenth-century manuscript, the *Theophrastus redivivus*, who was, indisputably, an atheist. For Kors, the significance of this text has been much overstated: its author is an isolated figure who has plundered the classics for atheistical arguments and has nothing new to say.[40] But it is worth pausing here to look at the opposing view, brilliantly developed by Tullio Gregory in a work that was the first of the major new histories of unbelief.[41]

Gregory set out to show what the author of the *Theophrastus redivivus* had read. Many of his sources were classical. But he was also familiar with many early seventeenth-century authors who were widely accused of being unbelievers: Machiavelli; Vanini (executed for atheism in 1619); sceptics such as Montaigne, Charron, and Naudé; philosophers who denied that one could demonstrate the immortality of the soul, such as Pomponazzi.[42] What Gregory had managed to do was to reconstruct the library of an atheist, and, strikingly, this turned out to consist of the very books that theologians such as Mersenne said were read by atheists: the 'imaginary' atheist of the theologians corresponded perfectly to the 'real' atheist. Moreover, Gregory could show how his atheist had read his books: how he had pulled subversive arguments from them, while ignoring the conventional statements of piety that often accompanied these arguments and appeared to take the sting out of them. The key question that arose from this line of enquiry was: Was this the right way to read these books? In the early modern period they had been widely read in this way, but was this what their authors had intended? Febvre's problem was: Were there really any unbelievers? Surprisingly, he thought that there were, but

[40] Kors, *Atheism in France*, 219–25.
[41] Tullio Gregory, '*Theophrastus redivivus*': *Erudizione e ateismo nel Seicento* (Naples, 1979).
[42] A major recent study of Pomponazzi is M. L. Pine, *Pietro Pomponazzi: Radical Philosopher of the Renaissance* (Padua, 1986).

that their unbelief was backward-looking, not modern (just as Kors dismisses the *Theophrastus*). The problem we inherit from Gregory's study is: Were the theologians and the unbelievers right to read so many published works as deliberately putting forward arguments against faith?

Earlier historians of unbelief had, like early modern theologians, been happy to 'read between the lines'. In recent decades this has seemed an indefensible strategy to most historians of ideas. The main school of thought to regard such readings as justifiable is represented by the followers of Leo Strauss.[43] It is therefore worth looking briefly at a book by a member of this school, Hiram Caton's study of Descartes.[44] Caton claims to find numerous inconsistencies in Descartes's work that point to the need to disinter Descartes's genuine teaching from his surface meaning. In the light of these inconsistencies he concludes that Descartes does not intend his *Metaphysics* to be taken seriously, only his physics. Thus Descartes does not intend seriously the proofs of the existence of God and of the immateriality of the soul that he offers: he is in fact a materialist and an atheist. In support of this analysis, Caton offers two additional arguments. In the first place he shows that Descartes was interpreted by many people in the late seventeenth and eighteenth centuries as fostering atheism and even as being an atheist. In the second he argues that, in a controversy with a disciple, Descartes explained how to read (and how to write) between the lines. This is both evidence that Descartes could have undertaken the project of writing between the lines and information on how to read his own work.

These two arguments are weak. Many of Descartes's contemporaries were impressed by his work because it seemed to constitute a bulwark for Christian faith: Bayle, for example, thought that Descartes had produced the first

---

[43] Leo Strauss, *Persecution and the Art of Writing* (New York, 1952; pbk. edn, Chicago, 1988). Two critical discussions of Strauss's views are contained in S. B. Drury, *The Political Ideas of Leo Strauss* (Basingstoke, 1988), and Stephen Holmes, 'Truths for Philosophers Alone', *Times Literary Supplement*, 1–7 Dec. 1989, 1319–24.

[44] Hiram Caton, *The Origin of Subjectivity: An Essay on Descartes* (New Haven, Conn., 1973); also id., 'The Problem of Descartes' Sincerity', *Philosophical Forum*, 2 (1971), 355–69.

serious arguments that might confound an atheist. If one turns to Kors's book, one discovers at once the true context of the accusations of atheism directed against Descartes and how little they tell us about Descartes's own intentions. Moreover, Descartes's account of how one should read between the lines tells us to ignore purely conventional echoings of established opinions and to concentrate on the arguments that are radical and novel, for it may well be that the conventional passages are a mere camouflage. The key problem with Caton's argument is that the *Metaphysics* is not a conventional work: as far as contemporaries were concerned, much of the novelty of Cartesianism was to be found in it. On Descartes's own principles of interpretation, it seems likely that its author meant what he said.[45]

Caton's book can stand as an example of an arbitrary and ahistorical interpretation. But there have been several recent attempts to establish 'reading between the lines' on a more historical basis.[46] A persuasive example, in my view, is Gino Bedani's interpretation of Vico.[47] Bedani shows that Vico was soon read as attacking Christianity. His milieu was one where (if we are to believe the records of the Inquisition) irreligious speculation existed and where fear of the Inquisition gave the strongest of reasons for concealment. Vico's *Scienza nuova* exhibits a suspicious pattern of acknowledging insignificant, orthodox sources, and of passing over in silence a much more important dependence on suspect authors such as Lucretius, Hobbes, and Spinoza. What appears to be 'conventional' in

---

[45] This does not mean that later authors may not have used Cartesianism as a conventional camouflage for materialism. It is even possible that Bayle is in this category.

[46] Stephen Zwicker, 'Language as Disguise: Politics and Poetry in the Later Seventeenth Century', *Annals of Scholarship*, 1 (1980), 47–66; id., *Politics and Language in Dryden's Poetry* (Princeton, NJ, 1984); Annabel Patterson, *Censorship and Interpretation: The Conditions of Writing and Reading in Early Modern England* (Madison, Wis., 1984): for criticism, see A. B. Worden, 'Literature and Political Censorship in Early Modern England', in A. C. Duke and C. A. Tamse (eds.), *Too Mighty to be Free: Censorship and the Press in Britain and The Netherlands* (Zutphen, 1987), 45–62; Lois Potter, *Secret Rites and Secret Writing: Royalist Literature, 1614–1660* (Cambridge, 1989); and Zagorin, *Ways of Lying*. An interesting case is that of the *Travels* of F. Mendes Pinto (ed. and trans. R. D. Catz (Chicago, 1989)), a work that pretends to be an autobiography but is not.

[47] Gino Bedani, *Vico Revisited* (Oxford, 1989).

Vico's argument often hides the unconventional: Vico's concept of providence, for example, turns out on close inspection to be indistinguishable from natural necessity. Vico's argument is that contemporary civilization derives, by a lengthy evolutionary process, from primitive men who were ignorant and brutish: his attempts to fit Adam, the Flood, and God's revelations to the Hebrews into (or rather alongside) this scheme seem so unconvincing as to be incredible.[48] In early drafts Vico experimented with a radical reworking of traditional pre-Deluge chronologies, an approach that he presumably abandoned as likely to bring him into conflict with the authorities. Bedani's case that Vico was an opponent, rather than an advocate, of established religion is well made: one is not surprised to discover that, in the last sentence of his autobiography, Vico says that when he had completed the *Scienza nuova*, 'enjoying life, liberty and honour, he held himself more fortunate than Socrates', implying that he had been lucky to escape condemnation for undermining belief in the established religion.[49] Nor is one surprised to find a long passage in the *Scienza nuova* discussing how fables (which Vico normally insisted were truthful) could be used to convey secret meanings.

It may be helpful at this point to ask what ideal body of evidence might justify an unshakeable 'reading between the lines'. It seems clear one would want the following:

(1) a text in which conventional sentiments seem to be at odds with unconventional ones;

(2) contemporary readings of the text that see it as suspect;

(3) a declared interest in 'writing between the lines';

(4) statements by the author (such as Vico's reference to Socrates) that seem to be intended to confirm suspicions about his own literary procedures or his own private convictions;

(5) independent contemporary evidence that the author was believed to be irreligious or at least moved in irreligious circles; and

[48] A valuable study of the collapse of belief in biblical chronology can be found in Paolo Rossi, *The Dark Abyss of Time* (Eng. trans., Chicago, 1984).

[49] Frederick Vaughan, '*La scienza nuova*: Orthodoxy and the Art of Writing', *Forum Italicum*, 2 (1968), 332–58 (p. 334).

(6) manuscript evidence that shows the author had more radical views than he dared to publish.

In Vico's case we can satisfy all six. An even stronger case is that of the early seventeenth-century scientist and historian Paolo Sarpi.[50] Here we have the strongest possible manuscript evidence that he was an agnostic, if not an atheist, and that he advocated telling lies to those who did not already possess the truth or who were not properly prepared to receive it. We have independent contemporary descriptions of him as irreligious, and contemporary attacks on his publications as subversive not only of Catholicism, but of any form of Christianity. Knowing what we do about him (which is far more than contemporaries did), we are bound to look again at his published work to see how far his private convictions were allowed to shape his published work, and how far he sought to keep his private philosophizing and his public writing separate. Read against this background, it becomes apparent why Sarpi's *Istoria del Concilio di Trento* was so admired by historians like Gibbon: it implies a totally secular and sceptical view of religion. Here the strong evidence as to Sarpi's private views authorizes a new reading of the text, one that brings out ambiguities of which its author must have been aware.

Authors like Sarpi and Vico necessarily present a double image to the world: from one point of view their arguments seem conventional; from another they seem to be saying something quite different and much more radical.[51] To see them from this double perspective is not to adopt an anachronistic, twentieth-century perspective, but rather to view

[50] David Wootton, *Paolo Sarpi: Between Renaissance and Enlightenment* (Cambridge, 1983). See now Vittorio Frajese, 'Sarpi e la tradizione scettica', *Studi storici*, 29 (1988), 1029–50, and *idem*, 'Sarpi interprete del *De la sagesse* di Pierre Charron: 1 *Pensieri sulla religione*', *Studi Veneziani*, 20 (1990), 59–85. A book that is in many respects comparable to my own is J. R. Jacob, *Henry Stubbe: Radical Protestantism and the Early Enlightenment* (Cambridge, 1983): for criticism, see A. B. Worden, *Times Literary Supplement*, 5 Aug. 1983, 837. Jacob is surely right to argue that Stubbe's *An Account of the Rise and Progress of Mahometanism*, ed. H. M. K. Shairani (London, 1911), is an attack on Christianity.

[51] It was not only unbelievers who resorted to such tactics. Kors provides an example of a superficially scholastic work that in fact offers a hidden Cartesian teaching: *Atheism in France*, 276–7.

them precisely as their contemporaries saw them: as puzzling, self-contradictory, and subversive.

Pierre Charron is a good example of an author who leaves us puzzling over his meaning. We have seen that Charron was part of the atheist's library, and in a chapter in this book Tullio Gregory shows just how unconventional some of the arguments of *De la sagesse* were. But are we justified in picking out these unconventional passages and regarding them as central to the argument of the entire book? On this question Charron sends a double message. On the one hand, in the introduction to the second edition, he warns us not to read the book as Gregory does and as readers of the first edition had done: to do so would be to confuse descriptions with value-judgements, hypotheses with conclusions, indirect speech with direct speech, reason with faith, virtue with grace. If these potential misunderstandings are borne in mind, then his true intentions will be recognized, and we will not, he tells us, have any difficulty in understanding him.[52]

Charron is offering us two alternative keys to the interpretation of his work: one irreligious, the other pious; one false (he says), the other sound. A very different tone, however, is struck in the preface to book II. There he remarks on how rare it is for anyone to dare to attack the prejudices of the day and to defend true wisdom. There are only two models of how to do so: Democritus and Heraclitus. Those who follow the model of Democritus mock folly but do not describe true wisdom. Those who follow the model of Heraclitus are feeble: they whisper and talk out of the side of their mouth; they disguise their language; they mix up and water down their true views so that they will pass unnoticed amongst the rest of what they are saying. They speak ambiguously, like oracles. But Charron himself is going to adopt a quite different mode. He is going to write bluntly, clearly, distinctly; he will not merely attack folly but portray wisdom.[53]

What is the reader to make of this? On the one hand Charron tells us to draw the claws of his text as we read it.

[52] Pierre Charron, *De la sagesse* (Rouen, 1623), 17.
[53] Ibid. 307–10.

On the other, he tells us that its unique merit is that the claws
are there for all to see. One moment he admits that it is easy
to read him as if he were following the model of Heraclitus;
the next he boasts that we will find it hard to do so, for his
book is anything but ambiguous.

The simple answer, I think, is that Charron is trying to
ensure that the first four of the six criteria mentioned earlier
as justifying 'reading between the lines' have been met. Here,
he tells us, we will find views that are at odds with conventional opinion; contemporaries have found these views to be
suspect; this is not surprising, for some authors (the followers
of Heraclitus) do indeed write between the lines; as for our
present author, he is bolder even than Democritus and
Heraclitus—both of them unbelievers. When the discussions
of reading and writing contained in the two prefaces are
juxtaposed, the tension between them can only be resolved
by concluding that his description of how *not* to read his
book in the first preface is in fact a description of how we
should read it: only then will he seem blunter and bolder
than all those who have gone before.

Much of the history of unbelief is, of necessity, lost to
sight. Few were eager to condemn themselves to death by
speaking openly. Those who fell under suspicion naturally
sought to defend themselves: it is impossible to be sure now
that the accusations levelled against Marlowe or Raleigh, for
example, were justified.[54] In the absence of explicit avowals,
reading between the lines becomes one of our most valuable
sources of information. To do this properly, however, we
have to pay close attention both to what the author tells us
about his own book and to what contemporaries found
remarkable in it.[55]

Thanks to David Berman's work, anyone who begins to take
an interest in reading between the lines is bound to turn to
an essay that John Toland published in 1720: 'Clidophorous,

---

[54] The two most useful surveys of accusations of atheism in pre-Enlightenment
England are G. E. Aylmer, 'Unbelief in Seventeenth-Century England', in Donald
Pennington and Keith Thomas (eds.), *Puritans and Revolutionaries* (Oxford, 1978),
22–46, and Michael Hunter, 'The Problem of "Atheism" in Early Modern England',
Transactions of the Royal Historical Society, 5th ser., 35 (1985), 135–57.
[55] For a case-study, see Wootton, 'Pierre Bayle: Libertine?'

or Of the Esoteric and Exoteric Philosophy'.[56] In it Toland
points out that many ancient philosophers had both esoteric
teachings, which they communicated only to their close
disciples, and exoteric teachings, which were public to all. In
Toland's view, these two different teachings did not always
occupy two separate worlds: often a text that appears to be
exoteric contains an esoteric message as well. How can one
tell when to read between the lines? When an author provides
strong arguments against a conventional view and only a
weak defence of it (this was an accusation frequently made
against Cardano and Vanini); or when an author provides a
'bounceing compliment' designed to ingratiate him with an
orthodoxy that he would otherwise be seen to be attacking.
In general, Toland agrees with Descartes: conventional views
may only be a camouflage and should not necessarily be
taken too seriously; unconventional ones, especially if they
are likely to get their author into trouble, almost certainly
reflect deeply held convictions. 'Clidophorous' is, amongst
other things, one of the first eloquent pleas for freedom of
speech; for until people can speak freely without fear of
punishment, true intellectual debate will be impossible.

The delight of Toland's essay is that all the time he is
practising what he is describing. He provides a 'bounceing
compliment' to Moses, insisting that he is not to be included
amongst the great statesmen in history who have invented
religions to serve worldly purposes; but the whole thrust of
his argument is that he should be. Sometimes, Toland tells
us, 'that I might hint it *en passant*', the key to the esoteric
meaning of a text is given by the author in the text itself.[57]
The key to 'Clidophorous' (which means 'key-bearer' in
Greek) is the following passage:

I have more than once hinted, that the External and Internal
Doctrine, are as much now in use as ever; tho the distinction is not
so openly and professedly approv'd, as among the Ancients. This
puts me in mind of what I was told by a near relation to the old
Lord Shaftesbury. The latter conferring one day with Major

[56] In John Toland, *Tetradymus* (London, 1720). On Toland see R. E. Sullivan,
John Toland and the Deist Controversy (Cambridge, Mass., 1982).
[57] Toland, *Tetradymus*, 76.

Wildman [the former Leveller] about the many sects of Religion in the world, they came to this conclusion at last; that notwithstanding those infinite divisions caus'd by the interest of the Priests and the ignorance of the People, All Wise Men Are of the Same Religion: whereupon a Lady in the room, who seem'd to mind her needle more than their Discourse, demanded with some concern what that Religion was? to whom the Lord Shaftesbury strait reply'd, Madam, wise men never tell. And indeed, considering how dangerous it is made to tell the truth, tis difficult to know when any man declares his real sentiments of things.[58]

Looking back over the text in the light of this passage, one quickly sees that Toland's whole purpose is to argue not simply that there have been esoteric philosophies, nor merely that there are appropriate ways of discovering these philosophies in exoteric texts; his central claim is that every philosopher has had the same esoteric teaching, namely (to use a term he himself invented), pantheism. This is Toland's esoteric message, concealed within an essay on esotericism.

Two generations earlier, the author of the *Theophrastus redivivus* had maintained that all philosophers had always been atheists—although many of them had sought to conceal their true beliefs from the public. The same view is held by present-day Straussians. It is not one I share. My claim is that the case for thinking that Charron, Sarpi, Bayle, and Vico were attacking Christianity is very different in character from the case for thinking Descartes was an atheist. In the case of Sarpi, the evidence is so strong as to be overwhelming. At the other end of the scale, in the cases of Charron and Bayle, an 'atheistical' reading makes the best sense of what would seem to be deliberately ambiguous texts.

Ambiguity is, however, not the only defence mechanism to which authors turned for refuge. Alan Charles Kors classifies as 'deist' the numerous volumes of the *Letters Writ by a Turkish Spy* (1684–94): let us accept the classification for the moment, although the work is sympathetic in its treatment of pantheism and atomism as well as deism. Its author—almost certainly, after the first volume, an Englishman writing at the time of publication—claimed to be

[58] Ibid. 94–5.

translating from an Italian text, which was itself supposed to be a translation from Turkish.[59] As if this were not protection enough, the letters all purport to have been written at an earlier date, an illusion that is built up through lengthy discussions of, by then, historical events. Thus responsibility is displaced in time and space: as a result, the author can write about sexual morals and religious beliefs as if he were indeed writing private letters, not a public text.

Traditions of Unbelief

Much the most widely admired of the recent books on unbelief has been Carlo Ginzburg's *The Cheese and the Worms*. Ginzburg's brilliant study of Menocchio, a sixteenth-century miller in northern Italy who fell foul of the Inquisition, showed that someone in the upper levels of peasant society could reject Christianity outright, dismiss with contempt the authorities in Church and State, and defend an irreligious cosmology that explained the origins of the gods and of the world: the gods (or angels) appeared by spontaneous generation out of chaos, as worms do out of rotting cheese. The main dispute provoked by Ginzburg's work has been over where Menocchio's ideas came from.[60] For Ginz-

[59] In favour of an English author: J. E. Tucker, 'On the Authorship of the *Turkish Spy*', *Papers of the Bibliographical Society of America*, 52 (1958), 34–57, followed by A. J. Weitzman in his introduction to G. P. Marana, *Letters Writ by a Turkish Spy* (New York, 1970); against: Guido Almansi, '"L'esploratore turco" e la genesi del romanzo epistolare pseudo-orientale', *Studi secenteschi*, 7 (1966), 35–65, followed by Betts, *Early Deism*, 97–114. None of these authors considers an obvious clue, *The Amours of Edward the IV: An Historical Novel by the Author of the 'Turkish Spy'* (London, 1700). There are obvious points of similarity between this work and the *Turkish Spy*, suggesting that they may indeed have the same author.

[60] Carlo Ginzburg, *The Cheese and the Worms* (1976; Eng. trans., Baltimore, 1980). For criticism, see Giorgio Spini, 'Noterelle libertine', *Rivista storica italiana*, 88 (1976), 792–802; Paola Zambelli, 'From Menocchio to Piero della Francesca: The Work of Carlo Ginzburg', *Historical Journal*, 28 (1985), 983–99. Ginzburg was perhaps wrong to assume that the case of Menocchio was comparable to the cases of conflict between popular and official culture that he had studied earlier in *The Night Battles: Witchcraft and Agrarian Cults in the Sixteenth and Seventeenth Centuries* (1966; Eng. trans., London, 1983). Also by Ginzburg on irreligion, 'The Dovecote Has Opened its Eyes', in Gustav Henningsen and John Tedeschi (eds.), *The Inquisition in Early Modern Europe* (DeKalb, Ill., 1986), 190–8.

burg, they are evidence of a hidden stratum of popular culture, and Menocchio's beliefs have, in his view, real continuities with popular beliefs in ancient Rome and in distant India. Ginzburg's notion of a set of popular beliefs extending so widely across time and space has met with much scepticism. Rather than conclude that Menocchio made up his own theories, some have wanted to see them as containing distorted versions of arguments drawn from élite culture, and have sought to stress Menocchio's fragile links with the world of learning (links that may have been less fragile than they seem, for his interrogators were noticeably reluctant to pursue his own hints that he had close contacts with members of the local establishment). In fact, argumentative unbelief seems almost always to have been linked to some measure of education, and the general opinion of early modern commentators was that free-thought was aristocratic rather than popular in character.[61]

Arguments against religion were clearly spread, in all social groups, primarily by word of mouth. Books, of course, were censored, but it was also a fact of early modern life that letters were often intercepted, opened, and read.[62] We need not be surprised that no sixteenth- or seventeenth-century letters discuss religion in the blunt terms employed by the fictional 'Turkish spy' or even by Hume when writing to his friends. But what happened when unbelievers met? Sarpi almost certainly met Hobbes, whose materialism, absolutism, and anticlericalism he shared. Did they discuss religion?[63] He had dealings with Vanini, who was to become, according to Bayle, Western Europe's only martyr for atheism, and seems to have been instrumental in helping him 'convert' to Protestantism and escape (temporarily) to England.[64] Were these

[61] On learned unbelief, see Kors, *Atheism in France*, 57–60. On aristocratic unbelief, see Jean de La Bruyère, 'Of Free-Thinkers', in his *Characters*, trans. H. van Laun (Oxford, 1963), 298–321.

[62] Jerome Christensen, *Practicing Enlightenment: Hume and the Formation of a Literary Career* (Madison, Wis., 1987), 191–4.

[63] Wootton, *Sarpi*, 117, 169; Richard Tuck, *Hobbes* (Oxford, 1989), 10–11, 82, 87. Alan Charles Kors argues in *D'Holbach's Coterie* (Princeton, NJ, 1976), 83–4, that even d'Holbach kept his convictions to himself when talking to close friends.

[64] Francesco de Paola, *Vanini e il primo Seicento anglo-veneto* (Taurisano, 1979). A Turkish martyr also interested Bayle and his contemporaries: see Kors, *Atheism*

links intimate enough to allow the exchange of ideas, perhaps even of manuscripts?[65] Were unbelievers isolated individuals, or did they have a sense of belonging to a wider intellectual community? Did Menocchio speak just for himself, or also for his fellow villagers?

Contemporaries make repeated reference to schools of irreligion.[66] In Raleigh's circle or in Vico's Naples we seem to find evidence of irreligious arguments passing from the educated to the semi-educated: from academics to pharmacists and on to their uneducated assistants. In such circles there must have been a sense of fellow-feeling which goes some way towards explaining the confidence with which the author of the *Theophrastus redivivus* and Toland set out to show that all philosophers had always been atheists. Even Vallée claimed to have acquired his beliefs from conversations with learned men while travelling abroad. We know enough to feel sure that unbelievers were not isolated, even if it is often hard to trace the links between them.

Margaret Jacob's *The Radical Enlightenment* aims to provide a detailed study of clandestine contacts between unbelievers.[67] According to Jacob, Toland, together with close friends and associates of his in Holland, formed a complicated network of semi-private societies within which their ideas could be communicated. They had a secret, proto-Masonic fraternity, set up before official Freemasonry was established on the Continent. They joined the Freemasons. They established a literary society. They met in coffee-houses. All these organizations provided a cover behind which like-minded people could discuss ideas that were subversive of Church and State. It was within this circle, Jacob argues, that the most famous of all the early modern clandestine manuscripts

---

in France, 151–2, 234–5, 256. For an English martyr, see the remarkable poem by Thomas Gilbert, 'A Decleration of the Death of John Lewes', in Emrys Jones (ed.), *The New Oxford Book of Sixteenth-Century Verse* (Oxford, 1990).

[65] We need more studies of the transmission of manuscripts. One example is R. H. Popkin, 'The Dispersion of Bodin's Dialogues in England, Holland, and Germany', *Journal of the History of Ideas*, 49 (1988), 157–60.

[66] Wootton, 'Lucien Febvre', 700.

[67] M. C. Jacob, *The Radical Englightenment: Pantheists, Freemasons and Republicans* (London, 1981).

attacking Christianity, the *Traité des trois imposteurs*, was produced. The Toland fraternity thus joins other groups of like-minded individuals for whom a central role has been claimed in the history of unbelief: the Boulainvilliers connection, the d'Holbach circle.

Ginzburg has admitted that his argument depends upon 'standards of proof different from the usual'.[68] He is clearly right to insist that every discipline establishes its own standards as to what constitutes adequate evidence, but certain standards nevertheless remain common to all disciplines that depend upon the interpretation of texts. It is at this basic level that much of Jacob's book has come under criticism.[69] In Chapter 7 of this book Silvia Berti provides a radically different account of the genesis and nature of the *Traité*. But Jacob is not only concerned to give an account of Toland, his Dutch associates, and their activities. One of her larger theses is that the radicalism of Toland and of the *Traité* was itself a by-product of the collapse of censorship during the English Civil War. At that time not only radical political arguments, but ideas subversive of all established religion were expressed: indeed, the two were linked, for the dualism of conventional Christianity encouraged the establishment of a hierarchial society in which the body was subordinated to the soul, the believer to the priest, and the subject to the king. Pantheism was the equivalent in religion of democracy in politics. Toland, who edited Milton and Harrington, did much to keep the radical political tradition of the English Civil War alive. His pantheism was a natural part of the same tradition. From England this tradition was transmitted to Holland (where Toland's associates were also involved in radical political movements), and from there to the more radical members of the French Enlightenment: d'Holbach in particular.

The evidential basis on which Jacob rests her assertion of a

---

[68] Ginzburg, *The Cheese and the Worms*, 155.
[69] Apart from the criticisms of Berti in this volume, and those she cites, one may also note G. C. Gibbs, 'The Radical Enlightenment', *British Journal for the History of Science*, 17 (1984), 67–81, and Roger Emerson, 'Latitudinarianism and the English Deists', in J. A. Leo Lemay (ed.), *Deism, Masonry and the Englightenment* (Newark, Del., 1987), 19–48.

link between Toland's pantheism and Civil War irreligion is slim at best.[70] But even if we leave aside the question of how much Toland knew about Civil War irreligion and how much it influenced him, we are bound to ask whether Jacob is entitled to claim that there is a natural link between pantheistic materialism and political radicalism, a claim that her references to Civil War radicalism are partly intended to support. Many unbelievers—Menocchio, Gruet, Toland, Meslier—had subversive political views. But others—Naudé, Hobbes, Sarpi, Bayle—were firm defenders of absolutism.[71] Jacob's argument depends on being able to draw a distinction between two types of unbelief: pantheistic materialism and mechanistic materialism; the one radical in its implications, the other potentially conservative. It is not clear that unbelievers can be divided on party lines in this way: materialists of all political persuasions owed a considerable debt to Hobbes, and both the radical and conservative Enlightenments were indebted to Bayle. The first published version of the *Traité* drew directly on three absolutist authors (Charron, Naudé, and Hobbes), whose views on religion it had no difficulty in placing alongside those of Spinoza. No one doubts that the author of the *Traité* was a radical: it is significant that Berti shows that he had little sympathy with Spinoza's pantheism, preferring a straightforward materialism. Thus Jacob's radical pantheist tradition proves remarkably elusive, and she fails, in my view, to make a case for thinking that there was a significant correlation between the alternatives that individuals proposed to orthodox Christianity and their political opinions. Above all, the attempt to classify unbelievers as pantheists or mechanists is as dangerous as the attempt to classify them as atheists or deists, in that it fails to take account of those who do not fit: Hume, for example, or Gibbon.

Despite the problems that Margaret Jacob's book presents, I think she is right to suspect that we need to give more thought to the English contribution to the irreligious Enlight-

---

[70] I hope to show elsewhere that the evidence is slighter than Jacob believes.

[71] The evidence for the unbelief of these 'conservatives' is (with the exception of Sarpi) of a different quality from the evidence for the unbelief of the 'radicals': but this is partly because they were happy to defer to the authorities.

enment. In Holland Benjamin Furly's library (which plays an important role in the work of both Jacob and Berti) contained, along with the manuscript of the *Traité* and works by Spinoza and Bayle, volumes by Hobbes, Toland, Trenchard, Collins, Gildon, and Blount, together with replies by their opponents and conventional defences of Christianity against atheism.[72] Toland, Collins, Woolston, and Mandeville appear in translation among the clandestine French manuscripts in widespread circulation by the second quarter of the eighteenth century. D'Holbach published translations of Hobbes, Toland, Collins, Woolston, and Annet. It was in England that the vocabulary of unbelief was undergoing a second wave of innovation, with the appearance of words such as 'priestcraft', 'materialist', 'free-thinker', 'pantheist'.

Part of England's influence, of course, derived from the end of pre-censorship of the press in 1695: publishing in England was less restrained than in any other country, probably including Holland.[73] But it is also likely that the collapse of the established Church and the crisis in established intellectual life that accompanied the Civil War were important factors in explaining the English contribution to the pre-Enlightenment. In particular, the widespread attack on Puritan 'enthusiasm' (which was held responsible for the Civil War) gave the pre-Enlightenment in England a superficial respectability that it lacked in other countries. At the same time, latitudinarianism and Newtonian natural theology encouraged a retreat from doctrinal theology, a retreat that made the dissemination of deism all the easier.[74]

Above all, we need a better understanding of the role of John Locke's philosophy in the development of an enlightened scepticism towards religion. Locke himself was probably a Socinian: which is to say that he believed in the Gospel narrative and in the Resurrection, but not in original sin or

[72] *Bibliotheca Furliana, sive catalogus librorum* (Rotterdam, 1714).

[73] There was more censorship in Holland than is generally recognized: S. Groenveld, 'The Mecca of Authors? States Assemblies and Censorship in the Seventeenth Century Dutch Republic' in Duke and Tamse (ed.), *Too Mighty to be Free*, 63–86, and Bayle, *Dictionary*, 'Socinus'.

[74] A valuable essay on the history of natural theology is N. C. Gillespie, 'Natural History, Natural Philosophy and Social Order: John Ray and the "Newtonian Ideology"', *Journal of the History of Biology*, 20 (1987), 1–49.

48 *David Wootton*

the Trinity.[75] But whatever his private beliefs, his uncompromising subordination of revelation to reason had revolutionary implications; moreover, he firmly rejected Cartesian arguments for the immateriality of the soul, and in the process gave legitimacy to materialism; he identified the good with the pleasurable, and morality with the pursuit of happiness; and (not to extend the list unduly) his attack on innate principles and universal consent gave the libertine critique of the hold of religion upon men's minds a solid philosophical foundation. Those who read Locke on custom must have believed him to be endorsing the views of Charron, custom being

a greater power than Nature, seldom failing to make them [children and young folk] worship for Divine, what she hath inured them to bow their Minds, and submit their Understandings to, it is no wonder, that grown *Men*, either perplexed in the necessary affairs of Life, or hot in the pursuit of Pleasures, should *not* seriously sit down to *examine their own Tenets*; especially when one of their Principles is, That Principles ought not to be questioned. And, had Men leisure, parts, and will, Who is there almost, that dare shake the foundations of all his past Thoughts and Actions, and endure to bring upon himself, the shame of having been a long time wholly in mistake and error? Who is there, hardy enough to contend with the reproach, which is every where prepared for those, who dare venture to dissent from the received Opinions of their Country or Party? And where is the Man to be found, that can patiently prepare himself to bear the name of Whimsical, Sceptical, or Atheist, which he is sure to meet with, who does in the least scruple any of the common Opinions?[76]

Locke had probably never heard of Geoffroy Vallée, who, accused of being whimsical, decided to bring upon himself the charge of atheism too, complaining that believers recited like parrots the irrational views with which they had been indoctrinated while still in the cradle. But he was soon to take an interest in the case of Aikenhead, who went too far in questioning common opinions. We should not be surprised

[75] John Marshall, 'John Locke and Socinianism', in M. A. Stewart (ed.), *Oxford Studies in the History of Philosphy*, 2 (Oxford, forthcoming).
[76] John Locke, *An Essay Concerning Human Understanding*, ed. P. H. Nidditch (Oxford, 1975), bk. 1, ch. 3, para. 25. The *Essay* was published in French in 1700.

if Locke himself was cautious and did not always spell out the radical implications for conventional theology of the *Essay concerning Human Understanding*.

The Emergence of Probability

In the years after the publication of Locke's *Essay concerning Human Understanding* the foundations were certainly shaken, and soon men would appear who were prepared to beareven the name of atheist. At the moment our knowledge of Locke's immediate reception is too patchy to give us an adequate understanding of his contribution to the spread of unbelief. We have no study, for example, of the influence of Locke in France that corresponds to the studies of the influence of Bayle and of Spinoza.[77] As a result, we have an insufficient grasp of just how the foundations came to crumble.

Nevertheless, it is clear that the period 1680–1715, the period Hazard labelled that of *La Crise de la conscience européenne*, represents a take-off point for irreligious speculation. In 1686 Jean le Clerc commented on the new confidence with which religion was being attacked: 'The libertines of centuries past maintained their opinions out of sheer moral depravity, and attacked the Christian religion with nothing more than coarse humour that could only influence those whose hearts and minds were already debauched. But nowadays they use the weapons of philosophy and [historical] criticism in order to demolish our most sacred and unshakeable doctrines.'[78] By the time of his death in 1714 Furly (who was not himself irreligious but who had an interest in anti-

[77] Pierre Rétat, *Le Dictionnaire de Bayle et la lutte philosophique au XVIIIᵉ siècle* (Paris, 1971); Pierre Vernière, *Spinoza et la pensée française avant la Révolution* (2 vols., Paris, 1954). We have two valuable studies of the reception of the *Essay* in England: J. W. Yolton, *John Locke and the Way of Ideas* (Oxford, 1956), and id., *Thinking Matter: Materialism in Eighteenth-Century Britain* (Oxford, 1984); and a number of accounts of Locke's reception in America, most recently S. M. Dworetz, *The Unvarnished Doctrine: Locke, Liberalism, and the American Revolution* (Durham, NC, 1990).

[78] J. le Clerc, *Défense des sentimens de quelques théologiens* (Amsterdam, 1686), 219–20.

establishment speculation) had a library that contained much
that would have been of interest to a Voltaire or a d'Holbach,
and that was, indeed, of interest to his friends, many of
whom are now regarded as founders of the Enlightenment—
including Locke (who stayed with him for a lengthy period),
Bayle, the third Earl of Shaftesbury, Collins, Trenchard, and
Toland. Here too, of course, one could find the works of
Cartesian and anti-Cartesian debate that have attracted the
attention of Alan Charles Kors.

There are a number of possible approaches one can take to
this take-off period. One can claim that, substantially, it is in
fact continuous with the unbelief of the early seventeenth
century: that the late seventeenth century had little to contribute that was not to be found in Naudé or the *Theophrastus
redivivus*.[79] One can see it, as Jacob does, as a long-term
consequence of the English Revolution, or, with Febvre and
Kors, as a consequence of the crisis provoked by Cartesianism. One can argue that the key event was the publication of
Bayle's *Pensées diverses*: this was, as we have seen, the first
book to maintain that atheism was not necessarily subversive
of the social order. Henceforward, unbelievers might fear
censorship, but they had no need to engage in self-censorship.
They could feel justified in circulating their arguments more
freely.

None of these arguments seems to me to be entirely
satisfactory. Bayle may have been much indebted to Montaigne and Naudé, but it is hard not to feel that there is a
qualitative difference between his discussions of the arguments for faith and theirs. The English Revolution hardly
helps to explain Spinoza or Bayle; while the crisis caused by
Cartesianism had few implications for biblical criticism
(pioneered by La Peyrère, Hobbes, Spinoza, and Richard
Simon), or for debates over whether atheists could make
good citizens.[80] The correct answer, of course, is almost

---

[79] This is Tullio Gregory's view: see his 'Il libertinismo della prima metà del
Seicento', in Gregory *et al. Ricerche su lettaratura*, 3–47.

[80] A useful history of biblical criticism is contained in H. G. Reventlow, *The
Authority of the Bible and the Rise of the Modern World* (Philadelphia, 1985). See
also Gerard Reedy, *The Bible and Reason: Anglicans and Scripture in Late
Seventeenth-Century England* (Philadelphia, 1985), and, on La Peyrère, R. H.
Popkin, *Isaac La Peyrère (1596–1676)* (Leiden, 1987).

certainly that the unbelief and atheism of the Enlightenment had many sources, not just one.

There are, however, two novel developments of the period after 1660 that had radical implications for a wide range of intellectual activities. The first is Jansenism. Bayle's account of how self-interest, not faith, held society together was derived in large part from the writings of Nicole, and was first published under the guise of Jansenist authorship. Hume's discussion of the credibility of miracles was couched in terms which derived from Arnauld and Nicole's *La Logique*. Pascal's *Pensées* marked the beginning of a new fideism, and appeared to suggest that Christianity could not rely on arguments drawn from reason.

Nor would it be right to see in Jansenist philosophy merely the continuing influence of Descartes. For one of the reasons for the impact of Nicole, Arnauld, and Pascal was their willingness to think in terms of probability theory rather than in terms of the deductive certainties advocated by Descartes. Masked by the omnipresence of Jansenist arguments in the origins of modern unbelief is a second, more fundamental development: the extraordinary shift that Ian Hacking has termed 'the emergence of probability'.[81] Pascal's wager was to be a continuing challenge for unbelievers. Arnauld's discussion of miracles in the *La Logique* treated historical evidence as a question of probabilities and shaped the historical methodology of the Enlightenment, leading to a new approach to source criticism, an approach with significant implications for biblical criticism. Finally, Nicole's account of self-interest and of market forces was a description of unintended consequences (services are provided, the economy grows, individuals find themselves better off merely because each seeks a short-term profit), and these unintended consequences had to be thought of as probable outcomes not necessary consequences. Probability theory made as important a contribution to Enlightenment unbelief as anything that went before. If we are looking for an epistemological caesura

---

[81] Ian Hacking, *The Emergence of Probability* (Cambridge, 1975). For a discussion of probability theory and unbelief, see Wootton, 'Hume's "Of Miracles"', and id., 'Lucien Febvre', 719–26.

separating the world of faith from the world of unbelief, probability, not Cartesianism, is our best candidate. Much of the importance of Locke lies in the fact that he isolated, crystallized, and secularized probability arguments that derived from Jansenist sources.

Let us turn, for the last time, to the sad fate of Geoffroy Vallée. Vallée's central claim was that there were two types of belief. One—belief in the evidence of our senses, for example—was imposed upon us by nature, and was rational. The other—belief in the Creed, for example—was imposed upon us by society and was irrational. But it was easy for his interrogators to catch Vallée in contradictions. Were there not things of which he had no direct experience but which he nevertheless believed to be real? If he was going to renege and admit the existence of heaven, hell, and purgatory, would he not have to admit that it was sensible to believe things of which one had no direct experience? At this point it was mental confusion, as well as fear, that reduced Vallée to the silence that represented the ultimate victory of his interrogators.

Febvre was right to claim that sixteenth-century unbelievers lacked some of the conceptual tools with which to defend unbelief. The situation was radically altered as the emergence of probability theory introduced the notion of (to use Locke's terms) degrees of assent: armed with such a notion, Vallée could quickly have separated out different types and degrees of rational belief. All he would have had to do to defend his unbelief was to deny that Locke was entitled to make one solitary exception to the rule that the more unlikely something was, the more evidence one should require before one believed it—the solitary exception being reports of miracles, which, Locke claimed, were events that became all the more credible the more unlikely they were. Vallée was not, as Kors terms him, an 'atheist without atheism'; rather, he was an unbeliever without probability theory. Probability judgements are not central to the positive arguments of atheism and deism; but they lie at the heart of the negative claims of unbelief.

Hacking points out that gamblers had a pretty good idea of the odds even before they had access to the mathematical techniques required to calculate them correctly. So too there were level-headed unbelievers before the emergence of probability theory. But they were at a constant disadvantage, often accused of being whimsical as well as sceptical. It was to be more than a century after Vallée's death before it became widely recognized not only that principles ought to be questioned, but also just how one should go about questioning them. In the history of ideas Vallée's clumsy arguments are of little importance, just as all those gamblers receive only a passing mention in the history of probability theory. What is important is the phrase that marks his defeat by his interrogators. That single phrase, 'N'a seu respondre', marks the edge of his conceptual world; by the end of the seventeenth century Vallée's silence was giving way to philosophical debate. Was it rational, Locke asked, for an Indian prince to believe in ice if he could have no experience of it? Should one believe, Hume asked a generation later, in a miracle that one had not seen with one's own eyes? These were identified as problems in probability theory, and by arguing in terms of probabilities, others were to answer the questions that silenced Vallée. In doing so, however, they were merely clarifying the distinctions he had wanted to make, between knowledge and credulity, experience and tradition, reason and superstition. His arguments may have been clumsy, but they were not beside the point. His real historical importance is not that he demonstrates, as Bayle supposed, the tendency of unchecked reason to lead to unbelief, but that he illustrates the historical limits within which reason operates.

2

Unbelief and Atheism in Italy, 1500–1700

NICHOLAS DAVIDSON

'Most of my friends are so well educated they can
scarcely believe God exists'.

L. Sozzini, *Opere*, ed. A. Rotondò, 136.

These words appear in a letter from Lelio Sozzini to John
Calvin written on 14 May 1549. Sozzini had been born in
Sienna in 1525; by 1549 he was living in Zurich, an exile 'pro
religionis causa'. For he was no orthodox Christian: having
submitted the received doctrines of the faith to the test of his
own reason, he had come to doubt the divinity of Christ, the
resurrection of the body, and the verbal inerrancy of Scripture. He was also, not surprisingly, aware of arguments in
favour of religious dissimulation.[1] But he was clearly no
atheist, and he attributes the remark about friends who do
doubt God's existence to a hypothetical third party.

The conviction that Italy was a breeding-ground for atheists was, however, commonplace in the early modern period,
especially among foreign visitors to the Peninsula. Roger
Ascham reported in 1551 that in Italy 'a man may freelie
discourse against what he will, against whom he lust: against

[*Author's Note*. Earlier versions of this paper were presented to seminars at the
Universities of Edinburgh and Birmingham, at the Institute of Historical Research
in London, and at Trinity University, San Antonio. I am grateful to Dr Richard
Mackenney, Professor Robert Knecht, Dr Robert Oresko, Dr John Martin, and to
all who participated in those seminars for their helpful and constructive comments;
and to Dr Michael Hunter, Professor Brian Pullan, and Professor David Wootton
for some wise advice on the final typescript.]

[1] L. Sozzini, *Opere*, ed. A. Rotondò (Florence, 1986), 25, 28, 49–56, 61–5, 67, 72,
134–7, 153–7; cf. D. Cantimori, *Eretici italiani del Cinquecento: Ricerche storiche*
(Florence, 1939), 137–8; C. Renato, *Opere, documenti e testimonianze*, ed. A.
Rotondò (DeKalb and Chicago, 1968), 328–9.

any Prince, agaynst any gouernement, yea against God him selfe, and his whole Religion'.[2] In the seventeenth century Gui Patin described Italy as a land of 'pox, poisoning, and atheism',[3] and in the eighteenth century the Countess of Pomfret reported that many Italians 'of parts and learning are tempted to throw off all tradition at once' and 'proceed to the other extreme: they assert the eternity of the world; deny the government of Providence; and . . . renounce the God of nature'.[4] Foreign writers liked to compile lists of celebrated Italian atheists: Johannes Micraelius named Aretino, Ochino, Poggio, Clement VII, Alexander VI, Pomponazzi, Cremonini, Vanini, and Galileo;[5] Thomas Philipps added Ermolao Barbaro, Ficino, Poliziano, Porzio, Berigardo, and Cardano.[6] The origins of Italian atheism were variously traced: to the new learning of the Renaissance or the survival of scholasticism; to the Lutheran Reformation or the influence of Catholicism; to the Calvinists or the Anabaptists; to the disciples of Machiavelli or the followers of Epicurus.[7]

---

[2] R. Ascham, *The Scholemaster*, in his *English Works*, ed. W. Aldis Wright (Cambridge, 1904), 236; cf. 222–33. The first edition was published in 1570, two years after Ascham's death. For his visit to Italy, see S. L. Lee, 'Ascham, Roger', *DNB*, ii. 154.

[3] 'L'Italie est un pays de vérole, d'empoisonments et d'athéisme', letter 452 (to André Falconet) in *Lettres de Gui Patin*, ed. J. -H. Reveillé-Parise (3 vols.; Paris, 1846), iii. 80; cf. 333. For Patin, cf. J. Delumeau, 'Croyants et sceptiques au XVIᵉ siècle', in his *Un chemin d'histoire: Chrétienté et christianisation* (Paris, 1981), 44–50 (p. 46).

[4] *Correspondence between Frances, Countess of Hartford and Henrietta Louisa, Countess of Pomfret, between the Years 1738 and 1741* (2 vols.; London, 1805), i. 208–10; cf. ii. 251. Other visitors who remarked on the prevalence of atheism in Italy include the author of the *Naudaeana et Patiniana ou Singularitez remarquables* (Paris, 1701), 6–7, 38, 90.

[5] J. Micraelius, *Historia ecclesiastica* (Magdeburg, 1699), 887–8.

[6] J. T. Philipps, *Dissertatio historico-philosophico de atheismo* (London, 1716), 75–96.

[7] For examples of these claims, separately or in groups, see *Naudaeana*, 233–4; T. Campanella, *Atheismus triumphatus, seu Reductio ad religionem per scientiarum veritates* (Paris, 1636), 167 and the dedication to Louis XIII; T. Campanella, *The Defense of Galileo*, trans. G. McColley, (Northampton, Mass., 1937), 21; D. Pastine, 'L'immagine del libertino nell'apologetica cattolica del XVII secolo', in T. Gregory *et al.* (eds.), *Ricerche su letteratura libertina e letteratura clandestina nel Seicento* (Florence, 1981), 143–73 (p. 149); Philipps, *Dissertatio*, 76–7; G. Spini, *Ricerca dei libertini: La teoria dell'impostura delle religioni nel Seicento italiano* (Rome, 1950), 75–6; Micraelius, *Historia ecclesiastica*, 887; F. M. Bonini, *L'ateista convinto dalle sole ragioni* (Venice, 1665), 302; J. Calvin, *Three French Treatises*, ed. F. M. Higman (London, 1970), 141.

Modern historians have normally preferred to doubt the reliability of such accusations. Lucien Febvre argued that a systematic atheism was actually impossible before the end of the seventeenth century; references to 'atheists' before that date should be understood, he said, as insults rather than accurate intellectual descriptions.[8] Certainly the word was used rather freely: for suicides and opponents of belief in witchcraft, for the immoral and the physically self-indulgent.[9] But contemporaries used a number of such representative words as insults. In 1533, for example, the Venetian Council of Ten warned their officials in Verona that the friars of S. Fermo, who were responsible for many 'filthinesses' (*spurcicie*) with the nuns of the Magdalene, 'do not want to live under the rule of their founder, but as sons of iniquity . . . as Epicureans and Lutherans'.[10] Yet nobody now suggests that, in the sixteenth century, the word 'Lutheran' did not refer to something that really existed, even though it could also be used inaccurately; and the appearance of the word 'atheist' similarly indicates a contemporary awareness of at least the possibility of serious unbelief. It would hardly have been effective as an insult unless it had conveyed some sort of agreed meaning.[11]

None the less, contemporaries do seem to have found the term difficult to apply consistently. Guillaume Postel used it in Greek in 1544 of Italians who denied that spiritual substances could exist independently of the material world

[8] L. Febvre, *The Problem of Unbelief in the Sixteenth Century: The Religion of Rabelais* (Eng. trans., London, 1982), 131–2, 135–9; cf. D. Wootton, 'Lucien Febvre and the Problem of Unbelief in the Early Modern Period', *Journal of Modern History*, 60 (1988), 695–730.

[9] See e.g. G. C. Nelli, *Saggio di storia letteraria fiorentina del secolo* XVII (Lucca, 1759), 117 (on Antonio Oliva); F. Fabbri, *Adversus impios atheos* (Venice, 1627), 1 ('ede, bibe, lude, post mortem nulla voluptas'); M. Squarcialupi, *Simonis Simonii Lucensis, primum Romani, tum Calviniani, deinde Lutherani, denuo Romani, semper autem Athei summa religio* (Cracow, 1588), 19 ('Ede, bibe, lude iam Deus figmentum est').

[10] Archivio di Stato, Venice (hereafter ASVen), Consiglio dei Dieci, *Secrete*, reg. 4, fo. 5ᵛ.

[11] Ludovico Ariosto used the accusation of unbelief against his opponents: see his *Sonnetti*, 39, l. 6, and his *Satire*, 6, ll. 34–66. Cf. the suggestions of H. Busson, 'Les Noms des incrédules au XVIᵉ siècle', *Bibliothèque d'humanisme et Renaissance*, 16 (1954), 273–83 (pp. 278, 281–3); D. Wootton, 'Unbelief in Early Modern Europe', *History Workshop Journal*, 20 (1985), 82–100 (p. 91); and Febvre, *The Problem of Unbelief*, 357.

and who therefore rejected belief in the immortality of the soul. Eight years later he used it in Latin of those unable to acknowledge the government of providence.[12] Other writers used the term to describe those who rejected the Scriptures or laughed at miracles.[13] And in 1586 the Inquisition tribunal in Venice used it in Italian when interrogating Girolamo Garzoni, the prior of S. Maria delle Grazie:

we can see very little devotion or reverence in you towards God or our sacred Christian and Catholic law; we can therefore draw the legitimate consequence . . . that you have not believed anything in our faith and that you are consequently an atheist—that is, that you do not believe there is any God in this world and that the world was created by chance [*chel mondo sia fatto à caso*].[14]

Obviously, such examples demonstrate a generalized fear of atheism in early modern Italy, even though there may have been no universally agreed definition of its meaning. But attacks on supposed (and often unnamed) 'atheists' do not by themselves prove its existence in fact, and it could be argued that evidence of opposition to 'atheism' tells us more about the preoccupations of its opponents than about the phenomenon to which they were opposed. Indeed, the ideas linked with atheism by contemporaries may at first sight seem to

[12] G. Postel, *Quatuor librorum de orbis terrae concordia primus* (Paris, 1544), fo. 67ʳ, and cf. fo. 83ᵛ; G. Postel, *Liber de causis seu de principiis et originibus naturae utriusque, in quo ita de eterna rerum veritate agitur, ut et authoritate et ratione non tantum ubivis particularis Dei providentia, sed et animorum et corporum immortalitate ex ipsius Aristotelis verbis recte intellectis et non detortis demonstretur clarissime: Contra atheos . . .* (Paris, 1552). In his *De fato* Pomponazzi argued that denying God's providence is the same as denying his existence: A. Poppi, 'Fate, Fortune, Providence and Human Freedom', in C. B. Schmitt *et al.* (eds.), *The Cambridge History of Renaissance Philosophy* (Cambridge, 1988), 641–67 (p. 656).

[13] Busson, 'Les Noms', 273–4; G. C. Vanini, *Le opere*, ed. L. Corvaglia, (2 vols.; Milan, 1933–4), i, pp. xix–xx. Cf. also Alberto Bolognetti's reference to the 'atheismo' preached at the Carmine in Venice during his nunciature, in A. Stella (ed.), *Chiesa e stato nelle relazioni dei nunzi pontifici a Venezia: Ricerche sul giurisdizionalismo veneziano dal* XVI *al* XVIII *secolo* (Vatican City, 1964), 280. Among other Italian texts against atheism, it is worth noting especially the unpublished *Trattato contra l'ateismo* by the celebrated Franciscan preacher Francesco Panigarola, mentioned in F. Argellati, *Bibliotheca scriptorum Mediolanensium* (2 vols.; Milan, 1745), ii. 1035; and Fausto Sozzini's *Contra atheos*: Sozzini considered this to be his best work, but the MS was lost during the sack of his Cracow house in 1598 (G. Pioli, *Fausto Socini: Vita, opere, fortuna* (Modena, 1952), 10).

[14] ASVen, *Santo Uffizio* (hereafter *SU*), b. 52, 'Garzoni, Girolamo', fos. 64ʳ–ᵛ.

have little do do with each other. Yet all of them are likely to appear in any systematic denial of God's existence. For a belief that there is no God must also require a rejection of any belief in a non-material creator and of the authority of the Bible which records the act of creation. It may lead to doubt about the independent existence of other spiritual beings, including the human soul, and so to a denial of the afterlife. Taken singly, none of these subsidiary ideas amounts to 'atheism' in the modern sense; yet if any one of them is absent, its development may be impossible. And if they are all current, even among men and women who are not self-consciously unbelievers, the possibility of atheism is at least conceivable.[15] More than twenty years ago Paul Oskar Kristeller suggested that the arguments of non-atheist writers might have helped to form the philosophy of atheist readers.[16] Certainly, in early modern Italy all the arguments necessary for a fully developed atheism were put into circulation by believers.

Arguments about God were not new in the early modern period. Philosophers were aware of debates in the ancient world about the nature of the divinity, and normally credited Epicurus with an outright denial of God's existence.[17] The legacy of Aristotle was more uncertain, however, for while some authors tried to defend his piety,[18] others claimed that

[15] Cf. the way in which Filippo Fabbri builds his description of atheism from a list of such beliefs (including the denial of God's existence) at the beginning of his *Adversus impios atheos*. This text is discussed by A. Poppi, 'Un teologo di fronte alla cultura libertina del Rinascimento italiano', *Quaderni per la storia dell'Università di Padova*, 4 (1971), 103–18. For the contemporary image of 'atheism' and 'atheists', see M. Hunter, 'Science and Heterodoxy: An Early Modern Problem Reconsidered', in D. C. Lindberg and R. S. Westman (eds.), *Reappraisals of the Scientific Revolution* (Cambridge, 1990), 437–60.

[16] P. O. Kristeller, 'The Myth of Renaissance Atheism and the French Tradition of Free Thought', *Journal of the History of Philosophy*, 6 (1968), 233–43 (pp. 242–3); cf. D. Wootton, *Paolo Sarpi: Between Renaissance and Enlightenment* (Cambridge, 1983), 3.

[17] See e.g. C. Berigardo, *Circulus Pisanus* (Padua, 1661), 174–5; cf. J. Kraye, 'Moral Philosophy', in Schmitt *et al.*, *Cambridge History*, 303–86 (p. 382), for the common Renaissance misunderstanding of Epicurus' teaching.

[18] Postel, *Liber de causis*; H. Busson, *La Pensée religieuse française de Charron à Pascal* (Paris, 1933), 244.

his work came close to atheism.[19] The influence of Aristotle's medieval commentators caused further problems: the twelfth-century Muslim Averroes, for example, had cast doubt on the ability of Aristotle's 'first cause' to influence events on earth, an argument that reappears in Renaissance philosophers such as Alessandro Achillini.[20] Pietro Pomponazzi took these ideas one stage further in his *De incantationibus* of 1520: if God has submitted all things on earth to a universal law, can he now alter or ignore that law without altering himself? If he alters himself, does he cease to be God? And if he will not alter his law or himself, can prayer serve any purpose?[21] Despite the problems associated with Aristotle's thought, his works remained authoritative—essential university texts—throughout the sixteenth century, so much so that Tommaso Campanella launched a campaign against them in the early seventeenth century, arguing that no pagan scholarship could be compatible with Christianity.[22]

---

[19] See e.g. B. Donato, *De Platonicae atque Aristotelicae philosophiae differentia* (Venice, 1540), 63; I. Zabarella, *In tres Aristotelis libros De anima commentarii* (Venice, 1605), iii, fos. 73ᵛ–74ʳ.

[20] See e.g. the comments of G. Saitta, *Il pensiero italiano nell'umanesimo e nel Rinascimento* (3 vols.; Bologna, 1949–51), ii. 328; Wootton, 'Unbelief in Early Modern Europe', 84. Achillini lived from c.1463 to 1512. Even Protestant Italians were influenced by Averroes: see Cantimori, *Eretici italiani*, 99–100.

[21] See e.g. P. Pomponazzi, *De naturalium effectuum admirandorum causis seu De incantationibus liber* (Basle, 1567), 120, 134, 222–3, 243–4 (see further in M. Doni, 'Il "De incantationibus" di Pietro Pomponazzi e l'edizione di Guglielmo Grataroli', *Rinascimento*, 15 (1975), 183–230, for the history of this text). Similar arguments appear in critics of Aristotle: see A. Cesalpino, *Quaestionum peripateticarum* (Venice, 1593), fos. 2ʳ, 31ᵛ–32ʳ. Cesalpino lived from c. 1524 to 1603.

[22] T. Campanella, *De gentilismo non retinendo* (Paris, 1636), 7–8, 16, 19–20, 30; Campanella, *Defense of Galileo*, 24–5, 30. Doubts about Aristotle's authority had already been raised in the 16th cent. by a number of Italian writers influenced by the Renaissance recovery and assimilation of texts by ancient Sceptics such as Sextus Empiricus: see especially C. B. Schmitt, 'The Rediscovery of Ancient Skepticism in Modern Times', in his *Reappraisals in Renaissance Thought*, ed. C. Webster (London, 1989), ch. 12. See also the arguments of Bernardino Telesio's *De rerum natura*, published in several editions from 1565, and the comments of L. De Franco in his modern edition of the text, *De rerum natura, libri* VII–VIII–IX (Florence, 1976), pp. xiv–xvii. De Franco's comments provide the best recent introduction to Telesio's thought; except where indicated, however, I cite from the Naples edition of 1587. An Italian translation of 1573 by Francesco Martelli appears in F. Palermo (ed.), *I manoscritti palatini di Firenze* (3 vols.; Florence, 1853–68), iii. 1–232. Despite his fame as a philosopher, Telesio never held an academic post. The *De rerum natura* was put on the Index, along with other titles by Telesio, 'donec expurgentur' (F.H. Reusch, *Die Indices Librorum Prohibitorum des Sechzehnten Jahrhunderts* (Tübingen, 1886), 542).

One aspect of Aristotle's thought that troubled Campanella was his denial of the creation.[23] Diodorus Siculus had indicated that a number of ancients believed that the world 'was not generated, and is incorruptible, and that men have existed *ab eterno*'.[24] In 1513 the Papacy condemned such teaching, but Italians such as Celio Secundo Curione and Girolamo Cardano continued (for different reasons) to put it forward.[25] Giordano Bruno was also accused of believing that 'God was not the creator of the world, for the world was eternal just like God';[26] during his trial he denied the charge, but in his *De l'infinito*, written in 1591, he had praised Democritus and Epicurus for arguing 'that everything throughout infinity suffereth renewal and restoration . . . alleging a constant and unchanging number of particles of identical material that perpetually undergo transformation one into another'.[27] Atomist ideas of this kind had been available in Italy since about 1417, when the manuscript of Lucretius' *De rerum natura* had been rediscovered by Poggio Bracciolini,[28] and they seem to lie behind passages in texts such as Bernardino Telesio's *De natura rerum* of 1565.[29] Galileo made use of them again in his *Saggiatore* of 1623,[30] as did Claudio Berigardo in the

[23] Campanella, *De gentilismo*, 7.

[24] I have used the translation by Francesco Baldelli: *Historia overo Libraria historica di Diodoro Siciliano* (Venice, 1574), 7.

[25] *Bullarium diplomatum et privilegiorum sanctorum romanorum pontificum* (25 vols.; Turin, 1857–72), v. 602; Cantimori, *Eretici italiani*, 100; G. Cardano, *Opera omnia* (10 vols; Lyons, 1663), iii. 358–60. Among others holding similar beliefs was Agostino Steuco, prefect of the Vatican Library from 1538: see D. P. Walker, *The Ancient Theology* (London, 1972), 38; C. B. Schmitt, 'Perennial Philosophy: From Agostino Steuco to Leibniz', *Journal of the History of Ideas*, 27 (1966), 505–32.

[26] A. Mercati, *Il sommario del processo di Giordano Bruno* (Vatican City, 1942), 79, 84.

[27] G. Bruno, *Opere italiane*, ed. G. Gentile (2 vols.; Bari, 1907–8), i. 274; I quote from the translation by D. W. Singer, *Giordano Bruno: His Life and Thought* (New York, 1950), 245. See also P. Redondi, *Galileo Heretic* (Eng. trans., London, 1987), 60–1, 64.

[28] H. A. J. Munro, *T. Lucretii Cari De rerum natura* (Cambridge, 1886), 2–3. The Latin text was first published in Brescia in 1473; an Italian translation was made by Alessandro Marchetti from 1664 and published in London in 1717. An early discussion of the implications of ideas associated with Epicurus and Democritus appears in Giannozzo Manetti's *Contra iudeos et gentes*, written in the 1450s: C. Trinkaus, *In our Image and Likeness* (2 vols.; London, 1970), ii. 727–8.

[29] B. Telesio, *De natura iuxta propria principia* (Rome, 1565), 80; Telesio, *De rerum natura*, 8–9.

[30] Redondi, *Galileo*, offers an exclusively atomist interpretation of this work (see

middle of the seventeenth century to support a belief in the
eternity of matter.[31] The adoption of atomism did not necessarily presuppose a rejection of Christian teaching; but the
Church took alarm none the less. In the 1570s the Jesuit
Benito Pereira criticized the atomist conception of matter,[32]
and the atomism in Galileo's *Saggiatore* was attacked in 1626
by Monsignor Orazio Grassi because, he said, it left no place
for the established Catholic doctrine of transubstantiation.[33]
From 1632 the Jesuit colleges were repeatedly warned not to
teach atomist physics.[34] But scientists such as Giovanni
Alfonso Borelli continued to promote it, and books by
scholars such as Gassendi that made use of atomist theories
were freely available in Tuscany after 1660.[35]

The ancient world had, in addition, provided an alternative
account of the creation that owed nothing either to theories
about the eternity of matter or to atomism. In a vivid passage
Diodorus Siculus had described how the earth and the sky
had separated at the beginning of creation, allowing the heat

---

e.g. pp. 14, 54–6, 58, 64–6), and Fulgenzio Micanzio certainly seems to have been
attracted by this aspect (A. Favaro (ed.), *Le Opere di Galileo Galilei* (20 vols.);
Florence, 1890–1909), xvi. 154–5). The text itself, however, deals with other matters
as well, as V. Ferrone and M. Firpo point out ('From Inquisitors to Microhistorians:
A Critique of Pietro Redondi's *Galileo eretico*', *Journal of Modern History*, 58
(1986), 485–524 (p. 502)). Galileo claimed that he had never studied Epicurus
(*Opere*, vi. 476).

[31] Berigardo, *Circulus Pisanus*, 83–4, 418–25. I agree with Paolo Casini (*Introduzione all'illuminismo: da Newton a Rousseau* (Bari, 1973), 271–2) about Berigardo's
subtle support for the atomist framework; cf. also N. Badaloni, 'Libertinismo e
scienza negli anni di Galilei e Campanella', in Gregory *et al.*, *Ricerche su letteratura*,
213–29 (pp. 220–2). I am aware that there were important differences between
various corpuscular or atomist theories, but, for convenience, I use the term 'atomist'
here for all of them.

[32] B. Pereira, *De communibus omnium rerum naturalium principiis et affectionibus*
(Paris, 1579), 268–70; an earlier edition was published in Rome in 1576.

[33] *Ratio ponderum librae et simbellae*, republished in Galileo, *Opere*, vi. 373–500,
especially pp. 486–90 (translated in Redondi, *Galileo*, 335–40).

[34] Ferrone and Firpo, 'From Inquisitors to Microhistorians', 511–12.

[35] Redondi, *Galileo*, 94, 306–7—though cf. also Ferrone and Firpo, 'From
Inquisitors to Microhistorians', 493–6, 519–20; Casini, *Introduzione all'illuminismo*,
272; G. Grandi, *Risposta apologetica* (Lucca, 1712), 175–6; U. Baldini, *Un libertino
accademico del Cimento: Antonio Oliva* (Florence, 1977), 30–1. For further scientific
theories that undermined traditional thinking, see Galileo, *Opere*, xi. 149; L. Firpo,
'Il processo di Giordano Bruno', *Rivista storica italiana*, 60 (1948), 542–97 (pp.
595–6); and Badaloni, 'Libertinismo', 225 (on Borelli).

of the sun to work on the residual mud so that it began to stagnate and decay like a swamp; life-forms were generated by the heat in bubbles on the surface, and eventually emerged as animals, birds, or fish.[36] This theory of spontaneous generation—a creationist theory that, at best, minimizes the role of God—was adopted by Italians such as Andrea Cesalpino, who was prepared to trace even the origin of mankind to decaying matter;[37] and several Italians believed in a continuing process of spontaneous generation, at least among lower creatures such as flies and mosquitoes, snakes, mice, and moles.[38]

These intellectual arguments cast doubt on some basic Christian doctrines—but the willingness to question established beliefs was not confined to philosophers and scientists. In the records of the sixteenth and seventeenth centuries we can frequently trace a scepticism about elements of Church teaching that owes more to a preoccupation with daily life than to academic speculation. A nice example is provided by the comment of Matteo de Vincenti, a turner in Venice, after a sermon on the doctine of the Real Presence on Palm Sunday 1576: 'it's nonsense, having to believe these things—they're stories. I would rather believe I had money in my pocket.'[39] Belief in transubstantiation seems to have caused particular difficulties in the minds of the laity, for, as Giuseppe Caretta was reported to have said a few years previously in Portobuffole, 'if Christ were truly present in essence in the Host, you would know—because when the priest breaks the bread, you would hear the bones snap.'[40] Such opinions may, of

---

[36] Diodorus, *Historia*, 7–8; Avicenna had used a similar explanation to account for the emergence of life after the Flood: G. B. della Porta, *Della magia naturale* (Naples, 1611), 52.

[37] Cesalpino, *Quaestionum peripateticarum*, fos. 104^v–109^v; cf. also P. Zambelli, *Une réincarnation de Jean Pic à l'époque de Pomponazzi* (Mainz, 1977), 42–5, and P. Zambelli, 'From Menocchio to Piero della Francesca: The work of Carlo Ginzburg', *Historical Journal*, 28 (1985), 983–99 (pp. 990–2).

[38] L. Fioravanti, *Della fisica* (Venice, 1582), 112; della Porta, *Della magia*, 52–65; Telesio, *De rerum natura*, 2–6, 9, 13–15, 17; Zabarella, *In tres Aristotelis libros*, ii, fo. 83^r. The first experimental denial of spontaneous generation was provided by Francesco Redi, *Esperienze intorno alla generazione degl'insetti* (Florence, 1668).

[39] ASVen, *SU*, b. 40, 'De Simon Marcantonio, Paluelo Francesco', denunciation of 1 May 1576.

[40] ASVen, *SU*, b. 35, 'Caretta Giuseppe', undated denunciation; cf. the conversation recorded in Archivio di Stato, Lucca, *Offizio sopra la religione*, 1, 90.

course, reflect the influence of Protestantism rather than an incipient atheism; but in either case they indicate a willingness to abandon the teaching inherited from established authority—a willingness that sometimes reappears among those who recognized that faith and reason might conflict. The problem was starkly expressed by the Florentine historian Francesco Guicciardini: 'to have faith is simply to believe firmly—almost as a certainty—things that are not reasonable.'[41] Perhaps in consequence, there was a common preference for natural, rather than supernatural, explanations of events. In 1497, for example, a physician called Gabriele di Salò was tried at Bologna for asserting that Christ's miracles were natural phenomena, an argument subsequently echoed by Pomponazzi and Bruno.[42] According to Girolamo Garimberto, writing in 1549, 'all those natural things that occur but rarely are held to be miraculous by men who lack understanding of their causes . . . the marvellous is born of ignorance.'[43]

A similar convergence of learned and non-academic thought can be found among attitudes to immortality. Even sincere believers seemed aware of problems associated with Christian teaching on the soul,[44] especially when set beside the teaching of the ancients. Aristotle's views on the soul were the subject of extensive debate in the sixteenth and seventeenth centuries, but it was generally agreed that he had bound the soul so intimately to the body that he had been obliged to deny it immortality. There could be no punishment for evil, therefore, and no reward for virtue, outside the present life.[45] In 1513 Leo X issued a condemnation of any

[41] F. Guicciardini, *Ricordi*, ed. R. Spongano (Florence, 1951), 1; cf. Galileo's comments in the *Saggiatore*, republished in his *Opere*, vi. 232, and Cardano's in the *De rerum varietate*, republished in his *Opera*, iii. 159.

[42] H. de Bursellis, *Cronica gestorum ac factorum memorabilium civitatis Bononie*, ed. A. Sorbelli (Bologna, 1929), 116 ('miracula que Christus fatiebat, asserebat non virtute divina illa fieri, sed virtute corporum celestium'): Borselli called Gabriele an Averroist; Pomponazzi, *De naturalium effectuum*, 43, 103–4, 131; Firpo, 'Il processo di Bruno', 593.

[43] G. Garimberto, *Problemi naturali, e morali* (Venice, 1549), 102–3; cf. Pomponazzi, *De naturalium effectuum*, 230, 242–3.

[44] Cf. comments of Saitta, *Il pensiero italiano*, 344–5, 348, 350 (on Porzio).

[45] A clear account of Aristotle's views was given by Francesco Vimercati, *Commentarii in tertium librum Arist. De anima: Eiusdem de anima rationali, peripatetica*

teaching that expounded the mortality of the soul;[46] but speculation continued none the less. Philosophers such as Pomponazzi, Cesalpino, Cardano, and Telesio discussed the problems in print,[47] and inquisitors regularly uncovered individuals—not always well-educated—who admitted their inability to believe in immortality or the afterlife. In 1574, for instance, the Venetian Inquisition received a denunciation against Commodo Canuove of Vicenza, in which he was accused of saying that 'we have never seen any dead man who has returned from the other world to tell us that paradise exists—or purgatory or hell; all these things are the fantasies of friars and priests, who wish to live without working and to pamper themselves with the goods of the Church.'[48]

Some of these suspects may have been influenced by Italian Anabaptists, who had developed a number of doctrines not shared by similar groups elsewhere. In September 1550 an Anabaptist synod in Venice determined that the souls of the

---

disceptatio (Paris, 1543), especially pp. 229, 268–74; and cf Zabarella, *In tres Aristotelis libros*, iii, fo. 23^r. For a characteristic assault, see Campanella, *De gentilismo*, 7. For Pomponazzi's changing understanding of Aristotle's teaching, see B. Nardi,*Studi su Pietro Pomponazzi* (Florence, 1965), 149–98, who suggests (on p. 194) that Cardinal Cajetan was broadly in agreement with Pomponazzi on these matters.

[46] *Bullarium*, v. 601–2.

[47] See Pomponazzi's *On the Immortality of the Soul*, translated in E. Cassirer *et al.*, *The Renaissance Philosophy of Man* (Chicago, 1948), 280–381, especially pp. 302–3, 317–18, 336; Cesalpino, *Quaestionum peripateticarum*, fos. 40^r–45^v (for which see also C. Colombero, 'Il pensiero filosofico di Andrea Cesalpino', *Rivista critica di storia della filosofia*, 32 (1977), 267–84 (pp. 272–9)); Cardano's *De immortalitate animorum* republished in his *Opera*, ii. 455–536; and Telesio's *De rerum natura*, 257, 332–4. Cf. also the implications of Bruno's references to the nature and fate of the soul in his *Cabala del cavallo pegaseo*, first published in 1585, and reprinted in his *Opere italiane*, ii. 213–83, especially pp. 276–83, and his suggestion in the *De vinculis* that hell can be identified with the fear that we conceive of it (A. Ingegno, *La sommersa nave della religione: Studio sulla polemica anticristiana del Bruno* (Naples, 1985), 128).

[48] ASVen, *SU*, b. 38, 'Casanova Commodo', denunciation of 2 Jan. 1574; Canuove was executed in June. Cf. also the charge against Costantino Tessera: 'l'anima nostra non e altro ch'il sangue nostro' (*SU*, b. 41, 'Tessera Costantino', denunciation of 23 Apr. 1571); the denunciation presented against the shopkeeper Valerio dalle Madreperle in the summer of 1572 (*SU*, b. 32, fo. 1^r); the sentence in Verona of the chemist Giovanni Francesco de Pegorari (Trinity College, Dublin (hereafter TCD), MS 1225, fo. 194^r, dated 1580); the case of Pomponio Rustico, executed in Rome in 1587 (Spini, *Ricerca dei libertini*, 32–3); or the discussion by Giovan Battista Gelli in his *Capricci del bottaio*, first published in 1546, and republished in his *Opere*, ed. A. C. Alesina (Naples, 1969), 81–246 (pp. 105–7).

impious die with their bodies, whilst the elect sleep until the Day of Judgement.[49] Like Pomponazzi, they questioned the existence of immaterial beings, such as angels and demons,[50] and cast doubt on the divine origins of the human soul.[51] They also denied the divinity of Christ. Antitrinitarian ideas had circulated in Italy since at least 1539,[52] and in 1550 the Anabaptists who met in Venice continued this tradition when they came to the conclusion that Christ was the natural son of Joseph and Mary, and had not therefore existed before his nativity.[53] But this rejection of Christ's divinity appears in many documents of the period, including some that have no obvious connection with Anabaptism.[54]

[49] C. Ginzburg, *I costituti di don Pietro Manelfi* (Florence and Chicago, 1970), 34–5; for other examples, see Renato, *Opere*, 203–4, 222, 231, 234–5, 244–5; ASVen, *SU*, b. 9, 'Manelfi Pietro (*et al.*)', abjurations of Marc'Antonio Prata and Bartolomeo della Barba; *SU*, b. 11, 'Merlara Francesco', fo. 4ʳ; *SU*, b. 20, 'Moian Vettore', denunciation of 25 Apr. 1565; *SU*, b. 50, 'Robino Achille', fos. 53, 55, 57, 61, 68, confession and abjuration of 3 Apr. 1582, denunciation of 25 Apr. 1583; A. Rotondò, 'Per la storia dell'eresia a Bologna nel secolo XVI', *Rinascimento*, 1–2 (1961–2), 107–54 (p. 135).

[50] Cf. Ginzburg, *I costituti*, 34–5, with Pomponazzi, *De naturalium effectuum*, 198, 200, 297–310.

[51] Ginzburg, *I costituti*, 35, and Pomponazzi in Cassirer, *The Renaissance Philosophy*, 325–6; cf. Vimercati, *Commentarii*, 273–4, 286; Telesio, *De rerum natura*, 177–80; and the unorthodox opinions of Matteo Palmieri's *Libro del poema chiamato Citta di Vita*, ed. M. Rooke (Northampton, Mass., 1927), 21–5. An orthodox opinion is provided by F. M. Bonini, *L'ateista*, dialogue 10.

[52] A. Stella, *Anabattismo e antitrinitarismo in Italia nel XVI secolo: Nuove ricerche storiche* (Padua, 1969), 134–5.

[53] Ginzburg, *I costituti*, 34–5; cf. ASVen, *SU*, b. 9, 'Manelfi Pietro (*et al.*)', interrogations of Paolo Beltramino in the spring of 1552, and the abjurations of the shoemaker Giulio on 17 Mar. and of Giovanni Maria Sartor on 12 Dec. 1552.

[54] For the Anabaptists, see ASVen, *SU*, b. 6, 'Processus contra hereticos de Asyllo', abjuration of Giuseppe Sartor, 1551; *SU*, b. 9, 'Manelfi Pietro (*et al.*)', abjuration of Marc'Antonio Prata; Renato, *Opere*, 234, 236. For the Italians in Poland, see A. Pirnát (ed.), *De falsa et vera unius Dei Patris, Filii et Spiritus Sancti cognitione Libri duo* (Budapest, 1988), a reprint of the 1568 Gyulafehérvár edition of texts compiled by Francesco David and Giorgio Biandrata: see especially Biandrata's challenge in the dedication to John Sigismund, pp. 5–6; S. Lubieniecio, *Historia reformationis Polonicae* (Freistadt, 1685), 109; D. Caccamo, *Eretici italiani in Moravia, Polonia, Transilvania (1558–1611): Studi e documenti* (DeKalb and Chicago, 1970), especially pp. 22–3; J. Miller, 'The Origins of Polish Arianism', *Sixteenth Century Journal*, 16 (1985), 229–56, especially p. 239. See also L. Firpo, *Ricerche Campanelliane* (Florence, 1947), 234–6, for a sonnet attributed to Campanella, and ASVen, *SU*, b. 41, 'Salvator Colombina', fos. 1ʳ, 2ʳ, for an antitrinitarian trial of 1577 that appears to have nothing to do with Anabaptism. Giordano Bruno also ridiculed the doctrine of Christ's divinity in his *Spaccio della bestia trionfante*, first published in 1584, and reprinted in his *Opere italiane*, ii. 1–212: see especially

The Italian Anabaptists linked their rejection of the doctrine of the Trinity to a respectful scepticism about the authenticity of the Scriptures;[55] but among some other Italians outright mockery of the Bible was not uncommon. Pomponio Rustico was executed in Rome in 1587 for suggesting, *inter alia*, that 'the stories described in the Bible . . . are worthy only of derision'.[56] Such ridicule had serious implications, for the Scriptures provided the ultimate authority for many of the central doctrines of the Christian faith, and for much of the established apparatus of religion. But none of these, it seems, was immune in the sixteenth and seventeenth centuries. In 1575, for example, Pietro Sigos, a physician, was denounced in Venice for arguing that images can work no miracles: 'it's simply not possible; it's all an invention of the priests to get more money.'[57] This assumption, that priests were thieves and liars, appears frequently, of course,[58] but what we are dealing with here is surely a much broader assault on the essential tenets of the faith, an assault that seems to be based on something more considered than mere anticlericalism. For a number of writers argued that 'superstition'—and particularly a belief in the afterlife—was nothing more than a human invention to keep order in society. Niccolò Machiavelli and Girolamo Cardano were

---

pp. 207–8. For an interpretation of the *Spaccio* as a sort of 'anti-Gospel', see Ingegno, *La sommersa nave*.

[55] Ginzburg, *I costituti*, 64, where Manelfi credits St Jerome with the early chapters of the first and third Gospels; see also pp. 68–9, and ASVen, *SU*, b. 9, 'Manelfi Pietro (*et al.*)', abjuration of Marc'Antonio Prata. Lorenzo Valla's *Collatio Novi Testamenti* had already raised doubts about the received text of the New Testament in the 15th cent.

[56] Spini, *Ricerca dei libertini*, 32–3. Cf. also ASVen, *SU*, b. 41, 'Drasa, Draso', deposition of 22 Mar. 1578, reporting that when, during a church service, 'li comenzorno cantar le profecie comenzando, In principio creavit Deus celum et terram . . . subbitto disse [Giacomo Profici] mogia mogia è chi è stato la'.

[57] ASVen, *SU*, b. 39, 'Sigos Pietro', denunciation of 1 Oct. 1575; cf. the similar arguments of Francesco Pucci's *Forma d'una republica catolica* of 1581, republished in *Gli scritti di Francesco Pucci*, ed. L. Firpo (Turin, 1957), 90–1, and the examples cited by R. Mackenney, *Tradesmen and Traders: The World of the Guilds in Venice and Europe, c.1250–c.1650* (London, 1987), 178–9. Pomponazzi's *De incantationibus* and Machiavelli's *Discourses* had also preferred a natural interpretation of miracles.

[58] See e.g. ASVen, *SU*, b. 34, 'Contra illos de Portusnaono', fos. 40[r], 41[r], 47[r], or *SU*, b. 39, 'Lefevre Zilio', denunciation of 8 Mar. 1575. Guicciardini had no very flattering view of the clergy either: *Ricordi*, 33.

probably the most notorious;[59] but the conviction that most people were virtuous because of fear, not belief, appears in several other writers too,[60] and a few individuals were even prepared to suggest that the great religions of the world, including Christianity, were merely fabrications designed to secure their founders' dominance over contemporaries.[61] If this were true, then all religions could be reduced to the same level of significance, and none could exercise any superior claim to human allegiance.[62]

A final element in this range of doubts was the denial of any external validity to Christian morality: as Angelico da Venezia, the prior of S. Antonio, was reported to have said: 'religions are nothing but hypocrisy, and the best man is the man who best knows how to dissemble.'[63] Such cynicism was traced by many to the influence of either Machiavelli or the Protestant Reformation—to the first, because he appeared to question the association of morality and worldly success,[64]

---

[59] Machiavelli, *Discourses* (first published 1531), book 1, ch. 11; Cardano, *Opera*, iii. 550.

[60] Pomponazzi, *De naturalium effectuum*, 103–4, 201–2, 243; P. Gaudenzio, *De philosophiae apud Romanos initio et progressu* (Pisa, 1643), 64–6; Berigardo, *Circulus Pisanus*, 116–7; and S. Bertelli, *Ribelli, libertini e ortodossi nella storiografia barocca* (Florence, 1973), 200–1 (on Davila's *Historia delle guerre civili di Francia*, published in Venice, 1630). The word 'superstitio' was used by F. Vimercati, *In quatuor libros Aristotelis Meteorologicorum commentarii* (Paris, 1556), 199.

[61] See e.g. Firpo, *Ricerche Campanelliane*, 236, or the reference to the *Libri de tribus magnis impostoribus* in Micraelius, *Historia ecclesiastica*, 888. Plethon had made the same accusation in the 15th cent. (E. Garin, *Astrology in the Renaissance: The Zodiac of Life* (Eng. trans., London, 1983), 19), and Bruno was charged with similar beliefs in the 16th (Firpo, 'Il processo', 585, 591–2).

[62] Some such thinking may lie behind the comments of Zorzi Carganello on the relative merits of Islam and Christianity, reported in ASVen, *SU*, b. 34, 'Contra illos de Portusnaono', fos. 47ᵛ–48ʳ, 49ʳ. Giulio da Milano accused the Anabaptist Silvio da Vicenza of believing that 'la fede non è altro che l'oppenione de l'huomo, secondo che la persona se l'imaggina et fabrica ne 'l suo cervello; di maniera che non afferma l'una fede l'essere più vera nè miglior de l'altra' (quoted by Ginzburg, *I costituti*, 43). The recent discovery of peoples in America, Africa, and Asia who had lived in harmony for centuries without Christianity seemed to suggest that God's revelation was unnecessary: Berigardo, *Circulus Pisanus*, 182.

[63] ASVen, *SU*, b. 28, 'Contra donum angelicum', fo. 6ʳ; cf. also fos. 1ʳ, 3ʳ for his moral reputation.

[64] See Machiavelli, *Discourses*, bk. 1, ch. 26; cf. Telesio, *De rerum natura*, 357–8, 360–2; Vanini, *Opere*, i, p. xviii; Febvre, *The Problem of Unbelief*, 116–18, 121. Guicciardini's opinion was similar (*Ricordi*, 53, 57). A curiously 'Machiavellian' statement is attributed to Alessandro Mantica in ASVen, *SU*, b. 34, 'Contra illos de Portusnaono', fo. 9ʳ.

and to the second, because it appeared to destroy the association of morality and the afterlife by denying that good works can be performed as an act of free will.[65] Some Italian Protestants in the sixteenth century, however, seem to have followed a tradition that recalls the medieval heresy of the free spirit. In the 1540s Giorgio Siculo taught that the redeemed cannot have any will to sin; therefore the flesh cannot war any longer with the spirit.[66] And in the seventeenth century some Italians argued, more broadly, that nothing that an individual felt impelled to do by instinct or nature could possibly be wrong. At a trivial level, this thinking could be extended to questions of etiquette and table manners;[67] but it could be transformed more dangerously into a repudiation of all established morality. Several members of the Venetian Accademia degli Incogniti led notoriously amoral lives, and their published work followed suit. Francesco Pona, for example, praised the freedom of the prostitute in *La Lucerna*, published in the 1620s,[68] and the *Novelle amorose* of his fellow academicians veer on occasion towards the pornographic.[69]

[65] For an Italian Protestant statement, see Francesco Negri's *Tragedia di F. N. B. intitolata, Libero arbitrio* (1546), sig. N4ᵛ; for the causal connection with unbelief, see Campanella, *Atheismus*, 167–8 and the dedication to Louis XIII. Postel likened Lutheranism to Islam for this reason: see his *Alcorani seu legis Mahometi et evangelistarum concordiae liber* (Paris, 1543), 21, 25–8. Pomponazzi also questioned free will—though for different reasons—and came to a similar conclusion about the impossibility of either morality or providence (*Libri quinque De fato*, ed. R. Lemay (Lugano, 1957), 53–4, 59–60, 69–73, 77–80, 106–9: this text was completed in 1520, but remained in manuscript until after the author's death). Cf. also Guicciardini, *Ricordi*, 103.

[66] ASVen, *SU*, b. 30, 'Nascimbene Nascimbeni', written confession of 6 Jan. 1570 (published in C. Ginzburg, 'Due note sul profetismo cinquecentesco', *Rivista storica italiana*, 78 (1966), 184–227 (p. 216). For the 'Spirit of Freedom' in Italy, see R. Guarnieri, *Il movimento del Libero Spirito* (Rome, 1965), especially pp. 404–97; and cf. Spini, *Ricerca dei libertini*, 22, on Zanino da Sòlcia.

[67] See the witty assault on 'quell'Alchimista delle Cerimonie nomato il Galateo', in the undated *Capitoli e precetti morali Da pratticarsi, et osservarsi nell'Accademia dei Disinvolti* of Pesaro (published in Brescia), especially pp. 3–5, 10–11, 13–15, and cf E. Benvenuti, 'Briciole secentesche', *Rivista delle bibliotheche e degli archivi*, 22 (1911), 1–17 (pp. 15–17).

[68] *La Lucerna di Evreta Misoscola* (Verona, [1625]), 38–9.

[69] F. Carmeni (ed.), *Novelle amorose de'Signori Academici Incogniti* (Venice, 1641); G. B. Fusconi (ed.), *Delle Novelle amorose* (Venice, 1643). Cf. G. Brusoni, *Vita di Ferrante Pallavicino*, published in F. Pallavicino, *Opere scelte* (4 vols.; 'Villafranca', 1660), i. 4–6, 9, 26, 28–9 (the set was probably published in

Such relatively public expressions were not necessarily very common; but we cannot argue from relative silence that doubts of this kind were therefore rare. In the age of the Inquisition and the Index we should not always expect contemporaries to have spoken their minds. Individuals who did not believe in an afterlife, or who denied that their fate there was determined by their behaviour on earth, can only rarely have perceived any great profit in suffering persecution for their convictions. In 1641, indeed, Torquato Accetto openly recommended an 'honest dissimulation' for the wise man who knows the truth but recognizes the benefit of silence.[70] An active dissimulation could thus become conscious policy—a policy similar to that already developed among the persecuted Protestants of the sixteenth century whom Calvin labelled 'Nicodemists'.[71] Siculo had actively encouraged a positive wariness of this kind, and his teaching was welcomed by followers such as Nascimbene;[72] many

---

Amsterdam); Spini, *Ricerca dei libertini*, 142–4; L. Puppi, '"Ignoto Deo"', *Arte veneta*, 23 (1969), 169–80 (pp. 171–2); N. S. Davidson, 'Theology, Nature and the Law: Sexual Sin and Sexual Crime in Renaissance Italy', in T. Dean and K. Lowe (eds.), *Crime and Disorder in Renaissance Italy* (Cambridge, forthcoming). Some of the Incogniti were more respectable: see *Le glorie de gli Incogniti* (Venice, 1647), 388–91, on Ridolfo Campeggi, the author of the *Racconto* of 1622 cited below (n. 126). A further tradition, however, is evident in Italian utopian literature, which sometimes recommends that women should be held in common (see e.g. A. F. Doni, *Mondi celesti, terrestri, et infernali, de gli academici pellegrini* (Venice, 1562), 175–6, 178–9).

[70] T. Accetto, *Della dissimulazione onesta*, with a preface by B. Croce (Bari, 1928), 28: 'pur si concede talor il mutar manto per vestir conforme alla stagion della fortuna, non con intenzion di fare, ma di non patir danno, ch'è quel solo interesse col quale si può tolerar chi si vuol valere della dissimulazione, che però non e frode'. Cf. Sarpi's famous comment, 'la falsità non dico mai mai, ma la verità non a ogni uno', recorded in his *Lettere ai protestanti*, ed. M. D. Busnelli (2 vols.; Bari, 1931), ii. 123.

[71] For Nicodemism, see A. Rotondò, 'Atteggiamenti della vita morale italiana del Cinquecento: La pratica nicodemitica', *Rivista storica italiana*, 79 (1967), 991–1030; C. Ginzburg, *Il nicodemismo: Simulazione e dissimulazione religiosa nell'Europa del '500* (Turin, 1970); A. Biondi, 'La giustificazione della simulazione nel Cinquecento', in *Eresia e riforma nell'Italia del Cinquecento*, Miscellanea 1 (Florence and Chicago, 1974), 7–68; C. M. N. Eire, 'Calvinism and Nicodemism: A Reappraisal', *Sixteenth Century Journal*, 10 (1979), 45–69; C. M. N. Eire, 'Prelude to Sedition? Calvin's Attack on Nicodemism and Religious Compromise', *Archiv für Reformationsgeschichte*, 76 (1985), 120–45.

[72] *Epistola di Georgio Siculo servo fidele di Iesu Christo alli cittadini di Riva di Trento contra il mendatio di Francisco Spiera, et falsa dottrina di protestanti* (Bologna, 1550), especially fos. 48ᵛ–49ᵛ; ASVen, *SU*, b. 30, 'Nascimbene Nascimbeni', Ferrara abjurations of 15 Jan. 1551 and 31 Oct. 1560.

years later, a French printer in Venice, Pietro d'Ochino, is reported to have argued 'that it was necessary to be seen going to Mass, to prevent anyone else becoming suspicious'.[73] Such a policy was often accompanied by a calculated ambiguity in conversation, and even by the use of hypothetical third parties to advance views that were known to be dangerous.[74] These tactics were the common property of the Italian Reformation; they could serve the purposes of anyone else of unorthodox belief—even atheists—equally well.

There was, then, within the community of believers, a startling willingness to question traditional beliefs about God, the creation, the world of the spirit, immortality, Christ's divinity, the authority of the Bible, and Christian morality. And since so many alternative theories were already in circulation, among both educated and uninstructed Italians, the materials for a fully developed atheism were, in a sense, already to hand. It was possible, of course, to doubt one or more of these doctrines without denying the existence of some sort of God; but it would have been difficult to reject all of them and still claim to be a believer in any sense recognized by the Western Church. Even the awareness of such daring alternatives may have brought about a shift in attitudes, and so helped to make 'atheism' a more plausible option.[75]

The problem for the historian in retrospect is to identify such thoroughgoing unbelievers, for, as was widely acknowledged at the time, they would probably have tried to hide their beliefs if at all possible.[76] Many of those we might suspect

[73] ASVen, *SU*, b. 39, 'D'Ochino Pietro', denunciation of 24 July 1575.

[74] A good example is provided by Rotondò, 'Atteggiamenti della vita morale', 1025–6.

[75] In his history of the Council of Trent Paolo Sarpi suggested that disputes about the existence of God had appeared in the work of medieval scholastic theologians (*Istoria del Concilio di Trento*, ed. C. Vivanti (2 vols.; Turin, 1974), i. 318—a point acknowledged by Cardinal Sforza Pallavicino in his reply to Sarpi (*Istoria del Concilio di Trento* (2 vols.; Rome, 1656–7), i. 652–5. Cf. the general argument of M. J. Buckley, *At the Origins of Modern Atheism* (New Haven, 1987), and A. C. Kors, *Atheism in France, 1650-1729: The Orthodox Sources of Unbelief* (Princeton, NJ, 1990).

[76] Lorenzo Magalotti referred to 'those closed-mouth Brutuses and Cassiuses' who 'keep quiet about their misbelief; instead of arguing, they just laugh': cited by E. Cochrane, *Florence in the Forgotten Centuries, 1527-1800* (Chicago, 1973), 302.

of atheism restricted their arguments to conversation and teaching, or left their most damaging written works in manuscript.[77] Some resorted to deliberate ambiguity. Lorenzo Magalotti, for example, once stated: 'I will never presume to demonstrate the existence of God—still less the intelligibility of the true religion.' Did he believe that such a demonstration was not necessary—or that it was not possible?[78] Others used history to frame their arguments: in the 1620s Giovanni Antonio Venier called all ancient prophecies fraudulent in his *De oraculis*; but he conspicuously failed to exclude identical Christian examples from his condemnation.[79] Giulio Cesare Vanini was accused of advancing atheism under cover of a debate; others were reprimanded for presenting atheism more forcefully than its Christian refutation.[80] Similar objections were made against books by Pompanazzi and Francesco Vimercati, which rehearsed arguments hostile to the faith and then finished with a lame reminder that the teaching of the Church must still be accepted none the less.[81]

[77] Cf. M. A. del Torre, *Studi su Cesare Cremonini: Cosmologia e logica nel tardo aristotelico padovano* (Padua, 1968), 41–2; Puppi, '"Ignoto Deo"', 175–7; H. Busson, *Les Sources et le développement du rationalisme dans la littérature française de la Renaissance (1533–1601)* (Paris, 1922), 206; Zambelli, 'From Menocchio to Piero della Francesca', 994. It seems to have been easier to publish more unorthodox texts in France than in Italy.

[78] Cited Casini, *Introduzione all'illuminismo*, 281. A similar ambiguity appears in Berigardo's comment that 'nothing is more difficult to prove, but easier to accept, than God's existence' (cited in D. C. Allen, *Doubt's Boundless Sea: Skepticism and Faith in the Renaissance* (Baltimore, 1964), 115).

[79] *De oraculis et divinationibus antiquorum, tractatus succinctus et exquisitus* (Basle, 1628), 12, 53, 55. Pomponazzi may also have been guilty of the same tactic in his *De naturalium effectuum*, 200–1, 283–6, 288.

[80] F. Garasse, *La Doctrine curieuse des beaux esprits de ce temps ou prétendus tels* (Paris, 1623), 43, 650, 652, 1007–8; *Naudaeana*, 38; G. Ernst, 'Campanella "libertino"?', in Gregory et al., *Ricerche su letteratura*, 231–2. Vanini used an assault on atheism as the excuse for the *Amphitheatrum*: see his *Opere*, i, pp. xviii, xx, and cf. 97–8 or 171–2, for particularly feeble assertions of the Christian case. In the *De admirandis* he relied on a hypothetical 'infelix atheus' to present atheist arguments (*Opere*, ii. 267–72, 313), as did Magalotti in his *Lettere familiare*, written in the 1680s and first published in 1719 (Casini, *Introduzione all'illuminismo*, 279–81). Vanini's extensive plagiarism from earlier authors may also have afforded him some protection (cf. E. Namer, *La Vie et l'œuvre de J. C. Vanini, Prince des Libertins, mort à Toulouse sur le bûcher en 1619* (Paris, 1980), 271).

[81] See the charges made in the Vatican manuscript cited by C. Dejob, *De l'influence du Concile de Trente sur la littérature et les beaux-arts chez les peuples catholiques* (Paris, 1884), 380; and by D. Durand, *La Vie et les sentimens de Lucilio Vanini* (Rotterdam, 1717), 37–8.

Historians are therefore often forced back on to second-hand evidence, casual comments, and even jokes, or they must divine belief from reports of actions or life-style. What are we to make, for example, of Bruno's refusal to focus on the crucifix held up to him during his execution at the stake, or Paolo Sarpi's reluctance to participate in 'superstitious ceremonies' on his death-bed?[82] How often did opposition to ecclesiastical authority or debate about doctrine mask committed atheism—and how much atheism was concealed by Nicodemism or indifference?[83]

At least one Italian, however, paraded his atheism fairly openly. Giulio Cesare Vanini was born in 1585; educated by the Jesuits and at the University of Naples, he joined the Carmelites in 1603, and took his doctorate in law about three years later. He was in Padua after 1608, and preached in Venice in 1611; but the following year, when rumours of his unorthodoxy reached the Carmelite General, he left Venice and moved to England. The rest of his short life was spent travelling: to Flanders from 1614, then to Paris, Liguria, Lyons, and Toulouse. He left two books at his death, both published in France: the *Amphitheatrum*, published in Lyons in 1615, and the *De admirandis*, published in Paris in 1616. In the first he argues from within the Christian tradition that God cannot have personality, and raises the familiar problem of his role in the creation of evil.[84] But in the second, a dialogue between 'Alexander' and 'Julius Caesar'—clearly identified as

---

[82] Spini, *Ricerca dei libertini*, 73; G. Cozzi, 'Sulla morte di fra Paolo Sarpi', in *Miscellanea in onore di Roberto Cessi* (3 vols.; Rome, 1958), ii. 387–96 (p. 396: Sarpi 'n'at vollu nulles ceremonies superstitieuses'). His friend Giovanni Francesco Sagredo was also reluctant to confess: Cozzi 'Sulla morte', 224. A similar report of the remarks of the former Cardinal Alfonso Petrucci before his execution in July 1517 is quoted in F. Winspeare, *La congiura dei Cardinali contro Leone X* (Florence, 1957), 157–8. Cf. too the comments of M. Firpo, 'Alcuni documenti sulla conversione al cattolicesimo dell'eretico lucchese Simone Simoni', *Annali della Scuola Normale Superiore di Pisa* (classe di lettere e filosofia), 4 (1974), 1479–1502 (p. 1490).

[83] Giovanni Targher da Modena was accused by witnesses in Venice of fornication, ferocious blasphemy, breaking Church fasts, and ridiculing miracles; but they all agreed that he attended Mass regularly (ASVen, *SU*, b. 20, 'Targher Giovanni', depositions of 13 Nov. 1565). For some helpful methodological considerations, see Spini, *Ricerca dei libertini*, 12, 76–7; Baldini, *Un libertino accademico*, 13; M. Gauna, *The Dissident Montaigne* (New York, 1989), 2, 4–5, 280, 283; and especially Delumeau, 'Croyants et sceptiques', 48–9.

[84] *Opere*, i. 5–7, 61

the author himself[85]—Vanini takes the debate outside orthodox theology altogether. He questions whether an immaterial
God can create a material world, and whether any spiritual
being can communicate with a corporal one;[86] eventually he
claims that the only true worship is the worship of nature.[87]
He accepts the eternity of matter[88] and mocks the doctrine of
creation, presenting instead a case for the origin of mankind,
as well as lesser animals, in putrefaction.[89] He argues against
the existence of non-material beings, such as ghosts, demons,
spirits, and the immortal human soul.[90] Religions, including
Christianity, are fictions, invented by rulers and priests to
secure their power;[91] miracles attributed to prayer have natural
explanations,[92] reason is instinct, and immorality the product
of illness or diet.[93] In one short volume, therefore, Vanini
presented virtually all the alternatives to Church teaching
discussed among believers, including some that cast doubt on
the very existence of God. In 1619, at the age of 34, he was
burned to death at Toulouse for blasphemy and atheism.[94]

[85] Ibid. ii. 287, 289, 304, 318–19.
[86] Ibid. 275, 286, 288, 302–4, 333, 361–2. For his denial of providence, see ibid. i. 45–6.
[87] Ibid. ii. 276; cf. the discussion, ibid. i. 167.
[88] Ibid. i. 17, 99.
[89] Ibid. ii. 143–4, 152–4. Interestingly, he also seems to adopt a theory of evolution (ibid. 156–7, 178–9).
[90] Ibid. 143, 260, 277–81, 318, 337, 365; for his view on immortality, cf. also ibid. i. 97–8.
[91] Ibid. ii. 276–7, 279. He quotes Statius' famous line, 'primus in orbe deos fecit timor' (ibid. 276; cf. Statius, *Thebaid*, iii, v. 661, for the original). Cardano used the same line (*Opera*, iii. 550), but both he and Vanini attribute it to Lucretius. J. H. Mozley called it a 'commonplace of the rhetoricians' (*Statius*, ed. J. H. Mozley, (2 vols.; London, 1928), i. 500).
[92] Vanini, *Opere*, ii. 322, 335 (on the sanctuary of S. Vito at Poligno a Mare).
[93] Ibid. 255–6, 258, 260–2 (the Tartars are cruel because they drink horses' blood, the British are gentle because they drink cold beer). For a recent account of Vanini, see Namer, *La Vie de Vanini*, especially pp. 248–70. The earlier discussions by Saitta, *Il pensiero italiano*, 441–8; Spini, *Ricerca dei libertini*, 121–34; and F. Berriot, *Athéismes et athéistes au XVIe siècle en France* (2 vols.; Lille, 1976), ii. 797–818, are all worth consulting. Vanini's *Amphitheatrum* was published during the debate that followed the death of another Italian in France accused of atheism, Cosme Ruggeri: for an account of his death, see Garasse, *La Doctrine curieuse*, 157. The *De admirandis* was put on the Index on 3 July 1623 (*Index librorum prohibitorum Alexandri VII . . . editus* (Rome, 1664), 93, 323).
[94] Accounts of Vanini's execution in *Le Mercure françois* (25 vols.; Paris, 1611–48), v. 64–5; Garasse, *La Doctrine curieuse*, 146–7; and G. B. Gramonde, *Historiarum Galliae ab excessu Henrici IV* (Toulouse, 1643), 208–9.

Alvise Capuano left no books, but his atheism also seems clear. He was born at Lesina; his parents came from Manfredonia. He had travelled widely in Italy, and had visited Geneva and France on his way to Santiago de Compostella. He was denounced to the Venetian Inquisition in 1577, and sentenced as an atheist in 1580. His sentence summarizes his confessions:

that the world was created by chance [*chel mondo sia stato fatto à caso*] . . . that when the body dies the soul dies also . . . that during the time that you were an atheist—that is, when you believed that the world was created by chance—you believed that Christ was the adopted son of the Madonna, born as other men are, and that angels and demons do not exist . . . that there are no true witches, and that belief in witchcraft arises from melancholic humours. At times you have believed that the world has neither beginning nor end, and that when you were an atheist you did not believe that God existed, or, indeed, any supernatural beings. And that Christ's miracles were not true miracles but natural acts . . . and that the only law that must be obeyed is the law of nature . . . and that the entire Old Testament is a superstition [*che tuto il testamento vecchio sia una superstitione*].[95]

Similar arguments against miracles and the doctrines of creation and immortality were attributed at Rome in the early seventeenth century to Monsignor Gaspar Varella.[96] He was said to have been influenced by Aristotle, and two other prominent Aristotelians with a claim to atheism were Francesco Vimercati and Cesare Cremonini. Vimercati was born in Milan, in about 1512, but by the 1530s he was teaching at the University of Paris; in 1542 he was appointed king's reader in Greek and Latin philosophy.[97] He makes a few

[95] ASVen, *SU*, b. 47, 'Capuano Alvise', sentence of 7 May 1580. He was condemned to perpetual imprisonment, but subsequently released. Both Vanini and Capuano were familiar with the work of Machiavelli—whom Vanini called 'atheorum facile princeps' (E. Namer, 'La vita di Vanini in Inghilterra', *Rinascenza Salentina*, 2 (1934), 113–42 (pp. 126, 140); Vanini, *Opere*, i, pp. xviii, 23; *SU*, b. 47, 'Capuano Alvise', fo. 3ʳ).

[96] Archivio Segreto Vaticano, *Borghese*, iv. 44, fos. 263ʳ–266ʳ; the denunciation is undated, but refers to the 'beato Ignatio', and so must fall between 1608 (Loyola's beatification) and 1622 (his canonization).

[97] For an account of Vimercati's career, see Busson, *Les Sources du rationalisme*, 202–31, with corrections in two articles by N. Gilbert: 'Francesco Vimercato of Milan: A Bio-Bibliography', *Studies in the Renaissance* 12 (1965), 188–217; and

references to God in his published work; but in his *De principiis rerum*, left in manuscript at his death, he virtually assimilates God and nature, and rejects the doctrine of creation *ex novo*.[98] Matter is eternal, with neither a beginning nor an end, though it constantly alters its form and appearance.[99] All that exists has a natural cause, and man can look forward to no personal immortality; religion is the product of fear, an invention of rulers.[100] Cremonini was equally cautious in his published work. He served as professor of philosophy at Padua from 1590 to 1629. Like Vimercati, he reduced religion to fantasy, and refused to adjust his Aristotelian teaching to Christian theology—even under pressure from the Inquisition.[101] Like Vanini, he denied personality to God, and eliminated his role in creation and the world. In his *De coeli efficentia*, a manuscript found after his death, he attributes all causation on earth to the heavens, which are eternal.[102] He clearly adopts a materialist position, and was investigated on several occasions between 1604 and 1626 by the Inquisition, on suspicion of denying immortality. His manuscripts certainly suggest that the individual soul cannot survive without the body, but Cremonini managed to evade

'Renaissance Aristotelianism and its Fate: Some Observations and Problems', in J. P. Anton (ed.), *Naturalism and Historical Understanding: Essays on the Philosophy of John Herman Randall* (Albany, NY, 1967), 42–52 (pp. 46–7).

[98] *De principiis rerum naturalium* (Venice, 1596), fos. 106ᵛ–107ʳ. He died in or before 1580.

[99] Ibid., fos. 48ᵛ–54ʳ, 144ᵛ. Both Vanini and Vimercati defended Epicurus in their writings, though neither seems to have adopted atomism (Busson, *La Pensée religieuse*, 418; H. Busson, *La Religion des classiques (1660–1685)* (Paris, 1948), 215).

[100] Vimercati, *De principiis*, fo. 91ʳ; cf. Vimercati, *In quattuor libros*, 299, and Busson, *Les Sources du rationalisme*, 209–13. For his attitude to death, see H. Busson, '*Consolation* de Francesco Vimercati à Cathérine de Médicis (1559)', in *Mélanges offerts à M. Abel Lefranc* (Paris, 1936), 320–38. During his residence in Paris the city had a reputation for atheistic speculation: cf. G. J. C. Henriques (ed.), *George Buchanan in the Lisbon Inquisition* (Lisbon, 1906), 42. Buchanan had friends in common with Vimercati: see I. D. McFarlane, *Buchanan* (London, 1981), 92, 96, 355–7.

[101] Del Torre, *Studi su Cesare Cremonini*, 54–62. This is probably the best study of Cremonini, and gives extensive attention to his manuscripts; Saitta, *Il pensiero italiano*, ii. 422–40 is still useful. Cf. also C. B. Schmitt, 'Cesare Cremonini: Un aristotelico al tempo di Galileo', in his collected essays, *The Aristotelian Tradition and Renaissance Universities* (London, 1984).

[102] Del Torre, *Studi su Cesare Cremonini*, 56, 61–2, 66–7, 74–9, 87–8.

arrest—partly because he had powerful protectors, and partly because he was careful to maintain a regular religious observance.[103]

Another intellectual accused of atheism was Simone Simoni, who, like Vanini and Vimercati, spent much of his life away from Italy.[104] He too refused to ascribe personality to God, and was expelled from his post at the University of Heidelberg in 1567 after suggestions that he had denied the doctrine of creation in his teaching—a charge later repeated by the Protestant Marcello Squarcialupi. He thought miracles absurd, and questioned personal immortality. He had attached himself to Protestantism in 1565, but reconverted to Catholicism in 1581; for the rest of his life, however, he avoided all religious ceremonies, appearing to have been almost contemptuous of religious commitment.[105]

The case of Paolo Sarpi, appointed the Venetian government's theological consultant in 1606, is rather different. He stayed in Italy, and despite his excommunication in 1607, he continued to demonstrate his religious observance in public, saying Mass regularly until his death in 1623. In his writings he elevates personal experience above the intellectual reasoning of any human author,[106] and the picture of the universe given in his unpublished *Pensieri* has no place for God at all.[107] His first *Pensiero sulla religione* baldly states that 'the

[103] ASVen, *SU*, b. 152, 'Sommario di leggi e decreti relativi all'Inquisitione', for the 1604 investigation; Galileo was suspected at the same time of believing that the stars could influence human free will. See also Saitta, *Il pensiero italiano*, ii. 435–6; Spini, *Ricerca dei libertini*, 146–7, 158; and del Torre, *Studi su Cesare Cremonini*, 35, 38, 44, 47–8.

[104] For Simoni, see above all Firpo, 'Alcuni documenti sulla conversione'. For Beza's concern about the influence of Aristotle on Simoni, see A. Pascal, 'Da Lucca a Ginevra; Studi sulla emigrazione religiosa lucchese nel secolo XVI', *Rivista storica italiana*, 51 (1934), 469–503 (p. 497 n. 3).

[105] Squarcialupi, *Simonis Simonii*, 9–11; Caccamo, *Eretici italiani*, 132–7, 139, 145; Firpo, 'Alcuni documenti sulla conversione', 1489–93; A. Dufour, 'Simonius entre le catholicisme et le protestantisme', in M. Lienhard (ed.), *Les Dissidents du XVIᵉ siècle entre l'humanisme et le catholicisme* (Baden-Baden, 1983), 155–62 (p. 157). Simoni's views on immortality were in line with Averroist thinking; Vanini, too, praised Averroes (*Opere*, ii. 264). All Simoni's published works were put on the Index in the 16th cent. (Reusch, *Die Indices*, 573).

[106] P. Sarpi, 'Arte de ben pensar', published in his *Scritti filosofici e teologici editi e inediti*, ed. R. Amerio (Bari, 1951), 121–44 (p. 142).

[107] Sarpi's *Pensieri* have been analysed by Wootton, *Paolo Sarpi*, 13–38.

end of man is to live, just like any other living being.'[108] He
warns against accepting any supernatural causation for events
on earth;[109] and like Cremonini, he was suspected by contemporaries of rejecting immortality.[110] The human sense of God,
he argues, springs from our ignorance and incapacity—it
articulates a human need;[111] but the wise can rise above this
level, and live a moral life without fear of God or the
afterlife.[112]

During the Venetian Interdict Sarpi was believed by Rome
to be the 'head of an atheist company' in Venice, whose
purpose was to introduce complete freedom of conscience.[113]
Sarpi himself told Christoph von Dohna that there were
many atheists in Venice,[114] and a number of his contemporaries in the city certainly had a reputation for infidelity. One
of them, Antonio Foscarini, Venetian ambassador in Paris
(1607–11) and London (1611–15), was reported to have
questioned whether paradise existed, mocked the doctrine of
the Trinity, and spoken and acted without respect for Christ,
Christianity, or the sacraments.[115] A few years later, Venice
housed another suspect group, the Accademia degli Incogniti,
who were gathered together by the patrician Giovanni Francesco Loredan. Their use of the motto 'Ignoto Deo' was
thought apt by one observer, 'because very rare among them

---

[108] P. Sarpi, *Opere*, ed. G. and L. Cozzi (Milan and Naples, 1969), 95.

[109] Ibid. 40 (no. 5), 49 (no. 114: 'la mente non . . . intende cosa, che corpo non sia'), 49–50 (no. 115); cf. his *Scritti filosofici*, 141.

[110] British Library, Add. MS 10,786, fos, 6ʳ–ᵛ.

[111] Sarpi, *Opere*, 56 (no. 251), 57–8 (no. 255), 60 (no. 308); cf. also 95–7.

[112] Wootton, *Paolo Sarpi*, 3, 5, 133–4.

[113] P. Savio, 'Per l'epistolario di Paolo Sarpi', *Aevum*, 10 (1936), 3–104 (pp. 42–5); cf. the anonymous 'Come Paolo Sarpi non fu Vescovo di Nona', *La civiltà cattolica*, 87 (1936), 196–206 (p. 198). R. Pintard, *Le Libertinage érudit dans la première moitié du XVIIᵉ siècle* (2 vols.; Paris, 1943), i. 261, quotes a manuscript comment by Naudé suggesting that Sarpi was an Epicurean: 'de sua fide nihil dico'. Cf. Wootton, *Paolo Sarpi*, 40–2, for other charges against him.

[114] Sarpi, *Lettere*, 123.

[115] A. B. Hinds (ed.), *Calendar of State Papers Venetian*, xiv (London, 1908), 29–30; S. Secchi, *Antonio Foscarini: Un patrizio veneziano del '600* (Florence, 1969), 87–94; Wootton, *Paolo Sarpi*, 65, 129, 138–42. Vanini's escape from imprisonment by the Archbishop of Canterbury in 1614 was assisted by Foscarini's chaplain (Namer, 'La vita di Vanini', 125–34, 141, 232; F. De Paola, *Vanini e il primo Seicento anglo-veneto* (Taurisano, 1979), 249–51).

are any who know God'.[116] One of their more notorious members was Ferrante Pallavicino, an ex-claustral Lateran canon. According to his biographer, Girolamo Brusoni, he had brought 'heresy and atheism' back to Italy from Germany after he had met an atheist French soldier: 'they disputed at length together about the truth of the Christian religion and about divine providence'.[117] Pallavicino was duly executed in France in 1644; his published works criticize the Church for keeping the laity in ignorance of the truth, and exalt sexual vice as natural.[118]

But, as the case of Alvise Capuano suggests, atheism could extend beyond the study and the academy. Pietro Strozzi was a Florentine exile, a cousin of Cathérine de Médicis; he served with the French military forces from 1536, becoming chamberlain to the King of France, colonel general of the infantry, general of the galleys, and commander of the French forces in the war of Sienna. He subsequently commanded Paul IV's troops against the Spanish in 1557.[119] He was evidently well educated—a mathematician who translated Caesar into Greek and collected books and antiquities. But he was also a man of action, a link between the study and the world. As he lay dying, in 1558, wounded at the siege of Thionville, he renounced God and denied immortality; the evening before, he had asserted that the Scriptures were a fiction.[120]

Strozzi, like most of the other figures discussed so far,

---

[116] Spini, *Ricerca dei libertini*, 162; cf. ibid. 142–5, and Puppi, '"Ignoto Deo"', 172–5.

[117] Brusoni, *Vita di Ferrante Pallavicino*, 22–4. Brusoni's biography is not an entirely reliable source, as it was written partly in self-justification (see 'Brusoni, Girolamo', in *Dizionario biografico degli Italiani* (Rome, 1972), xiv. 716).

[118] See e.g. *Il divortio celeste, cagionata dalle dissolutezze della sposa romana*, first published in 1643, and republished (and separately paginated) in his *Opere scelte*, 122–4: 'Gl'Ecclesiastici hanno cominciato a bramar ciechi i Fedeli . . .'; and *La retorica delle putane . . . dedicata alla Università delle Cortigiane più celebri* ('Cambrai', 1642) (probably published in Venice). *Il divortio* was prohibited on 18 Dec. 1646; *La retorica* on 4 July 1661 (*Index librorum*, 54). For an account of Pallavicino's life, see Spini, *Ricerca dei libertini*, 164–86.

[119] S. Pepper and N. Adams, *Firearms and Fortifications: Military Architecture and Siege Warfare in Sixteenth Century Siena* (Chicago, 1986), 214 n. 4.

[120] *Mémoires de la vie de François de Scepeaux, Sire de Vieilleville . . . composés par Vincent Carloix* (5 vols.; Paris, 1757), iv. 72–5; Busson, *Les Sources du rationalisme*, 511–13. Cf. Berriot, *Athéismes*, 207–8, for discussion of the sources on Strozzi.

had an educated background. It is rather more difficult to trace unbelief among the uneducated, for our knowledge of 'popular atheism' must normally be derived from trial records, which inevitably contain much false information.[121] Some examples seem overwhelming nevertheless. In 1550 an apostate Franciscan called Francesco Calcagno was denounced to the Inquisition in Brescia; the case was later transferred on government orders to Venice, where he was sentenced to death. He was charged with saying 'that God does not exist, nor the soul; when the body dies, the soul dies also'. Christ was merely human, and the Bible is an untrustworthy invention designed to frighten the laity. He claimed 'that he would rather worship a pretty little boy in the flesh than God'.[122]

Denial of God's existence was in fact a relatively common charge in Venice: in 1579 it was registered against Pietro 'fiammingo', a trimmer; in 1588 and 1590 against Giovanni Francesco Corfiut, a Franciscan Observant.[123] It reappears in the case against some of Campanella's followers after the collapse of the Calabrian conspiracy of 1599: Dionisio Ponzo 'said that there is no God apart from nature', and Cesare Pisano confessed that he 'had also come to believe that there was no God'.[124] It forms a significant part in the case against Costantino Saccardino in Bologna in 1622. He rejected the doctrine of creation, and believed in the spontaneous generation of the first human beings. He denied the existence of angels, demons, the immortal soul, and hell—which he saw

---

[121] Cf. N. S. Davidson, 'The Inquisition in Venice and its Documents: Some Problems of Method and Analysis', in A. Del Col (ed.), *Gli archivi dell' Inquisizione in Italia* (Trieste, forthcoming). My own archival research on this subject has concentrated on the records of the Inquisition tribunal in Venice; it would be interesting to know rather more about similar cases in the archives of tribunals in other cities.

[122] The trial records appear in ASVen, *SU*, b. 8, 'Fra Francesco Calcagno' and 'Fra Marco'.

[123] ASVen, *SU*, b. 45, 'Pietro fiammingo', denunciation of 14 July 1579; *SU*, b. 62, 'Corfiut, fra Giovanni Francesco', denunciations of 20 Feb. 1588 and 28 Sept. 1590: he was also charged with denying God's providence and the divinity of Christ.

[124] L. Amabile, *Fra Tommaso Campanella: La sua congiura, i suoi processi e la sua pazzia*, (3 vols.; Naples, 1882), iii. 248–50 (Cesare's confession stated that 'io venni anco in questa credenza che non ci fusse Dio'); cf. also p. 338. Other charges included a denial of the afterlife and the divinity of Christ, as well as sacrilege and blasphemy.

as a 'fable, an invention of rulers, so that men should abstain from doing evil'. Naturally, he did not believe in Christ's divinity, nor in divine providence, nor in the authority of the Bible, which he called 'a worthless book . . . he despised it as just so many lies'.[125]

A similar range of charges had been brought in the later sixteenth century against Domenico Scandella, known as Menocchio, a miller from Friuli. His cosmology, which has been fully discussed by Carlo Ginzburg, does not exactly deny the existence of a God, but it places him within creation, as the product of a natural process of spontaneous generation rather than its originator.[126] He denied immortality and the divinity of Christ, and was critical of the Scriptures. All religions were equally valid as a means of inducing civilized behaviour[127]—an opinion shared by two other figures discussed by Ginzburg, Pellegrino Baroni, another miller, investigated by the Inquisitions of Modena and Ferrara in 1561 and 1570, and the poet Scolio.[128]

A number of historians, including Ginzburg, have speculated recently about the relationship between this sort of 'popular atheism' and the more academic traditions discussed earlier. There was, we know, a high literacy rate among artisans in the bigger cities,[129] and the development of printing had made it possible, in theory at least, for anyone who could read to gain access to some of the most advanced intellectual writers of the day.[130] Saccardino could certainly read, for

[125] R. Campeggi, *Racconto de gli heretici iconomiasti giustiziati in Bologna* (Bologna, 1622), 80–4, 87–8, 91; the case is discussed by C. Ginzburg, 'The Dovecote Has Opened its Eyes: Popular Conspiracy in Seventeenth Century Italy', in G. Henningsen and J. Tedeschi, (eds.), *The Inquisition in Early Modern Europe: Studies in Sources and Methods* (DeKalb, Ill., 1986), 190–8. One of Saccardino's fellow conspirators was sentenced because 'non credeva se non quello, che di giorno in giorno sensatamente vedeva' (Campeggi, *Racconto de gli heretici*, 103–4).
[126] C. Ginzburg, *The Cheese and the Worms: The Cosmos of a Sixteenth Century Miller* (Eng. trans., London, 1980), 6, 11–12, 56–7, 63–5, 68–72, 75–6, 81, 101, 153–4. Menocchio was tried in 1584 and 1599.
[127] Ibid. 11–12, 39–41, 49.
[128] Ibid. 113, 119, 123–4.
[129] Cf. P. F. Grendler, *Schooling in Renaissance Italy: Literacy and Learning, 1300–1600* (London, 1989), 45–7, 71–8, 90–108; Mackenney, *Tradesmen and Traders*, 183–5.
[130] Cf. Ginzburg, *The Cheese and the Worms*, 59–60.

example, and he was familiar with the ideas of contemporary medical scholars.[131] Ginzburg has suggested that Baroni may have associated with heretical circles in Bologna,[132] and there is no reason in principle why Menocchio should not have come across some discussion of unorthodox ideas during visits to Venice and the Padovano.[133] Social contacts between Italians of widely differing backgrounds were frequent[134] and not necessarily restricted to formal occasions. Sometimes we can point to individuals who may have served as intermediaries. A rich Paduan university graduate attended the Venetian Anabaptist synod in 1550, for example;[135] Daniele de Melchiori, parish priest of Polcenigo in Friuli, was a friend of Menocchio, and had been tried by the inquisitor of Aquileia and Concordia in 1576 and 1579 for statements (and behaviour) that suggested a distinctly materialist approach to life.[136]

A 'filtering-down' of intellectual ideas was therefore possible, and Inquisition tribunals certainly tended to assume that atheist beliefs had to be learned from others rather than developed independently.[137] But there is some evidence that atheism could emerge without an external academic stimulus, in reflection on personal experience. A poignant example was revealed in 1581, when Evangelista de Vintura presented a written confession to the Venetian Inquisition stating that, for the previous twenty-five years, 'I have been forgetful of my salvation and have lived far from the true and correct Christian way of life.' He traced his desperation (*disperatione*) to the plague of 1555–6, when his mother, brothers, and sisters had been killed and he had lost all his property: 'I

---

[131] Ibid. 2, 28–30, 50; Ginzburg, 'The Dovecote', 191–2.

[132] Ginzburg, *The Cheese and the Worms*, 121–3.

[133] Cf. the suggestion of Zambelli, 'From Menocchio to Piero della Francesca', 992–3.

[134] Ginzburg, 'The Dovecote', 194–5.

[135] Ginzburg, *I costituti*, 66–7.

[136] ASVen, *SU*, b. 44, 'De Melchiori Don Daniele', fos. 3ᵛ–4ʳ; Ginzburg, *The Cheese and the Worms*, 73–4; cf. Zambelli, 'From Menocchio to Piero della Francesca', 994.

[137] TCD, MS 1225, fo. 194ʳ, sentence of the chemist Giovanni Francesco de Pegorari in Verona ('perseverando pur che per ignorantia, e per passione senza esser insegnato da nissuno e senza haver conferito con nissuno, eri cascato a credere e a dire che morto il corpo era morta l'anima').

doubted that God could have any providential control over events, since he had treated me so badly.'[138]

We should not underestimate the extent of such heartfelt original thinking, at all levels of society. As Menocchio's case suggests, it was possible for individuals to piece together a patchwork philosophy from sometimes contradictory sources, some written, some verbal: elements that matched their circumstances or conformed to their own prior conclusions were adopted, and the rest were discarded. The final pattern was original, though the component parts may well have been second-hand.[139]

The individuals discussed here rarely escaped investigation. Their published writings were censored or prohibited, their persons tried and convicted. As the sixteenth and seventeenth centuries progressed, the ecclesiastical authorities became increasingly alarmed by what they saw as a surge in unbelief. Statistics derived from Inquisition trials shows a matching increase in the numbers investigated for atheism and related offences.[140] By the later seventeenth century a campaign against the intellectual expression of unbelief had begun, in part co-ordinated from Rome. In 1670 Cardinal Leopoldo de' Medici discreetly alerted Pisan supporters of atomism to the fact that times were changing.[141] In the following year one of the cardinal inquisitors warned the Archbishop of

[138] ASVen, *SU*, b. 47, 'Arcudi Crisso', confession of 20 Apr. 1581. The experience of 'desperation' was familiar to English Protestants (cf. K. Thomas, *Religion and the Decline of Magic* (London, 1971), 199).

[139] Ginzburg, *The Cheese and the Worms*, pp. xi–xii, xxii, 27, 33–4, 36, 51, 61, 124–6; cf. Zambelli, 'From Menocchio to Piero della Francesca', 994–5, and the thoughts of Wootton, 'Unbelief in Early Modern Europe', 94–5. Popular atheism can also be found in 18th cent. Inquisition trials: see L. Accati, 'Lo spirito della fornicazione: Virtù dell'anima e virtù del corpo in Friuli, fra '600 e '700', *Quaderni storici*, 41 (1979), 644–72 (pp. 662–6).

[140] E. W. Monter and J. Tedeschi, 'Towards a Statistical Profile of the Italian Inquisitions, Sixteenth to Eighteenth Centuries', in Henningsen and Tedeschi, *The Inquisition*, 130–57 (pp. 144, 146). Pintard, *Le Libertinage*, 261, refers to the executions in Rome of Troilo Savella and the Marquis of Manzoli for atheism in the first half of the 17th cent.; Charles Coypeau wrote his *Pensées de Monsieur Dassoucy dans le S. Office de Rome* (Paris, 1676) against atheists while imprisoned in Rome by the Inquisition during the reign of Clement IX.

[141] Casini, *Introduzione all'illuminismo*, 272.

Naples against the implications of Cartesian philosophy,[142] and by 1676 the trials had started. In December of that year an atomist, Andrea Pisani, abjured in Rome.[143] In 1688 investigations were initiated in Naples against two groups (eleven persons in all) accused of denying the existence of God and the doctrines of creation, the afterlife, and the divinity of Christ; they had, it was said, adopted instead a belief in atomism and the eternity of the world.[144] The charges were not definitively proved, but the trials demonstrate the concern that already existed in the minds of the authorities. In Venice, meanwhile, Michelangelo Fardella was investigated for Cartesianism and atomist sympathies, and in 1690 the Roman Accademia dei Bianchi was investigated on suspicion of encouraging atheism.[145] In the same year Grand Duke Cosimo III prohibited the teaching of atomism at the University of Pisa, and by 1693, according to one Jesuit, 'all Rome' was opposed to the new physics, which was said to be 'most pernicious for both scholarship and sincere religion'.[146] There was to be no slackening in the campaign against atheism and related expressions of unbelief until the 1720s or even later.

I have tried to suggest in this chapter that, in sixteenth- and seventeenth-century Italy, elements of unbelief could be, and on occasion were, combined into atheism—that atheism was both conceivable and actual among the educated and the uneducated. Its sources were varied. Some ideas seem to have been drawn from the writings of ancient authors rediscovered by Renaissance scholars before 1500: especially important

---

[142] L. Amabile, *Il Santo Officio della Inquisizione in Napoli* (2 vols.; Città di Castello, 1892), ii. 53 n. 2. These early preoccupations were focused particularly on the Accademia degl'Investiganti.

[143] Redondi, *Galileo*, 318–19.

[144] They were also accused of sexual perversions: Casini, *Introduzione all'illuminismo*, 272, 291; A. Corsano, *Umanesimo e religione in G. B. Vico* (Bari, 1935), 17–21; L. Osbat, *L'Inquisizione a Napoli: Il processo agli ateisti* (Rome, 1974). Giacinto de Cristofaro's abjuration included the belief 'che non si dia Dio, ma che le cose del Mondo si reggono dalla natura', (Osbat, *L'Inquisizione*, 243. Osbat also refers to a series of sermons in Naples against atheists in 1685–6 (p. 77)).

[145] Casini, *Introduzione all'illuminismo*, 283–4; Baldini, *Un libertino accademico*, 50–61. The Bianchi were a secretive group of mostly young people who were opposed to the papal government; they were also suspected of atheism.

[146] Casini, *Introduzione all'illuminismo*, 272–3.

here were those which did not rely on the assumption of supernatural intervention to explain the existence, composition, and working of the natural world.[147] Others may have developed after 1500 in response to a growing awareness of alternatives to Catholicism, whether in Europe or overseas.[148] Yet the case of Evangelista de Vintura suggests that it was possible to create a personal synthesis of unbelief in response to experience, without any formal intellectual stimulus at all.

However, I would not want to claim that atheism was common in this period. For the majority, the teaching of the Church or the assumptions of 'popular religion' were sufficient. But for a few, they were not. François Garasse, who wrote in 1623 against atheism and 'the beautiful spirits of our time', called Giulio Cesare Vanini a 'poor butterfly'[149]—beautiful, presumably, but vulnerable and short-lived. And yet he was not alone.

---

[147] Professor Kors has also emphasized the availability of 'ancient sources of disbelief' in the early modern period (*Atheism in France*, 178–218, 222–5).

[148] Menocchio provides a nice example of this: Ginzburg, *The Cheese and the Worms*, 41–51, 101–2, 106–8. See also the experience of the communities of converted Jews and their descendants, some of whom were accused of believing nothing at all (B. Pullan, *The Jews of Europe and the Inquisition of Venice 1550–1670* (Oxford, 1983), 233, 235–7, 240, 245–6).

[149] Garasse, *La Doctrine curieuse*, 43.

3

Pierre Charron's 'Scandalous Book'

TULLIO GREGORY

'One cannot read Pierre Charron's *Sagesse* without running the risk of having one's Catholic faith shaken ... Some maintain that they have never read a better book. They admire its dry, taut style and its many incisive maxims. But for the most part they are libertines who mock the ceremonies of the Church.'

Pierre Charron's *De la sagesse* is omnipresent in libertine culture, as this passage from Mersenne reminds us. Charron is constantly denounced in French apologetic writings of the first half of the seventeenth century. His book is described as a 'dangerous book', brimming over with 'poison sweetened with honeyed words', a 'seminary of irreligion', that has caused 'much more harm than good' (according to Garasse and Mersenne); 'a scandalous book, which adopts the teaching of Machiavelli and is extremely dangerous to religion', as Buffalo, the papal nuncio in France, wrote to Cardinal Aldobrandini when he was attempting to have it withdrawn from the bookshops[1] *De la sagesse* was first published in

[*Editors' Note*. This chapter has been translated from Tullio Gregory, *Etica e religione nella critica libertina* (Naples, 1986) by permission of the publishers of the Italian version, Guida editore s.p.a., Naples. The bibliography on Charron that Gregory takes for granted is: Edward F. Rice, *The Renaissance Idea of Wisdom* (Cambridge, Mass., 1958); Hans Baron, 'Secularization of Wisdom and Political Humanism in The Renaissance', *Journal of the History of Ideas*, 21 (1960), 131–50; Richard H. Popkin, The *History of Scepticism from Erasmus to Spinoza* (Berkeley, Calif., and Los Angeles, 1979); Jean D. Charron, *The 'Wisdom' of Pierre Charron: An Original and Orthodox Code of Morality* (Chapel Hill, NC, 1960); Anthony Levi, *French Moralists: The Theory of the Passions, 1585 to 1649* (Oxford, 1964); and Anna M. Battista, *Alle origini del pensiero politico libertino: Montaigne e Charron* (Milan, 1966); see now also V. Dini and D. Taranto (eds.), *La saggezza moderna. Temi e problemi dell'opera di Pierre Charron* (Naples, 1987).]

[1] François Garasse, *La Doctrine curieuse des beaux esprits de ce temps ou prétendu tels* (Paris, 1623), 27, 1015; Marin Mersenne, *L'Impiété des déistes* (2 vols.; Paris,

1601. A revised edition that appeared in 1604 was censured by the Sorbonne; and in 1605 it was put on the Index. Despite such difficulties, it was an immense publishing success. Between 1601 and 1672 it was republished dozens of times (there were three editions in the years 1621–3, when the debate over libertinism was at its height). The abbreviated *Petit traicté de sagesse* went through twelve editions between 1606 and 1645. Garasse would have placed *De la sagesse* in 'the libertine's library'; it was held by Naudé to be the best book in the world, second only to the Bible; it was celebrated by Gassendi as one of his favourite books. *De la sagesse* treats in an exemplary way some of the themes of libertine culture.

The influence of Montaigne, who for many years was Charron's close friend, runs throughout *De la sagesse*. In it Charron often transcribes, summarizes, reshapes Montaigne's *Essais*, in order to make their meaning clearer, their impact greater. As Naudé put it: 'Of his [Montaigne's] wisdom he was to my knowledge the first admirably to summarize and order the precepts, an achievement of method, theory, and discernment . . . In the process he created something more noble than anything else produced by either the ancients or the moderns.'[2] Charron did not draw only on Montaigne, however: in addition, he was influenced by the classical moralists, as well as by a humanist tradition which ran from Machiavelli to Justus Lipsius.

De la sagesse is a text that reflects a crucial moment in the crisis of the metaphysical tradition, and a fundamental characteristic of the work is its defence of doubt, uncertainty, and enquiry. Man is not made for truth. His fulfilment is to be found in doubt and ambiguity: 'the world is a school of enquiry'. The quest for knowledge is an end in itself, 'whether one finds the mark is beside the point'. In nature there is nothing but doubt, and nothing is more certain than uncer-

---

1624), i. 184–5, 198, 210. Buffalo's opinion is to be found in J. B. Sabrié, *De l'humanisme au rationalisme: Pierre Charron (1541–1603)* (Paris, 1913), 131.

[2] Gabriel Naudé, *Bibliographia politica* (Venice, 1633), 15–16. For Gassendi's opinion, referred to above, see his *Opera omnia* (6 vols.; Lyon, 1658, vi. 1 B, 2 A. For the comparison with the Bible, *Naudaeana et Patiniana, ou Singularitez remarquables, prises des conversations de Mess. Naudé et Patin*, 2nd edn. (Amsterdam, 1703), 3–4.

tainty.[3] This scepticism—Montaigne and Charron were, of course, avid readers of Sextus Empiricus—leads to the defence and application of a non-dogmatic reason. Charron's critique of certainty destroys any pretence that we are able to bring the process of enquiry to a conclusion in a definitive and all-embracing system, or that we can lay claim to absolute and universal principles and values. The corollary of the defence of doubt is the injunction 'to be impressed by nothing', never to be blinkered by the presumption that one has attained the truth.

The *Petit traicté de sagesse* is both a summary of the larger work and at the same time a response to its critics. Here Charron replies to an objection that dogmatic minds have made through the ages: that the condition of doubt and uncertainty is stressful and unhappy. 'I maintain, on the contrary,' Charron replies,

that it alone can provide true repose and security for our spirits. Have all the greatest and most noble philosophers and wise men who have professed doubt been in a state of anxiety and suffering? But they [the dogmatists] say: to doubt, to consider both points of view, to put off a decision, is this not painful? I reply, it is indeed for fools, but not for wise men. It is painful for people who cannot stand freedom, for those who are presumptuous, partisan, passionate and who, obstinately attached to their opinions, arrogantly condemn all others . . . Such people, in truth, know nothing. They do not even know what it is to know something.

On the other hand, the state of doubt, of enquiry, 'is the science of sciences, the certainty of certainties'.[4]

Charron's outlook is of the utmost importance. It involves the rejection of all the claims of dogmatic reasoning and all the values associated with it. It is not merely the result of a new reading of the ancient sceptics. It is a self-conscious response to the discovery of the multiplicity and the diversity of intellectual and moral worlds, to the new civilizations and religions that one could learn about by reading the reports of

[3] Pierre Charron, *De la sagesse*, I. 16: 131; II. 2: 301 (I have used the Paris edition of 1783, which follows the first edition, printed in Bordeaux in 1601; references indicate book and chapter numbers as well as page numbers).

[4] Pierre Charron, *Petit traicté de sagesse* (Paris, 1635), 223–4, (first published in 1606).

travellers who had explored the Far East and the New World
('just think', Charron writes, 'how much we have learnt from
the discovery of the New World, the East and West Indies
... Who can doubt that in the foreseeable future there will
be further discoveries?'[5])

The exploration of these contrasting civilizations, from the
refined Mayans to the cruel inhabitants of Canada, from the
Egyptians to the Chinese, reinforced the impact of the rediscovery of the ancient sceptics. The result was to cast doubt on
the very category of 'barbarism', which, for more than two
thousand years, had been proudly defended as the line of
demarcation between what was held to be the only true
civilization and all the other ways of living which lay outside it.

It is a sign of stupidity and weakness to think that all should believe
and live as they do in one's own village and mother country, that the
things that happen here are of interest to, and shared by, the rest of
the world. The fool, when told that there are beliefs, customs, and
laws that are quite contrary to those which he is used to seeing revered
and practised, either attacks these novelties and immediately con-
demns them as barbarous, or else refuses to believe such reports. So
enslaved is his soul to his own local customs that he takes them to be
the only legitimate ones, believing them to be natural and universal.
We each call 'barbarous' whatever does not accord with our taste and
habits; it seems that there is no other touchstone for the identification
of truth and reason than the example of the customs and the habits of
mind of the country in which we live.[6]

This line of thought had been developed by Montaigne,
and it recurs throughout the writings of the *libertins érudits*.
The discovery of diversity—'nothing suits the nature and
spirit of man better than diversity', claimed Charron—
throws into relief the relativity of every criterion of judgement and every social custom.[7] It is therefore held to be the
pre-condition for that full liberty and open-mindedness
within which wisdom can be realized.

To acquire and preserve this universal, vigorous, free and open
spirit (a rare and difficult thing, of which not all are capable, just as
many can never attain wisdom), there are many things that are of

---

[5] Charron, *De la sagesse*, II. 2: 306.   [6] Ibid. 303–4.
[7] Charron, *Petit traicté*, 228.

assistance: above all . . . the great variety, diversity, and inequality amongst men . . . and the vast range of laws and customs that have established themselves in the world; there is no better school of life than to observe continuously the diversity of men's lives and to relish the perpetual variety to which our nature lends itself.[8]

Not surprisingly, in the libertine culture of the seventeenth century, travel—that is to say, the encounter with non-European peoples and customs, and, indeed, with the differing sects of Christians—is the paradigmatic route to a 'free philosophy'. La Mothe le Vayer recommends travel much as doctors advise a change of air, or botanists the transplanting of trees: 'this transplantation is no less beneficial for men than for plants'.[9] On the other hand, the defenders of orthodoxy are unanimous in holding that travel is a cause of libertinism and of atheism, for they too think that the experience of a diversity of customs and beliefs serves to dissolve religious convictions. In the second half of the seventeenth century La Bruyère, speaking of the *esprits forts* in his *Caractères*, is merely repeating a commonplace when he says that they 'complete the corruption of their minds by going on too long voyages, during which they lose what remnants of religious belief they had. Day by day they encounter new confessions, watch new ceremonies, study new customs,' until finally they become indifferent or incredulous because everything appears and seems possible.[10] They end up uninterested in religion or simply irreligious, having formed the impression that there is nothing to choose between one religion and another.

In Charron, too, the contemplation of the diversity of customs, rites, and religions leads to indifference, which he defines as the suspension of judgement. One should find nothing surprising, he maintains:

Nothing that is said, approved, believed in one time and place is not also said, approved, and believed elsewhere; but somewhere else it is denied, disapproved of, and condemned, for the human mind is capable of anything . . . Everything that happens occurs

[8] Charron, *De la sagesse*, II. 2: 304–5; III. 14: 637.
[9] [François de La Mothe le Vayer], 'De la vie privée', in Oratius Tubero, *Quatre dialogues faits à l'imitation des anciens* ('Frankfurt, 1506' [1632–3]), 177.
[10] Jean de La Bruyère, *Les Caractères*, in *Œuvres complètes*, ed. J. Benda (Paris, 1957), 450.

within the circumscribed world of natural events, within which events repeat themselves. Everything is subject to birth, alteration, and death, to the influences of changing times, places, climates, stars, airs, and territorial divisions. From this we learn not to wed ourselves to any belief, not to swear by anything, not to be surprised by anything.[11]

The insistence with which Charron returns to this theme throughout *De la sagesse* is significant. To the compact world of values that the Mediterranean civilizations had constructed, values that the Christian Church had reshaped into a theological system, there was now counterposed the relativity and singularity of manners, customs, and faiths, all equally the product of the human intellect, 'which is capable of finding an appearance of rationality in anything, witness the fact that whatever is held to be impious, unjust, disgraceful in one place, is pious, just, and honourable in another; one cannot name a single law, custom, or belief that is universally either approved or condemned.'[12]

This new relativism did not only entail a crisis in the concept of barbarism. It undermined the very idea of a human nature that all could be seen to have in common, along with the ideas of a common rationality and a universal natural law.

We can no longer recognize anything of nature in ourselves. If we had to say how many laws of nature there are, and what they ordain, we would be at a loss. The sign of a natural law must be the universal respect in which it is held, for if there was anything that nature had truly commanded us to do, we would undoubtedly obey it universally: not only would every nation respect it, but every individual. Instead there is nothing in the world that is not subject to contradiction and dispute, nothing that is not rejected, not just by one nation, but by many; equally, there is nothing that is strange and (in the opinion of many) unnatural that is not approved in many countries, and authorized by their customs.[13]

Human nature, rationality, and natural law are now supplanted by the idea of custom (*coustume*, *consuetudo*), which is held to be the only foundation for ethical and religious

---

[11] Charron, *De la sagesse*, II. 2: 308.
[12] Ibid. I. 16: 132.   [13] Ibid. II. 3: 325.

norms and practices, for the laws of states, and the ceremonies of religions. Fundamentally custom, as Montaigne had already said, was not rational, but mystical: that is to say, it was a brute fact, and therefore was endowed with an irresistible authority.

Custom . . . is another powerful and imperious mistress. She lays claim to her authority in a violent and treacherous fashion. She installs herself little by little. She establishes her power surreptitiously and almost unnoticed from modest, sweet, and humble beginnings; having ensconced herself with the assistance of the passage of time, she discloses a furious and tyrannical aspect. One finds oneself without the will or the strength even to look her in the face. She draws her authority from present possession and from habit; she grows larger and more powerful as she advances, like a river on its way to the sea; and it is dangerous to trace her back to her origins.

Who would believe how great, how imperious is the authority of custom? He who defined it as a second nature did not have the last word on the subject, for custom is more powerful than nature, and overrides her . . . Against the opposition of both reason and justice, it legitimizes and imposes upon the world opinions, religions, beliefs, practices, habits, and ways of life that are truly fantastic and ridiculous.[14]

Charron's polemic against custom is of central importance throughout *De la sagesse*. *La coustume* is the totality of ideas, and of ways of judging and behaving, that draw their strength from habit, often from deception, but never from reason. They are taken to be incontestable truths, functioning as laws that govern conscience and thought. Thus custom deprives men of their individual identity, turning them into 'herd animals', sheep in a flock (*la sotte multitude*), governed by unreason.[15] From Charron's attack on custom follows not only his denunciation of the tyranny of public opinion, but also his more specific criticism of 'universal assent'. Universal assent had been regarded in the Stoic tradition as a criterion of truth, and, having been taken up by Christian theology, was used in the seventeenth century as a proof of natural theology: a reflection of divine inspiration. Charron's view of it was quite different: 'the strongest and most effective method of

---

[14] Ibid. II. 8: 386–7, 392–3.   [15] Ibid. II. 1: 293.

winning assent, the best touchstone of truth, is the appeal to arguments from antiquity and from widespread agreement. However, there are so many more fools than wise men, *santitatis patrocinium est insanientium turba.*'[16] 'The strongest argument for truth is from the universal assent of the whole world. However, fools greatly outnumber wise men. Moreover, one has to ask how this consensus has been reached: the answer will be by contagion, approval being bestowed without judgement or knowledge of the issues, but merely by following the lead of someone who has begun the dance.'[17]

The theme of custom had already been explored by the classical sceptics and developed by Montaigne. Alongside cultural diversity, it recurs throughout the libertine literature. In the very years in which Descartes wrote his famous pages on how common sense is 'the most fairly distributed' of all characteristics, 'by nature equal in all men', La Mothe le Vayer declared that common sense was no longer freely available, having become 'contraband': 'nothing is more popular than self-deception', and one should therefore flee from anything that claims to be common or popular. 'When it is said that everyone says, believes, or does such and such,' Charron writes, 'he [the wise man] should say to himself: so much the worse for them.'[18] More technically, Gassendi argued against the Platonism of Herbert of Cherbury and the 'innatism' of Descartes. He insisted on the diversity of laws and customs in order to deny that there were any beliefs that received universal assent, even the idea of God—which stemmed, he maintained, from tradition and authority. Ethical and political principles, too, he held, following Epicurus, to be derived not from nature but from convention.

Besides the experience and valorization of diversity, with, as already mentioned, all its disruptive implications, Charron had a profound sense of the distinction, even the discrepancy, between different spheres of experience, thought, and behaviour. Significant in this context is the preface to *De la sagesse*,

---

[16] Ibid. I. 7: 66.
[17] Ibid. I. 16: 135.
[18] [François de La Mothe le Vayer], 'De la philosophie sceptique', in Tubero, *Quatre dialogues*, 53; id., 'Le Banquet sceptique', ibid. 133–4; Charron, *De la sagesse*, II. 1: 292. For Descartes, see the opening lines of *Discours de la méthode*.

where Charron explains that in attacking popular beliefs that are universally accepted, he intends to educate men not 'for the cloister', but 'for the world', 'for civic life'. Consequently he is not writing as a theologian or preacher, and feels free to make use of 'philosophical and intellectual freedom'.[19] He wants to be read, not by 'weak minds', but by *'esprits forts'* who understand 'how the world goes'. Thus he does not want to offer an abstract plan for the education of men in general, nor a sketch of unrealizable ideal; instead, he proceeds from a realistic consideration of the 'human condition' ('a good anatomy of the mind', as Naudé put it): 'I present things as they are, and lay them out on the counter-top', Charron wrote, adding in the *Petit traicté* that it is a mistake to confuse 'matters of fact with questions of right and duty', 'questions concerning men's private beliefs and independent thoughts with questions concerning public behaviour and social propriety; questions that are matters of human judgement with those which concern revealed truth and religious belief'.[20]

These dichotomies—the world and the cloister, civic life and monastic life, the *esprit fort* and the weak-minded, the intellectual freedom of the philosopher and the theologians' deference to authority, private independence and public conformity—these run parallel to each other, culminating in the supreme distinction between reason and religion in which Charron encapsulates the difference between *De la sagesse* and the earlier *Les Trois Verités*. At the end of the *Petit traicté* Charron returned to the theme of the preface of *De la sagesse*, insisting that throughout his book

I do not intend to oblige anyone to agree with me, nor do I aim to persuade them. I do not argue dogmatically. I simply lay out my views, as a stall-holder displays his wares in a market . . . I make no claims without the backing of reason, although [pedants] may not be able to recognize the fact or accept my conclusions. If anyone puts forward a better argument than mine, I will listen to it with pleasure and delight. But they must not expect me to retreat

[19] Charron, *De la sagesse*, preface, p. xxvii.
[20] Ibid., p. xxv, and 'Advertissement de l'autheur', pp. xx–xxi; Charron, *Petit traicté*, 196; for Naudé's view, see *Lettres de Gui Patin*, ed. J.-H. Reveillé-Parise (3 vols., Paris, 1846), ii. 480.

in the face of quotations from others and appeals to authority, for I
do not consider this the right way to argue, except where religion
is concerned, for there authority alone, unsupported by reason,
carries the day. That is the true kingdom of authority, but elsewhere
reason alone, unsupported by authority, is victorious.[21]

This may simply seem like a variation on an old theme. If
we pay close attention to the various comparisons and
contrasts drawn by Charron, however, we will recognize that
they are incompatible with the fideistic interpretation of his
writings that is often put forward, which seeks to assimilate
his views to those of contemporary religious apologists.
Among contemporary apologists one never finds a comparable defence of the critical capacity of sceptical reason, nor a
similarly radical denial of the existence of universal values,
nor a rejection of anthropocentrism that goes so far as to
regard animals as superior to men, nor an attack on superstition that extends to the whole of religious practice, nor a
renunciation of proselytizing and of efforts to save sinners:
all these are themes that Charron develops from his sceptical
premisses, and they ensure that his defence of 'philosophical
freedom' has no parallel among the fideistic theologians of
his own day.

The best way to understand Charron is to take his dichotomies seriously: between weak, simple, commonplace minds
and *esprits forts*; between reason and philosophical liberty on
the one hand, and religion and dogmatism on the other. In
the very act of withdrawing religion from the realm of reason,
denying the possibility either of a science of theology or of
the capacity of human reason to establish an elementary
natural theology (even the immortality of the soul and the
existence of God cannot be proved), he in fact identifies
religion with custom. Thus he reduces the rites and doctrines
of religion to products of tradition, with the necessary
implication that they are irrational, mystical, arbitrary, and
rooted in deceit. Custom, remember, 'against the opposition
of both reason and justice, legitimizes and imposes upon the
world opinions, religions, beliefs, practices, habits, and ways

---

[21] Charron *Petit traicté*, 227–8.

of life that are truly fantastic and ridiculous'. Withdrawn from the realm of reason, religion—all religions, for Charron accords privilege to none—goes 'beyond common sense, far surpassing what human reason can accomplish; consequently it should not and cannot be established or survive amongst mankind by natural and human means ... but must be brought to men through an extraordinary and heavenly revelation, and must be accepted on the basis of divine inspiration from heaven.' In fact, Charron goes on, this is not the real state of affairs:

Despite what they say, religion is maintained by human means and preserved by human hands. One has only to look at the way in which the various religions have been established in the world, and in which even now they win over particular individuals. One's nation, one's country, one's home determines one's religion. One is of the religion of the place where one was born and brought up. We are circumcised or baptized—Jews, or Muslims, or Christians—before we know we are human beings. It is not we who choose our religion ... If religion was of divine establishment ... shining out with God's glory, it would be solidly established in our hearts, and would have consequences that would seem, and would indeed be, miraculous.[22]

Readers of these pages, as Mersenne remarked, might easily conclude that 'the true religion is no better than the false religions. Instead we ought to thank God we are Christians, for Christianity comes not from our homeland and our mother's womb, but from the blood of our redeemer Jesus Christ, which works through baptism, the gateway to the true religion.'[23]

Montaigne had already written in a very well-known passage:

We adopt our religion in our own way and according to our own methods, no differently from the way in which others adopt other religions. We find ourselves in a country in which it is the established faith. We may respect its antiquity, and the authority of the men who have upheld it. Or we may fear the punishment it foretells for unbelievers. Or we may be attracted by the rewards it

---

[22] Ibid. II. 5: 346–7.   [23] Mersenne, *L'Impiété des déistes*, i. 208–9.

promises to the faithful . . . We are Christians for the same reason that we are Perigordians or Germans.[24]

But in Charron this line of thought acquires a particular polemical force by virtue of his continuous references to the incompatibility of religion and common sense, and his insistence on the fact that all religions, without exception, share the same characteristics: 'all discover and publicize miracles, prodigies, oracles, sacred mysteries, saints, prophets, festivals, articles of faith, and beliefs necessary for salvation;' 'each pretends to be better and truer than the others'.[25] Charron constantly stresses the practical and political purposes that religions fulfil. In religion 'one finds the most extraordinary claims and the most transparent impostures', but these only serve to inspire greater reverence and more unquestioning admiration.[26]

These themes were promptly taken up by libertine polemicists. Thus Crucé was soon to echo Charron's sentiments ('all these religions claim to be able to prove their truthfulness by appealing to the evidence of miracles, and each pretends to be better than the others'), denouncing the preoccupation of the dogmatists with the conversion of others at any cost ('why must we make war on each other over differences in rituals? . . . We should not persecute those who refuse to adopt our ceremonies'), and their presumption that whatever the custom of their country, it could be claimed to be true ('this is the typical vice of the lower classes, who have never travelled outside the territory surrounding their own town; they believe that everybody should live as they do').[27] Similarly, La Mothe le Vayer referred to Charron in the course of an iconoclastic survey of the various religions, which followed his praise of atheism as the norm during civilized epochs.[28]

Those who have argued that Charron was a fideist, and have sought to place him within the ranks of contemporary

---

[24] Michel de Montaigne, *Essais*, ed. M. Rat (3 vols.; Paris, 1952), ii. 123.
[25] Charron, *De la sagesse*, II. 5: 342, 344.
[26] Ibid. II. 8: 388; II. 5: 346.
[27] Éméric Crucé, *Le Nouveau Cynée* (Paris, 1623), 52.
[28] [François de La Mothe le Vayer], 'De la divinité', in Oratius Tubero, *Cinq autres dialogues du même autheur* ('Frankfurt, 1606'), 173.

apologists for Roman Catholicism, have first to find equally
blunt passages in the contemporary apologists' analysis of the
religious phenomenon, its origins, and its diffusion; passages
that are comparable in continuously stressing the analogies
among the different historical forms of religion; and that
evidence, finally, a willingness to advocate respect for the
established religion of one's country on comparable terms to
those employed by Charron:

all religions have this in common, that they are an outrage to
common sense, for they are pieced together out of a variety of
elements, some of which seem so unworthy, sordid, and at odds
with man's reason that any strong and vigorous intelligence laughs
at them; but others are so noble, illustrious, miraculous, and
mysterious that the intellect can make no sense of them, and finds
them unpalatable. The human intellect is only capable of tackling
mediocre subjects: it disdains petty subjects, and is startled by large
ones. There is, therefore, no reason to be surprised if it finds any
religion hard to accept at first, for all are deficient in the mediocre
and the commonplace, nor that it should require skill to induce
belief. For the strong intellect laughs at religion, while the weak
and superstitious mind marvels at it but is easily scandalized by it
. . . This is why there are so many unbelievers and scoffers, for
these pay undue attention to their own judgement, wishing to
examine and weigh religious questions according to the capacities
and abilities of their own intellects, and to judge them with the
means that nature has given them. To accept religion one must be
simple-minded, obedient, and easygoing; one must believe out of
reverence and obedience, and be prepared to subject oneself to the
law, subordinating one's own judgement, and allowing oneself to
be shepherded and guided by public authority, *captivantes intellec-
tum ad obsequium fidei.*[29]

The particular use to which Charron puts this well-known
Latin tag is noteworthy. He sees faith not as the acceptance
of a set of doctrines derived from supernatural revelation, but
as deference to public authority, an authority embodying the
traditions of the country in which one has been raised.
Obsequium fidei thus means obedience to custom. One forms
the impression that, for Charron, religion is both the

---

[29] Charron, *De la sagesse*, II. 5: 345–6.

expression of custom and its ultimate guarantor, giving it
continuity and strength. Charron describes the sovereign as a
'perpetual and absolute power, subject to neither restrictions
nor conditions . . . subject to no human laws, even those it
has itself decreed', 'an absolute power, free to make and
impose laws as it pleases'.[30] Moreover, his actions are not
governed by the same principles as those of private individuals: the 'justice, virtue, and probity of the sovereign are
to be assessed somewhat differently from these qualities in a
private individual.'[31] Yet even the sovereign finds a limit to
his powers in the religious traditions of his country: 'The
prince should ensure that religion as embodied in the ancient
ceremonies and established laws of the country is protected,'
for this is required by the law of God and of nature.[32]
Wherever the sovereign tries to change the established religion, or to violate the conscience of its adherents, he becomes
a tyrant: then, and only then, those with responsibility in the
government, the princes, the magistrates, the Estates General,
can oppose him; private citizens should either flee or pas-
sively submit.[33]

   Charron's polemic against the Reformation, and against
innovation in general, is thus not inspired by theological
principles. Since religion lies outside the range of the human
intellect, religious traditions cannot be assessed as true or
false, just or unjust. What human judgement can assess,
however, is the damage that all innovation does to the ordered
structure of society, for it is in religion that society is
grounded, and through religion that it maintains itself. 'Religion is the bond and cement of human society.'[34] The
reformers, moreover, share the same faults as the dogmatists.
They are always agitated, wanting to lay down the law for
the whole world. They try to persuade people to their point
of view by laying claim to a truth that they alone possess.
When persuasion fails, they resort to all kinds of violence and
oppression.

---

[30] Ibid. I. 45: 247.   [31] Ibid. III. 2: 458.
[32] Ibid. 457.   [33] Ibid. III. 16: 659–61.
[34] Ibid. 655; III. 2: 456.

Anyone who believes in something thinks he is doing others a favour by persuading them to believe it too; to this end, he does not hesitate to invent whatever he considers necessary to obtain his object and to overcome the incapacity and the resistance that he believes he sees in those around him . . . When normal means fail, he resorts to peremptory commands, to force, to beating and burning. This vice is characteristic of the dogmatists and of those who want to make laws for others and usurp the right to govern.[35]

The wise man's response to this madness—Charron's thinking plainly bears the scars of the Wars of Religion—was to retreat into silence and solitude, to wear a mask, 'to conceal one's mind and thoughts from everyone'.[36] Behind this mask he could continue the free exercise of his reason, making responsible choices in the light of his own conscience, and leaving the world to its fate, which would be determined by the ridiculous predominance of weak spirits, slaves to custom. The price of this secret freedom was external conformity to established laws and traditions.

The advice I give to those who wish to be wise is that their words and actions should obey the established laws and customs of the country in which they live . . . not because these laws and customs are necessarily just and equitable, but simply because they are established. One should not lightly condemn or take exception to the laws of others. One should freely and objectively examine both one's own laws and theirs, for one's private judgement and personal belief should be governed by reason alone . . . First, all wise men hold that the rule of rules and the overriding law of laws is to obey and preserve the laws and customs of the country in which one finds oneself, *sequi has leges indigenas honestum est.* Every form of behaviour that diverges from the norm is to be suspected as foolish or ambitious, a threat to stability and security. Secondly, laws and customs maintain their reputation not because they are just, but because they are laws and customs. This is the mystical—and the sole—foundation of their authority.[37]

Deprived of any basis in reason and of any independent ethical validity, laws depend upon custom to sustain themselves. They therefore reflect the errors and prejudices of

---

[35] Ibid. I. 7: 64–5.   [36] Ibid. II. 9: 401.
[37] Ibid. II. 8: 394.

custom. The wise man is thus obliged to dissociate his public behaviour from his private judgement, the one following custom, the other reason. This dissociation marks a fundamental crisis in the European conscience. It reflects the climate of intimidation that was imposed by 'public opinion' in the early modern period, tyrannically expressed through the courts of the Church and State, which made frequent use of censorship, imprisonment, and execution.

It is a characteristic of the brave-hearted and wise man (and it is wisdom that I am trying to portray here) that he examines everything, that he assesses all the laws and customs of the known world one by one, comparing them with one another in order to judge them . . . objectively and unemotionally by the standards of truth, reason, and the universal principles of nature to which we owe our primary obligation of obedience. He does not take shelter in illusions, or betray his own judgement by accepting falsehood as truth. But he is content to render obedience and respect to those laws and customs that, as citizens of particular countries, we are also obliged to obey. Thus no one will have grounds for objecting to our behaviour. It will sometimes happen that, because of our individual obligation to obey the laws and customs of our country, we will do things that are contrary to our primary and fundamental obligation—contrary to the law of nature and the universal principles of reason. But we satisfy our obligations to nature and reason if we keep our private judgement and personal convictions just and sound, according to the precepts of these higher laws. This is the limit of our freedom: our private judgement is all that we control, for the world has no right to interfere with our thoughts. Our behaviour, however, is a matter of public concern, and we are held accountable for it. Thus it will often be right for us to do things of which we rightly disapprove. There is no remedy for this, for it is in the nature of things.'[38]

Two roles, two faces, the stage and the behind-the-scenes, or, as Montaigne had expressed it, 'the shop, and the workshop out of the customer's sight'. 'Each of us plays two roles and lives two lives, one external and public, the other private and real. One must distinguish between a man's skin and his clothes.'[39]

[38] Ibid. 396–7.   [39] Ibid. II. 2: 314.

Thus, that disarticulation of a cohesive system of values and behaviour that characterized Charron's experience leads to an extreme outcome. We are no longer facing cautious distinctions, but a clear-cut opposition between political behaviour, which corresponds to municipal obligations, and ethical behaviour, which is radically different, governed by universal reason and justice, and sharply at odds with one's political obligations. Only the wise man can obey reason and justice, and out of the dissociation and conflict between these two and custom is formed the life of the *esprit fort*, who, through his external behaviour, 'justly' fulfils obligations that his reason denounces as unjust and contrary to natural law. Only the *esprit foible* knows no uncertainties and internal conflicts, protected by his rash conviction that he is entitled to act in accordance with his own beliefs.

The conservative implication of Charron's critique has been overly stressed. Through the sharp distinction that it draws between internal freedom and external conformity to the established law, it provides no criticism of the existing order, which, indeed, it seeks to uphold. But during the course of the first half of the seventeenth century it came to be seen that to deny that existing values had any foundation in universal and absolute principles was to imply that every moral system was the product of a historical process, which varied from place to place. Laws derive their validity from their very existence, not from their inherent justice, as Charron kept repeating. Thus the concept of justice loses all ethical significance, becoming a question merely of current practice and social utility; similarly, the State ceases to be conceived as an organism that incorporates and expresses ethical and religious values that are antecedent to, and properly override, the needs of individuals. It becomes simply a coercive power, dependent on its own laws. Consequently, the state can demand only external conformity. It cannot make claims over the individual's conscience, which retains and demands complete independence. Thus, recognition of the 'mystical' or irrational foundation of the laws and of the state lays them open to direct criticism. La Mothe le Vayer formed part of a recognizable line of descent from Charron when he accused states and governments of having 'caused wars, persecutions, plagues, dearths, and virtually all the evils from which we suffer . . . one thing cannot be denied, that they have shackled man's natural liberty, and there can be no compensation for this loss.'[40] Shortly after 1650 the *Theophrastus redivivus* drew on what was by then a long tradition of libertine speculation in denouncing the state as a horrible monster, founded on a *iustititia legalis* imposed by the powerful and sustained by religious myths, in direct contravention of the rights of nature, which have been destroyed or distorted.

It is this tradition that Hobbes's political theory sought to modify by offering a defence both of natural liberty and of established authority. Indeed, Hobbes was not without influence on the libertine tradition, particulary when his work was taken up by Sorbière. His authority converged with that of Epicurus, who was seen as upholding a theory of the just as the useful, and the legal as the conventional. Gassendi's admiration for Hobbes thus follows naturally upon his defence of Epicurus. He wrote that Hobbes's *De cive* was a book that was 'far from commonplace, and deserved to be in the hands of all those who sought profound knowledge'. He hoped that all Hobbes's works would soon be published, 'for I know no other philosopher who is as free of prejudice, or who looks more deeply into the subjects that he seeks to analyse'.[41]

Finally, one should note how the progressive secularization of the idea of law combined with the relativization of moral values to make room for a new definition of morality as an autonomous form of behaviour, depending not on values established outside either ethics or the individual, but rather on the private convictions of one's conscience. Far from being morally ambiguous, as it seemed at first, the libertine tradition offered a sharp distinction between the heteronomous and the autonomous, the political and the moral. The world of public life was seen in terms of practical needs detached from any ethical foundation.

---

[40] [François de La Mothe le Vayer], 'De la politique', in Tubero, *Cinq autres dialogues*, 252.

[41] Letter of Pierre Gassendi to Samuel Sorbière, in Gassendi, *Opera omnia*, vi. 249B.

It is very dangerous to judge the morality or immorality of an individual on the basis of his actions ... We must not look at his actions alone, for they are only an external and crude indication of the man. Indeed, they are often completely misleading, masking his true self. One must penetrate his internal self, learning to recognize the motives that govern his heart and underlie his actions. It is these one should judge ...[42]

Thus one could distinguish between a true and a false wisdom (*preud'hommie*). False wisdom, which corresponds to that mode of behaviour that is widely taught and generally admired, is 'scholastic and pedantic, a slave to the laws, constrained by hope and fear. It is acquired and taught through respect and submission to religion, law, and custom, the commands of one's superiors, and the examples of one's associates. It involves subjection to the prescribed forms. It is effeminate, fearful, and leaves one perturbed by scruples and doubts ... It varies from one part of the world to another, for each has its own religion, laws, and customs.' True wisdom, on the other hand, is 'free and frank, manly and generous, smiling and happy, stable, uniform, and constant. It walks with a steady step ... without hesitation or changes of pace accompanying every shift in the direction of the wind, every change in circumstances or fashions ... What governs this *preud'hommie* is the law of nature, that is, equity and the universal principles of reason.'[43]

One immediately notes the contrast between the local, provincial (*municipal*), arbitrary ('the laws of civilized behaviour, which we have made for ourselves'), 'diverse and variable' character of false *preud'hommie*, and the 'universal' significance of the behaviour of the wise man (founded in 'full, complete, universal liberty of spirit').[44] Scepticism, by stressing the relativity of ethical and political norms, and denouncing custom as the ineradicable vice of every social group, invites the wise to flee 'the contagion of the world'. In silence and solitude, where the intellect can be freed from popular mystification, it discovers a true universality,

---

[42] Charron, *De la sagesse*, II. 3: 316–17; also II. 2: 299.
[43] Ibid. II. 3: 317–18. [44] Ibid. 324; II, preface, 290.

founded not on universal consent, but on the law of nature and of reason, of which most people have no understanding.

> True *preud'hommie*, which is the foundation and pinnacle of reason, lies in following nature, that is reason . . . *Preud'hommie* is a sound and firm commitment by the will to follow reason. This is within man's capacity, for he is master of his own will, and can direct it and form it according to his beliefs. This is the peculiar capacity of man, to require his will always to conform to reason.[45]

Thus, while at first sight it would seem that the invocation to seek solitude implies a radical individualism, acting *selon soy* becomes a universal norm, one that is not to be identified with any of the ethical systems established by existing religions and laws. It corresponds instead to the requirements of reason, which is the very essence of man (*anima ratio legis*), and constitutes the only possible defence (*rempart, mur d'airain*) against the triumph of corruption and fanaticism. 'If our reason is as it ought to be, we are invulnerable.'[46]

The extent of the influence of Stoicism on Charron's moral philosophy is suggested by his repeated references to Cicero and Seneca. But I should emphasize that his account of *vraye preud'hommie* is sharply opposed to any subordination of ethics to religion. This represents a radical break with traditional moral philosophy, which had been firmly tied to transcendental principles, requiring faith in the existence of God and in rewards and punishments after death. 'I want everyone to be a man of goodwill, quite independently of their hope of heaven or fear of hell,' Charron writes. He attacks those who 'think only of religion . . . [who] believe that the definition of integrity should be adapted to serve the needs of religion, and do not recognize any *preud'hommie* beyond that which is motivated by religion'.[47] These are weak intellects, presumptuous and dogmatic,

> having no love or undersanding of *preud'hommie* except when it is enslaved to religion, and believing that to be a good man one need only be concerned to advance one's own religion and further its cause, convinced that any means—betrayal, dishonesty, sedition, rebellion, or any conceivable crime—is not only legitimate, if

[45] Ibid. II. 3: 326.   [46] Ibid. 320; III. 20: 685.
[47] Ibid. II. 5: 359, 361.

inspired by religious fervour, but is even praiseworthy, meritorious, and saintly if it serves the advancement of religion and the destruction of her adversaries.[48]

Worse still, precisely because he shapes his own behaviour in the light of his fear of punishment in the next world, 'the superstitious man does not allow either God or his fellow man to live in peace ... He trembles with fear ... anxious that God may not be pleased with him, he tries to placate him and conquer him with adulation, importuning him with prayers, vows, offerings, inventing miracles of his own, and easily giving credence to those invented by others.' Thus he abases and vilifies God, attributing to him emotional behaviour that is peculiar to man.[49]

This polemic against the misleading consequences of religious belief yet again places Charron quite apart from contemporary theologians. It is striking that his whole discussion of true and false *preud'hommie* is conducted in terms that make no reference to the fundamental Christian principles of original sin and divine grace, and is free of eschatological tensions. Precisely because it is an expression of the true universality of human nature, *preud'hommie* is conceived by Charron as being antecedent to, and independent of, religious faith. Its foundation is the private conscience, its goal the welfare of the individual and the community: 'virtue seeks no wider or more distinguished audience before which to perform than its own conscience,' 'the conscience of having acted well', without seeking 'the reward of which it is worthy outside its self'.[50] Any other mode of behaviour involves 'sending one's conscience to work in a brothel', and denies the true nature of man.[51] 'I want men to be good and to be solidly and firmly dedicated to what is right and to *preud'hommie*, motivated by love of themselves and by the desire to live up to their nature as men. Any other commitment is a betrayal of one's self and leads to the destruction of one's self.'[52]

[48] Ibid. 360–1.
[49] Ibid. 350–1.
[50] Ibid. III. 42: 741.
[51] Ibid. II. 3: 325.
[52] Ibid. 316. (I am quoting here from the Paris edition of 1836, which reproduces the second edition (1604), and gives variant readings of the first edition in an appendix).

This insistence on the autonomy of ethical choice marks the secularization of morality, its separation from the sphere of the sacred. It is echoed throughout the libertine literature: in the *Quatrains du déiste* to take one example.[53] For La Mothe le Vayer, it is a fundamental characteristic of philosophical reflection: 'most philosophers have maintained that virtue is to be chosen for its own sake, and that it depends on nothing outside itself, for the conscience of the virtuous man is his only audience, and he is satisfied with its applause. His own congratulations are reward enough for doing good.'[54] That this theory is characteristically libertine is confirmed by the theologians who denounce the view that virtue is sufficient unto itself, attacking appeals to an autonomous conscience as showing a presumptuous pride, and leading straight to the abyss of atheism: 'they [the atheists] should not be listened to,' says Mersenne, 'even when they lay claim to a semblance of virtue.'

If it seems to you that they follow virtue for its own sake, let me tell you that it is not so. In fact, though they cover their behaviour with a semblance of virtue, they act as though they do because they are eaten up with ambition and pride. They are children of the present age, children of darkness . . . You can often hear them say that they never act against their own conscience, that they always follow the light of reason, that they would prefer to die than break an oath or to be devious. But they lie.[55]

This attack on the theory of the autonomy of virtue indicates its importance. In libertine circles, the idea of the autonomy of virtue acquired a meaning quite different from that which it had had in classical Stoicism, whence it had been reintroduced in the sixteenth century. It was the outcome of the attack upon traditional moral values, which had led not to the immoralism that the theologians denounced, but to the discovery of conscience as the principle of an

---

[53] 'Quatrains du déiste', in Antoine Adam (ed.), *Les Libertins au* XVIIe *siécle* (Paris, 1964), 107.
[54] [François de La Mothe le Vayer], 'De l'ignorance louable', in Tubero, *Cinq autres dialogues*, 100.
[55] Marin Mersenne, *Quaestiones celeberrimae in Genesim* (Paris, 1623), cols. 155–6.

autonomous moral behaviour. The abandonment of the ethics of the sacred marked the birth of that 'theology of man'—which—as Yves de Paris protested in horror—freed reason from the heavens.

4

The 'Christian Atheism' of Thomas Hobbes

RICHARD TUCK

The title of this chapter comes from a letter that Henry Hammond, the Anglican theologian and a former friend of Hobbes, wrote to Matthew Wren, Bishop of Ely, on 14 October 1651 (about six months, that is, after *Leviathan* was published). The letter ends: 'Have you seen Mr Hobbes' Leviathan, a farrago of Christian Atheism?' A week later he wrote again, remarking that Hobbes,

having in France been angered by some Divines, and having now a mind to return hither, hath chosen to make his way by this book, which some tell me takes infinitely among the looser sons of the Church, and the king's party, being indeed a farrago of all the maddest divinity that ever was read, and having destroyed Trinity, Heaven, Hell, may be allowed to compare ecclesiastical authority to the kingdom of fairies.[1]

Such a reaction to *Leviathan* was not, of course, uncommon, and became more strident as the work was studied more closely. But Hammond's response is of particular interest precisely because he had been a friend of Hobbes in the 1630s, and had (apparently) no particular quarrel with the theology of Hobbes's earlier works. Moreover, his description of Hobbes's theology as 'Christian atheism' was a very apt and perceptive one—perceptive, perhaps, in a way that only an old friend could have manifested.

We can find similar reactions from other former acquaintances of Hobbes. The most interesting is that of Robert

---

[1] [Anon], 'Illustrations of the State of the Church during the Great Rebellion', *Theologian and Ecclesiastic*, 9 (1850), 294–5.

Payne, who had been chaplain to the Earl of Newcastle at Welbeck in the 1630s, a period when Hobbes spent much time with the Earl and began to develop his philosophical ideas. Payne kept in touch with Hobbes during the 1640s, and in 1650 he found what turned out to be a pirated edition of the last part of Hobbes's *Elements of Law* in an Oxford bookshop. Payne mistakenly took the book to be an unauthorized translation of *De cive*, and wrote at once to Hobbes, urging him 'to prevent that translation by one of his own' (a clear indication, incidentally, that the arguments of *De cive* were perfectly acceptable to royalist Anglicans like Payne). Hobbes replied, so Payne reported to their mutual friend Gilbert Sheldon on 13 May 1650, that 'he hath another trifle on hand, which is Politique in English, of which he hath finished thirty-seven chapters, (intending about fifty in the whole,) which are translated into French by a learned Frenchman of good quality, as fast as he finishes them.'[2] This 'trifle' was, of course, *Leviathan*. Payne wrote again to Hobbes about the content of this new work, and was most disconcerted by what he learned. On 19 August 1650 he told Sheldon that

I have written to my friend abroad again and again since I writ to you last, and heard from him; he assures me he hath no particular quarrel to that tribe,[3] only this position he shall set down and confirm, that the Civil sovereign (whether one or more) is chief pastor, and may settle what kind of Church government he shall think it fit for the people's salvation; which will be enough to justify those who have cassierd Bishops already, and may tempt others who have not, to follow their example. The truth is, I fear, he is engaged too far, already to retreat, and therefore I have small hopes to prevail, yet in my last I commended this consideration to him, that all truths are not fit to be told at all times, and if the argument he had undertaken did necessarily require that he should publish it, yet I should expect even for the antiquity's sake of that order, (which by the confession of those who most opposed it had been received in all Christian Churches of the world, for near 1600 years,) it should not be so indifferent with him, but that it should find at least so much favour with him in regard of Presbyterians

---

[2] Ibid. 6 (1848) 172.   [3] By 'tribe', Payne meant episcopalians.

and Independents, as monarchy had done in respect of Democr. and Aristoc.[4]

It is clear from the reactions of both Hammond and Payne that they saw something special, and specially dangerous, about the religious arguments of *Leviathan* that they had not seen in *De cive*. Others seem to have agreed with them: the translation of *De cive* that did appear, in March 1651, was (it is now almost certain) not by Hobbes himself, nor authorized by him. Instead, it was produced by a group of Anglican royalists, published through the famous royalist printing-house of Richard Royston, and adorned with a set of engravings in which the dead King Charles I is depicted as the personification of *Religion*.[5] Moreover, Edward Hyde, Earl of Clarendon, who had read both the *Elements of Law* and *De cive* with appreciation, was warned by Hobbes himself when they met in Paris in April 1651 that *Leviathan* was in the press, and that (Clarendon recorded) 'he knew when I read his Book I would not like it, and thereupon mention'd some of his Conclusions.'[6] And writing to a friend in 1659 in an attempt to get Matthew Wren's son to provide a critique of *Leviathan*, Clarendon observed that 'I dare say he [Wren] will find somewhat in Mr. *Hobbs* himself, I mean in his former Books, that contradicts what he set forth in this, in that Part in which he takes himself to be the most exact, his beloved Philosophy.'[7]

These Anglican readers of Hobbes were right, for the *Elements of Law* and *De cive* do indeed set out a fundamentally orthodox Anglican theology, while *Leviathan* breaks dramatically with that tradition. Furthermore, the theological space that Hobbes carved out for himself in *Leviathan* did to

---

[4] 'Illustrations of the State of the Church', 173. Payne had already been made aware by Hobbes of his current views on Church government, before he realized that they were part of a new book: see his letter to Sheldon of 4 February 1650, ibid. 167.

[5] See my 'Warrender's *De cive*', *Political Studies*, 33 (1985), 310–11.

[6] Edward Hyde, Earl of Clarendon, *A Brief View and Survey of the Dangerous and Pernicious Errors to Church and State, in Mr Hobbe's Book, entitled Leviathan* (Oxford, 1676), 7.

[7] Peter Barwick, *The Life of the Reverend Doctor John Barwick* (London, 1724), 430. I am indebted to Martin Dselzainis for this reference; see his 'Edward Hyde and Thomas Hobbes's *Elements of Law, Natural and Politic*', to be published shortly.

an extent entitle Hammond to describe him as a Christian atheist. To show this, I will first discuss the theology of Hobbes's earlier works.

All that Hobbes has to say about religion, in each of his works, takes place against the background of a fundamental and quite familiar distinction between *faith* and *reason*. It is customary, among those Hobbes scholars who take any interest in these matters, to suppose that Hobbes allowed very little scope for *reason* in religion; J. G. A. Pocock, for example, has written that 'Hobbes's relgious heterodoxy is of a fideist-sceptical kind, very characteristic of its age, but not to be confused with the deist rationalism of the next century.'[8] But in fact, particularly in *De cive*, Hobbes put forward a consistent and important theory of a 'natural' or 'rational' religion that is very similar to the deism of the Enlightenment. Everything that Hobbes says about Christianity must be interpreted in the light of this.

The *locus classicus* for Hobbes's discussion of natural theology is chapter 15 of *De cive*, 'Of the Kingdoms of God, by Nature'. As Warrender observed, this is much more detailed than the otherwise quite comparable account in chapter 31 of *Leviathan*.[9] In this chapter of *De cive* Hobbes argued that philosophically or rationally speaking, we can say that God exists, for 'by the word *God* we understand the *Worlds cause*' (15:14), and it is a philosophically acceptable proposition that there must be a first cause to the universe. Whatever made the universe, and therefore ourselves, must be incomparably more powerful than anything else we can imagine; and power of this kind necessarily elicits worship (15:9). All the descriptions of God (other than that he exists and is the first cause), and all the rites found in human religions are simply expressions of honour and worship, and cannot be said to have any *truth value* at all. Hobbes applied

---

[8] J. G. A. Pocock, 'Time, History and Eschatology in the Thought of Thomas Hobbes', in his *Politics, Language and Time* (London, 1972), 192. See also Willis B. Glover, 'God and Thomas Hobbes', in K. C. Brown (ed.), *Hobbes Studies* (Oxford, 1965), 162: 'His many affirmations of a rational knowledge of God are undermined by the scepticism and more dependent for support on the fideism than Hobbes usually makes clear.'

[9] Thomas Hobbes, *De cive: The English Version*, ed. Howard Warrender (Oxford, 1983), 195 n. 8.

this reasoning in particular to the traditionally vexed questions of how God could be the author of evil, and in a remarkable passage written shortly after *De cive*, he remarked:

Personally, while I hold that the nature of God is unfathomable, and that propositions are a kind of language by which we express our concepts of the nature of things, I incline to the view that no proposition about the nature of God can be true save this one: *God exists*, and that no title correctly describes the nature of God other than the word 'being'. Everything else, I say, pertains not to the explanation of philosophical truth, but to proclaiming the states of mind that govern our wish to praise, magnify and honour God . . . Therefore [the words 'God sees, understands, wishes, acts, bring to pass'] are rather oblations than propositions . . . Neither propositions nor notions about His nature are to be argued over, but are a part of our worship and are evidences of a mind that honours God. Propositions that confer honour are correctly enunciated about God, but the opposite ones irreligiously; we may reverently and as Christians say of God that He is the author of every act, because it is honourable to do so, but to say 'God is the author of sin' is sacrilegious and prophane. There is no *contradiction* in this matter, however, for as I said, the words under discussion are not the propositions of people philosophising but the actions of those who pay homage. A contradiction is found in propositions alone.[10]

On the basis of this fascinating argument. Hobbes was able to claim that all religions are simply ways of worshipping this inscrutable creator, and that their differences are merely the consequences of societies' different beliefs about the constitution of honour. In particular, because Hobbes believed that in general the *civitas* or its sovereign must have the power to determine the public meanings of all words, 'the City therefore by Right (that is to say, they who have the power of the whole City) shall judge what *names* or *appellations* are more, what lesse *honourable* for God, that is to say, what doctrines are to be held and profest concerning the nature of God, and his operations' (15:16). There is, according to Hobbes, a *natural* reason for worship and theology, but their determinate content is a *civil* matter. With this theory, he establishes

[10] Thomas Hobbes, *Thomas White's De mundo Examined*, trans. H. W. Jones (Bradford, 1976), 434 (slightly adapted by myself). See the *Critique du De mundo*, ed. J. Jacquot and H. W. Jones (Paris, 1973), fos. 396 ʳ⁻ᵛ.

himself as belonging to a tradition that began among six-teenth-century Italian humanists and stretched to Rousseau, in which a form of deism was allied to support for a 'civil religion' (though it should be said that there was at this stage in Hobbes's life an important caveat about this). Like every-one else in that tradition, Hobbes drew explicitly on ancient societies to serve as examples of what he favoured, remarking in the *Elements of Law* that 'amongst the Grecians, Romans, or other Gentiles . . . their several civil laws were the rules whereby not only righteousness and virtue, but also religion and the external worship of God, was ordered and approved; that being esteemed the true worship of God, which was κατά τα νόμιμα (i.e.), according to the laws civil.'[11]

It should be said that Hobbes was not tremendously unusual in espousing a position of this kind. The most relevant comparison to draw, as in many other features of Hobbes's thought, would be with Grotius (relevant also, as we shall see presently, in the *limitations* of this position). In *De iure belli ac pacis* (1625) Grotius described the 'true Religion, which has been common to all Ages', as

built upon four fundamental Principles; of which the *first* is, that *There is a GOD, and but one GOD only*. The *second*, that *GOD is not any of those Things we see, but something more sublime than them.* The *third*, that *GOD takes Care of human Affairs, and judges them with the strictest Equity.* The *fourth*, that *The same God is the Creator of all Things but himself* . . . And from these speculative Notions follow the practical, as, that *GOD is to be honoured, loved, worshipped, and obeyed* . . . Now the Truth of these speculative Notions . . . may, no Doubt, be demonstrated by Arguments drawn from Nature, amongst which this is one of the strongest, That it is evident to Sense that some Things are made, or have a Beginning; now the Things that are made do necessarily lead us to acknowledge something that was never made . . .[12]

And Grotius accompanied this theory with an equally confi-dent assertion that the *civil* magistrate has, in all times and

[11] Thoms Hobbes, *Element of Law*, ed. Ferdinand Toennies, 2nd edn. (London, 1969), 145.
[12] Hugo Grotius, *The Rights of War and Peace . . . translated into English* (London, 1973), 442–3. See also his *De veritate religionis Christianae*, 1:2, in his *Opera theologica* (3 vols.; London, 1679), iii. 4.

places, had ultimate responsibility for religious matters, an assertion made most plainly in his *De imperio summarum potestatum circa sacra*, which was not published until 1647 but which circulated as a manuscript in England amongst groups with which Hobbes was familiar.[13] Together with other points, Grotius observed there that the Twelve Tables of the Roman Republic dealt with matters of religion as well as secular matters.[14]

Neither for Grotius nor for Hobbes, it should perhaps be said, did the fact of a natural religion mean that the natural laws governing human behaviour were applicable only to theists. The proposition of God's existence was independent of other necessarily true propositions, and men could believe in the force of laws of nature without believing in a God. In chapter 14 of *De cive*, Hobbes argued that the 'sin' of an atheist is that of 'imprudence or ignorance', and that an atheist does not 'sin ... against the Law of nature' (any more, one might say, than an incompetent mathematician does).[15] He was aware that this argument laid him open to the accusation that he had not 'declared my selfe an enemy bitter enough against Atheists', but he countered it by saying that it was by his unbelief that an atheist made himself an enemy of God, and that he would be punished by him, or by a sovereign who recognized the truth of the natural religion. But the implication of this argument is that a sovereign who did not recognize the existence of a natural religion would have no other reason for punishing atheists. The practical application of this argument came in *De cive*, chapter 2 where Hobbes proposed that atheists are disabled only from *making an oath* and not from making a *promise*, and that oaths add nothing to the obligatory force of a

[13] Grotius gave a copy to Lancelot Andrews while visiting England in 1613; Andrews later returned it, but had a number of copies made, two of which survive among John Selden's papers in the Bodleian (MSS Selden, *supra* 126 and 127). See Selden's *De synedriis veterum Ebraeorum*, in his *Opera omnia*, ed. David Wilkins (3 vols.; London, 1726), i, col. 1014. This fact has not been known to students of Grotius who have generally concluded, on the basis of references in his letters, that he wrote the *De imperio* in 1617. A new edition of the work is badly needed.

[14] Grotius, *Opera theologica*, iii. 206.

[15] Hobbes, *De cive*, 179.

promise or contract.[16] As for Grotius, we need only recall the most famous sentence in the *De iure belli ac pacis* (prolegomena 11): 'all we have now said would take place, though we should even grant, what without the greatest Wickedness cannot be granted, that there is no God, or that he takes no Care of human Affairs.'[17]

However, neither Grotius nor—in 1640 and 1642—Hobbes pressed these naturalistic arguments too far beyond orthodoxy. Grotius's views were well-known and greatly admired in just those Anglican circles in which Hobbes seems to have mixed when in England (for example, the so-called 'Tew Circle'); Hammond in particular stood forward as a champion of what came to be called 'the Grotian Religion'.[18] For Grotius argued that on top of this natural religion, the truth of which can, in principle, be philosophically demonstrated, we have good reasons for believing in the particular claims of Christianity. These are *reasons* for having *faith*, and are to be distinguished from the ahistorical and universal reasons underpinning the natural religion.

> The Truth of the Christian Religion, in those Particulars which are additional to natural and primitive Religion, cannot be evidenced by mere natural Arguments, but depends upon the History we have of CHRIST'S Resurrection, and the Miracles performed by him and his Apostles, which have been confirmed by unexceptionable Testimonies, but many Ages since, so that the Question now is of Matters of Fact, and those of a very antient Date . . .[19]

We can capture the distinction by saying that if someone chooses not to believe in the truth of the scriptural accounts, there is no way in which his fundamental beliefs about the world can dictate his assent to Scripture; but this is not true of the natural religion.

In common with almost all Christians, however, Grotius had quite a complex theory about what we must believe in in order to count as Christians. Scripture requires interpretation, and he was clear that we should act entirely as our own

---

[16] Ibid., 60–1.
[17] Grotius, *The Rights of War and Peace*, p. xix.
[18] See particularly H. R. McAdoo, *The Spirit of Anglicanism: A Survey of Anglican Theological Method in the Seventeenth Century* (London, 1965), 358 ff.
[19] Grotius, *The Rights of War and Peace*, 447.

interpreters. To understand his position on this matter, and the early Hobbes's rather similar position, we ought to remind ourselves of the principal Christian theories of interpretation in the early seventeenth century. The oldest theory was, of course, that officially espoused by the Roman Catholic Church, namely, that Scripture was unintelligible unless interpreted by a Church standing in the apostolic succession from Christ. Our 'faith' as Christians is not grounded purely in the truth of the scriptural stories, therefore, but rather in a *modern* history of the Church constantly transmitting and refining an authoritative message. To be a Christian was thus to have faith in the authority of a *Church*, so that ecclesiological matters could not be disentangled from what might now seem purely theological ones.

Against this view was ranged the central commitment of the sixteenth-century reformers to a direct understanding of Scripture without the aid of an apostolic Church; but here we must be careful not to misrepresent the reformers' ideas. As systematized by Calvin in particular, their ideas did not countenance a wholly individualist interpretation of Scripture: the ministers of the existing Church still had a special authority over the public promulgation of the Gospel message. But they were vested with this authority not because of some supernatural link with Christ himself through the apostolic succession, but through the continued policing by the ministers of one another's interpretations of Scripture, and the generation of some agreed (or at least concerted) interpretations to impose upon the general public. It was, one might say, more like the authority of a professional body of experts than the authority of a Catholic priesthood; but it was still intended to foreclose general lay debate about the interpretation of Scripture. As a consequence, the *ceremony* of ordination—the laying of hands by one minister on another—still had significance for Calvin, for it represented the acceptance of the new minister into the existing ministerial society. To be a Christian (for the Calvinist) was thus to have faith in the learning and professional expertise of the ministers—including a faith that those ministers would be able to recognize such knowledge and true understanding of the Scriptures in any candidate for the ministry. Once again, however, the defining characteristic of a Christian was not naked faith in Scripture, but an informed faith, based on authoritative, modern, and professional guidance.

Appropriately enough, Anglicanism took a *via media* between these positions, for the Church of England never abandoned its reliance on the apostolic succession, and never placed the authoritative character of its interpretations solely in the expertise at scriptural exegesis of its current ministry. On the other hand, it had a different account of the essence of the apostolic Church from that of the Roman Catholics; increasingly, Anglicans came to insist that truly authoritative interpretation of Scripture could initially be found only in the writings of the early Fathers of the Church (during the first four or five centuries), and that modern interpretations had to conform to those writings. In a sense, the more recent apostolic succession mattered less, and Anglicans could write rather like Calvinists on the subject of authority, with the important proviso that the texts upon which Anglican ministers were to exercise their intelligence were much wider and fuller than Scripture alone. But in another sense, Anglicans found themselves opposed to a coalition of Calvinists and Catholics, for both the latter groups (though for different reason) allowed the modern Church to exercise unaided interpretative skills on Scripture alone.

Only among the forerunners of later Independency at this time do we find the idea that a Christian is simply someone who believes in the truth of Scripture (as interpreted by himself). Such a view seemed shocking to almost all contemporaries, and even more conservative Independents shied away from its full implications; it might be said that only the Quakers eventually accepted the substance of this idea, and to many contemporaries they effectively ceased to be Christians at all because of it. Properly to understand the question of faith in the seventeenth century, we constantly have to bear in mind the fact that the Church (however defined) was not ancillary to faith but constitutive of it: in general, one could not be thought to be a Christian outside an authoritative Church.

In his later writings, where he confronted these issues directly, Grotius increasingly came down in favour of (approximately) the Anglican view, which stressed the authority of the truly universal early Councils (something that contributed to his popularity among Anglicans like Hammond).[20] He had always accepted that the Church and 'tradition' (however defined) had an essential role to play in interpreting Scripture (see, for example, *De iure belli ac pacis*, II. 20: 50), and he had also always accepted the importance of ordination as a means of securing the true Church.[21] It might be thought that this view of the constitution of Christianity could not be squared with Grotius's sympathy with a 'civil religion' to which I referred earlier. But Grotius, like the Anglicans, was perfectly able to hold both views. The civil sovereign is entitled to make the rules on religious matters for his society; but the coming of Christianity had introduced a new set of considerations to which the sovereign had to attend. The orderly worship of a primitive God is not all that a Christian sovereign has to think about, for he now has access to a set of supplementary truths about God that he ought to make public. Moreover, these truths are equally well known to those of his subjects who follow the teachings of the Church, and so if the sovereign does not make them part of the public religion of the society, his Christian subjects will still have reason to believe in them. This did not, however, make the Church into an authority *like* the sovereign: in the analogy that Grotius used consistently throughout the *De imperio summarum potestatum*, the true Church was in the position of a doctor who has medical knowledge and is advising a ruler on what to do. The doctor has no authority of his own to enforce public health measures, but the judgement as to whether to follow his advice or not can reasonably be said to be up to the ruler alone. He might, indeed, make quite the wrong decision; but Grotius was clear that, in that case, the doctor, or the Church, simply had to put up with it, and hope that God's providence would

[20] See his 'Annotata ad consultationem Cassandri', in his *Via as pacem ecclesiasticam* (1642), *Opera theologica*, iii. 628; *Votum pro pace ecclesiastica* (1642), ibid. 674; and particularly *Rivetiani apologetici . . . discussio* (1645), ibid. 685–6.
[21] See Grotius, *De imperio summarum potestatum*, 20: 2, *Opera theologica*, iii. 257.

eventually correct the ruler.[22] An important point for our present purposes, however, is that neither Grotius nor the Anglicans assumed that civil authority in any way defined faith for the individual Christian: such an individual was not a Christian because he believed what the sovereign told him, but because he believed in the interpretative authority of the Church over Scripture, just as the sovereign himself did if he were a Christian.

It has, I think, not generally been recognized that Hobbes too, in his works of 1640–2, argued that the coming of Christianity had made a difference to natural religion, and that the essence of the Christian faith was a confidence in the authoritative teachings of the apostolic Church. Yet just this is stated explicitly in the third part of *De cive*, on 'Religion'. In chapter 17, for example, Hobbes argues that the civil sovereign must be the authoritative judge of the meanings of all the terms involved in natural matters (including, as we have seen, natural *religion*); but there are also controversies over 'spiritual matters, that is to say, questions of faith, the truth whereof cannot be searcht into by naturall reason; such are the questions concerning *the nature*, and *office of Christ, of rewards and punishments to come, of the Sacraments, of outward worship*, and the like'.[23] These controversies are, for Christians, questions of scriptural interpretation, and Hobbes argued that they are *not* to be decided by the sovereign, at least not in the same way that he decides issues of natural religion.

For the deciding of questions of Faith, that is to say, *concerning God*, which transcend human capacity, we stand in need of a divine blessing (that we may not be deceiv'd at least in necessary points) to be deriv'd from CHRIST himselfe by the imposition of hands. For, seeing to the end we may attaine to aeternal Salvation, we are oblig'd to a supernatural Doctrine . . . which therefore it is impossible for us to understand; to be left so destitute, as that we can be deceiv'd in necessary points, is repugnant to aequity. This infalibility our Saviour *Christ* promis'd (in those things which are necessary to Salvation) to his *Apostles* untill the day of judgement; that is to say, *to the Apostles, and Pastors* succeeding the *Apostles* who were

---

[22] Ibid. 243.   [23] Hobbes, *De cive*, 248.

to be consecrated *by the imposition of hands.* He therefore who hath the Soveraigne power in the City, is oblig'd as a Christian, where there is any question concerning *the Mysteries of Faith,* to interpret the Holy Scriptures by *Clergy-men* lawfully ordain'd . . .[24]

A similar point is made in the *Elements of Law*: 'Seeing then the acknowledgement of the Scripture to be the word of God, is not evidence, but faith; and faith . . . consisteth in the trust we have in other men: it appeareth plainly that the men so trusted, are the holy men of God's church succeeding one another from the time of those who saw the wondrous works of God Almighty in the flesh . . .'[25] So Hobbes was completely in line with his Anglican friends: to be a Christian was, at least in part, necessarily to have faith in the interpretative authority of the Christian *Church*, a Church (moreover) defined in impeccably orthodox terms as the vehicle of the apostolic succession of the priesthood (see *De cive*, 17: 24). There is a whole realm of belief, and belief of a most important kind, that is determined by people and institutions quite separate from the civil sovereign.

In chapter 18 of *De cive* Hobbes faced up, in effect, to the problem posed by the multiplicity of modern Christian Churches. If the sovereign makes authoritative for Christians under his command those interpretations of Scripture agreed on by the apostolic Church in his dominion (which is clearly the practical implications of Hobbes's view, and indeed of Anglicanism in general), then does this create as many religions as there are sovereigns? Hobbes's answer here was that all Christians, whatever else they believe, must believe that 'Jesus is the Christ'—in other words, belief in Jesus's existence and historical role will secure eternal life. Here at least there can be no dispute about the reading of Scripture, and hence no problem of interpretation will arise. Where problems do arise, the Christian must accept the determination of *his* Church, and not be troubled by the disparity between his Church's interpretations and those of another: his fundamental commitment must be to accept the public

---

[24] Ibid. 249.   [25] Hobbes, *Elements of Law*, 58.

doctrine of his Church. Hobbes's argument here is precisely parallel to his general argument about the sovereign's role in establishing *moral* truths: those truths, too, will vary from state to state, but in all states there will be a minimal common core of morality consisting of the right of nature and the law of nature. Articles of the Christian faith will vary from Church to Church, but all Churches will agree that Jesus is the Christ. Once again, this is very close in spirit to Grotius's view that there was a minimal, ecumenical Christianity to be discovered within the competing Christian sects—a vision to which he devoted the last years of his life.

It is often assumed that Hobbes's materialism was in some way incompatible with an orthodox Christianity of this kind; but the theory of these early works contradicts that assumption. Hobbes was, of course, an avowed materialist in all of them, insisting in both the *Elements of Law*, and *De cive* that there could not be immaterial substances. But he also asserted that this was perfectly compatible with the Christian articles of faith.

We who are Christians acknowledge that there be angels good and evil; and that they are spirits, and that the soul of man is a spirit; and that these spirits are immortal. But, to know it, that is to say, to have natural evidence of the same: it is impossible ... But though the Scripture acknowledge spirits, yet doth it nowhere say, that they are incorporeal, meaning thereby, without dimensions and quantity ...[26]

And he sought to show that his entire metaphysics and moral philosophy was in agreement with orthodox Christianity as promulgated by his own Church. On the face of it, he was right: it is hard to find a single truly heretical opinion in either the *Elements of Law* or *De cive*.

We can now, I think, see why Anglicans should have read Hobbes's early works with approval and befriended their author (and also why Aubrey should have said, otherwise very strangely, that 'Bp Manwaring (of St David's) preach'd *his Doctrine*'[27] But now we also have to consider the character

---

[26] Ibid. 55.
[27] John Aubrey, *Brief Lives*, ed. Oliver Lawson Dick (Harmondsworth, 1962), 230.

of the change of thought represented by *Leviathan*, and the reasons for it.

The change can be described very simply, but it had profound consequences. The new theory is set out at length in chapter 42 of *Leviathan*, 'Of Power Ecclesiastical', namely that the civil sovereign and *not* the Church had the power to interpret Scripture, and that this power was essentially the same as civil sovereigns had enjoyed before the coming of Christianity.

In all Common-wealths of the Heathen, the Soveraigns have had the name of Pastors of the People, because there was no Subject that could lawfully Teach the people, but by their permission and authority. This Right of the Heathen Kings, cannot bee thought taken from them by their conversion to the Faith of Christ; who never ordained, that Kings for believing in him, should be deposed . . .[28]

The apostolic succession of the priesthood ceased to matter:

every Soveraign, before Christianity, had the power of Teaching, and Ordaining Teachers; and therefore Christianity gave them no new Right, but only directed them in the way of teaching Truth; and consequently they needed no Imposition of Hands (besides that which is done in Baptisme) to authorize them to exercise any part of the Pastorall Function, as namely, to Baptize, and Consecrate . . .[29]

And Hobbes summed up his new position thus: 'It is the Civill Soveraign that is to appoint Judges, and Interpreters of the Canonicall Scriptures; for it is he that maketh them Laws.'[30]

Effectively, what had happened in *Leviathan* was that the sphere of *natural* religion (discussed in chapter 31 of *Leviathan* in terms very close to chapter 15 of *De cive*) had expanded to include *all* religion: Christianity was no longer a special case, but a civil religion like the religions of antiquity. In one respect it did remain distinctive, and a source of beliefs that was outside the control of the commonwealth: though

[28] Thomas Hobbes, *Leviathan*, ed. C. B. Macpherson (Harmondsworth, 1968), 568.
[29] Ibid. 574.   [30] Ibid. 575–6.

the Christian was to be guided by his sovereign's interpretation of *Scripture*, he could not accept any interpretation that contradicted the proposition that 'Jesus is the Christ', as it remained true that this statement could not be denied by any conceivable interpretation of the Scriptures. So if the sovereign either forswore the practice of interpreting Scripture and sought to impose instead a wholly non-biblical religion on his citizens, or alleged that 'Jesus is the Christ' is not a proposition of Scripture, the Christians among the citizens (Hobbes argued) could reasonably accept martyrdom.[31]

Martyrdom had been an obvious possibility in the earlier works, and it had been rendered particularly plausible by the interpretative independence of the Church; as Hobbes said in Chapter 18 of *De cive*, the fact that obedience

is due in all *temporall matters* to those Princes who are no Christians, is without any controversie; but in *matters spirituall*, that is to say, those things which concern Gods worship, some *christian Church* is to be followed. For it is an hypothesis of the Christian Faith, that God speaks not in things supernaturall, but by the way of Christian Interpreters of holy Scriptures. But what? Must we resist Princes when we cannot obey them? Truly no; for this is contrary to our civill Covenant. What must we doe then? Goe to Christ by Martyrdome.[32]

In *Leviathan* it remained a possibility, but Hobbes now stressed the unlikelihood of any infidel sovereign actually persecuting Christians, defined as Hobbes now defined them; and with good reason, for it is hard to see what kind of judgement the private Christian of *Leviathan* could advance against that of his sovereign: Even the very definition of Scripture was now in the hands of the sovereign: 'those Books only are Canonicall, that is, Law, in every nation, which are established for such by the Soveraign Authority.'[33] The sovereign (if Hobbes was consistent) did not have the power to declare, say, the Koran canonical for Christians, since that book denies that Jesus is the Christ; but he could do anything short of such an act. And since it is unclear, without a lot of interpretative superstructure, quite what

---

[31] Ibid. 625.   [32] *De cive*, 262.
[33] Ibid. 415.

'Jesus is the Christ' actually *means*, most of the important practices and dogmas of religion are designated in *Leviathan* as part of the material of a civil religion.

Having established that the Church had no interpretative authority, Hobbes was able to give free rein to his own metaphysical speculations within the much looser regime of modern England. In fact, the question of precisely what public doctrine was proclaimed by the sovereign in 1651 is somewhat complicated, and is part of a wider question (very relevant to Hobbes) about the point at which England ceased legally to be a Christian country. The Long Parliament in May 1648, under Presbyterian influence, had passed a most extensive and savage Ordinance against blasphemy and atheism, effectively restricting public religion in England to orthodox trinitarian Christianity (and, *inter alia*, prescribing the composition of the canon of Scripture). The Ordinance actually resembled the Bill against atheism introduced to the Commons in 1666, which was specifically aimed at *Leviathan*. But an Act of the Rump in August 1650 defined blasphemy in much narrower terms, principally as the claim that a living person is God, and it seems to have been thought that this Act abrogated the Presbyterian Ordinance of 1648 (though this was not stated in the Act). In September 1650 the Rump also passed its famous Act repealing all previous Acts of Uniformity, though it still required Englishmen to attend a service at which God was worshipped each Sunday.[34] So Hobbes could write in a famous passage of *Leviathan* that

we are reduced to the Independency of the Primitive Christians to follow Paul, or Cephas, or Apollos, every man as he liketh best: Which, if it be without contention, and without measuring the Doctrine of Christ, by our affection to the Person of his Minister, (the fault which the Apostle reprehended in the Corinthians,) is perhaps the best: First, because there ought to be no Power over the Conscience of men, but of the Word it selfe, working Faith in every one, not alwayes according to the purpose of them that Plant and Water, but of God himself, that giveth the Increase; and secondly, because it is unreasonable in them, who teach there is

---

[34] For these Acts and Ordinances, see C. H. Firth and R. S. Rait, *Acts and Ordinances of the Interregnum 1642–1660* (3 vols.; London, 1911), i. 1133, and ii. 409, 423.

such danger in every little Errour, to require of a man endued with Reason of his own, to follow the Reason of any other man, or of the most voices of many other men; Which is little better, than to venture his Salvation at crosse and pile.[35]

Hobbes seems to have assumed that scriptural Christianity was still the civil religion of his country, and in view of the uncertainty over the law in 1651, this was probably wise; but he was also clear that the old refinements of doctrine were no longer enforceable by the civil authorities and that there was no point in resting one's faith on the decisions of the Church. So in *Leviathan* he could consistently debate idiosyncratic interpretations of Scripture without being guilty of publicly disputing the doctrines established by his sovereign, and he could break through the philosophical constraints that he had imposed upon himself earlier in deference to traditional Christianity. The two interpretations that caught his first readers' attention most urgently were his new statement of 'mortalism'—the view that the soul is not only material but also *mortal* (though capable in some way of being revived)—and his remarkable claim that Christ 'represented the person' of God in exactly the same way as Moses had done.[36] Both arguments went to the very limits of what was possible within the civil religion that Hobbes took to have been established in 1650, but Hobbes was very careful to ensure that, at least arguably, they stayed within it.

Having outlined the main features of Hobbes's religious thought and how it changed between his earlier and later works, it is now time to take stock and consider whether Hammond was right. Was Hobbes a 'Christian atheist'? It seems to me that in *Leviathan* he had indeed effectively become an atheist, at least of a kind. The natural religion to which Hobbes subscribed all his life, and which we might reasonably term 'deism', was very far from an orthodox theism. God, on his account, was like the modern 'big bang' at the start of the universe; and though it was psychologically right for men to worship this phenomenon, our inability to

[35] Hobbes, *Leviathan*, 711.   [36] Ibid. 483, 520.

attribute to it any human properties whatsoever (except as performative utterances in an act of worship) meant that this was an extremely 'atheistical' religion. The closest parallel would indeed be with the 'religions' of the French revolutionaries and early nineteenth-century socialists, who wished to turn the human psychological capacity for worship to a better end than traditional religion. This view of religion was kept from overwhelming Hobbes's orthodox Christianity in the *Elements of Law* and *De cive* by a continued insistence on the special character of the doctrines propounded by the Christian Church; but in *Leviathan* this insistence faltered, and Christianity became in effect the civil religion of modern England, with no other meaning to its doctrines than the performative ones attached to any worship. Payne's alarm at Hobbes's ecclesiology was part of the same response as Hammond's alarm at Hobbes's atheism, for it was Hobbes's ecclesiology which made him into an atheist.

The last question to ask is, why did this happen? As we saw at the beginning of this chapter, Hammond explained the change in Hobbes's thought in terms of squabbles at the exile court (something Payne agreed about); and though that seems a trivial base for such a major development, he may have been right. Certainly, the behaviour and views of the exiled Anglicans are likely to have reinforced a dislike of their conduct that Hobbes had voiced privately as early as 1641 (at the same time, that is, as he was publicly defending an Anglican theory of church government),[37] and the new ecclesiastical regime of England after 1650 represented security from clergymen of all kinds. It is worth reminding ourselves that the last words of the main body of *Leviathan* are directed expressly against the possibility of a *Presbyterian* take-over in England, something against which the Rump was probably a better safeguard than any other regime on offer.[38] It is, perhaps, hard for modern writers (whether theists or atheists themselves) to realise that questions of ecclesiastical authority are intimately bound up with religion

---

[37] Ferdinand Toennies, 'Hobbes-Analekten', *Archiv für Geschichte der Philosophie*, 17 (1903–4), 302.

[38] Hobbes, *Leviathan*, 714–15. This is the point of the reference to 'an Assembly of Spirits'.

itself. But, as we have seen, for many pre-modern people, faith in God *was* a faith in a Church and a particular tradition of doctrine. Once that faith went, there were only two plausible directions in which to go: either into true Independency, and the theory that every individual in some sense makes his own faith (an idea whose 'ideal type' is Quakerism, but which is (I suspect) really believed by all modern theists); or into deism, civil religion, or atheism. Hobbes could not take the former course, for all his moral and political philosophy held him back from countenancing radical pluralism of doctrine; it was natural, therefore, for him to take the latter one. Apparently small shifts in ecclesiology could thus start an avalanche, beneath which Christianity itself was ultimately buried.

5

The Charge of Atheism and the Language of Radical Speculation, 1640–1660

NIGEL SMITH

Historians of mid-seventeenth-century English radicalism (political and religious) are fond of repeating an accusation often made at that time—that those whose opinions and behaviour put them at an unacceptably anti-establishment, anti-orthodox, or democratic extreme were atheists, even if they claimed to believe in a (Christian) God. In his most accomplished study, *The World Turned Upside Down* (1972), Christopher Hill repeats the fears of the heresiographers of the 1640s: 'Religious toleration is the greatest of all evils, thought Thomas Edwards in 1646. It will bring in first scepticism in doctrine and looseness of life, then atheism;' 'Walter Charleton in 1652 said that the present age in England had produced more swarms of "atheistical monsters" than any age or nation.'[1] While Hill is judicious in juxtaposing what the radicals actually said with what was said about them, we sense that he would like to believe the heresiographers—that is, like them confuse heresy, unorthodox belief, and anticlericalism (but not unbelief) with atheism—as he hints in a more speculative essay: 'Well then: I have established to my own satisfaction, and I hope to yours, that there was a good deal, if not of atheism, at least of positive irreligion in the English Revolution.'[2] Other historians have betrayed similar convictions. David Wootton, for instance, talks of the Leveller William Walwyn's conception of a loving

---

[1] Christopher Hill, *The World Turned Upside Down* (London, 1972), 98, 179.
[2] Christopher Hill, 'Irreligion in the "Puritan" Revolution', in J. F. McGregor and B. Reay (eds.), *Radical Religion in the English Revolution* (Oxford, 1984), 191–211 (p. 209).

God, but cannot resist the caveat: 'I remain to be convinced that Walwyn was not a sceptical disciple of Montaigne and no Christian.'[3]

Clearly, there is a double viewpoint at work here: some historians accept an affirmation and a language of faith in radicalism, but they cannot help but agree that the hostile contemporary view was, to a greater or lesser extent, true—that some radicals were atheists. The picture is complicated by the fact that many records of interrogations and many publications by radicals tend, in the face of persecution, to stress their orthodoxy: sometimes we have no means of knowing what the religious radical 'really thought'.

One reason for the modern doubleness of vision is that some of the more extreme radical beliefs, ideas, and expressions of the mid-seventeenth century resemble opinions that were professed by atheists both before 1640 and towards the end of the century. Mortalism (the belief that the soul remains with the body after death), annihilationism (that after death people are entirely annihilated or return to the prime matter of the universe), antiscripturalism, and versions of pantheism look like some of the beliefs of those who attacked Christianity in the name of atheism later in the century and in the eighteenth century.[4] Also, seemingly modern 'materialism' and 'cultural relativism', often associated with atheism, can be detected in contemporary radical thought.

Among others, J. C. Davis has successfully demonstrated the success of early modern literary stereotypes in forging a widely held belief in the association of atheism and religious sectarianism. By ignoring the distinction between philosophical and practical atheism (that is, immoral behaviour), it was possible to project the image of atheism upon anyone of whose conduct or beliefs one disapproved. To hostile observers, toleration and sectarianism were immoral and led to

[3] David Wootton, (ed.), *Divine Right and Democracy: An Anthology of Stuart Political Writings* (Harmondsworth, 1986), 272.

[4] See the subsequent essays in this book, and N. T. Burns, *Christian Mortalism from Tyndale to Milton* (Cambridge, Mass., 1972).

atheism: *ergo*, all sectarians were atheists.[5] The image of the atheist was a precursor of the image of the Ranter, and both expressed the fears of imminent social disorder on the part of the perpetrators of those images. Whatever the expressions and ritualized practices of the Ranters actually were, most people understood them in large part through the hostile and immoral depiction of the libertine atheist.

Such an appreciation of the power of projected images has gone a long way towards dispelling the simple image of the dissolute, 'irreligious', radical sectarian, but as the dominant view stands, historiographical double vision leaves us with an ambiguous and inconsistent understanding of an important aspect of the English Revolution; an ambiguity that is rooted, more often than not, in modern ideological conflict between commentators sympathetic to the emergence of secular society and others sympathetic to radical Christianity, sometimes because it constitutes a root of their own faith.[6] Worse still, some 'progressive' historians have been guilty of bad faith towards the radicals: displaying admiration for the apparently near-secular nature of their heresies, yet equal sympathy for the strength of conviction that sectarians manifested in their suffering of persecution; two aspects that would have been regarded as inconsistent and incomprehensible from a sectarian point of view. At the same time, sceptical historians (Davis) seem to think that exposing the operation of stereotypes is sufficient, without attempting to probe further in order to discover whether there is anything behind the veil cast by the stereotype that might enable us to see a genuine, as opposed to an imaginary, connection between atheism and radicalism.

The purpose of this chapter is not to produce a single vision, but to remove the blurring of images in our current understanding of radicalism by examining the circulation of atheistical and sceptical ideas and opinions in radical religious

---

[5] J. C. Davis, *Fear, Myth and History: The Ranters and the Historians* (Cambridge, 1986), 113–20.

[6] For an example of the former, see James Turner, *One Flesh: Paradisal Marriage and Sexual Relations in the Age of Milton* (Oxford, 1987), 98–100; for the latter, see B. W. Ball, *The English Connection: The Puritan Roots of Seventh-Day Adventist Belief* (Cambridge, 1981), 13–24.

and political activities and writings. It is possible to reach a
new position in our perception both of atheism and of radical
religion. This new view puts paid to the simplistic notion of
an autochthonous 'mechanic atheism', a font of folk-beliefs
concerning the natural world, which surfaced in the guise of
radical sectarianism after 1640.[7] While not denying the possibility of an original popular irreligion, this chapter seeks to
comprehend more effectively the character of radical religious
speculation. It emphasizes the significance of the dissemination of philosophical, occult, and scientific texts in unlearned
religious culture, a printed literature that had usually enjoyed
only an élite and, therefore, highly restricted circulation
before 1640. Religious and political radicalism can rightly
claim large areas of autochthony, but its multifarious nature
was possible in large part through the presence of printed
material, some of it sceptical, some of it encouraging speculative thinking dangerous to the integrity of orthodox and
institutional structures of belief. The radicals either used or
parodied these materials. The new view accounts for nothing
less than the interaction of radical Puritan belief (especially
the notion that the individual is personally subject to the
visitation of the Holy Spirit) with the sceptical and speculative thinking of late humanism in the arena of popular religion
and politics in the English Revolution.

To be regarded as an atheist in the seventeenth century did not
require a denial of the existence of God, but the denial of a
'divine economy of rewards and punishments, in heaven and
hell'.[8] Michael Hunter similarly defines the 'atheism' of
opinion as it was regarded in the early and mid-seventeenth
century: 'irreligion in the sense of a more or less extreme attack
on orthodox Christianity from a cynical or Deistic viewpoint'.[9] He proceeds to argue that this phenomenon was
distinguishable from sectarian heresy. But as he admits, even if
it was distinguishable, it was not distinct. In *A Single Eye All*

---

[7] See e.g. Hill, *The World Turned Upside Down*, 295.

[8] David Wootton, 'Unbelief in Early Modern Europe', *History Workshop Journal*, 20 (1985), 82–100 (p. 86).

[9] Michael Hunter, 'The Problem of "Atheism" in Early Modern England', *Transactions of the Royal Historical Society*, 5th ser., 35 (1985), 135–57 (p. 136).

Light, No Darkness (1650), ordered to be seized and burnt by Parliament shortly after its appearance, the Ranter Laurence Clarkson sought to replace a dualistic conception of the universe with a monistic one, looking at the 'center', with the 'single eye'.[10] In this pamphlet Clarkson maintains that the perfect creature is already able to see that darkness (so-called 'evil') is the same as light ('good'), since both emanate from the same source, God. Clarkson first admits the duality of light and darkness, but then subverts it by referring to scriptural exegesis that finds contradictions in points of grammar. The Scriptures and the book of nature are continuous: 'From hence you may observe the connexion hereof run in the plural, not Power, but Powers; a Power of darkness, a Power of light, a Power in the wicked, a Power in the Godly; yet you have held forth in the same Scripture but one God.'[11] Damnation is redefined as the individual's realization that sin simply belongs with God, though this is incorrectly seen as a moral negative by the unenlightened.[12] Clarkson is peculiar here, in that he admits the absolute truth of neither dualistic myth nor Scripture, as all is subordinated to his impulse to regard any act, good or bad, as an emanation from God. Clarkson later looked back at this Ranter phase in his career, admitting that he had had no faith in Scripture because it was self-contradictory. Instead, he converted biblical metaphors and myths into a description of a 'ground of being' for the self. There is no God 'but onely nature' (God is an 'infinite nothing'), and 'that which was life in man, went into that infinite Bulk and Bigness, so called *God*, as a drop into the Ocean, and the body rotted in the grave, and for ever so to remain.'[13]

---

[10] Along with Abiezer Coppe's *A Fiery Flying Roll* (1649), the tract was a victim of the Blasphemy Act of 9 Aug. 1650, which defined an 'Atheistical, Blasphemous and Execrable' opinion as one which denied the 'necessity of Civil and Moral Righteousness amongst Men', or which affirmed that any man or creature was God, or which affirmed that God lived inside living beings: *A Collection of Ranter Writings from the Seventeenth Century*, ed. Nigel Smith (hereafter *CRW*) (London, 1983), 14.

[11] Laurence Clarkson, *A Single Eye All Light, No Darkness* (1650), in *CRW*, 167.

[12] Ibid. 172.

[13] Laurence Clarkson, *The Lost Sheep Found* (1660), in *CRW*, 185. In this account, something called 'life' survives the eventual annihilation of the body. It imitates, of course, the transcendental journey of the soul after death. Some religious radicals did translate 'life' as 'soul': see John Brayne, *The Unknown Being of the Spirit, Soul, and Body; Anatomized* (London, 1654), 3.

In so far as Clarkson's God is an all-beneficent nature, it is hard to see how his position differs so greatly from what was to become deism, in the sense of a non-revelatory 'natural religion', except that he consistently uses the Bible as part of his evidence. In so far as Clarkson rejects the metaphysical dualisms and the adherence to Scripture that had hitherto reinforced all orthodox European religions, he is cynical.

Clarkson makes his observations in a context common to extreme sectarians, in which Scripture is allegorized so that it represents a state of inner being in the individual and in the universe. Epistemological commonplaces were challenged as a consequence. The anonymous pamphlet *Divinity and Philosophy Dissected, and set forth, by a Mad Man* (1644) speaks of a hell that is not a place but takes shape in the individual's mind or conscience, of a symbolic state of elementary birth and of further symbolic states such as the first birth and its loss, of the external world as living death, and of the annihilation of all things into the prime substance of the universe.[14] The oscillation between the literal and the figurative interpretation permits the realization of human perfection:

As for the creation of the world, it is in Mans heart, as Ecclesiastes saith in the third Chapter, it is internally; and in the first of the Hebrews, he saith that God hath created the worlds, speaking in the plurall number; that is he makes a first and second creation of Man; now the creation of Gods first world in man, is Man and God joyned together from eternity; and this was that deep silence and waters that God moved or brooded on, and he separated the waters from the waters for God is that light and holy spring, and Man is that darke and blacke water.[15]

Pantheism, annihilationism, the internalization of scriptural figures so that heaven and hell are delocalized, and a highly individualized subjectivity are introduced, as the Bible

---

[14] Mystical or near-mystical treatises that set out a schematic process of personal illuminations or 'deification' were often labelled 'Familist' in the Interregnum, although this was not usually accurate; see G. F. Nuttall, *James Nayler: A Fresh Approach* (London, 1954), 2; Nigel Smith, *Perfection Proclaimed: Language and Literature in English Radical Religion 1640–1660* (Oxford, 1989), 144–84.

[15] *Divinity and Philosophy Dissected, and Set Forth, by a Mad Man* (Amsterdam, 1644), 1.

becomes a map of the self's inner life. Above all else, in this world of speculation it is not Church discipline but cosmology that is being reordered or reimagined. A destabilized or reordered universe could have been a rather more threatening prospect to the orthodox believer than simply separated congregations—if, indeed, the heresiographers took this kind of perfectionism seriously. Moreover, Clarkson himself openly linked his practice of free love (for him a political freedom, too) with this cosmology: 'I say I lye with none but my wife, according to Law, though in the unity of the spirit, I lye with all the creation.'[16]

How did Clarkson come to develop these opinions? It is clear from his autobiographical writings that he moved in circles in which opinions and interpretations were exchanged through the media of preaching, the printed word, and discussion. Somebody with relatively little education (his earliest publications reveal very elementary writing skills) came to terms with comparatively sophisticated conceptions outside the institutional structures (the Church and the universities) in which those conceptions usually circulated. *A Single Eye* is a kind of vulgar parody of scholastic logic that none the less seeks to affirm a perfectly serious mystical and antinomian truth.[17] The tract finishes with a list of 'queries' concerning the nature of God, a speculative habit that Clarkson claims he did not have when he was still in Lancashire listening to lectures in the established Church. What he did have was what he later regarded as a simplistic, child's-eye view of God: 'God was a grave, ancient, holy, old man, as I supposed sat in Heaven in a chair of gold.' The capacity to speculate, to 'try all things', be they in the Bible, other books, or the opinions of other men, came only slowly, as Clarkson moved through the burgeoning Churches and sects of the 1640s:

About these things I was searching the truth thereof, and labored in the letter of the Scripture to satisfie my judgement; in the interim hearing of one doctor *Crisp*, to him I went, and he held forth

---

[16] Clarkson, *The Lost Sheep Found*, CRW, 183.

[17] On the sectarian imitation and appropriation of the textual procedures and conventions of devotional discourse, see Smith, *Perfection Proclaimed*, 312–27.

against all the aforesaid Churches, that let his people be in society or no, though walked all alone, yet if he believed that Christ Jesus died for him, God beheld no iniquity in him: and to that end I seriously perused his Bookes.[18]

After his time as a Ranter, Clarkson practised as an astrologer and physician in Cambridgeshire and Essex, using 'magical' manuscripts to help him divine the whereabouts of stolen goods, 'to raise spirits, and fetch treasure out the earth'.[19] Here, radical speculation elided with the practice of a technology that relied for its effect upon the continuity of widespread popular superstition. What is important is the presence of the text in endowing Clarkson with magical powers of healing and divination. He also says that at this time he accepted that there were men before Adam, an idea that he may have received from discussion, from autochthonous deduction, or, like the royalist prophet Arise Evans, from the published English translation of the *Prae-Adamitae* of Isaac de La Peyrère.[20]

Beyond the bounds imposed by any form of consociated Church discipline, Clarkson was free to speculate as far as the conditions in which he lived, the milieux in which he moved, and the printed information available to him permitted. As a Ranter, he became his own God, as he claimed to be part of the Godhead, complete with a metaphysic that was part and parcel of his religion of the free spirit and free love.

One other radical close to the technology of print was the mortalist and Leveller Richard Overton. Overton was related to a printing family, and he may have been a Cambridge undergraduate.[21] Where Clarkson speculated in a language on the margins of literacy, and in a parody of forms of learned and social authority, Overton deliberately challenged orthodoxies and accepted hierarchies in a contemptuous manner. The scurrilous jesting of his political pamphlets is anticipated

---

[18] Laurence Clarkson, *The Lost Sheep Found* (London, 1660), 9.

[19] Clarkson, *The Lost Sheep Found*, CRW, 185.

[20] See David S. Katz, *Philo-Semitism and the Readmission of the Jews to England, 1603–55* (Oxford, 1982), 221–4.

[21] For Overton's life, see R. L. Greaves and R. Zaller (eds.). *A Biographical Dictionary of British Radicals in the Seventeenth Century* (3 vols.: Brighton, 1982–4).

in the prefatory poem by 'N.C.' to Overton's *Mans Mortali-tie* (1643) in a manner that is Lucianic and Marlovian:

> The Hell-hatch'd Doctrine of th'immortall Soule
> Discovered, makes the hungry Furies houle,
> And teare their snakey haire with grief appal'd,
> To see their Errour-leading Doctrine quail'd,
> Hell undermin'd, and Purgatory blowne
> Up in the aire, and all the spirits flowne,
> Pluto undone, thus forced for to yeeld
> The frightned Soules from the Elizian Field.[22]

But this interesting prediction of the fall of hell in festive terms, where a general resurrection is imagined as an inversion of traditional divisions, does not end in literary play. Overton's own writing displays a rational treatment of scriptural interpretation:

Mans immortality is in *Actuall Being*, whose beatitude and infelicity comes through Faith and infidelity. So that Death reduceth this *productio Entis ex Non-ente ad Non-entem*, returnes Man to what he was before he was; that is, *not to Be: Psal.* 115.17. *the Dead prayse not the Lord, neither shall they go down into silence . . .*[23]

Overton argues for the inseparable integration of body and soul, and of form and matter. Drawing on Aristotle, Nemesius, and the French medical authority Ambrose Paré, Overton claims that the soul is 'the internall and externall Faculties of Man joyntly considered: or *Man Anatomized*'.[24] Traces of formal logic appear in his writing, as he seeks to demonstrate his argument from Scripture and from reason. Reason, fragile 'common-sense', empirical observation, and argument from natural analogy combine in a way that seems uneven, inconsistent, and troubling to us today:

They [soul and body] must as well end together as *begin* together; and *begin* together as *end* together. Moreover, experience further tells us, that they neither can *Be*, nor consist without other: For if Nature be deprived more, or lesse in her work of conception of her

---

[22] Richard Overton, *Man Mortalitie* (1643), ed. Harold Fisch (Liverpool, 1968), [4].

[23] Ibid. 9.

[24] Ibid. 18–20. Nemesius (*fl.*). 390), an early bishop, developed a view on the soul that was to influence scholastic thought.

due, ... her Effect is accordingly: If membrally impedited, a membrall impediment; if totally impedited, a total frustration.[25]

While maintaining that the soul is really part of the body, Overton does not deny God, but, like Clarkson, he tends to reduce the concept of a deity, as with that of death, to a metaphysical and cosmological abstract that in itself is materialistic. The sun, for instance, becomes literally a veil between man and God, a shadow and reflector of his glory, while hell is either *'outer darknesse'*, or 'Earth reduced to its *prima materia* or *created matter*, which he saith cannot be consumed'. Although Overton's mortalism cannot be connected with pantheism or deism, he was none the less absolutely certain of the fictionality of the soul.[26]

While Overton denied any extra-material existence, the self-proclaimed prophet (and King of the Jews) Thomas Tany said that even the soul does not represent substance. Bodies are shadows and *non ens*.[27] But both positions, at extremes from each other at face value, are closely linked in terms of the particular definition of the individual or subject that they offered; definitions that were characteristic of sectarian thought. While the Seekers, Ranters, and Quakers were extreme spiritualists, regarding only the spiritual world as having any absolute reality, the Muggletonians (like Overton, 'soul-sleepers') gave bodies to supernatural entities. John Reeve regarded the identities of Christ and God as one, and both Reeve and Muggleton stressed the necessity of belief in a personal Christ and a personal God rather than in an 'Indwelling Essence'.[28] To the extent that both the spiritualists and the materialists made all reality into a higher nature, then all of them are nominalists as opposed to realists. What both groups are doing is making the distance between the human and the divine much smaller than before, a not

---

[25] Ibid. 23–4.

[26] Ibid. 41, 49–50; Overton's distance from deist positions is considered by Burns, *Christian Mortalism from Tyndale to Milton*, 159–61.

[27] For Tany's epistemological and linguistic theories, see Smith, *Perfection Proclaimed*, 299–307.

[28] John Reeve, *The Prophet Reeve's Epistle to his Friend* (London, 1654), 20; Lodowick Muggleton and John Reeve, *A Divine Looking-Glass* (London, 1656; repr. 1661), 55.

uncommon habit of seventeenth-century idealists. By a kind of paradox, the Ranters and Quakers placed the Godhead within the individual, while the Muggletonians realized divine bodies in human terms. For Overton, the soul was naturalized, and rationality with it, so that existence was to be viewed as a wholly natural and developmental process; the work of grace did not come in this life, but after all deaths.

The patterns of thought that typify extreme religious radicalism in England, then, involve attempts to reshape the cosmos and the self in a manner that could only offend the orthodox and the traditional. But how were these patterns determined? The problems encountered by individuals when their own definitions altered with their evolving religious positions are well illustrated by Laurence Clarkson's changing sense of his sexual identity, mythology, and practice. In his final resting-point as a Muggletonian, the Fall is conceived of as the literal rape of Eve by Satan. This allows the Muggletonian notion of spirits as superior forms of bodies to be accommodated, and makes real as opposed to 'verbal' the notion that the human race is divided into two seeds, good and evil, the 'Seeds of Faith and Reason'. The treatment combines literal truth with metaphor.[29] The evil seed in Satan is seen as venereal disease. Though Clarkson talks in a figurative sense of redemption coming from the womb of Mary with the seed of faith (Christ), he is also in another sense using the language of sexual pollution to exonerate his sexually licentious past as a Ranter. Clarkson was obsessed by the conflict between sectarian morality and sexual desire, specifically in the case of the Baptist preacher Thomas Gunne, who shot himself after he had committed adultery with his landlady.[30] The episode is repeated by Clarkson in more than one pamphlet of the late 1650s, when he had seen a pattern in his own religious development; this episode triggered Clarkson's vision of a monistic reality, an attempt to accommodate in positive terms what he saw as the inevitable presence of

---

[29] 'So that from the seed of Gods own body, I say, ye had better been generated a Snake, or a Toad, then a rational, understanding man, as in the day of an account, when it is too late, you will acknowledge, but then in vain:' Laurence Clarkson, *A Paradisical Dialogue Betwixt Faith and Reason* (London, 1660), 120.

[30] Clarkson, *The Lost Sheep Found*, CRW, 177.

sin in all men. With Clarkson, it is possible to interpret the development of his 'heresies' as a continuing attempt to explain, in metaphysical terms, the drama of sin, salvation, and sexuality that he saw in himself and in others. Increasingly, the analogies and imagery in Clarkson's thought are derived from the language of procreation, insemination, and pollution. Much of this language was scripturally based (which did not stop it attracting the 'atheist' label), but the scriptural is developed to become a description of the self in a mythology of 'natural' terms.

As a Muggletonian, Clarkson saw that his justification for sin was part of the operation of the seed of reason in him. Faith here means the acceptance of the myth of the two seeds as both literal and figurative, the acceptance of the corporeality of all forms, and the acceptance of Reeve and Muggleton as the two last witnesses referred to in the Book of Revelation. Muggletonian corporeality is based upon the sceptical argument that seeing is believing. God has a body because it is impossible to imagine a spirit without a body, just as you cannot make love to a woman as a spirit without her body.[31] Again, sexual experience provides the means by which reality is judged, though much of the argument is inconsistent or open-ended: when the body dies, the soul dies with it, which is to say that it rises up with a new, more spiritual body, but the sexual status of the latter, and whether such a resurrection is immediate or not, is not defined. As a Muggletonian, Clarkson described the Fall in terms of Ranter sexuality: Eve persuaded herself that all men and women were of one flesh, so that it represented purity to be freely available to all. God honoured the womb of the Virgin Mary, removing in part the disease of sin that Adam had caught from the polluted Eve in the first place.[32] Clarkson's career in the 1650s marks the transposition to an acceptance of the continuity of being between soul and seed, from the uncertain revelation of identity in difference as he realizes he is God making love to God:

---

[31] Laurence Clarkson, *The Quakers Downfall* (London, 1659), 72.
[32] Clarkson, *The Lost Sheep Found*, 60–1; id., *Look about You, For the Devil that You Fear is in You* (London, 1659), 3, 11, 14.

Oh then my Creature, let me speak to thee:

. . . .

Fie then for shame, look not above the Skies
For God, or Heaven; for here your Treasure lies
Even in these Forms . . .[33]

Beneath the stereotype of the sectarian as atheist was a form
of speculation, part bookish, part not, that deified man, or
materialized the divine, in a series of speculative responses to
the economy of sexuality.[34]

So far, the case has been made for the emergence within
radical religion of cosmological and epistemological redefini-
tions that were regarded as atheistical, and that, in other
contexts, earlier and later, would be recognized as atheistical
by those who propounded them. That this was an effect of
the circulation of knowledge in print (and in manuscript) is
as important as, if not more important than, the autochthonous generation of heretical and atheistical opinions. Indeed,
the higher the degree of literacy and education within radical
religion, the greater the likelihood of engagement with one
or more of the major intellectual traditions, a phenomenon
too often overlooked in the historiography of Puritanism. In
fact, the *crise pyrrhonienne*, that recuperation of Greek
scepticism which played a large role in the emergence of
modern atheism, did not leave the radicals untouched.[35] In
particular, the tolerationist and democratic arguments of the
Leveller party of the mid- to late 1640s were in part the result
of the impact of scepticism upon radical Puritan thought and
sensibility. The engagement of some of the Levellers with
sceptical humanist literature has been noted before, but its
ramifications have never been fully or correctly realized.

William Walwyn, merchant, tolerationist, and sometime
prominent Leveller, was labelled 'atheist' in an attempt to

---

[33] Clarkson, *A Single Eye*, CRW, 162.

[34] The inscription of bodily economies into discourse is explored in Piero
Camporesi, *The Incorruptible Flesh: Bodily Mutation and Mortification in Religion
and Folklore*, trans. Tania Croft-Murray (Cambridge, 1968). I intend to explore this
topic with regard to sectarians (and Ranters especially) at greater length in a future
article.

[35] See Richard H. Popkin, *The History of Scepticism from Erasmus to Spinoza*
(Berkeley, Calif., 1979).

discredit him after he had challenged Independent arguments for scriptural authority.³⁶ In fact, his belief in God's free grace and man's free justification was the strongest component in a powerfully articulated theology. Man was capable of achieving his own salvation, without any intervention from the divine. Once he had realized his justification, he would behave virtuously in acts of charity, and, by following natural standards, he would contribute to the founding presence of divinely instilled love in society. Walwyn associated himself with no particular radical religious group, and offended some Independents and sectarians by refusing to join a specific congregation.³⁷ He preferred to use his knowledge in debates with the many sectarians and separatists he met in London, and continued to worship in his parish church (St James, Garlickhythe) for most of the Interregnum. He believed in the possibility of justification and toleration for all—including Catholics—and liberty of the press.³⁸ Altogether, his thinking appears contradictory, his statements containing a rather broader range of thought than is usually to be found in the pages of religious radicalism. A. S. P. Woodhouse paid tribute to the subtlety of Walwyn: 'His aim is to inculcate a sentiment. He adapts (sometimes almost out of recognition) such parts of Puritan doctrine as he can use, while undermining, rather than openly assailing, the rest.'³⁹ What Woodhouse does not say is that this undermining was made possible by Walwyn's knowledge of scepticism, and that such undermining was itself a sceptical procedure.

³⁶ John Price, *Walwins Wiles* (1649), in William Haller and Godfrey Davies, (eds.), *The Leveller Tracts* (hereafter *LT*) (New York, 1944; repr. Gloucester, Mass., 1964), 291. See also Thomas Edwards, *Gangraena*, (3 vols.; London, 1641) i. 96, and ii. 26–30, where Walwyn is described as a dangerous man, a Seeker, and a 'man of an equivocating Jesuiticall spirit, being full of mentall reservations and equivocations' (ii. 26), and the satirical character given by John Bastwick, in *The Just Defence of John Bastwick* (London, 1645), 16–17.

³⁷ For Walwyn's biography, see 'Introduction: The Life and Thought of William Walwyn', in Jack R. McMichael and Barbara Taft, (eds.), *The Writings of William Walwyn* (hereafter *WWW*) (Athens, Georgia, and London, 1989), 1–51.

³⁸ For Walwyn's activities as a member of parochial and political committees, see William Walwyn, *A Whisper in the Eare of Mr. Thomas Edwards* (1646), in *WWW*, 176–7; and Valerie Pearl, *London and the Outbreak of the Puritan Revolution* (Oxford, 1961), 252–3, 260.

³⁹ A. S. P. Woodhouse, (ed.), *Puritanism and Liberty* (London, 1938; new edn., with preface by Ivan Roots, London, 1986), [55].

The sources of this thought, as his enemies said, and as he himself admitted, were in humanist, particularly sceptical, writings, ancient and modern.[40] In his library could be found Plutarch, Seneca, Lucian, Machiavelli, Montaigne, Charron, all in English translation, since Walwyn read no foreign or ancient languages.[41] Walwyn was also familiar with radical religious thought, especially antinomianism, though his theological reading matter consisted also of the episcopalians Hooker, Hall, and Ussher (from whom he derived arguments for toleration), and the Puritans Perkins and Downame.[42] It has been argued that Walwyn threw over his humanist-inspired doubt in order to embrace antinomianism,[43] but it is more accurate to say that he made subtle use of an extensive and familiar knowledge of the sceptical tradition to arrive at a unique radical religious and political position. The sceptical and humane authors enabled him to conceive of toleration for the sake of a complete liberty of conscience, a position at odds with Protestant and Puritan polity: Walwyn's forms of reasoning were regarded by the Independents as most dangerous when they were used to turn soldiers' minds from the necessity of defeating the Catholic threat in Ireland.[44]

Walwyn's ignorance of Latin, Greek, and French, despite his gentry roots, meant that he had an apprehension of literature in other languages that set him apart from the etymological and rhetorical dispositon of the classically learned. This, together with the extent of his reading and his refusal to be trammelled by any one authority, resulted in a very general treatment of ideas and perceptions in his own expression, so that it is often very difficult to determine the presence of a particular mode of thought. Walwyn was interested in the abstract qualities of love and virtue that were anterior to speech, language, and action: he stressed that the

[40] Price, *Walwins Wiles*, *LT*, 297; William Walwyn, *Walwyns Just Defence*, in *WWW*, 395–403.
[41] *Walwyns Just Defence*, *WWW*, 395–403; Humphrey Brooke, *The Charity of Church-Men* (1649), in *LT*, 362.
[42] William Walwyn, *The Humble Petition of the Brownists* (London, 1641), 5–6; *Walwyns Just Defence*, *WWW*, 97.
[43] Lotte Mulligan, 'William Walwyn', in Greaves and Zaller, *Biographical Dictionary*.
[44] Price, *Walwins Wiles*, *LT*, 310.

Bible could impart all its truth in whichever language it was
written.[45] The spirit and the love were paramount, sentiments
that went against the general assumption in English society
that a godly commonwealth was as much to do with justice
and punishment as with mercy:

The proper object of *Love* is vertue, the more vertuous, the more it
loveth; the lesse vertuous, the lesse it loveth: what so ever *justly*
deserveth the name of infirmity, *Love* can beare with all: but it is
contrary to its nature to beare with wickedness, because mercy to
the wicked, tends to the ruine of the just, and so becomes the
greatest cruelty: *Love* is just, as God is; spares not the greatest . . .
and you can never be partiall in judgement.[46]

Walwyn's urging of a kind of Christian communism has been
identified by David Wootton as the relegation of religion to
a role of public utility.[47] If this is the case, it does not nullify
Walwyn's conception of the efficacy of the abstract power of
love. Nor, as we shall see, does it disqualify what is clearly
the merging of a civic humanist notion of good action and
the cultural relativism of scepticism with a certain kind of
antinomian spiritual libertinism.

Walwyn's reading list is relatively austere: he says that he
thought Cicero, in particular the *Oratione*, vainglorious,
despite the recommendation of a friend. But the sense of
intense familiarity with some texts is very prominent. That
he owned Plutarch's *Moralia* for twenty years but only read
it, he reckoned, for forty hours and no more, implies that he
knew other works in his library in greater depth.[48] It is
probably overstating his commitment to humanism to say,
along with one commentator, that he was fascinated and
sustained by the myth of the lost golden age.[49] But it was his
reading that enabled him to be labelled an atheist by the

[45] William Walwyn, *The Vanitie of the Present Churches* (1649), in *WWW*, 321.
[46] William Walwyn, *A Parable, or Consultation of Physitians upon Master
Edwards* (1646), in *WWW*, 260.
[47] David Wootton, 'Leveller Democracy and the Puritan Revolution', in J. H.
Burns, (ed.), *The Cambridge History of Political Thought*, ii (Cambridge, 1991),
412–42.
[48] *Walwyns Just Defence*, *WWW*, 410.
[49] Wilhelm Schenk, *The Concern for Social Justice in the Puritan Revolution*
(London, 1948), p. 54.

Independents, particulary his knowledge of pagan writers.[50] How Walwyn might have used this knowledge in public disputes with others is another matter.

As far as we can tell, Walwyn found in the text of Lucian a means to discover the vanity of 'things of wordly esteem', of ambition, pride, and covetousness.[51] Humphrey Brooke, Walwyn's defender and son-in-law, repeated the assertion that Walwyn held wit in low esteem, but he also said that he read Lucian's 'Tyrant' or 'Megapenthes' dialogue in Walwyn's company, which portrayed the 'fouleness and deformity of Tyrannie in a third person', so informing people of the 'wickedness of such under whom they lived'.[52] This is entirely consistent with a general Renaissance sceptical perspective, particularly that of Cornelius Agrippa in *De incertitudine et vanitate omnium artium et scientiarum*, who Walwyn also regarded as having been unjustly persecuted.[53] Of course, many others were also familiar with Walwyn's reading material. As he himself admitted, Lucian was popular in the universities. The use of fables and the same exemplary figures recalled by Walwyn (see below, p. 148) were recommended and employed in the rhetoric books of the previous century, and had long been embedded in the humanist tradition.[54] It is the particular context that matters, however: Walwyn was using translations (thus justifying the perennial fear of the privileged that the vulgar should not be permitted to have ideas that they might use to a subversive end), which were introduced into a radical religious context where they were largely unknown and could be employed in a radically critical way.[55]

Walwyn also believed in the reading of classical histories as

---

[50] Price, *Walwins Wiles*, LT, 296.

[51] *Walwyns Just Defence*, WWW, 398.

[52] Brooke, *The Charity of Church-Men*, LT, 334, referring to the accusation made in *Walwins Wiles*, LT, 296.

[53] William Walwyn, *The Fountain of Slaunder Discovered* (1649), in WWW, 352.

[54] See e.g. Richard Rainolde, *A Booke called the Foundacion of Rhetoricke* (London, 1563), fos. ii[v]–x[r], xl[r]–xliii[v].

[55] *Walwyns Just Defence*, WWW, 397–8. For the circulation of translations of mystical and occult works in radical religious circles, see Smith, *Perfection Proclaimed*, part 2. Popular Lucianic satire had flourished since the early 1640s, in the attacks on Laud, Strafford, and sectarians. Godly ire may have been enhanced by associating Walwyn's use of Lucian with these kinds of writing.

a means of drawing attention to immoral and intolerant behaviour. To this end, he sent a friend turned enemy, Richard Price, a copy of Thucydides. Much more significant was his use of Montaigne. From the *Essais* he extracted the examples of Tiberius and Epaminondas to explain the relationship between tyranny, deceit, public or civic virtue, and grace. Tiberius refused to poison Arminius because the Romans dealt openly with their enemies, while Epaminondas never slew his vanquished enemies in battle and never killed a man without legal sanction.[56] Above all, it was Montaigne's own self-denying statements that facilitate Walwyn's most sophisticated expressions in this instance. Montaigne says that his verbal assurance and his faith are part of the community, at their best when serving the public good. However, as a virtuous man, he should only do what is fitting for his skills and his station, and if asked to rob, let alone murder, he would rather go to the galleys. Monetary analogy is attractive to Walwyn: as with the Lacedaemonians under Antipater, heavy tax burdens are acceptable, but commands to shameful or dishonest action are not. Typically with Montaigne, it is the double negative that counts, demanding of the reader a greater effort to appreciate the positive and negative aspects of the situation: 'What is lesse possible for him to do, then what he cannot effect without charge unto his faith.'[57]

Montaigne's discourse gave Walwyn a particular way of perceiving the connection between scepticism and free grace. Walwyn takes Montaigne's reasoning for not having sects, and uses it to justify the opposite position. If all human thoughts are inevitably reducible to contradiction by other human thoughts, what really matters is divine grace reflected in virtuous behaviour: 'If this ray of Divinity, did in any sort touch us, it would every where appear: not only our words, but our actions, would bear some shew, & lustre of it. Whatsoever should proceed from us, might be seen inlightened, with this noble and matchlesse brightnesse . . .'[58] Given

---

[56] See Michael de Montaigne, *Essais*, trans. John Florio (London, 1600), bk. ii, ch. 36.

[57] *Walwyns Just Defence*, *WWW*, 401. Richard Price, not to be confused with the minister John Price, was a scrivener.

[58] Ibid. 399; see Montaigne, *Essais*, ii. 12: 389.

this, all factions must appear shameful. Further, it might be said that God is unknowable not because of man's inability to know him, but because he is infinite.[59] Walwyn has chosen a passage that amply rejects the claim of some modern commentators that Montaigne was an anti-essentialist, and the notion that Montaigne put man at the centre of the providential plan.[60] Yet the passage goes on to take in a piece of cultural relativism: though Turks and pagans are not Christians, they still display such charitable manners among themselves that they put factional Christians, who have a superior witness, to shame. Unlike the cannibals (here Walwyn follows another famous Montaigne essay), Christians are not devoid of all evil and pernicious traits of behaviour.[61] Taking the two readings together, Walwyn's argument does not hark after the golden age, because Turks do not live in a state of nature. Rather, Walwyn turns Montaigne's argument around, so that the Independents are asked to see the ideal principles in Catholics, Turks, and cannibals, and to extend their own principles in that direction. The xenophobia of Protestantism, and the exclusiveness of covenant theology, is undermined:

These, and the like flowers, I think it lawful to gather out of his Wildernesse, and to give them room in my Garden; yet this worthy Montaign was but a Roman Catholique ... Go to this honest Papist, or to these innocent Cannibals, ye Independent Churches, to learn civility, humanity, simplicity of heart; yea, Charity and Christianity.[62]

Although Montaigne (after Erasmus) wrote to discourage sectarianism, Walwyn took Montaigne's belief in the possibility of the attainment of virtue and charity through following natural principles, found it compatible with—or,

---

[59] In 'An Apology of Raymond Sebond', Montaigne cites Hermes Trismegistus on the admirable activity of exploring divine nature, something that would have been attractive to the speculative enthusiasts among the Puritans, if not to Walwyn himself: *Essais*, bk. II. 475.

[60] Jonathan Dollimore, *Radical Tragedy: Religion, Ideology and Power in the Drama of Shakespeare and his Contemporaries* (Brighton, 1984), 18.

[61] *Walwyns Just Defence*, WWW, 399. Walwyn was familiar with Islamic history and governance from his reading of a biography of Muhammad, perhaps Sir Walter Raleigh's *The Life and Death of Mahomet* (London, 1637).

[62] *Walwyns Just Defence*, WWW, 400.

indeed, responsible for—his own version of antinomianism, and used it to argue for near-total toleration. Free grace, free justification, scepticism, and toleration are here mutually interdependent.

Reading Montaigne's text is usually said to result in an undermining of confidence in the power of reason to arrive at any truth. Yet here is Walwyn seeing in Montaigne not fideism, but the use of reason and moderation in human affairs, each massively determined by the power of grace in nature to produce virtuous action in people. This is, of course, a partial comprehension of Montaigne's writing. When Walwyn addressed his Independent opponent John Price, he pointed out that he did not accept everything in the *Essais*. The Leveller, having changed the title of 'An Apologie for *Raymond Sebond*' to 'Of Christian Religion', is playing down the radical critique of reason here, highlighting the exhortation to virtuous action through free justification.[63] But from an orthodox point of view, Walwyn's use of Montaigne could only appear as a devious application of sceptical thought processes to bolster up spiritual libertinism.

Traditionally, Montaigne's insights were supposed to lead to two attitudes. First, that man cannot transcend the relativities in which he is placed by history, a position more compatible with Catholic teaching. Second, that man is inadequate to grasp anything, so that grace must vouchsafe access to a divine truth as a gift in the form of faith, which was considered to result in a tepid faith.[64] While there is undoubtedly a stress on the practical effects of good works in Walwyn, there is no lack of conviction based upon faith *and* reason: 'I judge no man beleeveth any thing but what he cannot chuse but beleeve: it is misery enough to want the comfort of true beleeving, and I judge the most convincing argument that any man can hold forth unto another . . . is to practice to *the uttermost* that which his faith binds him unto.'[65]

[63] Ibid. 399.
[64] See Terrence Penelhum, 'Skepticism and Fideism', in Myles Burnyeat (ed.), *The Sceptical Tradition* (Berkeley, Calif., 1983), 287–318 (p. 297).
[65] William Walwyn, *A Still and Soft Voice from the Scriptures* (1647), in *WWW*, 274.

At this point, Walwyn's thought begins to show the influence not of Montaigne, but of Montaigne's disciple Pierre Charron, who effectively reduced the complex flux of his master to a more straightforward, if less exciting, expression of the dependence of reason upon nature as being that of a guide, until a superior revelation from God arrived: 'Nature hath disposed all things in the best state that they could be, and hath given them the first motion to good, and the end which they should seek, in such sort, that he that will follow her need not obtain and possess his own good and his own end.'[66] Such notions were set forth in two works, *Les Trois Veritez* (1593) and *De la sagesse* (1601), Samson Lennard's translation of the latter going through nine editions during the course of the seventeenth century. In his reading of Charron, Walwyn would have come across strong attacks on witnesses to possession and ecstasy, and on excessive formalism, two extremes of devotional behaviour that were present in English radical religion.[67]

'To judge of all things, not to be assured of any', says Charron. The first use of nature is that nothing is certain: 'we do nothing but search, enquire, and grope after appearances'. Resisting the demands of the passions, the wise man achieves 'Universality of spirit, whereby a wise man taketh a view, and entreth into consideration of the whole universe'.[68] Charron recommends a form of secular self-preservation, which, within the assumption of a general beneficence of nature, is predicated upon a Pyrrhonistic doubt of human abilities, and the surety of perceptual phenomena.

The opening of one of Walwyn's first works, *The Power of Love* (1643), though framed by the text of Titus 2: 11–12 (an assurance of universal salvation), clearly repeats Charron's precept: 'It is evident (though it be little regarded or considered, the more is the pity) that in naturall things all things whatsoever that are necessary for the use of mankinde, the use of them is to be understood easily with out study or difficulty.' And this simplicity of perception was entirely

---

[66] Pierre Charron, *Of Wisdome*, trans. Samson Lennard (London, 1606), 243.
[67] Ibid. 32, 152. [68] Ibid. 217, 223.

congruent with the positive statements of Leveller political
theory, voiced here by Overton:

By natural birth all men are equal . . . born to like propriety, liberty
and freedom, and as we are delivered of God by the hand of nature
into this world, every one with a naturall innate freedom and
propriety . . . even so we are to live, every one equally . . . to enjoy
his birthright and privilege, even all whereof god by nature hath
made him free.[69]

At the height of Leveller activity, Walwyn still considered
doubt to be part of a thinking process congruent with nature:
'Nor will it in any measure satisfy the Conscience, to Gods
justice, to go on in uncertainties, for in doubtfull cases men
ought to stand still, and consider, untill certainty do appear,
especially when killing and sleying of men (the most horrid
worke to Nature and Scripture) is in question.'[70] The sources
for the Leveller rooting of inalienable popular rights in the
law of nature were derived from a variety of texts, not least
of which was parliamentarian apology itself.[71] The specific
contribution of Walwyn's appropriation of scepticism (especially Charron) was that his conception of nature was not
simply part of the language of legal precedent, or a mythology
of lost, perhaps reclaimable, perfection, but part of a judgement process eternally available to mankind—an ethical and
moral predisposition. Pyrrhonism had suddenly become part
of the intellectual locomotion of London radicalism and,
ultimately, of New Model Army agitation—a very different
context from the aristocratic associations that Charron's book
had carried at the beginning of the century.[72]

In effect, Walwyn antinomianized Pyrrhonism, making the
language of doubt and relativism justify an enlightened
pacifism. Consequently, Charron's wisdom is replaced with

[69] Richard Overton, *An Arrow against All Tyrants* (London, 1646), 3–4.
[70] William Walwyn, *The Bloody Project: or A Discovery of the New Designe, in
the Present War* (1648), in *WWW*, 297.
[71] On the derivation of Leveller rights theory, see Richard Tuck, *Natural Rights
Theories* (Cambridge, 1979), 149–50; Wootton, 'Leveller Democracy and the Puritan
Revolution'.
[72] Lady Anne Clifford was painted holding a copy of *Of Wisdome*. Information
dervied from Graham Perry's paper on Lady Anne Clifford, at the Oxford
Renaissance Graduate Seminar, Jan. 1989.

love based upon virtue and experience, 'the best Schoole-master in things naturall and morall'.[73] Part of Walwyn's intent is to remove pejorative categories imposed upon radi-cals. Separatists are not wild, irrational enthusiasts in their beliefs, says Walwyn. Their open meetings and their rea-soned, level-headed arguments mark them out as figures of virtue, worthy of toleration.[74] Here, Walwyn's reason is beginning to be associated with a power of grace, a combina-tion that he launches against the esoteric mysticism of other radicals (see below). Rather than being a separate entity, reason is connected to the perception of divine love, so merging the contemplative or affective with the practical and moral: 'he made him naturally a rationall creature, judging rightly of all things, and desiring only what was necessary, and so being exempt from all labour, and care of obtaining things superfluous, he passed his dayes with aboundance of delight and contentment: until he sought out unto himselfe many inventions.'[75]

Finally, Walwyn's greatest debt to the sceptical humanists is that characteristic argumentative equilibrium and equivo-cation. It is a matter of perception and a style that facilitate the dismissal of superstition, just as the sceptics had rejected dogmatism.[76] Of course, this manner has neither the com-plexity of Montaigne nor the ordered edifice of Charron, but it represents a synthesis of scepticism and humanism that is designed to imply a persona of considered good sense and goodwill.

Such a style was responsible for Walwyn being accused of using Jesuitical and casuistical subtlety to pervert the honest Protestantism of Levellers like Lilburne and Prince and turn them away from the necessity of fighting the Irish.[77] Walwyn does not overtly attack the syllogism, but he does develop a personally authenticated source of reasoning that suggests, more than the simple denial of truths in some radical religious

---

[73] Walwyn, *A Still and Soft Voice*, WWW, 265.
[74] William Walwyn, *The Compassionate Samaritaine* (1644), in WWW, 103–4.
[75] William Walwyn, *The Power of Love* (1643), in WWW, 82.
[76] Hence the detection of passion in Edwards: Walwyn, *A Whisper in the Eare of Mr. Thomas Edwards*, WWW, 180–2.
[77] Price, *Walwins Wiles*, LT, 310.

disputation, that those without love and virtue cannot think or write correctly:

> If their ignorance and superstition appear so grosse and palpable, that (in loving tearmes, and for their better information,) you demand how they come to know there is a God, or that the scriptures are the word of God: their common answer is, *doe you deny them*: *it seems you do*? *otherwise why doe you aske such questions*?[78]

It is Walwyn's humanism that allows him to posit an absolute standard to which all men should adhere, and his scepticism that permits him to undermine relentlessly the 'weak argument'.[79] Also, many of Walwyn's pamphlets, such as *The Power of Love* (1643), are unsigned. The persona who speaks is anonymous, and has been supposed to be Walwyn's fictional creation of a member of the Family of Love.[80] In this way, Walwyn is able to put his method and his stance— the conjunction of scepticism, free grace, and toleration— into the mouth of a particular sectarian stance. Additionally, without Walwyn's name on the tract, we are more readily convinced of a relative lack of distortion of ideas, since Walwyn is not writing under the pressure to defend himself against a particular charge. Walwyn was not an atheist or an unbeliever, but he did manage to make the most extreme language of doubt in the seventeenth century work on behalf of extremely radical religious and political positions.

Walwyn's thought and his role in London radicalism were very specific consequences of the freedoms of the 1640s.[81] Without the chance to read as he did, to circulate among the London churches, and then to put his experience into practice as a committee-man and Leveller, his sceptical free justification and tolerationism would not have developed. But further behind this were the personal means by which Walwyn enjoyed the space to speculate. As a merchant, he

---

[78] Walwyn, *A Still and Soft Voice*, WWW, 266–7.

[79] Ibid. 271.

[80] See William Haller (ed.), *Tracts on Liberty in the Puritan Revolution, 1638–1647* (3 vols.; New York, 1933), i. 42.

[81] For the wider perspective of popular participation in 1640s London, see Keith Lindley, 'London and Popular Freedom in the 1640s', in R. C. Richardson and G. M. Ridden (eds.) *Freedom and the English Revolution* (Manchester, 1986), 111–50.

had the freedom to buy books, to read them, and to have an establishment wealthy enough to entertain acquaintances at will. Before 1640 his own reading had led him in private to his 'antinomianism'. The relative economic independence of the merchant facilitates an openness to different kinds of literature and opinions, which could be acquired as often as means would allow. In Walwyn's own writings there is a sense of mercantile habit being transferred from the economic to the moral sphere. A good bargain has to be found: Cicero's *Oratione* were disliked by Walwyn because they were 'vainglorious' and 'verball', a rejection of their eloquence, and a mark of Walwyn's adherence to the Senecanism so typical of the time.[82] The merchant is able to slide across different positions and ideas as represented in print and in debate, assimilating and redefining as he proceeds. The individual, centred and assured by the knowledge of God's free justification, with rights guaranteed in law, lives a virtuous and charitable life, testing each truth as it appears before him. Toleration and the separation of Church and State permit the circulation of as many viewpoints as arise, and in a true exercise of *epochē*, the man of charity 'tries all things'.

Although Walwyn thought that believers should join a gathered Church if they were so persuaded, such associations should only be voluntary—he himself refused to become part of any one congregation.[83] This refusal to 'ingraft' into the body of Christ, as the Independents would have said, was certainly one reason why he and the Levellers were finally dropped by the more powerful Independent and Particular Baptist Churches in 1649, so effectively ending the possibility of a Leveller success in the late 1640s.[84] Indeed, Walwyn was attacked primarily on religious and not political grounds. As he said, when the split with the gathered Churches came, the charges of atheism, once made against him by Presbyterians,

---

[82] If Walwyn was a true adherent of Senecanism, he would have learnt of it from his copy of Joseph Hall's *Meditations and Vowes*, 1st edn. (1605).

[83] William Walwyn et al., *A Manifestation* (1649), in *WWW*, 338.

[84] For the history of Leveller-seperatist collaboration and its breakdown, see Murray Tolmie, *The Triumph of the Saints: The Separate Churches of London 1616–1649* (Cambridge, 1977), 144–91.

returned in the mouths of those whom he had spent most of the past decade defending.[85]

Some of these charges reflect sceptical views of claims for the absolute authority of the Scriptures. Walwyn was accused of saying that the bible was not worth reading because it was contradictory, and he said that he found extant arguments for the divine authority of Scripture (as well as the existence of God) weak. He knew God by inner experience; and it was further alleged that he regarded the Song of Solomon as a mere epithalamium of love.[86] Humphrey Brooke says that Walwyn followed John Goodwin in regarding the Scriptures, either in the original or translated languages, as not being the word of God, which could only exist 'divers' in every man.[87]

Walwyn's friend, Clement Writer, shared these views to some extent. Writer, originally a clothier from Worcester, sometime General Baptist and Seeker, pointed to problems of translation and inconsistency. Like the Quaker scriptural sceptic Samuel Fisher, he used the heresiographer Daniel Featly, and Jeremy Taylor's *The Liberty of Prophesying* (1647) to emphasize the errors in all scriptural translations: 'Can any make Fundamentals of Uncertainties?'[88] He felt that divine evidence (by which he meant the presence of the Holy Spirit in the individual) was necessary before any commitment could be made to any belief, rather than simply accepting the words of the Scripture.[89] In 1646 this was a political issue, which turned upon the rejection of accrued tyranaical authority: 'Parliament must protect this gift of the spirit for the people, since *"The safety of the people is the supream Law."*'[90] The sophistication of biblical textual criticism, and the interpretation of a body of writings the truth of which one could regard with no final certainty, was a form

[85] *Walwyns Just Defence*, WWW, 425–6.
[86] A view notoriously associated with the sixteenth-century Calvinist turned tolerationist, Sebastian Castellio.
[87] Price, *Walwins Wiles*, LT, 294–6; Brooke, *The Charity of Church-Men*, LT, 333–7.
[88] For Writer's life, see *DNB*; Greaves and Zaller, *Biographical Dictionary*; Clement Writer, *An Apologetical Narration*, 2nd edn. (London, 1658), 2, 7, 16, 65, 68, 76.
[89] Clement Writer, *Fides divina* (London, 1657), 77.
[90] Id., *The Jus Divinum of Presbyterie* (London, 1646), 28.

of tyranny imposed upon simple people, 'the poor *Herds-man*, the labouring *Plow-man*, and Country *Huss-wife*', who should each be entitled, with the help of toleration, to their own inner knowledge of the working of the spirit.

Scriptural scepticism, deeply offensive to most orthodox Protestants, and certainly to those in gathered Churches and Baptist conventicles, was, for Writer, part of a theological and epistemological perfectionism and political radicalism. The similarity with Walwyn is apparent: 'In reading of the Scriptures, let us never be induced to understand any Text in such a sense as shall contradict either the Law of Nature written in our hearts, or the love and goodness of God.'[91] As with Leveller political theory, that which is natural according to personal experience or evidence, and that which equates with the manifest love of God, has precedence over literally interpreted biblical injunctions. Writer's humane scepticism is in fact a defence against self-contradiction: having to accept scriptural truths means that the individual is permanently at odds with himself—'in a Scripture-sense a man at one and the same time may be said to believe, and not to believe, (that is) to believe intellectually, and not to believe obedientially, whereby he becomes a self-condemner.'[92] Like Clarkson, Writer seeks a certainty of truth without contraries, a typical habit for a radical religious thinker, but the means he was able to employ to do this were the product of an entirely different kind of thinking that was prepared to admit doubt and uncertainty.

Historians now recognize the power of stereotypes in the formation of identities in early modern England. The 'atheist' as sectarian is no exception, but it would be a great mistake either to believe the stereotype or to accept that it was neither accurate nor applicable, and to reject the problem of 'atheism' in radical religion as a projection of contemporary hostile fears. Those godly ministers who so feared the lay antinomi-anism and political libertinism of the merchants and the speculations of artisanal preachers were reacting to the devel-

[91] Ibid., 2nd edn. (London, 1655), 88–9.
[92] Writer, *Fides divina*, 77.

opment of forms of questioning that dispelled a rigid ecclesiology and a disciplinarian theology, though also without
forgetting God. Perhaps that was more threatening still, and,
in the eyes of Featly, Pagitt, and Edwards, impossible to
understand. In the writings of extreme religious radicals like
Clarkson, Overton, Muggleton, and Reeve, forms of speculation were developed concerning the organization of existence that located the divine and the hitherto transcendental
in the natural world, or that construed the divine in terms of
very basic human identities and processes. In William
Walwyn and in Clement Writer scepticism of a very refined
nature was appropriated, reorganized, and put to use in a far-
sighted criticism of institutional forms of obedience, of
persecution and exploitation, to produce a vision of society
in which the presence of justice and punishment was practi-
cally replaced by overriding goodness. Radical religion had
assumed forms of speculation, of analysis, reasoning and
ultimately of enlightenment, that were to have a lasting
impact on the reality and the memory of mid-seventeenth-
century English radicalism. We must begin to rewrite the
biographies of the radicals in terms that are appropriate to
the kinds of knowledge they were able to deploy, and to the
broader intellectual movements of which those kinds of
knowledge were a part.

6

Jewish Anti-Christian Arguments as a Source of Irreligion from the Seventeenth to the Early Nineteenth Century

RICHARD H. POPKIN

Since the mid-first century, Jews have offered arguments as to why they do not accept Christianity as the fulfilment of Judaism. In both the New Testament and the Talmud there is ample evidence of this. Strong efforts are made in the Gospels to show the Jews that prophecies in the Old Testament have been fulfilled in the life of Jesus of Nazareth, and strong efforts are made in the Talmud to show that this is not the case.

As the Christian Church became more powerful, in both the Western and Eastern empires, these efforts to convince became more forceful, and Jewish answers became more circumspect. In medieval Europe staged disputations occurred, often inspired by Jewish converts. The Jews were offered a no-win situation. If they put forward any strong arguments, they were subject to prison or death for insulting Christianity. If they offered weak arguments, they were subject to severe pressures to convert. In spite of the odds, both sides usually claimed victory, and surviving documents demonstrate how each side provided a record of the encounter that would make them the winner. The Christians often tried to show that, at an earlier stage, Jews had admitted that the Messiah had come, and were now covering this up by changing the texts of the Talmud or hiding documents.[1]

[1] On the history of Jewish–Christian polemics, see Hans Joachim Schoeps, *The Jewish–Christian Argument: A History of Theologies in Conflict* (London, 1963), and Haim Hillel Ben-Sasson, 'Disputations and Polemics', in *Encyclopedia Judaica* (16 vols.; Jerusalem, 1971–2), vi. 79–103.

The disputes took on a different character after the massive effort in Spain and Portugal to convert the Jews to Christianity by force, as a prelude to the Second Coming. From the pogrom of 1391, led by the Catholic millenarian St Vincent Ferrar, onwards, a large percentage of Spanish and Portuguese Jewry were dragged into churches, threatened with death if they did not convert, and then converted against their will. It was in this atmosphere that the great Tortosa disputation occurred in 1415, a debate between converted rabbis and unconverted ones.[2]

The Iberian situation produced a new world of disputants, namely, *conversos*, or New Christians, who did not accept the religion they found themselves in. The original forced converts and their descendants found that, as 'Christians', their opposition now became heresy and blasphemy. The Spanish and Portuguese Inquisitions were established to police, and punish, them for any sign that they were still Judaizers, that is, that they were persons who accepted any Jewish views or practices, or aided and abetted those who did.[3]

This state of affairs produced a hostile group within Christianity, seeking some way of expressing their opposition. In Spain and Portugal and their colonies there were constant discoveries of conspiracies to undermine Christianity. Among the forms of conspiracy uncovered by the Inquisition were anti-Christian views expressed in the context of supposedly Christian writings, and expressions of Jewish anti-Christian views in such works. It was, of course, extremely dangerous to produce such works, and many authors were either arrested or were forced to flee outside the jurisdiction of the Inquisition. It is those who fled to parts of Europe that allowed the free practice of Judaism who will be the subject of this chapter, principally some of those who went to Amsterdam in the seventeenth century.

[2] On the history of the Jews of Spain, see Yitzhak Baer, *The Jews in Christian Spain* (2 vols.; Philadelphia, 1961). On the Tortosa disputation, see *Encyclopedia Judaica*, xv. 1270–2.
[3] See Cecil Roth, *A History of the Marranos* (Philadelphia, 1960), and I. S. Revah, 'Les Marranes', *Revue des études juives*, 118 (1959–60), 29–77.

One further background element that needs to be mentioned is that the drive to convert the Jews took on a new immediacy in the sixteenth and seventeenth centuries, because of the increasing conviction on the part of Christian millenarians, Catholic and Protestant, that the 'end of days' was imminent, and that the penultimate event before its coming was the prophesied conversion of the Jews.[4] The results of forced conversion in Spain and Portugal had been so counterproductive that most serious European millenarians were now adamant that the Jews should be brought to convert through genuine conviction. This could only be accomplished by rational discourse and goodwill projects (and by God's intervention, making the Jews see the light). The great English theorist, Joseph Mede of Cambridge, contended that only a symbolic conversion was necessary, the genuine and sincere conversion of *one Jew*, as a type, just as the conversion of one Jew, Saul of Tarsus, had realized the possibility of the conversion of the Gentiles. So, on Mede's theory, effort should be expended on those Jews who would listen and who had enough background and training to understand Christianity as Jewish fulfilment.[5]

The Spanish and Portuguese *conversos* had been raised and trained as Christians. They went to Christian schools and read Christian texts. When they escaped and went to The Netherlands and reverted to Judaism, they still had this background knowledge, so that serious discussion could be held with them. In seventeenth-century millenarian literature there is an on-going dispute as to whether the conversion would or might occur in England, The Netherlands, France, or a regenerated Portugal.

Two developments that made some Sephardic Jews secure enough to start presenting their side of the story was the protection of a Jewish 'cell' within the court of Marie de'

---

[4] On Christian millenarian expectations, see Norman Cohn, *The Pursuit of the Millennium* (New York, 1961); Marjorie Reeves, *The Influence of Prophecy in the Late Middle Ages* (Oxford, 1969); and Marion L. Kuntz, *Guillaume Postel: The Prophet of the Restitution of All Things* (The Hague, 1971).

[5] On Mede, see Katherine R. Firth, *The Apocalyptic Tradition in Reformation Britain, 1590–1640* (Oxford, 1979), ch. 7, and R. H. Popkin, 'The Third Force in Seventeenth-Century Thought: Skepticism, Science and Millenarianism', in E. Ullmann-Margalit (ed.), *The Prism of Science* (Dordrecht, 1986), 21–50.

Medici in Paris, and the establishment of a free Jewish community in Amsterdam.

When Marie de' Medici married Henri IV, she brought with her to the Paris court some old friends, including the Jewess Leonora Galigai and her husband Concino Concini. After the murder of Henri IV, she also brought her favourite doctor, Elijah Montalto, a Portuguese Jew who had escaped from Iberia and was flourishing in Italy. He was not only a prominent medical scientist, but also a leader in the movement to exhort *conversos* to escape and revert to Judaism, and to prevent those who did so from relapsing back into some form of Christianity.[6] Montalto came to Paris in 1610 with his secretary, Saul Levi Mortera, a young Italian Jew who was to become the chief Sephardic rabbi of Amsterdam. Montalto asked for, and got from the queen, a guarantee that he could practise his religion freely and that he would have police protection from Christians if he argued with them about religion. Montalto engaged in several disputes with Catholic priests, the reports of some of which have been preserved.[7] It was learned after his death, and after Louis XIII killed Concini in 1617, that there was a Jewish 'cell' in the Louvre, headed by Montalto, and including Concini's widow (Leonora Galigai), the 'convert' professor of Hebrew at the Collége Royale, Philippe d'Aquin, and Mortera. Concini was disinterred, and cooked and eaten on the Pont Neuf, and his bones ground to dust and cast into the Seine. His wife was burned alive. Some other participants were later punished by the Spanish Inquisition.[8]

Montalto's attacks on Christianity exist in manuscript form. A version was published in the eighteenth century. He wrote in Spanish and Portuguese, and concentrated on showing that the Christians had misinterpreted their crucial 'proof text', Isaiah 53, by claiming that the 'suffering servant'

---

[6] On Montalto, see Cecil Roth, *A History of the Jews in Venice* (Philadelphia, 1930), 242–4.

[7] See the article on Montalto by Isaac Broyde in the *Encyclopedia Judaica*, viii. 662–3.

[8] See Fernand Hayem, *Le Maréchal d'Ancre et Leonora Galigai* (Paris, 1910), and Pierre Bayle's article on the Maréchal d'Ancre in his *Dictionnaire historique et critique* (Rotterdam, 1695–7).

described there was Jesus. Montalto's open, blunt challenge made him a hero in the Marrano (secret Jewish) world, as well as in the newly emerging world of free Judaism in the northern Netherlands.[9] When Dr Montalto died in 1616 on his way to a royal wedding in Tours, his body was carried to Amsterdam by his secretary, Saul Levi Mortera, because there was no Jewish cemetery in France. Montalto was one of the first persons to be buried in the Jewish cemetery at Ouderkerk, outside Amsterdam.[10] Mortera decided to stay in Holland, and became a leader of the developing Spanish and Portuguese community of Jewish refugees. As the Dutch emancipated themselves from Spanish rule, Jews and secret Jews fled from Iberia, the southern Netherlands, and elsewhere to Holland. The Dutch tolerated a free Jewish community, the only one in Western Europe that was not ghettoized or put under any disabilities. The members of the Jewish community were recognized as legal residents, but not as Dutch citizens. They could keep up their religious and cultural practices as long as they did not cause scandal to the Dutch Protestant citizenry.[11]

Amsterdam became the New Jerusalem. Jews flocked there from all over Europe. Soon there was a thriving intellectual community, with schools for young and old to study Judaism and the kind of subjects that would have been studied in Spain and Portugal at the time. Some important thinkers and scholars were there, including the most important philosophical kabbalist, Abraham Cohen Herrera;[12] the most renowned Jew in the Christian world, Menasseh ben Israel,[13] who began

[9] Manuscript copies of his writings are to be found in Amsterdam in the Ets Haim and Rosenthaliana collections, in Paris in the Bibliothéque Nationale, in London in the British Library, as well as in New York at Columbia University and at the Jewish Theological Seminary.

[10] Herman P. Salomon, 'Inleiding' to Saul Levi Mortera, *Traktaat betreffende de Waarheid van de Wet van Mozes* (Braga, 1988), p. xxxiii.

[11] On the state of affairs of Dutch Jewry, see Jonathan I. Israel, *European Jewry in the Age of Mercantilism, 1550–1750* (Oxford, 1985).

[12] On Herrera, see Kenneth Krabbenhoft, 'Vida de Abraham Cohen de Herrera', in Abraham Cohen Herrera, *Puerta del cielo* (Madrid, 1987), 12–19.

[13] On Menasseh ben Israel, see the introduction by Henry Mechoulan and Gerard Nahon to Menasseh ben Israel, *The Hope of Israel* (Oxford, 1987); Cecil Roth, *The Life of Menasseh ben Israel* (Philadelphia, 1934); and Y. Kaplan, H. Mechoulan, and R. H. Popkin (eds.), *Menasseh ben Israel and his World* (Leiden, 1989).

Hebrew printing in The Netherlands; Judah Leon Templo, the builder of a famous model of Solomon's Temple;[14] Saul Levi Mortera;[15] Isaac Orobio de Castro;[16] and many others. Almost all these figures had either been Christians earlier in their lives, or they had been raised in Christian communities and had studied at Christian institutions.[17] Many of them did not know Hebrew when they arrived, nor had they had a traditional Jewish education.[18]

They did know that they rejected Christianity, and they expressed their rejection in terms of the intellectual tools at their disposal. Hence their anti-Christian literature was of a different kind from that which had developed earlier, in that they were not familiar with either the established Talmudic answers or the tradition of rabbinical answers during the Middle Ages. But they were acquainted with what Christians of their time took as evidence that the Jews were wrong in not recognizing Jesus as the promised Messiah.

The conditions of their happy settlement in The Netherlands required that they should not scandalize their Christian neighbours, and they lived in a section of Amsterdam that was contiguous with the rest of the city and had no walls. Rembrandt van Rijn lived at 1 Joodenbreestraat (Jewish Broad Street), in a house belonging to Baron Francis Boreel, the Dutch ambassador to France. This house is only a short distance from the great Portuguese Synagogue and the school where Spinoza studied. In the early years the Jewish house of worship was shared with some of the English dissenters who

---

[14] On Templo, see A. K. Offenburg, 'Jacob Jehuda Leon (1602–1675) and his Model of the Temple', in J. van den Berg and E. G. E. van der Wall, *Jewish–Christian Relations in the Seventeenth Century* (Dordrecht, 1988), 95–115.

[15] On Mortera, see Salomon, 'Inleiding'.

[16] On Orobio, see Yosef Kaplan, *From Christianity to Judaism: The Life and Work of Isaac Orobio de Castro* (Jerusalem, 1982) (in Hebrew). An English translation of this work, published by the Oxford University Press, appeared in 1989.

[17] See R. H. Popkin, 'The Historical Significance of Sephardic Judaism in 17th-Century Amsterdam', *American Sephardi*, 5 (1971–2), 16–32.

[18] See Henry Mechoulan's 'Abraham Pereyra: Esbozo biobibliografico', in his *Hispanidad y Judaismo en tiempos de Espinoza: Edicion de La certeza del camino de Abraham Pereyra* (Salamanca, 1987), 49–54, Pereyra, who was one of the most important figures in the Amsterdam Jewish community, did not know Hebrew. Pereyra pointed this out himself in his 'Prologo al lector', ibid. 103.

had fled to Holland. When they built their great synagogue, these were open to the public, and many Christians came to services and discussed religious matters with them.[19] Hence they were on public display, and had to be careful about expressing their views about Christianity lest they offend their fellow inhabitants.

As a result, a literature emerged in Amsterdam that was written but not printed, and that circulated primarily amongst members of the Jewish community. There are only a couple of cases, which will be discussed below, of non-Jews who knew of this literature before the end of the seventeenth century. And it will be the claim of this chapter that it was the increasing discovery of this material by non-Jews that intensified the developing scepticism about, and/or denial of, Christianity by deists and proto-atheists. Most of the material has still not yet been printed, and a scholarly edition of only one item has just been published for the first time in 1988![20] Greatly diluted versions have appeared, sometimes with a preface stating that the material is only for the use of the Jewish community and that, if it is found by anyone else, it should be returned unread; then it is said that the work is printed but not published.

Apparently, the earliest items of this genre are polemics by Elijah Montalto, and a slightly earlier work, *Chizzuk emunah* by Isaac ben Abraham Troki. The latter work was published in 1681, with a Latin translation by the anti-Semitic German orientalist Johann Christoph Wagenseil, as a horrendous example of what the Jews thought about Christianity. Wagenseil had obtained a copy in North Africa.[21]

Chizzuk emunah, or *The Fortification of the Faith*, or *Faith*

---

[19] Menasseh ben Israel remarked that more than half the people who attended Synagogue services were Christians, and the paintings of services at the Portuguese Synagogue in the 17th century seem to bear this out. Various Christians like Peter Serrarius and Samuel Fisher described attending services.

[20] This is H. P. Salomon's edition of Mortera's *Tratado da verdade da lei de Moises*, cited in n. 10 above (hereafter Mortera, *Tratado*). Salomon intends to publish editions of other works of Mortera, plus the sermons of his which are at UCLA.

[21] It appears in Johann Christoph Wagenseil, *Tela ignae Satanae* (Altdorf, 1681).

Strengthened—the title of the nineteenth-century toned-down version that is currently available in paperback[22]—is not part of the Jewish tradition at all. It was written in 1593 by a Lithuanian Karaite teacher, who was arguing with Roman Catholics, Lutherans, Greek Orthodox Catholics, Socinians, and others in Vilna (Vilnius).[23] The Karaites are a group that broke with traditional Judaism in the eighth and ninth centuries AD over their refusal to accept the authority of the Talmud. They were fundamentalists *avant la lettre*, and based their religion solely on the Old Testament. They were apparently sufficiently strong for several centuries to warrant many orthodox Jewish attacks, and a total refusal by rabbinical Jews to recognise Karaites as Jews. Rabbis would, and still will, refuse to marry a Jew and a Karaite.[24] Hence, the views of a Karaite teacher would usually be of little or no interest to Jews.

However, in the case of Isaac Troki's work, one finds that it exists in Spanish, Portuguese, Dutch, and French translation in the Jewish archives in Amsterdam, in elegantly prepared manuscript versions.[25] No other anti-Christian text was treated with such respect. This may be due to the special circumstances of the Sephardic Jews in Amsterdam and the Karaites in Lithuania. Troki, just a few miles from Vilna, was the centre of the oldest and most important Karaite community in the country. During the sixteenth and the first half of the seventeenth century Troki was the intellectual and religious centre for the Karaites in Lithuania and Poland. They had been given full equality with Christians, and, as Isaac Troki's text indicates, they frequently conversed and argued with Christians.[26] In offering his arguments, Isaac Troki apeals only to what is in the Bible and to the facts of

---

[22] Isaac Troki, *Faith Strengthened*, trans. Moses Mocatta, introd. Trude Weiss-Rosmarin (New York, 1970). On the cover it says, '1200 Biblical Refutations to Christian Missionaries'.

[23] Weiss-Rosmarin, 'Introduction', to Troki, *Faith Strengthened*, pp. viii–ix.

[24] See the article by Leon Nemoy, 'Karaites', in the *Encyclopedia Judaica*, x. 761–83. It is rumoured that Lavrentia Beria's mother was a Karaite.

[25] L. Fuks and R. G. Fuks-Mansfeld, *Hebrew and Judaic Manuscripts in Amsterdam Public Collections*, ii (Leiden, 1975), entry nos. 188, 192, 211, 212, 217, and 222.

[26] Weiss-Rosmarin, 'Introduction', pp. viii–ix.

history, ancient and modern, and not to Talmudic interpretations. His material was therefore perfectly intelligible to the
Amsterdam Jews who had emerged from their Christian
backgrounds. Once the work was translated into languages
they knew, they saw that it contained a host of powerful
arguments against the Christian reading of Jewish prophecies, and against the Christian claims that historical developments showed that they were right and the Jews were
wrong.

On the first score, Isaac Troki argued that it was evident
that Jesus was not the Messiah, 'firstly, from his pedigree;
secondly, from his acts; thirdly, from the period in which he
lived; and fourthly, from the fact that during his existence,
the promises were not fulfilled which are to be realised in the
advent of the *expected* Messiah, whereas the fulfilment of the
conditions alone can warrant a belief in the identity of
Messiah.'[27]

With regard to interpreting historical developments in
Jewish and non-Jewish history from the first century
onwards, Isaac Troki insisted that these do not constitute
evidence for the truth of Christianity. The disasters of Jewish
history are judgements on Jewish actions at various times,
and have nothing to do with the story of Jesus.[28] But the fact
that, in spite of the disasters, the Jews still exist as a
recognizable group shows that they are still under divine
protection.[29] On the other hand, Christian history is fraught
with negative developments that suggest that God is not
protecting Christendom. Its great rival, Islam, has flourished
for a thousand years and has conquered many of the oldest
and most important Christian centres. At this very moment,
the Ottoman Turks have entered the heartland of European
Christianity and are threatening to overwhelm it. Do the
successes of Islam and the Turks disprove Christianity?[30] If
not, then why should the problems of Jewish history disprove
Judaism, or constitute a judgement upon its merits? (One can
understand why the victims of the Spanish Inquisition should
find this sort of argument congenial, and should want to

[27] Troki, *Faith Strengthened*, ch. 1: 5.   [28] Ibid., ch. 2: 14–17.
[29] Ibid., ch. 5: 20–2.   [30] Ibid. 21.

make it known to brethren who could only read Spanish, Portuguese, French, or Dutch.)

As mentioned earlier, Isaac Troki's text has not been an important one for Jews, except in seventeenth-century Amsterdam and in mid-nineteenth-century England.[31] However, it seems to have been powerful enough to be seriously refuted in Germany both in the seventeenth century and by conversionist groups just before the Nazi era.[32]

The two anti-Christian writings of Marie de' Medici's doctor, Elijah Montalto, were also popular among the Amsterdam Jews. There are quite a few copies in Spanish and Portuguese of his analysis of the so-called proof text, Isaiah 53, and a copy of his Latin answer to Catholicism.[33] The first, carefully argued against the Christian interpretation, was interesting enough to be published in English in 1790 by a deist, 'Philo-Veritas', as a critique of intolerant Christianity.[34]

During the seventeenth century many anti-Christian works were written, but not published, in Amsterdam by scholars who settled there. These indicate a broad knowledge of the contemporary Christian literature and of Christian critiques of Judaism. Historical, textual, and theological–political historical arguments are offered against Christianity and against specific Christian authors, some of whom were known personally to the Jewish scholars. The two most important Jewish authors of this genre of disputative writings were Saul Levi Mortera and Isaac Orobio de Castro. The former had been Montalto's secretary in Paris, and became chief rabbi and *haham* (wise man) of the Portuguese Synagogue in Amsterdam. The latter had been a royal physician in Spain and a professor of philosphy and of medicine, first in Spain and then in Toulouse, before fleeing to Amsterdam.[35]

Until now, Mortera has been chiefly known in Western

---

[31] It was translated by Moses Mocatta, and issued in London in 1851.

[32] Weiss-Rosmarin, 'Introduction', pp. vi–vii.

[33] Fuks and Fuks-Mansfeld, *Hebrew and Judaic Manuscripts*, nos. 198, 214, 225, and 226. Other copies exist in libraries in Europe and America.

[34] *A Jewish Tract on the Fifty-Third Chapter of Isaiah, Written by Dr. Montalto in Portuguese and Translated from his Manuscript by Philo-Veritas* (London, 1790).

[35] On Orobio's career, see R. H. Popkin, 'Orobio de Castro', *Encyclopedia Judaica*, 1475–7, and Kaplan, *Christianity to Judaism*.

thought for his role in the excommunication of Spinoza. He was the leader of the Synagogue tribunal that ratified the expulsion of the young rebel. In the relevant literature Mortera appears as Spinoza's chief persecutor. In the earliest biography of the philosopher, attributed to Jean Maximilien Lucas, Mortera is portrayed as a rigidly orthodox Talmudist, completely out of touch with the modern world.[36] As we have already seen, he was in fact quite different. He had been court secretary to Elijah Montalto at the Louvre in Paris for several years, and *then* became one of the leading teachers and preachers of the new Jewish community of Amsterdam.

Until recently, it was not known for certain where Mortera came from, some surmising that he was a Portuguese New Christian, like Montalto.[37] The recent study of him by H. P. Salomon has revealed that Mortera was an Ashkenazic Jew from Venice who became involved with Montalto and became his secretary, writing down some of his scientific medical works. Mortera had apparently had some Jewish training in Venice, and knew more Hebrew than Montalto.[38] He joined Montalto when he was about 13 years old, and went to Paris with him then. When Montalto died, Mortera carried his body to Holland for burial, and stayed there as a teacher and a leader of the Jewish community.

He wrote several treatises in Portuguese defending Judaism, including a debate with a priest at Rouen.[39] In the last year of his life he wrote his *Tratado da verdade da lei de Moises (Treatise on the Truth of the Law of Moses)*. Many manuscripts of this work exist in the original Portuguese and in Spanish translation, often with elegant illustrations. The holograph manuscript is in the collection of Ets Haim, the school of the Portuguese Jewish community of Amsterdam. It is over 400 folios long. It has just been published in a

---

[36] This picture of Mortera is presented in [Jean Maximilien Lucas], 'The Life of the Late Mr. de Spinosa', published in Abraham Wolf (ed.), *The Oldest Biography of Spinoza* (New York, 1928), 44–56.

[37] H. P. Salomon, 'Haham Saul Levi Morteira en de Portuguese Nieuw-Christenen', *Studio Rosenthaliana*, 10 (1976), 127–41.

[38] H. P. Salomon, La Vraie excommunication de Spinoza', in H. Bots and M. Kerkhof (eds.), *Forum Literarum* (Amsterdam-Maarsen, 1984), 181–99.

[39] For a list of Mortesa's writings, see Mortera, *Tratado*, pp. xvii–xx and lxi–lxiv.

facsimile edition, with transcription, by Salomon—the first
actual printing of this work.[40]

Salomon describes it as 'the most extensive and comprehensive book produced until then by a Jewish author about all
forms of Christian dogma; the first critical analysis of the
New Testament couched in the vernacular; the only work of
its kind ever written in Portuguese'.[41] Mortera explained that
the primary purpose of the work was to convince the less
rigid Dutch Protestants, the 'Chrétiens sans église', the
Mennonites, the Collegiants, and similar groups that the New
Testament was not a divine document, and that they should
adopt a Jewish kind of Christianity, derived from, or inspired
by, the Old Testament.[42] (There were Judaizing Christians or
philo-Semitic Christians, like Peter Serrarius, Adam Boreel,
John Dury, who were in close contact with the Jewish
community and often attended Jewish religious services.
Elsewhere I have attempted to show that some of them tried
to work out a joint Jewish-Christian formulation of their
religious expectations with Jewish leaders like Menasseh ben
Israel and Nathan Shapira.[43])

The beginning of the *Tratado* aims to show why it is that
Jews accept the Old Testament as God's message, but do not
accept the New Testament in the same way. Presumably the
Judaizing Christians, who root their religion *first* in the Old
Testament, are able to recognize that that alone is enough,
and that the New Testament is not a divine sequel. The first
thirty chapters concentrate on presenting the Jewish case for
the divinity of the Old Testament, and for the total adequacy
of the divine message contained therein to guide mankind.[44]
Mortera ends this section by citing some Christian authors

[40] This is the manuscript listed as no. 187 in Fuks and Fuks-Mansfeld, *Hebrew
and Judaic Manuscripts*, 91–2. Salomon gives a facsimile reproduction and transcription of the text in his edition.

[41] H. P. Salomon, in a proposed blurb announcement for the forthcoming
Portuguese edition of his introduction and Mortera's text.

[42] Mortera, *Tratado*, ch. 2.

[43] See R. H. Popkin, 'Some Aspects of Jewish–Christian Interchanges in Holland
and England 1640–1700', in van den Berg and van der Wall, *Jewish–Christian
Relations*, 3–32, and 'Rabbi Nathan Shapira's Visit to Amsterdam in 1657', in J.
Michman and T. Levie (eds.), *Dutch Jewish History* (Jerusalem, 1984), 185–205.

[44] Mortera, *Tratado*, chs. 1–30: 1–119.

on this, including John Calvin on the divinity of the law of Moses.[45]

Next Mortera argued that the difference between the Mosaic law and what is found in the New Testament is essentially the difference between what is divine and what is merely human. Then he contended that God's word is misrepresented in the New Testament in order to justify the separation from the Mosaic law.[46] The last chapters insist that the law of Moses is all that is needed to live a godly life, and Calvin is used to justify this claim of the self-sufficiency of Jewish law.[47]

Mortera exhibited a great knowledge of Jewish and Christian biblical texts, and of Jewish and Christian history, derived from sources that would be familiar to Christian exegetes and from Christian explanations of texts. He used materials from the Church Councils to rebut claims of Jesus' divinity, and he used Calvin to buttress the Jewish basis of Christianity and, as in chapter 41, to attack the alleged idolatrous Catholic interpretations and practices.[48]

Mortera's text is genuinely formidable, and, as we shall see, was regarded as such as soon as it became known to the Enlightenment world. Another kind of attack on Christianity appears in the writings of Isaac Orobio de Castro, who had been trained as a scholastic philosopher in Spain. He offered a more theoretical attack on the 'metaphysics' of Christianity (as well as on the metaphysics of naturalism in his answers to Prado and Spinoza).

Orobio was born in 1620 in Braganza, Portugal; today the town has a Rua Orobio de Castro, where he is identified as 'om dos maias sabios do seu tempo'.[49] He studied philosophy and medicine in Spain, became a professor of metaphysics at Alcala, and a royal physician and counsellor. He was arrested by the Inquisition for practising Judaism, and was tortured

---

[45] Ibid. 119.

[46] Ibid., chs. 31–62: 119A–356.

[47] Ibid., chs. 63–71: 357–419.

[48] Ibid., ch. 41: 185–92.

[49] The entire text of the inscription on a tablet on the Rua Orobio de Castro is reproduced in a handwritten note by Augusto d'Esaguy to a presentation copy of his article, 'The Dramatic Life of Orobio de Castro', *Bulletin of the Institute of the History of Medicine*, 5 (1937), 822–6. This copy of the offprint is in my possession.

and forced to confess. He fled to France, where he became royal professor of pharmacy at the University of Toulouse. Finally, deciding to renounce his Christian existence, he moved to Amsterdam, where he was circumcised and joined the Jewish community in 1662. He quickly became one of its leading intellectual figures. He wrote poetry and also composed philosophical defences of Judaism.[50] He began by attacking Juan de Prado, whom he had known as a doctor in Spain before the latter came to Holland and became an intimate of Spinoza, and he probably induced the young Spinoza to become a rebel. In a work that has not yet been found, Prado had argued that the law of nature takes precedence over the law of Moses. Orobio presented a rationalistic rejoinder to Prado and his son.[51] He also wrote a metaphysical defence of Judaism, using mainly Spanish scholastic materials, in answer to Alonso de Cepeda.[52]

His two most famous works are, first, his answer to Spinoza in geometrical form, *Certamen philosophicum propugnatum veritatis divinae ac naturalis* (1684), which was published in Fénelon's collection of answers to Spinoza, and appeared in several versions[53] (it is the only known answer to Spinoza by a member of the Spanish-Portuguese community of Amsterdam[54]); second, his major anti-Christian work, *Prevenciones divinas contra la vana idolatria de las gentes*, which circulated in manuscript form. There are many transcripts of it

[50] Full details on Orobio's career are in Kaplan, *From Christianity to Judaism*.

[51] Orobio wrote *Epistola invectiva contra Prado, un philosopho medico que dudava a no creva la verdad de la divina escriture, y pretendio encubir su malicia con la afectada confession de Dios y la ley de naturaleza: Carta apologetica al Doctor Prado* (against Juan de Prado), and a letter to Prado's son, who tried to defend his father. These works are in manuscript in Amsterdam and Paris. Some of the text appears in Israel S. Revah, *Spinoza and Juan de Prado* (The Hague, 1959).

[52] This work is entitled *Repuesta a una persona que dudaba si el libro de Raimundo Lulio nuevamente traducido y comentato, por don alonso de Zepeda era intelligible, y si concluyan sus discursos.* It exists in manuscript in Amsterdam; Fuks and Fuks-Mansfeld, *Hebrew and Judaic Manuscripts*, no. 198. Revah found that the work was published with a Latin translation in Brussels in 1666 by Cepeda in his defence of Raimund Lull: Revah, *Spinoza*, 31 n.

[53] It was published several times both separately and as part of Fénelon's collection of answers to Spinoza. Bayle commented on it in his article on Spinoza, in the *Dictionnaire historique et critique*. A French manuscript of it is in Bordeaux.

[54] There are indications that there is also an answer by Pinhero, but it has not been found.

in European and American libraries, some of them most carefully copied with illustrations.[55] In the Ets Haim collection there is one copy that has a note on the flyleaf in Orobio's hand, stating that he did not publish the work for fear of causing scandal, but that he had sent it to the Jesuits in Brussels, who liked it very much.[56] The work constitutes the most philosophical Jewish answer to Christianity, challenging the metaphysics of Trinitarianism as well as developing the historical and textual arguments of contemporary Jews against Christian interpretations of Scripture, religious history, and world events. At the height of the Enlightenment, the *Prevenciones divinas* was partly abridged in a work attributed to Baron d'Holbach, *Israel venge* (1770).[57] Two English translations of the French appeared in the nineteenth century, one entitled *Israel Defended, or The Jewish Exposition of the Hebrew Prophecies Applied by the Christians to their Messiah by Isaac Orobio. Translated from the French; and Printed Expressly for the Use of Young Persons of the Jewish Faith.* [NOT PUBLISHED], *London 1838*.[58] Although the text is much toned down from the French, the translator, Grace Aguilar, said that the work was not intended for controversies or to make converts; it was only to make Jews aware of the principles of their own faith. 'Should these pages ever meet the eye of other religionists, the translator earnestly entreats these facts may be remembered.'[59] A minister actively engaged in trying to convert Jews, Alexander McCaul of Trinity College, Dublin, put out a less toned-down text, *Israel Avenged: By Don Isaac Orobio*, with a line-by-line refutation.[60]

[55] There are copies in Holland, Paris, London, Iberia, and America. Many are noted in Kaplan, *From Christianity to Judaism*.

[56] See no. 234 in Fuks and Fuks-Mansfeld, *Hebrew and Judaic Manuscripts*. This is HS. EH48 E42 of the Ets Haim collection, presently located at the National Library of Israel in Jerusalem. On p. 1 it says: 'Este papel admirable no se imprimio por no permitirlo los de la nacion hebrea por no causar el menor Escandalo en materia de religion, mas se remitio manuscripto a Bruselas donde fue my aplaudido de los Jesuitas que otro hombres doctos todo sea en honra de Dios y Gloria de su santissima Ley.'

[57] Isaac Orobio de Castro, *Israel vengé, ou Exposition naturelle des prophéties hébraïques que les chrétiens appliquent à Jesus leur prétendu Messie* (London[?], 1770). This work was reprinted in Paris in 1845.

[58] There is a copy in the British Library, shelf-mark 4034 b. 18.

[59] Isaac Orobio de Castro, *Israel Defended* (London, 1838), p. vi.

[60] Alexander McCaul, *Israel Avenged: By Don Isaac Orobio* (London, 1839–40), British Library shelf-mark 4034 g. 37.

Perhaps more famous than his writings was the disputation that Orobio had with the Dutch Remonstrant Philip van Limborch in 1686. This was published by the latter under the title *Amica collatio cum erudito Judaeo* in 1687, the year in which Orobio died.[61] Limborch appended to the text of the debate the first publication of the autobiography of the Jewish heretic Uriel da Costa, to show both how badly the Jews had treated him and how irreligious a Jewish heretic could become.[62] John Locke was apparently present at the disputation, and both the correspondence between Limborch and Locke and Locke's review of the episode seem to imply that Limborch had won.[63] However, as the text—which was published twice—indicates, Orobio deftly put down all the Christian arguments against Judaism. The Synagogue worried about the effect of the affair, and forbade members to carry on disputes with Christians, while, as Jacques Basnage indicated, Christian intellectuals in The Netherlands tended to give up trying to convince or convert Jews through disputation.[64]

The best of the anti-Christian polemicists, who were forced converts, had scholastic and humanist training. They knew about syllogisms and about humanist criticism, and could put

[61] Philip van Limborch, *De veritate religionis Christianae: Amica collatio cum erudito Judaeo* (Gouda, 1687).

[62] Uriel da Costa, *Exemplar humanae vitae*. There is some question as to whether the autobiography is genuine. It does not correspond to some of the facts in da Costa's life, and it omits large parts of his career. The text published by van Limborch is from a manuscript that his father-in-law possessed. It is not in da Costa's hand, and it is not a continuous text. The manuscript is in the collection of the University of Amsterdam.

[63] In *The Correspondence of John Locke*, ed. E. S. De Beer, iii (Oxford, 1978), Locke and van Limborch discussed the debate in letters 958, 959, 963, and 964 (pp. 258–61 and 268–72). The letters are all from Sept. 1687, when the debate was published. There is some question as to whether Locke wrote the long review of the debate in the *Bibliothèque universelle*, 7 (1687), 289–330. In a set of that journal that belonged to Robert Shackleton of Oxford, I saw marks made either by Locke or Jean le Clerc, indicating which of the reviews were by Locke. Such a mark appears at the head of the review of the Orobio–Limborch debate.

[64] After the debate, members of the Portuguese Synagogue were forbidden to debate with Christians. Locke and van Limborch (see the letters cited in the previous note) took this as a sign of victory for the Christians. In the last chapter of Jacques Basnage's *Histoire des juifs* (15 vols.; La Haye, 1715) he discussed the sad fact that debates with Jews did not help the Christian cause. On the debate, see also P. T. van Rooden and J. W. Wesselius, 'The Early Enlightenment and Judaism; The "Civil Dispute" between Phillipus van Limborch and Isaac Orobio de Castro', *Studia Rosenthaliana*, 21 (1987), 140–53.

the traditional Jewish reasons for rejecting Christianity in terms of powerful objections to Christian claims. Jacques Basnage's despairing concluding remarks to the *Histoire des Juifs*, in which he surveyed the debates that had transpired in the seventeenth century, pointed out that the Jews usually won because they knew the material better and had better arguments.[65] After the Orobio–van Limborch debate of 1687 he advised giving up debating, and letting God take charge of converting the Jews.[66] Later on Jean-Jacques Rousseau suggested that the Jews must have good arguments for not becoming Christians, but that they are not given the chance to express them.[67]

In fact, in 1782 a Dutch society offered a prize to any Jew who would present his arguments. Zalkind Hourwitz, a royal librarian to Louis XVI, sent in his arguments and kept demanding his prize, since the society apparently found no way of answering him.[68] Moses Mendelssohn, who was being urged to convert by the Swiss physiognomist Lavater, threatened to publish his objections against Christianity. This led Lessing, Kant, and Herder to support Mendelssohn's refusal to convert.[69]

In the course of the sixteenth and seventeenth centuries Catholic and Protestant philo-Semites thought that by making Jews more aware of their beliefs, and, in John Dury's phrase, 'making Christianity less offensive to the Jews',[70] the Jews would convert.[71] a great deal of collaboration therefore occurred in editing, annotating, explaining, and publishing Jewish non-biblical texts, such as the Talmud, the Mishna,

---

[65] Basnage, *Histoire des juifs*, xv, bk. IX, ch. 89, esp. s. 28.

[66] Ibid. 113: 'Il semble aussi que Dieu les reserve à une Conversion, qui ne se peut faire que par une Direction extraordinaire de la Providence & de la Grace.'

[67] Cited in Zalkind Hourwitz, *Apologie des juifs* (Paris, 1789), 30.

[68] Ibid. 31–2.

[69] On this, see Alexander Altmann, *Moses Mendelssohn: A Biographical Study* (University of Alabama, 1973), ch. 3.

[70] John Dury [and Samuel Hartlib], *Englands Thankfulnesse, or An Humble Remembrance Presented to the Committee for Religion in the High Court of Parliament* (London, 1642). This rare pamphlet is reprinted in Charles Webster, *Samuel Hartlib and the Advancement of Learning* (Cambridge, 1970), 90–7. The reference to making Christianity less offensive to the Jews is on p. 95.

[71] On these views of Dury and Hartlib, see R. H. Popkin, 'The First College of Jewish Studies', *Revue des études juives*, 143 (1989), 351–64.

the Zohar, and the Lurianic cabbalistic works. Rabbis and Christian Hebraists worked together, editing these works in Hebrew, Latin, and Spanish.[72]

This increase in knowledge about what the Jews believed seems to have produced few conversions of Jews, but it did lead to the reinforcing of Jewish objections and to the stirring of doubts among some Christians, partly because of the Jewish anti-Christian arguments. Some of these arguments were heard in debates. It was rumoured that stronger refutations existed, especially by Mortera and Orobio de Castro, but Christians could not obtain copies of the works (except for the Jesuits in Brussels). Anthony Collins complained that he was unable to obtain a copy of Mortera's most important anti-Christian work.[73] A couple of years ago I discovered how and when, but not why, the Amsterdam documents began to be passed into the general Christian world.

The Jewish arguments to show that the Christians were wrong provided part of the irreligious arsenal of the Enlightenment. These arguments were slightly known: one scholar at Leiden had a manuscript of one of Elijah Montalto's tracts;[74] the Jesuits in Brussels had read Orobio; when he was in England, Menasseh ben Israel passed on a couple of anti-Christian polemics to Ralph Cudworth;[75] Anthony Collins had heard about Mortera's arguments, and later used some of

---

[72] Cf. R. H. Popkin, 'Some Aspects of Jewish–Christian Theological Interchanges', in van den Berg and van der Wall, *Jewish–Christian Relations*; David S. Katz's forthcoming study of Rabbis Isaac and Joseph Abendana; and Allison Coudert's discussion of the co-operative effort involved in the publication of the *Kabbala denudata*, in 'A Cambridge Platonist's Kabbalist Nightmare', *Journal of the History of Ideas*, 35 (1975), 635–45.

[73] Cf. Anthony Collins, *A Discourse of the Grounds and Reasons of the Christian Religion* (London, 1724), 82–3 n.

[74] P. T. von Rooden, *Constantin l'Empereur 1591–1648* (Leiden, 1985), 186–7, indicated that Constantin l'Empereur, professor of Hebrew and theology at Leiden, had seen some of Montalto's writings.

[75] This is discussed in Richard Kidder, *A Demonstration of the Messias; In which the Truth of the Christian Religion is Proved Especially against the Jews* (3 vols.; London, 1684–1700), ii, sigs. A4–A4ᵛ, and iii, pp. iii–iv. The preface to Ralph Cudworth's *The True Intellectual System of the Universe* cites a letter from Cudworth to Thurloe describing the former's outraged reaction to the manuscripts he received from Menasseh. See David S. Katz, *Philo-Semitism and the Readmission of the Jews to England, 1603–1655* (Oxford, 1982), 234 and n.

the Jewish material in challenging Christianity;[76] part of Orobio's answer to Christianity came out in his debate with Philip van Limborch. But the thoroughgoing attack on Christianity passed into general European information only when a collection of Jewish manuscripts in Amsterdam entered Christian hands.

In 1716, in the last edition of his *Histoire des Juifs*, Jacques Basnage explained that a further edition of his book was needed because he had suddenly come into possession of manuscripts hitherto unknown to Christian scholars, works by Montalto, Orobio, Mortera, Judah Leon, and others. He cited these from something called the *Biblioteca Sarraziana*.[77] I searched for such a library, and, finally, I found that it belonged to Sarraz, Basnage's son-in-law, a Protestant minister who became the private secretary to the Elector of Saxony, who was also the King of Poland. Sarraz sold his library at auction in September 1715 in The Hague, and the *Biblioteca Sarraziana* is the catalogue of the auction sale, about 800 pages long.[78] It lists as one of its treasures these Jewish manuscripts from Amsterdam that had never been available before.[79] (There is no information on how or when Sarraz obtained them.[80]) The copies of the auction catalogue at Wolfenbüttel, Oxford, The Hague, and Harvard list the prices paid. Some of the Jewish manuscripts fetched great sums.[81] It is not yet possible to tell who bought them, but soon the Duke of Sussex owned a copy of Mortera's chief

---

[76] Collins's attack on Christianity in *A Discourse of the Grounds and Reasons of the Christian Religion* (1724) appears to borrow heavily from the Jewish polemics.

[77] Basnage, *Histoire des juifs*, pp. xlvii, lxxiii, and xv, chs. 36 and 39.

[78] *Bibliotheca Sarraziana distrahenda per Abr. de Hondt et H. Scheurleer, Bibliop: ad 16 diem Septb. 1715* (The Hague, 1715). For further details, see R. H. Popkin, 'Jacques Basnage's *Histoire des juifs* and the *Bibliotheca Sarraziana*', *Studia Rosenthaliana*, 21 (1987), 154–62.

[79] The first example of the rare items in the sale is described as 'Manuscripts aliquot Hispanics, quae celeberrimos habent Judaeos Authores': *Bibliotheca Sarraziana*, s. 3, p. 19.

[80] Gerald Cerny, who recently published *Theology, Politics and Letters at the Crossroads of European Civilization*: *Jacques Basnage and the Baylean Huguenot Refugees in the Dutch Republic* (The Hague, 1987), is investigating the matter.

[81] Orobio's masterpiece sold for 64 guilders, Mortera's for 30, and Montalto's for 10. On the prices listed in the copies of the catalogues, see Popkin, 'Basnage and the *Bibliotheca Sarraziana*', 159–60.

work,[82] Baron d'Holbach published a portion of Orobio's work, entitled *Israel vengé*, as part of his anti-Christian campaign,[83] and Voltaire was using material from Mortera.[84] Hamburg University had some of the items in the mid-nineteenth century.[85]

The radical Enlightenment bolstered its sceptical attack on Christianity by using the anti-Christian Jewish polemics. By 1724 Anthony Collins was familiar with some of the material, and he used the central theme that appears, among others, in both Mortera and Orobio, namely that, since the Old Testament prophecies were not literally fulfilled by Jesus, there is therefore no connection between the Old and New Testaments, and Christianity is groundless.[86] In the copy of *Israel vengé* in the Bibliothéque Nationale in Paris there is a manuscript note saying that 'Orobio prouve par l'histoire sacrée et les passages de l'Ecriture que le messie n'est pas encore venu' and that Jesus was not he.[87] At the end of the volume there is a letter from the *philosophe* Burigny to the Abbé de Saint-Leger, dated Paris, 2 March 1780, stating that the Christians cannot answer Orobio.[88] Burigny said that he had copied two of Orobio's manuscripts, apart from the ones that d'Holbach had published.[89] So, late in the Enlightenment, some of the Jewish anti-Christian manuscripts were being spread among the *philosophes*.

An interesting example of the effect that this anti-Christian

---

[82] It is listed in the *Bibliotheca Sussexiana* (London, 1827). On it, see Popkin, 'Basnage and the *Bibliotheca Sarraziana*', 160 n. 39.

[83] As cited above in n. 57, this was published in 1770 and printed again in 1845.

[84] Voltaire used some of the Jewish anti-Christian material in his article 'Messie', in his *Dictionnaire philosophique* (1764). Some of his points seem to come from Mortera's work, which he could have known about through Collins's use of items in it.

[85] Moritz Steinschneider, *Catalog der hebraischen Handschriften in der Stadtbibliothek zu Hamburg* (Hamburg, 1878), 170, lists an item (no. 352) with a title much like that of a work by Rabbi Judah Leon cited by Basnage. The work is no longer listed in the new Hamburg catalogue, but a work by Mortera on the Talmud, as well as Drobio's *Prevenciones* and Montalto's treatise on Isaiah 53, are listed. See the catalogue of Hebrew manuscripts edited by Ernest Roth and Hans Strelle.

[86] This is part of Anthony Collins's attack on Christianity in his *Discourse of the Grounds and Reasons of the Christian Religion*.

[87] Bibliothèque Nationale, rés. D2. 5193. This is the first handwritten note in the book.

[88] Ibid., MS letter at end of volume.

[89] Ibid., letter of Burigny. Another note in another hand mentions Rabbi Isaac [Troki]'s *Chissuk emunah*.

material had is provided by a minister trained at Harvard, George Bethune English (1787–1828), who came across items in the Harvard Library. He studied them, and then took them to Rabbi Gershom Seixas in New York in order to discuss the points at issue.[90] English returned to Boston and published a disproof of Christianity, a work entitled *The Grounds of Christianity Examined by Comparing the New Testament with the Old*, in 1813.[91] He said that he found the Jewish reasons for rejecting Christianity unanswerable.[92] He was immediately dismissed from his ministry, went to the Middle East, became a Muslim in Egypt, and was involved in various Turkish affairs.[93]

The seventeenth-century Jewish critique of Christianity became part of the religious scepticism of the Enlightenment. The use of some of the Jewish arguments led the deists to challenge Christianity as the fulfilment of Judaism and as a supernaturally based religion. Since Judaism was not a live option for them, what was left of scriptural religion was only an ethical view. As Zalkind Hourwitz, the royal librarian of the oriental collection in Paris at the time of the Revolution, said, one either has to give up Christian claims of superiority over the Jews or one furnishes victorious arms to Pyrrhonism and irreligion;[94] either one accepts Jewish history shorn of the supernatural or one has only deism or atheism. Even Tom Paine claimed that he was saving what was good in religion with his deistic theophilanthropy opposed to the atheism of the Reign of Terror—in his case, doing so at the price of doubting the historicity of both the Old and New Testaments.[95]

The Jewish anti-Christian literature coming out of The Netherlands and its effects on Christian thinkers are part of

[90] On his career, see Walter L. Wright, jun., 'English, George Bethune', *Dictionary of American Biography* (20 vols.; London and New York, 1928–36), iii, 165.
[91] George Bethune English, *Grounds of Christianity Examined* (Boston, printed for the author, 1813).
[92] Ibid., p. xii.
[93] Wright, 'English, George Bethune'.
[94] Hourwitz, *Apologie des juifs*, 59.
[95] Tom Paine, *The Age of Reason*, in *The Writings of Tom Paine*, ed. Moncure Daniel Conway (4 vols.; New York, 1894–1896), iv. 205.

the story of how scepticism turned from friend to foe of religion. The forceful arguments, stated in modern form and backed by modern standards of evidence, indicated that reasonable people could not find a real, solid connection between the Jewish expectations in the Old Testament and the events portrayed in the New Testament. The theologies that tried to make these two stories part of the same theodicy became less than credible. And if Christianity lost its link to the Old Testament, what did it rest on, and what could be its meaningful content?

This, of course, is just part of the development, and it has to be seen in relation to the role played by the ideas in clandestine works such as Bodin's *Colloquium heptaplomeres*,[96] *Les Trois Imposteurs*,[97] *Theophrastus redivivus*,[98] and the use that deists and incipient atheists made of them in the late seventeenth and throughout the eighteenth century. Perhaps, when all these pieces are put together, we shall be in a better position to understand the amazing change that took place over two hundred years in attitudes towards scripturally based religion, and the reasons for that change. I suggest that one of the factors involved was the ability of Jewish thinkers, schooled in modern Christian thought, to raise the possibility that Christians were misreading the biblical texts, misinterpreting the prophecies made in the Old Testament, and failing to see that those prophecies had not been fulfilled in the New Testament. If one could give this serious consideration, then Christianity was not the fulfilment of Judaism, and was not

[96] On Bodin's *Colloquim heptaplomeres*, see the introduction by Marion L. Kuntz to Jean Bodin, *Colloquium of the Seven about the Secrets of the Sublime* (Princeton, NJ, 1975); François Berriot, 'La Fortune du Colloquium heptaplomeres', in Jean Bodin, *Colloque entre sept scavans qui sont de differens sentiments des secret cachez des choses revelez* (Geneva, 1984), pp. xv–l; and R. H. Popkin, 'Could Spinoza have known Bodin's *Colloquium heptaplomeres*?', *Philosophia*, 16 (1986), 307–14, and 'The Dispersion of Bodin's Dialogue in England, Holland and Germany', *Journal of the History of Ideas*, 48 (1988), 157–60.

[97] On *Les Trois Imposteurs*, see Silvia Berti's chapter (Ch. 7) in this book; Bertram E. Schwarzbach and A. W. Fairbairn, 'Sur les rapports entre les éditions du "Traité des trois imposteurs" et la tradition manuscrite de cet ouvrage', *Nouvelle de la République des lettres*, 2 (1987), 111–36; and R. H. Popkin, 'Spinoza and *Les Trois Imposteurs*', in E. M. Curley (ed.), *Proceedings of the International Spinoza Congress (Chicago 1987)* (Leiden, 1990).

[98] On the *Theophrastus redivivus*, see the edition of Guido Canziani and Gianni Paganini (2 vols.; Florence, 1982).

based upon it. Then, one could ask, did it have any genuine historical or theological basis at all? One could even come to the question raised by Napoleon Bonaparte and Bruno Bauer, of whether Jesus ever actually existed as a person[99] let alone as a divine being, and to the question raised by David Hume, Tom Paine, and a host of others, of whether the Old Testament was anything more than superstitious folk-literature?[100] When such questions could be asked, one had entered a world outside of traditional Judaism and Christianity, a world in which many of us are still floundering.

[99] This is asserted several times in Napoleon's table-talk, and became a notorious 'scholarly' view when advanced by Bauer a few decades later.

[100] See David Hume, 'Of Miracles', in his *Enquiry Concerning Human Understanding* (1748), and Paine, *The Age of Reason*.

7

The First Edition of the
Traité des trois imposteurs, and its
Debt to Spinoza's *Ethics*

SILVIA BERTI

A Missing Book

'The book about the three impostors has itself been the subject of a singular imposture. It is a question on which opinions differ.'[1] B. G. Struve's deliberately ironic and mysterious statement applies not only—as he intended—to the medieval and Renaissance literary myth of the three impostors, but also to the strange fate of an impious little book best known by the title under which it was reprinted several times during the last forty years of the eighteenth century, *Le Traité des trois imposteurs*. It was, however, first published in 1719, entitled *La Vie et L'Esprit de Spinosa*. Though the editor's name and the place of publication did not appear on the title-page, we know that it was published by Charles Levier at The Hague.

This edition includes a document of great importance for the history of Spinozism in the early eighteenth century, one that has until now escaped the attention of historians: the first printed French translation (indeed, probably the first French translation altogether) of a part of Spinoza's *Ethics*, the appendix to the first section. Though published, it was scarcely made public. In the *Avertissement* of this first edition

---

[*Editors' Note*. This is a substantially revised and partially abbreviated translation of Silvia Berti, '"La Vie et L'Esprit de Spinosa" (1719) e la prima traduzione francese dell' "Ethica"', *Rivista storica italiana*, 98 (1986), 5–46.]

[1] B. G. Struve, *Dissertatio historico litteraria de doctis impostoribus* (Jena, 1703), 16.

there appears a declaration that has only been confirmed by the assiduous but fruitless researches of generations of scholars: 'So few copies have been printed that the work will be scarcely less rare than it would have been if it had remained in manuscript.' *La Vie* and *L'Esprit* were in fact two distinct texts, probably by different authors, but they are often to be found together in the numerous manuscript copies that survive.

La Vie was a biography of Spinoza written around 1678 by one of his most devoted disciples, almost certainly Jean Maximilien Lucas (1636 or 1646–97), a French journalist who had emigrated to Holland and who was well known for his violent campaign against the absolutism of Louis XIV, which he waged in the columns of the numerous newspapers he edited, beginning with the *Quintessence*.[2] It was in *La Vie* that there first appeared a portrait of Spinoza as a mythical epitome of virtue—faultless, indifferent to poverty, and dedicated only to the solitary quest for truth. Thus, this image of Spinoza was being disseminated, if only amongst members of a restricted circle and through manuscript copies, almost twenty years before Bayle drew heavily upon it in his *Dictionnaire historique et critique* (1697).[3] There Bayle was sharply critical of the philosophy of this 'systematic atheist', but eloquent in praise of his virtue. In 1719 the text of *La Vie* was published twice, for it also appeared as an article in the *Nouvelles littéraires* (volume 10, pp. 40–74), edited in Amsterdam by du Sauzet. This publication caused such scandal that the volume was quickly withdrawn, and only a few copies were saved from destruction.

L'Esprit, the second and more substantial part of our barely published volume, is one of the most important documents

---

[2] On Lucas's life, see W. Meyer, 'Jean Maximilien Lucas', *Tijdschrift voor Boeken Bibliotheekwezen*, 4 (1906), 221–7, and the same author's entry on Lucas in P. C. Molhuysen and P. J. Blok (eds.), *Nieuw Nederlandsch biografisch Woordenboek* (10 vols.; Leiden, 1918), iv. 934–6.

[3] On Bayle as a reader and interpreter of Spinoza, see P. Vernière, *Spinoza et la pensée française avant la Révolution* (Paris, 1982; 1st edn., 1954), 287–306, and the excellent essay by L. Kolakowski, 'Pierre Bayle: Critique de la métaphysique spinoziste de la substance', in P. Dibon (ed.), *Pierre Bayle: Le Philosophe de Rotterdam* (Amsterdam, 1959), 66–80. Also helpful is A. Corsano, 'Bayle e Spinoza', *Giornale critico della filosofia italiana*, 56 (1977), 319–26.

for the early history of Spinozism, all the more important because it was the most widely available of all the clandestine manuscripts that circulated during the eighteenth century, usually appearing under the title *Traité des trois imposteurs.* Numerous copies survive in European and North American libraries. The argument of *L'Esprit* is bold and uncompromising. Its style is uncultivated, but highly effective. Its language is cutting and violent. The views it expresses are surprising, for its arguments, despite the occasional clumsiness with which they are expressed, are already those of the Enlightenment. In particular, the text tightly links the criticism of religion to the question of political freedom. The author maintains that blind prejudice preserves the ridiculous conceptions of God that men are brought up to believe, and that they never pause to examine. Ignorance and fear have given birth to superstition, have created the gods, and, assisted by the impostures of rulers, have transformed laws that are actually human into inviolable divine decrees. Thus the ideas that men form regarding the nature of the world are the products of imagination, not of reason.

The alternative conception of God that is constructed out of a critique of popular superstitions is of a being who is absolutely infinite, one of whose attributes is to be an infinite and eternal substance. Nevertheless, people still consult the Bible, although it is full of ridiculous fables, and still maintain the principles of Christianity, established on the basis of a book that survives only in unreliable copies and that is full of supernatural events—in other words, impossibilities. Thus, renouncing reason and adopting a superstitious faith, men subordinate themselves to the phantasms of their own imaginations.

'Religion' is the term for this subordination of reason to imagination, a subordination motivated by fear. Building on this foundation, Moses, the descendant of a magician, legitimated his role as a legislator by laying claim to a divine investiture, which he confirmed by carrying out fraudulent miracles. Later, Jesus Christ drew men to him by offering them the illusory expectation of a life after death. The Christians believed him to be God, although they recognized him as a man: which is equivalent to believing that a circle could be a square. Finally, the imposture was perfected by Muhammad, whose authority derived from force of arms and who claimed to be a prophet for all nations, sent to give witness to the true law of God, which had been corrupted by the Jews and Christians. Other beliefs that men have acquired over time, such as the belief in the immortality of the soul or in the existence of immaterial beings, are equally groundless.

Only some of these theses were derived from Spinoza. The whole of chapter 4 is drawn from Hobbes's *Leviathan*, chapter 12, 'Of Religion'. The last chapter is mainly a collage of passages taken from chapter 45 of *Leviathan*. Most of the passages that make up the four chapters on Jesus Christ are from Vanini's *De admirandis naturae reginae deaeque mortalium arcanis* and from La Mothe le Vayer's *De la vertu des payens*: their common source is Celsus (via Origen's *Contra Celsum*). The two chapters on the soul draw largely on Guillaume Lamy's *Discours anatomiques*.[4] When they published the book, Levier and his collaborators also added six chapters drawn from the principal works of Charron and Naudé. In addition, they wrote a wholly new chapter on a legislator they thought deserved more attention, Numa Pompilius.

We can now begin to grasp the political and intellectual significance of this extraordinary publishing enterprise, and the risk that those engaged in it ran. Their purpose was to construct and disseminate the first portable philosophical compendium of free-thought, at once anti-Christian and anti-absolutist. Drawing on texts of varying date, they sought to publicize their intellectual inheritance and to guarantee its survival.

We have a detailed and learned account of this first edition of *L'Esprit* in the article 'Impostoribus (liber de tribus)', in Prosper Marchand's *Dictionnaire historique*, which is also the primary and indispensable source for studying the centuries of accounts of legendary works on the three impos-

---

[4] For a more thorough study of the text's sources and structure, see my French-Italian edition of *Trattato dei tre impostori: La vita e Lo Spirito del Signor Benedetto de Spinoza* (Turin, forthcoming; an English translation of this edition will be published by Van Gorcum, Assen).

tors.[5] Marchand's vast learning made it hard to believe that he had invented this edition; nevertheless, throughout the nineteenth century no copy of it could be found. An ancient curse seemed to be at work, whereby those who dismissed the three great historical religions of the world as fraudulent would themselves be proved guilty of fraud.

One fact that suggested that Marchand was guilty of deliberately combining authentic learning with fantasy, to the point where the two could no longer be distinguished, was his claim that the second edition had been published under the title of *De tribus impostoribus* by Michel Böhm at Rotterdam (with a false Frankfurt-am-Main imprint) in 1721: no copy of this edition has ever been found.[6] When Brunet published the first monograph devoted to the *Traité* in 1860, he made it clear that he knew the 1719 edition only at second-hand, through Marchand's account.[7] So too Meinsma, in his superb book on Spinoza's circle: there he dedicated a few valuable pages to Lucas's biography of Spinoza, which he had read in a 1735 reprint, but he was obliged to confess that he had never succeeded in laying his hands on a copy of the *Nouvelles littéraires* of 1719.[8]

Only at the end of the century, in the course of research carried out by various distinguished Spinoza scholars and directed primarily towards establishing the authenticity of *La Vie* and dating its composition, was a copy of the 1719 Levier edition located in the library of Halle (an der Saale) University. This exciting discovery was made by Freudenthal, who went on to publish a critical edition of *La Vie*, in which he established the variant readings between the Levier edition and the text published in the *Nouvelles littéraires*.[9] This gave

[5] P. Marchand, *Dictionnaire historique* (2 vols.; The Hague, 1758–9), i. 312–29. On Marchand, see C. Berkvens-Stevelinck, *Prosper Marchand: La Vie et l'œuvre (1678–1756)* (Leiden, 1987).

[6] Marchand, *Dictionnaire historique*, i. 324.

[7] Philomueste Junior [P. Brunet], *Le Traité des trois imposteurs* (Paris, 1860). Also, J. C. Brunet, *Manuel du libraire*, 5th edn. (6 vols.; Paris, 1860–5), v. 944–5.

[8] K. O. Meinsma, *Spinoza en zijn Kring: Historisch-kritische Studiën over Hollandsche Vrijgeesten* ('s-Gravenhage, 1896). I cite the recent French translation, which has an updated editorial apparatus: *Spinoza et son cercle* (Paris, 1983), 6–9 and *passim*.

[9] J. Freudenthal, 'Die Lebensgeschichte Spinozas', in *Quellenschriften, Urkunden und nichtamtlichen Nachrichten* (Leipzig, 1899), 1–25 and 239–45.

rise to a lively debate between Freudenthal and Dunin-
Borkowski that resulted in a rigorous analysis of the available
facts about Spinoza's first biography, of continuing use to
later researchers.[10]

These authors, however, wasted few words on *L'Esprit*.
They felt for it that ill-concealed contempt that philosophers
often express towards documents in the history of ideas, even
those of the foremost importance, which they feel entitled to
dismiss as 'scarcely original' or 'lacking in unity of thought'
(historians, of course, are guilty of an opposite failing, often
paying no attention to the quality and originality of an
argument). As far as one can tell, neither Jacob Presser nor
Abraham Wolf (who, as we shall see, assumed a rather
peculiar attitude towards the text) was seriously interested in
establishing the heterodox and radical milieu within which
the *Traité* had been written.[11] They were the last to consult
the Levier edition.

The 1930s were years of extraordinary intellectual vigour,
during which an immense contribution was made to the
history of ideas. Between 1935 and 1939 seminal works
appeared by Paul Hazard, Ira O. Wade, and Franco Venturi.[12] These works transformed eighteenth-century studies,
placing the political and anti-Christian elements in the
Enlightenment in the foreground. Consequently, it became
essential to clarify the intellectual components of Spinozism,

[10] S. von Dunin-Borkowski, 'Zur Textgeschichte und Textkritik der ältesten
Lebensbeschreibung Benedikt Despinozas', *Archiv für Geschichte der Philosophie*,
18 (1904), 1–34. Through a study of a number of manuscripts, supplemented by
internal evidence, Dunin-Borkowski established that Lucas's *La Vie* had been
written in 1678 (pp. 20–1). See also J. Freudenthal, 'Ueber den Text der Lucasschen
Biographie Spinozas', *Zeitschrift für Philosophie und philosophische Kritik*, 126
(1905), 189–208, and id., *Spinoza: Sein Leben und seine Lehre* (Heidelberg, 1927;
1st edn., 1904), 256–8, 313–14. See also Dunin-Borkowski's *Der Junge De Spinoza:
Leben und Werdegang im Lichte der Weltphilosophie* (Münster, 1933; 1st edn.,
1910), 46–51, 530–2; and C. Gebhardt, *Spinoza: Lebensbeschreibungen und Ges-
präche* (Hamburg, 1914).

[11] J. Presser, *Das Buch 'De tribus impostoribus' (Von den drei Betrügern)*
(Amsterdam, 1926); *The Oldest Biography of Spinoza*, ed., trans., and introd. A.
Wolf (London, 1927; repr. New York, 1970).

[12] P. Hazard, *La Crise de la conscience européenne: 1685–1715* (Paris, 1935);
I. O. Wade, *The Clandestine Organization and Diffusion of Philosophic Ideas in
France from 1670 to 1750* (Princeton, 1938); F. Venturi, *La Jeunesse de Diderot (de
1713 à 1753)* (Paris, 1939).

and the process by which it was disseminated, for this seemed the most promising strategy for understanding the uncompromising attack upon revealed religion that lay at the origins of the Enlightenment.

It was with this question in mind that Wade dedicated an important chapter to the manuscript tradition of *Les Trois Imposteurs*. Wade could have made an invaluable contribution to the study of the first edition of *L'Esprit*, but, as far as one can tell, he never became acquainted with the German literature on the question, nor with Wolf's book.[13] He therefore remained ignorant of the existence of the Halle copy. The same was true of John Spink, who, in a 1937 article, reported on his extensive but fruitless enquiries: 'these editions [those of 1719 and 1721] cannot have been widely disseminated, for I have not been able to locate a single copy of either.'[14]

No one has seen the Halle copy since the war, for reasons that remain obscure. It is paradoxical that this crucial volume has disappeared again just as historiographical developments have at last led to the systematic study of the clandestine culture of the early Enlightenment. Nevertheless, it was much discussed. In its absence, other—much later—editions were called upon to testify in its stead, most commonly that of 1777. Such editions, however, contained numerous and sometimes substantial differences from that of 1719; most important, they all lacked the six additional chapters that had been spliced into the first edition.

Vernière, in his invaluable study of *Spinoza et la pensée française avant la Révolution*, wrote (following Marchand) that 'no work was to give rise to more commotion than the *Vie et L'Esprit de M. Benoit de Spinosa*'.[15] Through a perceptive analysis of various chapters in the 1768 edition, he demonstrated both the author's debt to Spinoza and also his deep-seated misinterpretation of his ideas, exposing the dis-

[13] Wade, *The Clandestine Organization*, 124–40, 277–321.

[14] J. S. Spink, 'La Diffusion des idées matérialistes et antireligieuses au début du xviiiᵉ siècle: Le *Theophrastus redivivus*', *Revue d'histoire littéraire de la France*, 44 (1937), 248–55 (p. 254).

[15] Vernière, *Spinoza et la pensée française*, 362.

crepancies between the arguments and intentions of Spinoza and those of his disciple. In more recent years interest in *L'Esprit* has continued to be lively.[16] Of particular interest are the contributions of Margaret Jacob and Richard Popkin. Jacob's study, based on manuscript sources, of the intellectual milieu that was responsible for the edition of 1719 claimed to be able to identify the author of *L'Esprit* as Jean Rousset de Missy, a collaborator of Levier's.[17] Popkin, in studying the theme of the three impostors and the manuscript tradition of *L'Esprit*, has brought to light new evidence, and has suggested that the text can be dated as early as 1656.[18] I shall deal with both of these claims below.[19]

So far, the fate of *L'Esprit* is like a story by Borges: a book with the characteristics of a manuscript, impossible to locate, known only through unreliable copies, and yet written about as if it had been widely consulted. From this fate, however, it is now released. The present author, working in the Research Library of the University of California at Los Angeles, with the help of a good deal of what Spinoza called the *auxilium Dei externum*, has found a copy of the first edition of *La Vie*

[16] J. S. Spink, *French Free-Thought from Gassendi to Voltaire* (London, 1960), 240–2; G. Ricuperati, *L'esperienza civile e religiosa di Pietro Giannone* (Milan, 1970), 423–31 (see also G. Ricuperati, 'Il problema della corporeità dell'anima dai libertini ai deisti', in S. Bertelli (ed.), *Il libertinismo in Europa* (Milan, 1980), 369, 392, 400); P. Rétat (ed.), *Traité des trois imposteurs: Manuscrit clandestin du début du XVIII⁰ siècle (éd. 1777)* (Saint-Étienne, 1973); J. Vercruysse, 'Bibliographie descriptive des éditions du *Traité des trois imposteurs*', *Tijdschrift van de Vrije Universiteit Brussel*, 1 (1974–5), 65–70.

[17] M. C. Jacob, *The Radical Enlightenment: Pantheists, Freemasons and Republicans* (London, 1981).

[18] R. H. Popkin, 'Spinoza and the Conversion of the Jews', in C. de Deugd (ed.), *Spinoza's Political and Theological Thought* (Amsterdam, 1984), 171–183.

[19] Even Jacob believed that the two editions of 1719 and 1721 'appear not to have survived': *The Radical Enlightenment* 219. Ann Thomson, too, described them as 'unlocatable' in a collection of studies on 18th cent. clandestine literature; the same collection contains Miguel Benitez's lengthy list of manuscript copies of the *Traité*, a supplement to Wade's list published almost half a century before: O. Bloch (ed.), *Le Matérialisme du XVIII⁰ siècle et la littérature clandestine* (Paris, 1982), 16–25. More recently, Benitez listed some other unknown copies in his 'Matériaux pour un inventaire des manuscrits philosophiques clandestins des XVII⁰ et XVIII⁰ siècles', *Rivista di storia della filosofia*, 43 (1988), 519–20. On the manuscript tradition, see also B. E. Schwarzbach and A. W. Fairbairn, 'Sur les rapports entre les éditions du *Traité des trois imposteurs* et la tradition manuscrite de cet ouvrage', *Nouvelles de la république des lettres*, 2 (1988), 111–36.

et L'Esprit de Spinosa (1719).[20] The little volume forms part of the Library's Special Collections: Spinoza Collection, call-mark A4L96.[21]

The Los Angeles copy is not the same as the lost Halle copy. It is a second copy, the only other one so far to be studied.[22] It is worth reporting briefly how this little repository of antique heterodoxy came to be hidden in a high-technology building constructed to house one of the newest intellectual institutions of the New World. Why was its existence unsuspected for so long? The Los Angeles volume formerly belonged to Abraham Wolf, a Spinoza scholar and director of the Department of History and Philosophy of Science at University College, London. Wolf's most important contributions to Spinoza scholarship were his English edition of the *Korte Verhandeling*, and his edition (with English translation) of Lucas's *La Vie*, published under the title *The Oldest Biography of Spinoza*.[23] This edition was based on a collation of MS 2236 of the Bibliothèque de l'Arsenal in Paris with the Codex Towneley, then in his possession and now in the University Research Library (Special Collections), Los Angeles, which he took to be the oldest surviving copy.[24] His vast collection represented the largest private library of works relating to the life and work of Spinoza and his milieu, and included books that had belonged to Spinoza himself. I became aware of this important collection which Wolf had assembled in the course of forty-five years of

[20] Spinoza's definition of fortune appears in the *Tractatus theologico-politicus*. He continues: 'Per fortunam nihil aliud intelligo, quam Dei directionem, quatenus per causas externas et inopinatas res humanas dirigit': B. de Spinoza, *Opera*, ed. C. Gebhardt (4 vols.; Heidelberg, 1924), iii. 46: 22–4.

[21] A full description of the University Research Library copy of *La Vie et L'Esprit de Spinosa* ([The Hague], 1719) appears in Berti, '"La Vie et L'Esprit"', 14–21.

[22] Vercruysse cites a copy of the 1719 edition, in the Bibliothèque Royale de Bruxelles ('Bibliographie descriptive', 66). I noticed this reference (which others had overlooked before me) only just in time to include it in the original (1986) version of this chapter. In 1987 I identified two more copies of the 1719 edition: one in Frankfurt (Stadtbibliothek, R7), and the other in Florence (Biblioteca Marcelliana, RU1). I am indebted to Sergio Landucci for the last reference.

[23] *Spinoza's Short Treatise on God, Man and his Well-Being*, trans. and ed. A. Wolf (London, 1910; 2nd edn., New York, 1963); *The Oldest Biography*.

[24] Call-mark 170/2: *La Vie de feu Monsieur de Spinosa* (*L'Esprit* follows the text of *La Vie*). This manuscript is described in Berti, '"La Vie et L'Esprit"', 12.

research, from a book-dealer's catalogue (entitled *Spinozana and Logics*), but I had long been unable to trace its fate.[25]

Apparently, Wolf's collector's passion for sole possession of a priceless object was more powerful than his commitment to the history of philosophy, for he made only the coyest reference to his discovery of a copy of the Levier volume, referring to it only in this aside: 'Of the complete Levier volume there is a copy in the University Library in Halle-Saale, *and another is at present in London*; no other copies are known of.'[26] It would thus seem that during Wolf's lifetime he was the only person to make use of his copy. After his death his entire collection was put up for auction in 1950 by the famous Amsterdam book-dealer Menno Hertzberger.[27] Part of it was acquired by the University Research Library of Los Angeles, where *La Vie et L'Esprit de Spinosa* lay hidden for thirty-five years (its existence not even being recorded by the National Union Catalogue).

In addition to a collector's jealous pride of possession, there may have been a more profound reason why Wolf, who had taken such pains to establish the original text of *La Vie*, paid no attention to his own copy of *L'Esprit*. As I have already suggested, this may reflect a misconceived commitment to serious philosophy, which, in its deference to the theoretical and moral eminence of Spinoza, obstructed any proper understanding of the text. This prevented Wolf from recognizing that the entire second chapter of *L'Esprit*, entitled 'Reasons that have led men to imagine an invisible Being, generally called God', was, with the exception of only a few brief passages, the first printed translation in French of the appendix to the first part of the *Ethics*. Afraid that a reader might mistake the radical intellectual position that shines forth on any reading of the complete text of *L'Esprit* for a reliable summary of Spinoza's own views, Wolf preferred to abandon the work to oblivion with these words:

[25] S. S. Meyer, *Spinozana and Logics*, Antiquariaat 'Pampiere Wereld', Amsterdam.

[26] *The Oldest Biography*, 29 (my italics). Again, in a note to the preface that precedes *La Vie*, he wrote 'only in *some copies* [!] of the Levier edition' (pp. 131–3).

[27] See the sale catalogue, known to scholars as 'The Wolf Catalogue': *Spinoza (1632–1677): The Library of the Late Professor Dr A. Wolf* (Catalogue No. 150, International Antiquariaat (Menno Hertzberger), Keizersgracht 610, Amsterdam).

This so-called *Spirit of Spinosa* is a very superficial, tactless, free-thinking treatise, which may betray the spirit of Lucas, but certainly does not show the spirit of Spinoza. It contains an attack on the founders of the three historic religions, and roundly charges all three with having been impostors . . . It also illustrates the kind of thing that tended to bring the name of Spinoza into disrepute. Unfortunately it is the common fate of great teachers to be betrayed by weak disciples. Lucas would have deserved more if he had written less. But having his *Life* we may endeavour to forget his *Spirit.*[28]

Thus, for more than fifty years we were deprived not only of a critical edition of *L'Esprit*—which Wolf was in an ideal position to prepare, having all the necessary skills and a vast body of material at his disposal—but even of the very text itself.

The Editorial Undertaking

To give an idea of the structure and content of the printed version of *L'Esprit*, it may be helpful to reproduce the table of contents. This differs from that of later editions and from almost all the manuscript copies.

1) Of God; 2) Reasons which have led men to imagine an invisible Being, generally called God; 3) What God is; 4) The meaning of the word 'religion'. How and why so many religions have slipped into the world; 5) Of Moses; 6) Of Numa Pompilius [added by the editors]; 7) Of Jesus Christ; 8) Of Christ's politics; 9) Of Christ's moral philosophy; 10) Of Christ's divinity; 11) Of Muhammad; 12) Of religion in general [Charron, *Les trois véritez*, II, 1–2]; 13) Of the diversity of religions [Charron, *De la sagesse*, II, 5]; 14) Of the divisions amongst Christians [Charron, *Les trois véritez*, III, 1]; 15) Of the superstitious, superstitions, and popular credulity [Charron, *De la sagesse*, II, 5; Naudé, *Considérations politiques sur les coups d'estat*, IV]; 16) On the origin of monarchies [Naudé, *Considérations*, III]; 17) Of legislators, politicians, and the uses to which they put religion [Naudé, *Considérations*, III; IV]; 18) Truths which may be experienced with the senses and are evident; 19) Of the

---

[28] *The Oldest Biography*, 27.

soul; 20) What the soul is; 21) Of those spirits which are called demons.

Crucial assistance in understanding the motives and structure of this edition, and the milieu in which it originated, is provided by Marchand, whose work on the three impostors is like an Ariadne's thread for any scholar lost in this labyrinth, but which seems to be consulted in inverse proportion to its usefulness. The principal characters in his story, apart from Levier and his friend and probable co-editor Johnson, are Jean Rousset de Missy and Jean Aymon.[29] To reconstruct Marchand's view of events, we must also refer to a number of letters he received from Gaspar Fritsch. Margaret Jacob has already used these in *The Radical Enlightenment*, but my interpretation differs from hers.[30] Marchand was a personal friend of all the leading characters involved in this undertaking (except Aymon, whom he disliked); he is therefore an authoritative source.

Rousset lived from 1686 to 1762.[31] His first published work was a translation of Collins's *Discourse of Free Thinking* (1713) together with Toland's rare work, *A Letter from an Arabian Physician* (1706). Within a few years he became the

[29] The evidence for Johnson's role is to be found in a letter that Fritsch wrote to Marchand, responding to a claim made by Marchand: 'If it was Messrs. Johnson and Levier who published *La Vie et L'Esprit de Spinosa* in 1719, it was entirely without my knowledge'. (Leipzig, 17 Jan. 1740: Leiden, Universiteitsbibliotheek (UB), March. 2.) Thomas Johnson, an Englishman who had taken up residence at The Hague, was probably the most interesting publisher of the early Enlightenment, and deserves further study. He published Toland's *Adeisidaemon* in 1709, and from 1713 to 1722 he was the publisher of the *Journal littéraire*. His widow published Radicati's *Recueil de pièces curieuses*.

[30] Jacob, *The Radical Enlightenment*, 217–20. The original text of one of these letters, dated 7 Nov. 1737 (of which a translation appears in Jacob's book), has been published by C. Berkvens-Stevelinck in a sharp attack on Jacob: 'Les "Chevaliers de la Jubilation": Maçonnerie ou libertinage? A propos de quelques publications de Margaret C. Jacob', *Quaerendo*, 13 (1983), 65–7, 24–48. For Jacob's reply, see 'The Knights of Jubilation: Masonic and Libertine. A Reply', *Quaerendo*, 14 (1984), 63–75. See also my review (written prior to the Berkvens–Jacob debate) in *Rivista storica italiana*, 96 (1984), 248–53.

[31] On Rousset, see Jacob, *The Radical Enlightenment*, passim. The Dutch Freemasons have published a volume dealing with Rousset's Freemasonry: W. Kat, *Een Grootmeestersverkiezing in 1756* (n.p., 1974). Still valuable (but not cited by Jacob) is the discussion of Rousset, and particularly of his *Les Intérêts présens et les prétentions des puissances de l'Europe* (1733), in F. Meinecke, *Die Idee der Staatsräson in der neueren Geschichte*, 2nd. edn. (Munich, 1957), 302–20.

combative journalist of the *Mercure historique et politique*, one of the leaders of Dutch Freemasonry, a subtle commentator upon foreign policy and upon reason of state, and finally a leading conspirator in the Orangeist revolution of 1747. Undoubtedly he was the brains behind the publishing project with which we are concerned, and he was fully aware of its intellectual and political significance.

Little is known about Jean Aymon (1661–1734?): but enough to be sure he was far from being a conventional character. Descended from a Piedmontese noble family, he was ordained a Catholic priest at Grenoble. Later he converted to Protestantism at Geneva and wrote a number of works that, like Rousset's, are characterized by their concern to defend Protestantism and by their fascination with international relations.[32]

To carry out their project, Rousset and Aymon only needed an editor who shared their commitment: 'It was Charles le Vier, bookseller in this town, who printed the work.'[33] Like his friends, Levier was a refugee from France. In 1715 he established himself in Rotterdam and became a partner in a bookselling business with Gaspar Fritsch of Leipzig, and with Michel Böhm. All three were members of the secret society of the Chevaliers de la Jubilation, of which Fritsch was the grand master. Levier also published works by Rapin Thoyras and by Basnage. Marchand was so closely tied to Levier that he inherited many of the latter's manuscripts when he died in 1734; these are now preserved in the University Library in Leiden. They show that he was a committed *esprit fort*: amongst them, for instance, is the *Critique du chapitre des esprits forts de La Bruyère* (shelfmark March. 68). But there is no need to hunt down concealed evidence of Levier's commitment to Spinozism: one need only open Marchand's *Dictionnaire*. 'It is quite

---

[32] Aymon was, apparently, accused of stealing manuscripts from the Bibliothèque Royale. He was the author of such works as *Le Tableau de la cour de Rome* (The Hague, 1707), and *Lettres historiques contenant ce qui s'est passé de plus important en Europe depuis l'an 1712 jusqu'en 1718* (The Hague, 1719). Cf. E. and E. Haag, *La France protestante* (repr. 9 vols.; Geneva, 1966), i. 202–4.

[33] Marchand, *Dictionnaire historique* i. 325. On Levier, see E. F. Kossmann, *De Boekhandel te 's-Gravenhage tot het einde van de 18de eeuw* ('s-Gravenhage, 1937), 239–41.

certain, at any rate, that the second [disciple] was Richer la Selve [an anagram for Charles Levier], a man completely infatuated with the philosophy of Spinoza, although he was quite incapable of reading it in the original, and although he had none of the theoretical background required to understand it properly.'[34]

Marchand's acute intellect would not spare even his own friends: especially because he was himself a reader of Spinoza and was certainly fascinated by his works, even if he was never convinced by them. Well aware of the conceptual difficulties that Spinoza's philosophy presented, he clearly considered Levier incapable of mastering it.[35] Marchand left another piece of evidence regarding both his assessment of Levier as a Spinozist and his own critical detachment from Spinozism. In a note in his hand in a copy of G. de Foigny's *Les Aventures de Jacques Sadeur dans la decouverte et le voiage de la terre australe* (Paris, 1705), he refers to some manuscript pages written by Levier and bound into the end of the volume: 'The manuscripts added at the end of this volume were put there by a disciple of Spinoza who failed to notice that this book does not go beyond deism. But it is a characteristic of all sects that their members think that they find support for their views wherever they turn.'[36]

It is thus not difficult to understand that Levier might have been proud to publish *L'Esprit de Spinosa*. Moreover, he and his associates would certainly have been aware that, apart from demonstrating their intellectual courage and willingness to take risks, the publication of the *Traité des trois imposteurs* would well prove remunerative. At that time there was a

---

[34] There can be no doubt about Marchand's interest in Spinoza. In 1711, while Levier and Rousset were obtaining a copy of *L'Esprit*, Marchand was annotating a copy of the *Tractatus* (Leiden, UB, March. 77). Nevertheless, none of his short essays on theological matters justifies describing him (as some have done) as a follower of Spinoza, or as a pantheist.

[35] Marchand, *Dictionnaire historique*, i. 325. At Leiden there is a copy of the French translation of the *Tractatus*, *Traité des cérémonies superstitieuses des juifs* (Amsterdam, 1678: UB, 512 G11) annotated by Levier.

[36] Leiden, UB, 701 F16. Levier's comments are libertine in character, referring to works by Montaigne, Cyrano de Bergerac, La Mothe le Vayer, and Charron. On Gabriel de Foigny's own version of Spinoza's philosophy, and on his theories of 'l'être des êtres' and 'le génie universel', see Vernière, *Spinoza et la pensée française*, 215–16.

voracious appetite for the works of Toland and Collins and for clandestine works with a veneer of French anti-Christian deism, sometimes decorated with Spinozist themes. So it was that they resolved on an enterprise that was slow indeed to come to fruition, for they began work in 1711 and published only in 1719.

Rousset himself undertook the task of arousing interest in, and expectations of, the coming edition; to this end, he carried out what amounted to a brilliant advertising campaign. His idea was to respond publicly to a work written by de la Monnoye in 1712 and published in the *Menagiana* in 1715. There de la Monnoye had maintained that the famous treatise *De tribus impostoribus*, which for centuries had been a subject of discussion and speculation, was in fact a mere fiction. In search of its presumed author, he surveyed an illustrious company, considering in turn representatives of Renaissance naturalism, Protestant heresy, and hermetic philosophy, from the Emperor Frederick II to Averroes, from Aretino to Machiavelli, from Bruno to Postel, from Servetus to Bodin, from Ochino to Erasmus, from Cardano to Pomponazzi, from Campanella to Vanini. 'But there is no trace of it to be found', he concluded, nor had anyone ever offered any serious documentary evidence of its existence.[37] No such book had ever been refuted by the defenders of orthodoxy, nor did its name appear on the Index. Why should one believe that it had ever existed?

Under the initials J.L.M.N., Rousset replied with the only proof that an empiricist could not fault, that of an appeal to the senses. 'I have seen with my own eyes the famous little treatise *De tribus impostoribus*, and . . . I have it in my study.'[38] Indeed, this was true, but of course he was speaking of a copy of *L'Esprit de Spinosa*.

---

[37] 'Lettre à Monsieur Bouhier, Président au Parlement de Dijon, sur le prétendu livre des trois imposteurs', in *Menagiana, ou Les bons mots et remarques critiques, historiques, morales & d'érudition de Monsieur Menage. Recueillies par ses amis*, 3rd edn. (4 vols.; Paris, 1715), iv. 283–312 (p. 308).

[38] [J. Rousset de Missy], *Réponse à la dissertation de Mr de la Monnoye, sur le traité des trois imposteurs* (Leiden, 1716), 132 (I cite from Rétat's edition of the 1777 edition of the *Traité*. All editions of the *Traité* since 1768 have included the texts by de la Monnoye and by Rousset. A copy of the first edition of the *Réponse* ([Leiden?] The Hague, 1716) is in the Koninklijke Bibliotheek at The Hague. The attribution of

Having begun by stretching the truth, Rousset's *Réponse* ended by telling a wholly fantastic story, claiming that while visiting Frankfurt in 1706, and while in the company of someone called Frecht and another friend, he had met a bookseller called Trausendorff. Trausendorff had allowed him to inspect an ancient Latin manuscript if he swore not to copy it; relying on a Jesuitical distinction, he had felt free to translate it while it was in his possession. This manuscript was nothing less than the treatise composed by Frederick II in 1230! As Fritsch wrote later to Marchand: 'As for the story about Frecht and Tausendorf, the whole thing is a complete fabrication.'[39] But Rousset did not hesitate to press on and give 'the anatomy of the famous book we are concerned with', describing in some detail the chapters that make up *L'Esprit de Spinosa*. He added: 'This book is ready to be printed [it would thus seem that the volume was ready for the press in 1716] . . . nevertheless, I doubt whether it will ever see the light of day.'[40] In the same year Sallengre published a letter giving *L'Esprit* further publicity in the *Mémoires de littérature*, a periodical published by du Sauzet, a friend of Rousset's and later his associate in Dutch Free-masonry, even though Sallengre maintained that the treatise 'is written and argued according to the method and principles of the new philosophy', and that consequently it 'could not be very old'.[41]

Perhaps the original idea was to publish the text of *L'Esprit* under the title of *Traité des trois imposteurs*, as Böhm did in Rotterdam in 1721, and other editors did from 1768 onwards. In any event, the intended publicity has been gained. Evidently, commented Marchand, prevented by his Calvinist scruples from approving of his friends' claims: 'some impos-

---

this work to Arpe (1682–1748) is rejected by J. Presser (*Das Buch 'De tribus impostoribus'*, 94–5) on the grounds that Arpe did not know French. Marchand, too, had noted that Arpe did not write in French and could not be the author (*Dictionnaire historique*, i. 323 n. 71). Arpe was the author of an interesting *Apologia pro Julio Caesare Vanino Neapolitano* (Cosmopoli, 1712). For evidence that Rousset was the true author, see the letter from Fritsch to Marchand of 7 Nov. 1737 (below, p. 203).

[39] Fritsch to Marchand, Leipzig, 7 Nov. 1737 (Leiden, UB, March. 2).

[40] [Rousset], *Réponse*, 145.

[41] Cited from *Traité*, ed. Rétat, 148–9.

tor . . . thought it a good idea to change the title in this way, in order to sell it under two differing descriptions, and thereby to trick the same people with it more than once.'[42]

One final mystery about our little volume needs to be clarified: why was no surviving copy traced for almost two centuries, until Freudenthal found a copy in Halle? The answer is to be found, yet again, in the pages of Marchand, who this time was not simply a witness but the leading actor in the events he recorded. Fritsch wrote to him about his article 'Impostoribus': 'this little piece deserves publication, not omitting the funereal ceremony of the destruction of *La Vie et L'Esprit de Spinosa*'.[43] It was Marchand, we learn, who, when Levier died in 1734, burnt 300 copies of the book: 'What is certain is that after the death of one of his booksellers, his heirs handed over to me three hundred copies of this edition, which, according to their wishes, were all burnt; with the exception, however, of *La Vie de Spinosa*, which did not require destruction.'[44]

The text of *La Vie* was reprinted in 1735, although this edition too is very rare. The title-page and the introduction make it clear that it was prepared by Levier, but it carried a fictitious place of publication: 'Hamburg, Chez Henry Kunrath'.[45] It was a final, affectionate homage to Spinoza: the first edition of the *Tractatus theologico-politicus*, which we

[42] Marchand, *Dictionnaire historique*, i. 324.

[43] Fritsch to Marchand, 17 Jan. 1740 (Leiden, UB. March. 2). Jacob mistranslates this passage, led astray by her own assumptions. The original reads: 'ce morceau merite pourtant que vous y missiés la dernière main pour le rendre publiq, sans oublier la Cérémonie funebre de l'anéantissement de *La Vie et L'Esprit de Spinosa*'; which she translates: 'But this essay is perhaps such that you should disavow any hand in it when you make it public; while not forgetting the sad spectacle of the banning of *La Vie et L'Esprit de Spinosa* [by the Walloon Churches]' (The *Radical Enlightenment*, 218).

[44] Marchand, *Dictionnaire historique*, i. 325. After this conflagration, surviving copies of the book were worth the astronomical price of 50 florins. A note on the *Avertissement* of a manuscript of *La Vie et L'Esprit* at Göttingen (Hist. Lit. 42) states that 70 copies of the 1719 edition were printed, 'in favour of seventy apostles'.

[45] *La Vie de Spinosa, par un de ses disciples: Nouvelle édition non tronquée, augmentée de quelques notes et du catalogue de ses ecrits, par un autre de ses disciples* (Hamburg, 1735). At the end of the volume there is a 'Recueil alphabétique des Auteurs, et des Ouvrages condamnés au feu, ou qui ont merités de l'être', which includes (remarkably) the Bible, the Talmud, and some works in support of the Bull Unigenitus. There is a copy of this edition in Los Angeles (A4L96/1735).

know was printed by the firm of Jan Rieuwertsz, carried on its title-page the same fictitious name: 'Henr. Künrath, 1670'. Perhaps it was a homage not only to Spinoza, but also to the alchemico-cabbalistic philosophy of the real Heinrich Khunrath, a friend of Dee's and author of the remarkable *Amphitheatrum sapientiae aeternae solius verae* (Hanover, 1609).[46]

Authorship and Dating of L'Esprit

That the mythical Latin tract and *L'Esprit de Spinosa* were two quite distinct works was known at least from the time of publication of Marchand's *Dictionnaire historique*, in which *L'Esprit* was described as 'entirely modern'.[47] But when, and by whom, was it written?

I shall show in the next section that the references to Spinoza in *L'Esprit* are numerous and significant, and these are of central importance in dating the text. But in the chapters explicitly dedicated to Moses, Christ, and Muhammad, the influence of the libertine theory of the political origins of false religions (which the author took from Vanini and Naudé) is much more important. Let me take one example now, in addition to those I shall give later: 'The celebrated Moses, grandson of a great magician, according to Justin Martyr, having established himself as leader of the Hebrews . . .'.[48] This is nothing less than a translation of a passage in the 'De iudaica sive mosaica religione' of the *Theophrastus redivivus*.[49] As for Rousset and Levier's chapter on Numa, that refers explicitly to Machiavelli's *Discorsi*, but is probably based on Naudé's *Considérations* or even perhaps on the *Theophrastus*.[50]

[46] On Dee, see F. A. Yates, *The Rosicrucian Enlightenment* (London, 1972), 38–9, and C. Vasoli, 'Riflessioni sul "problema" Vanini', in Bertelli, *Il libertinismo in Europa*, 145–7.

[47] Marchand, *Dictionnaire historique*, i. 325.

[48] *Trattato dei tre impostori*, ed. Berti, 5:15–16.

[49] G. Canziani and G. Paganini (eds.), *Theophrastus redivivus* (2 vols.; Milan, 1981), ii. 436.

[50] *Trattato dei tre impostori*, ed. Berti, 6:1–41. Cf. G. Naudé, *Considérations politiques sur les coups d'estat* (Rome, 1639), ch. 3; *Theophrastus redivivus*, ii. 351.

Thus, two distinct traditions are welded together in *L'Esprit*. Undoubtedly, its debt to the arguments of Spinoza makes it a text that is, in Marchand's words, 'entirely modern'. But at the same time this modernity is grafted on to an older stock, the legend of the three impostors, which could be traced back to Averroes and Pomponazzi, but which had been recently reworked within the libertine tradition.[51] First there had been the *Theophrastus*, shortly after the middle of the century, then, around 1680, the *De tribus impostoribus*, which was finally published by the firm of Paul Straube in Vienna in 1753 (with a false publication date of 1598). There was also a *De imposturis religionum breve compendium*, to which Leibniz referred in a letter to the librarian of Eugene of Savoy. Leibniz, who was familiar with the whole of this literature, recognized the novelty of *L'Esprit*, remarking to his correspondent as he sent him a copy of Rousset's 1716 *Réponse* 'on the famous book' that 'it was doubtless preferable to the Berlin work, if what this letter says is true'.[52]

The last two decades of the century saw a proliferation of works echoing this theme. In the books of Kortholt and Kettner it was Spinoza himself who was given the role of impostor; in that of Jean-Baptiste de Rocoles it was Sabbatai Sevi.[53] Nevertheless, the motif had been present, even if often concealed from public view, in the previous decades.

In my opinion, this needs to be taken into account when assessing Richard Popkin's recent hypothesis concerning the composition of the *Traité* (that is to say, of the text that we have been calling *L'Esprit*). In an interesting article on the young Spinoza and his connections with the Quakers and the

[51] A recent discussion of the medieval origin of the notion of the three impostors is contained in F. Berriot, *Athéismes et athéistes au xvi*ᵉ *siècle en France* (2 vols.; Lille, 1985), ii. 310–545.

[52] Leibniz to the librarian of Eugene of Savoy, Hanover, 30 Apr. 1716: inserted at fo. 15 of MS 10450 of the Oesterreichische Nationalbibliothek, Vienna. On the diffusion of this Latin manuscript, see M. Faak, 'Die Verbreitung der Handschriften des Buches *De imposturis religionum* im 18. Jahrhundert unter Beteiligung von G. W. Leibniz', *Deutsche Zeitschrift für Philosophie*, 18 (1970), 212–28.

[53] B. C. Kortholti, *De tribus impostoribus magnis: Ed. Herberto de Cherbury, Th. Hobbesio & Spinoza* (Köln, 1680); F. E. Kettneri, *De duobus impostoribus: Spinoza et Balth. Beckero* (Leipzig, 1694); J.-B. de Rocoles, *Les Imposteurs insignes* (Amsterdam, 1683).

Collegiants, who shared the same milieu, one pervaded by the millenarian hopes of Serrarius and of Rabbi Nathan Shapira, Popkin invokes a letter that Oldenburg wrote to Boreel in 1656.[54] Alarmed at the spread of unbelief (*acuuntur cavilla profanorum*), Oldenburg remarked that the greatest danger came from the thesis that Moses, Christ, and Muhammad had all three been impostors, and expressed the hope that Boreel would save Christianity by refuting this view. Popkin adds that Spinoza wrote the *Tractatus* during the years in which Boreel (who died in 1665) was writing his defence of Christianity. Popkin concludes from Oldenburg's letter, and from the fact that 'in the *Tractatus* Spinoza seems to have been dealing with themes from this original form of *Les Trois Imposteurs*', that the earliest version of the *Traité* may date to 1656, and that it was against this that Boreel's polemic was directed.[55]

As I understand it, the evidence does not support this thesis. First of all, there is the fact that, as we shall see, not only the 1719 edition, but also some of the earliest manuscript copies of *L'Esprit*, such as the Codex Towneley and MS 2236 in the Bibliothèque de L'Arsenal, include whole passages drawn not merely from the *Tractatus*, but also from the *Ethics*, which was not published until 1677. Secondly, I know of no documentary evidence that Spinoza began writing the *Tractatus* before 1665 (the first reference to it in his correspondence is in a letter to Oldenburg of 1665; there is a facetious reference to it in the preceding letter from Oldenburg). Boreel died the same year. Thus, we would have to conclude that *L'Esprit* was written nine years before the *Tractatus*, and that Spinoza copied from it rather than vice versa. I find this quite implausible.

As for Oldenburg's letter to Boreel in 1656, I am inclined

---

[54] Popkin, 'Spinoza and the Conversion of the Jews', 171–83. On the same subject, see R. H. Popkin, 'Un autre Spinoza', *Archives de philosophie*, 48 (1985), 37–57. On the Collegiants, there are two fine and complementary studies: Meinsma, *Spinoza et son cercle*, 147–304; L. Kolakowski, *Chrétiens sans Église* (Paris, 1969), 136–249 (Boreel is discussed at pp. 197–9). Also relevant, though not always reliable, is M. Francès, *Spinoza dans le pays néerlandais de la seconde moitié du XVIIe siècle* (Paris, 1937). Oldenburg's letter is in A. Rupert and M. Boas Hall (eds.), *The Correspondence of Henry Oldenburg* (13 vols.; Madison and London, 1965–86), i. 89–92.

[55] Popkin, 'Spinoza and the Conversion of the Jews', 177.

to think that it refers to the *Theophrastus redivivus*, which develops the imposture argument at length. Though dated 1659, this consists of six erudite treatises, and we can easily suppose that early drafts existed before 1656.[56] As far as I can see, there is no evidence at all that *L'Esprit* existed in mid-century.

The acknowledged modernity of *L'Esprit* does not mean that it was necessarily the work of its first publishers, particularly of Rousset, as Margaret Jacob maintains.[57] Since we now know that part of the text is a direct translation of the *Ethics*, the best one could claim for Rousset is authorship only of the rest of the work. But we shall now consider evidence that even this is not the case. The key to the whole issue is a letter from Fritsch to Marchand of 7 November 1737:

La Vie de Spinosa is copied in every jot and tittle from the copy that Levier made of the manuscript belonging to Mr Furly. All that is new is a few notes, the short introduction, and the bibliography of Spinoza's works. But the *Esprit de Spinosa* has been revised and expanded. May one know who did it? I am certainly pleased to learn that Mr Rousset is the author of the *Réponse* . . . As for your belief that the imaginary translation whose existence is reported in the *Réponse* has something in common with the *Esprit de Spinosa*, I entirely agree with you. Levier copied it in 1711, this sort of book being his speciality. If, since then, he has had dealings with Rousset, then any suspicions one might have become certainties. The Book of the *Three Impostors* is like the *Clavicules de Salomon*, of which I have seen several manuscripts, no two of them alike.[58]

Fritsch confirmed and clarified his claims in a letter of 1740: 'You will, perhaps, remember that it was my brother who brought to our house the manuscript belonging to Mr Furly. Levier copied it very hurriedly. I still have the copy he made, and I do not know that he ever made another, though I may

---

[56] The theme of the three impostors had been circulating in England for more than a decade. Thus Sir Kenelm Digby, in *Observations upon 'Religio medici'* (2nd. edn. (London, 1644), 33, said of Bernardino Ochino that he 'at last wrote a furious invective against those whom hee called the three *Grand-Impostors* of the world, among whom hee ranked our Saviour Christ as well as Moses and Mahomet'.

[57] 'At a later point I shall be arguing that Levier and Jean Rousset de Missy are in effect the authors of that clandestine manuscript': *The Radical Enlightenment*, 161.

[58] Fritsch to Marchand, Leipzig, 7 Nov. 1737 (Leiden, UB, March. 2).

be mistaken.'[59] From these passages it is evident that Levier copied both *La Vie* and *L'Esprit*, and a copyist is something quite different from an author.

It thus seems clear that the bibliography of Spinoza's works that appeared in the edition of 1719 was Levier's work. As for *L'Esprit*, its text had only been revised and augmented. Marchand's response to Fritsch's explicit enquiry as to whether Levier had had dealings with Rousset is to be found in a phrase in the *Dictionnaire*: 'Aymon and Rousset polished [*L'Esprit*'s] prose'. Clearly, Marchand did not think they were its authors. Nor can one deduce from either Marchand or Fritsch, as Jacob claims, that 'Levier got the treatise from Rousset de Missy', still less that 'Fritsch strongly implies that Rousset was its author'.[60]

This does not, of course, detract from the significance of the extraordinary project that Rousset and Levier undertook. By printing the first translation of part of the *Ethics*, modernizing the text of *L'Esprit*, and supplementing arguments drawn from Spinoza with a few apposite chapters extracted from Charron and Naudé, they had publicized and popularized the 'new philosophy'. But it does clarify what, in the present state of the evidence, we may term the real facts of the matter.

I shall now present my own view on the date and authorship of *L'Esprit*, drawing upon new evidence. Buried in the text of Marchand's article 'Impostoribus' is a note about an article in the *Journal des sçavans* for August 1752, referring to the thesis defended by the Abbé de Prades at the Sorbonne.[61] Since Marchand refers to the 'affaire de Prades' as something that has just occurred, 1752 or 1753 should be taken as the date at which Marchand made the final revisions to his article. (He died in 1756, and the *Dictionnaire* was published posthumously two years later.) Working from this, we can arrive at a fairly exact date for *L'Esprit*. Further on in the same

---

[59] Fritsch to Marchand, Leipzig, 17 Jan. 1740 (ibid.). On Furly and his library, see W. I. Hull, *Benjamin Furly and Quakerism in Rotterdam* (Swarthmore, Pa., 1941).

[60] Jacob, *The Radical Enlightenment*, 218–19.

[61] Marchand, *Dictionnaire historique*, i. 320.

article Marchand describes *L'Esprit* as 'a work that has circulated in manuscript for around forty or fifty years'.[62] If this information is correct, and, given Marchand's general accuracy, there is no reason to doubt it, *L'Esprit* would seem to have been written in the decade between 1702 and 1712. But, as we know from Fritsch's letter of November 1737, Levier copied the manuscript in 1711: this, then, is the latest possible date for the composition of the text.[63] As for the earliest, 1702 could perhaps be pushed back to the last years of the seventeenth century, since Marchand's statement is not to be interpreted too rigidly.

As far as the question of the authorship of the text is concerned, I think we can exclude Boulainvilliers (who Wade thought was undoubtedly the author), for reasons relating to his translation of the *Ethics*, which I shall discuss in the next section. But there is some evidence in Marchand's article that perhaps points us in the right direction. After categorically denying that Lucas or Aymon had written *L'Esprit*, Marchand writes: 'At the end of a manuscript copy of this treatise that I have seen and read, the true author is said to be a Mr Vroese, councillor at the court of Brabant at The Hague. *Aymon and Rousset polished up his prose*, and the second of them added the *Dissertation* or *Réponse* that has since been published by the company of Scheurleer.'[64] Following up the references to Brabant, a number of scholars have looked for evidence relating to the mysterious Mr Vroese in the Belgian archives, but without success. So they suspected that Marchand had invented the name in order to safeguard the true

---

[62] Ibid. 324.

[63] In Jan. 1740 Fritsch wrote to Marchand: 'I will return to you your draft for the dissertation on the 3 impostors' (Leiden, UB March. 2). If one took this to be the date of the final draft, one would have to date *L'Esprit* a decade earlier, to 1690–1700. But the reference to the thesis of the Abbé de Prades in the printed text is evidence of the lengthy and complex evolution of the work (confirmation for which can be found in the dense mosaic formed by the numerous different manuscript fragments that are kept in Leiden under the call-number March. 15:1). Hence my preference for the first decade of the 18th cent.

[64] Marchand, *Dictionnaire historique*, i. 325. Almost identical words are to be found in a manuscript page, in Marchand's handwriting, 'Notice d'un manuscrit "De Tribus Impostoribus"', which gives the table of contents of a manuscript of the *Traité* that is obviously of importance but has not been located. See UB, March. 39:3, fo. 134.

identity of the author. But they were looking in the wrong place. In the archives of The Hague it is easy to pick up the track of Mr Vroese. Brabant, as a territory conquered by the United Provinces, was not included in the Union of Utrecht until 1795. Its most important courts sat at The Hague, where their records remain. A Jan (also variously written as Jean or Johan) Vroesen was born in Rotterdam in 1672. His father, Adriaen Vroesen, was a member of the Council of Citizens and later burgomaster of the city of Rotterdam. Jan studied law at the University of Utrecht, and then became secretary to Coenraad van Heemskerck. He had diplomatic responsibilities in France as a *chargé d'affaires* from 1701 to 1702. In June 1705 he was named an extraordinary member of the court of Brabant. He died in 1725.[65]

This is evidently the person to whom Marchand was referring, even if he made a slight error in copying the name, for the biographical details regarding his activity in the court of Brabant match and he was an adult when *L'Esprit* was written. Nor should we be surprised that the author of *L'Esprit* was a young Dutch diplomat, not a man of letters: the example of Coenraad van Beuningen (1622–93) reminds us that diplomats could move in the same circles as philosophers.[66] Indeed, it seems likely that Vroesen was ideally placed to write *L'Esprit*.

[65] The principal sources for the life of Jan Vroesen are in O. Schutte, *Repertorium der nederlandse vertegenwoordigers Residerende in het Buitenland 1584–1810* ('s-Gravenhage, 1976), 27, and A. J. Veenendaal, jun. (ed.), *De Briefwisseling van Anthonie Heinsius 1702–1720*, ('s-Gravenhage, 1976), 4. His nomination on 30 June 1705 as an extraordinary member of the court of Brabant, followed by his nomination as an ordinary member on 18 July 1705, are recorded in Algemeen Rijksarchief Den Haag (ARA), Staten-Generaal 12280, fos. 184–6. The date of his death is derived from a document in Gemeente Archief 's-Gravenhage, OITB, inventory no. 3, fo. 57ᵛ, according to which a tax of 30 florins was paid for his burial on 30 Aug. 1725. In ARA, Archief van A. Heinsius 766, there are some 50 letters from Vroesen to Heinsius written between 6 Jan. and 19 June 1702. Other information regarding his diplomatic activity is to be found in T. Thomassen, *Inventaris van Gezantschapsarchieven van Coenraad van Heemskerck* (The Hague, 1983).

[66] Van Beuningen was 3 times ambassador of the United Provinces to the King of France (during the period 1660–8). He was de Witt's close associate, and was hostile to absolutism and the France of Louis XIV. He defended the Collegiants of Rijnsburg, and expressed millenarian views. Works by van Beuningen appear in the catalogue of Benjamin Furly's library (see below, n. 68). On van Beuningen's complex personality, see at least C. W. Roldanus, *Coenraad van Beuningen: Staatsman en Libertijn* (The Hague, 1931).

As a member of one of the most eminent families of Bayle's Rotterdam, it seems highly likely that Vroesen would have met Benjamin Furly and had access to his library. Furly (1636–1714) was a Quaker from Colchester who had emigrated to Holland. He was a friend of Locke, of Algernon Sidney, of Shaftesbury, and of Bayle, and he was the founder of the most important philosophical and literary society in the city, known as The Lantern. This group met in his house and drew together heretics and free-thinkers; in this context, the fact that the French translation of Shaftesbury's *Sensus communis* was dedicated to Vroesen throws new light on the latter's connection with The Lantern.[67] Furly translated the work of a close friend of Spinoza, Peter Balling's *Het licht op de kandelaar (The Light on the Candlestick)* (1662). The families of Furly and of Vroesen certainly knew each other; a document survives (dated 9–10 June 1704) recording the transfer of ownership of 1,000 acre of land in Pennsylvania from Adriaen Vroesen, father of Jan, to Benjohan Furly, son of Benjamin. It is more than possible, then, that Jan Vroesen had access to Furly's astonishing library, which contained over 4,400 volumes. Furly's library had extensive holdings of the writings of Quakers, Mennonites, Socinians, Anabaptists, Collegiants, and Quietists, and it contained the key works of More, Fludd, Charron, Campanella, Hobbes, Cudworth, Bayle, Spinoza, and Locke, to name only a few.[68]

During the years 1701–2 Vroesen, now a diplomat in Paris, would have been able to make contact with those French intellectuals who were opposed to absolutism and familiar with libertine culture. Such a double background, both Dutch and French, is precisely what one would look for in the

[67] On Furly and the remarkable group of heterodox intellectuals who gathered around him, see Hull, *Benjamin Furly and Quakerism in Rotterdam*. For further evidence on Vroesen, see S. Berti, 'Jan Vroesen, autore del "Traité des trois imposteurs"?', *Rivista storica italiana*, 2 (1991), 528–43.

[68] On Furly's death, the publishers Fritsch and Böhm, friends of Levier and of Marchand, published the catalogue of his library that was auctioned on 22 Oct. 1714: *Bibliotheca Furliana, sive catalogus librorum honoratiss. & doctiss. viri Benjamin Furly* (Rotterdam, 1714). At least 2 copies survive: 1 in the British Library, and 1 in Amsterdam, in the Bibliotheek van de Vereeniging ter Bevordering van de Belangen des Boekhandels.

author of *L'Esprit*. Nor should we be concerned by the fact that the treatise is written in French: Vroesen's French was good, as can be seen from his private diplomatic notes, which survive at The Hague and which are written in French.[69] In any case, *L'Esprit* is far from being a masterpiece of style, for it is often wordy and laboured.

To maintain that Vroesen is the author of *L'Esprit* fits well with yet another piece of evidence. We have already seen that, according to a letter from Fritsch to Marchand (7 November 1737), Levier carefully copied the texts of *La Vie* and of *L'Esprit* (the latter retouched and extended by Rousset and Aymon) in 1711, and that his copy-text was a manuscript belonging to Benjamin Furly. This is another link to Vroesen's home town and to Furly's library. Jan returned to Rotterdam in 1702. There he would have been able to settle down to write his treatise, or complete it, if he had started writing it in Paris. We can say that the internal evidence of the text, the external testimony of Fritsch and Marchand, and the biography of Vroesen fit together perfectly.

As if this were not enough, there is another important witness, someone who is completely independent of Marchand but who agrees with him in attributing *L'Esprit* to Vroesen. The evidence is to be found in the introduction by the Lutheran pastor F. G. C. Rütz to the Dutch translation of *Einleitung in die göttlichen Schriften des Neuen Bundes*, a famous book by Johann David Michäelis, the great German Bible scholar who was professor of oriental languages at Göttingen.[70] Rütz was very knowledgeable when it came to deistic and anti-Christian works. He wrote an entire book about the most radical and disturbing author of the Italian Enlightenment, Alberto Radicati of Passerano, in which he claims to possess five different manuscript copies of the *Traité des trois imposteurs*.[71] In his introduction to Michäelis he describes a quarto manuscript,

[69] ARA, Archief C. van Heemskerck 284.

[70] J. D. Michäelis, *Inleiding in de godlijke Schriften van het Nieuwe Verbond* ('s-Gravenhage, 1778).

[71] F. G. C. Rütz, *Kleine Bydragen tot de dëistische Letterkunde, eerste Stuk: Behelzende eenige Byzonderheden, raakende de Schriften en Lotgevallen van den geweezen' Dëeist Albert Radicati, Graaf van Passeran* ('s-Gravenhage, 1781), 11. On the life and work of Rütz (1733–1803), see J. Loosjes, *Naamlist van Predikanten, Hoogleeraaren en Porponenten der Luthersche Kerk in Nederland* ('s-Gravenhage,

forty-eight pages long, containing sixteen different fragments attacking Christianity. Amongst them is a long note by Aymon on the *Traité*, followed by a 'Reflexion sur la précédente Remarque', written in 1737 by the anonymous compiler. This is what he has to say:

The author of these previous remarks (of considerable significance, about a thesis that attributes the religion[s of] M[uhammad], C[hrist], and the M[osaic] to three impostors) was Mr Aymon, well known both for his learning and for changing his religion. He could not possibly be ignorant of the true author of the MS that is known under the title *Of Three Famous Impostors*, and that was printed under the title *De l'esprit et de la vie de Spinosa*, for this Mr Aymon himself, along with Mr Rousset, corrected the original text by Mr Vroese, councillor of the Council of Brabant at The Hague, who was the true author of the manuscript in question. Mr Rousset, in order to make his friend's manuscript more valuable and market-able, and to entertain the public, added to it a dissertation on the three impostors which he then had printed by Sr. Scheurleer, bookseller at The Hague, etc.[72]

This testimony is of considerable value, for it is much earlier than Marchand's, but identical to it. From it we learn an even more essential fact, that Vroesen was a friend of Rousset de Missy, and it would appear that our information comes from someone in direct contact with Aymon.

Thus, although there is no definitive documentary proof that Vroesen was the author of *L'Esprit*, the evidence seems to me to make this almost certain.

Reading L'Esprit

The historical importance of *L'Esprit* does not consist in the theory of imposture, which was of ancient origin (and which was in large measure taken over from Vanini, Naudé, and the

---

1925), 272–5. On Rütz and Radicati, see S. Berti, 'Radicati in Olanda: Nuovi documenti sulla sua conversione e su alcuni suoi manoscritti inediti', *Rivista storica italiana*, 96 (1984), 510–22.

[72] Cf. Rütz's foreword to Michäelis, *Inleiding in de godlijke Schriften*, pp. xxix–xxx.

relatively recent *Theophrastus redivivus* (1659), so much as
in the Spinozist foundations that underlie it and crucially
affect its significance.[73] Spinoza is present not merely in the
section of the *Ethics* that is reprinted in its entirety, but also
in other quotations drawn from his metaphysics, together
with numerous passages from the *Tractatus theologico-politicus* and even from the letters.

L'Esprit is not a text that is all of a piece, a fact that makes
it a valuable test case in the history of ideas, and a true puzzle
for an interpreter. Nevertheless, it marks a new age. In it we
are far from the purely naturalistic criticism of miracles to be
found in libertine authors who, comparing the origins of the
different religions, rendered them all relative, and ended up
with a static and, indeed, lifeless religious indifferentism.
Cautious and faint-hearted, the exponents of erudite libertinism, relying on Paduan Averroism, on ancient Greece and
Rome, sought to strengthen the weapons of unbelief. But
they remained Catholics, preaching the need for external
conformity to the established religion, and generally offering
historical and theoretical defences of absolutism.[74] Thus, in
Vernière's apt phrase, 'they wore themselves out in sterile
compromises'.[75]

---

[73] On the *Theophrastus redivivus* see: T. Gregory, *Theophrastus redivivus:
Erudizione e ateismo nel Seicento* (Naples, 1979); id., '"Omnis philosophia mortali-
tatis adstipulatur opinioni": Quelques considérations sur le *Theophrastus redivivus*',
in Bloch, *Le Matérialisme du XVIII* siècle, 213–17; G. Paganini, 'La critica della
"civiltà" nel *Theophrastus redivivus*: I. Natura e cultura', followed by G. Canziani,
'La critica della "civiltà" nel *Theophrastus redivivus*: II. Ordine naturale e legalità
civile', in O. Bloch (ed.), *Ricerche su letteratura libertina e letteratura clandestina
nel Seicento* (Florence, 1981), 49–118; J. Vercruysse, 'Le *Theophrastus redivivus* au
18ᵉ siècle: Mythe et réalité', ibid. 297–303. There is now a critical edition (Canziani
and Paganini, *Theophrastus redivivus*).

[74] R. Pintard, *Le Libertinage érudit dans la première moitié de XVIIᵉ siècle* (2 vols.;
Paris, 1943).

[75] Vernière, *Spinoza et la pensée française*, 207. Pintard himself commented, in
the concluding pages of his classic study (*Le Libertinage érudit*, 566–9), on the
effective lack of intellectual development amongst his authors, whose attention was
turned to the past and who were weighed down by their own erudition. Lucien
Febvre, in a stimulating review of Pintard published in 1944, was harsher in his
judgement. Where Pintard had voiced a 'suspicion' and made some critical comments
in passing, Febvre spoke of 'failure' and 'defeat': 'Aux origines de l'esprit moderne:
Libertinage, naturalisme, mécanisme', in *Au cœur religieux du XVIᵉ siècle* (Paris,
1957), 337–58. For a different view, see T. Gregory, 'Il libertinismo della prima metà
del Seicento: Stato attuale degli studi e prospettive di ricerca', in *Ricerche su
letteratura libertina*, 3–47.

Spinoza's approach was quite different. He developed a historico-critical method for the interpretation of Scripture, which he outlined in the preface to the *Tractatus* and in its fifteenth chapter. This called for an interpretation of the Scriptures based on an examination of the text and of the history of its composition and transmission. Thus it would become possible to separate the true word of God from the corruptions of the theologians and the arbitrary accretions of men. Spinoza's contempt for the ceremonial aspect of religion, and for the superstitious respect paid to the Bible as a physical object rather than to its true message, would soon invigorate the Enlightenment attack upon superstition. It is not difficult to imagine the impact that Spinoza's invitation to 'begin a new, complete, and free examination of the Scriptures' must have had among Huguenots who had taken refuge in Holland.[76]

The first chapter of *L'Esprit* draws on these and other themes from the *Tractatus*, such as the attack on the supposedly divine character of prophecy (along with other more specific topics, to which we shall return). Like the first chapter of the *Ethics*, it is entitled 'Of God'. Ignorance, which is entirely responsible for false ideas of God, must be combated with natural reason. But the text immediately takes on a radical tone, attacking those who 'are paid to defend the established beliefs'. It continues: 'If the people could understand the abyss into which they fall due to ignorance, they would soon throw off the yoke of these venal characters who, in their pursuit of private profit, lead them astray. To do so, they would need only to make use of reason, for if one allows its full scope it is impossible not to discover truth.'[77]

The author of *L'Esprit* knew his Spinoza too well not to understand how the *Tractatus* was structurally and intellectually tied to the theory of the *Ethics* (Spinoza was already working on the *Ethics* in 1661, and did not begin the *Tractatus* until 1665, as we have seen). In order to provide a theoretical foundation for his critique of revealed religion and his theory of imposture, therefore, he decided it would be a

[76] *Tractatus theologico-politicus*, Preface (*Opera*, iii. 9: 20–5).
[77] *Trattato dei tre impostori*, ed. Berti, 1: 25–9.

good idea to let Spinoza speak directly, through those pages of the *Ethics* that, recalling the definition of God as *causa sui* and as a necessary being whose essence implies existence, amounted to a cogent criticism of the theory of final causes and the presumption that God must be conceived in the image of man. What Levier and Rousset found themselves publishing as the second chapter of *L'Esprit*, therefore (and we must presume that they recognized what they were doing), was the first French translation of the appendix to the first part of the *Ethics*.[78] (A few brief excisions were made, for various reasons, but these do not affect the substance of the argument.)

This was the first time that a French translation of a complete section of the *Ethics* had been made available in print; previously, the argument of the *Ethics* had been disseminated primarily through attempted refutations, such as those of François Lamy, Bayle, and Fénelon.[79] The first text to provide an accurate account of Spinoza's theories for a wide public was the *Essai de métaphysique dans les principes de B . . . de Sp . . .* Though written by Boulainvilliers in 1712, it was published only in 1731, twelve years after the Levier edition, under the title *Réfutation de Spinosa*. Moreover, notwithstanding its tremendous significance for the development of Spinozism in France, what Boulainvilliers offered was only a paraphrase, not a translation. *L'Esprit* may have contained only a small extract from the *Ethics*, but it was an important one, for it presented a complete and powerful argument. Its significance is underlined when one considers that no complete French translation of the *Ethics* was published until 1842.

Moreover, it seems likely that this was not only the first translation to be published in French, but the first to be written. Boulainvilliers's, published for the first time by

---

[78] Compare 'Raisons qui ont porté les Hommes à se figurer un Etre invisible, ou ce qu'on nomme communement Dieu', ibid., ch. 2, with the text in Benedict de Spinoza, *Opera posthuma* ([Amsterdam], 1677), 33–9.

[79] F. Lamy, *Le Nouvel Atheisme renversé, ou Refutation du sytsême de Spinoza* (Paris, 1696); P. Bayle, *Dictionnaire historique et critique*, 3rd. edn. (4 vols.; Rotterdam, 1720), iv, art. 'Spinoza'; F. Fénelon, *Démonstration de l'existence de Dieu* (Paris, 1713).

Colonna d'Istria only in 1907, was made long after 1704, for Boulainvilliers writes in his introduction to the *Essai*: 'the posthumous works of Spinoza came into my hands in 1704, when I sought them out to make use of a Hebrew grammar that is to be found in them.'[80] Boulainvilliers probably devoted several years of hard work to translating Spinoza's 'mathematical dryness' into elegant French. If his translation is compared with that of two of the oldest manuscripts of *L'Esprit* (Codex Towneley and MS 2236 of the Bibliothèque de L'Arsenal), their French is noticeably less cultivated, and is sometimes hesitant and archaic. Looking at these two translations, it would seem that they are quite different, and are mutually independent of each other. Moreover, there is a world of difference between the high esteem that Boulainvilliers evinces for the purity and simplicity of Muhammad's monotheism, and the derision with which *L'Esprit* refers to the founder of Islam. Boulainvilliers therefore had nothing to do with the writing of *L'Esprit* (contrary to Wade's view[81]).

Vernière remarked that Boulainvilliers's translation, had it been published in the early years of the century, 'could have given a valuable boost to the dissemination of true Spinozism'.[82] Rousset and Levier partly filled this gap. Why, then, has the translation of the appendix—which was after all reprinted, with only minor modifications and stylistic changes, in the various late eighteenth-century editions of *L'Esprit*—not been identified until now? One factor helping to obscure it was its relatively discursive style, so untypical of the *Ethics*. More important were the measures taken by its translator to camouflage it.

Thus Spinoza's opening passage, where he reviews his account of God as one and necessary, acting through the sole necessity of his nature and being the free cause of all things, is omitted. Instead a paragraph reminiscent of Hobbes's

[80] H. de Boulainvilliers, 'Essai de métaphysique dans les principes de B . . . de Sp . . .', in his *Œuvres philosophiques*, ed. R. Simon (2 vols.; The Hague, 1973), i. 84. Benedict de Spinoza, *Éthique*, trans. H. de Boulainvilliers, ed. F. Colonna d'Istria (Paris, 1907).

[81] Wade, *The Clandestine Organization*, 127: 'The author of the treatise was undoubtedly Boulainvilliers.'

[82] Vernière, *Spinoza et la pensée française*, 316.

Leviathan is substituted, in which 'the chimerical fear of invisible powers' is described as 'the seed from which religion grows'.[83] *L'Esprit* moves on at once to the central polemical argument of the appendix against teleological presuppositions. The translator, to clarify the meaning, breaks it up into short sentences: 'Men have believed that they [the Gods] resembled them, and that, like them, they did everything with some purpose in view. For they all agree in saying that God has made nothing except for man, and, conversely, that man is only made for God.'[84] The argument continues by identifying an indubitable principle upon which to build, namely:

that all men are born in profound ignorance of the causes of things, and that the only thing they know is that they have a natural inclination that leads them to seek out that which is useful and convenient for them, and to avoid that which is harmful . . . Men, feeling that they are capable of wishing and hoping, falsely conclude that this is all that is required to make them free. This error is one that they fall into all the more easily because they never take the trouble to consider the causes that determine their wishes and hopes, for they are incapable of thinking of them, or of conceiving of them, even in their dreams.[85]

Thus, by a strange reversal, men mistake efficient causes for final causes, and, not recognizing that they are necessarily determined in what they do, imagine themselves to be free.

The teleological presumption also infects their understanding of God. 'They presumed the Gods to be like themselves . . . instead of showing how nature does nothing in vain, they did the opposite, maintaining that God and nature dream [of unfulfilled purposes] just as men do.'[86] In truth, nature pursues no end, because to do so would be to destroy the perfection of God: 'If God were to act for a purpose, whether for his own sake or for someone else's, he would be wanting

---

[83] *Trattato dei tre impostori*, ed. Berti, 2: 18–19. Compare with *Leviathan*, ch. 11 'And this Feare of things invisible, is the naturall Seed of that, which every one in himself calleth Religion.'

[84] *Trattato dei tre impostori*, ed. Berti, 2: 25–9; Spinoza, *Opera posthuma*, 34.

[85] *Trattato dei tre impostori*, ed. Berti, 2: 38–49; Spinoza, *Opera posthuma*, 34; *Traité*, ed. Rétat, 14, reads somewhat differently: its text is identical to that of the Codex Towneley, fos. 14–15.

[86] *Trattato dei tre impostori*, ed. Berti, 2: 82–5; Spinoza, *Opera posthuma*, 35. Codex Towneley, fos. 16–17, and the edition of 1719 are identical at this point.

something that he did not have, and it would be necessary to admit that there was a time when God did not have that which he seeks to obtain by his actions, and when he wanted to have it; which is to make God imperfect.'[87]

The passage that precedes this argument in the *Ethics* was left out by the translator, for it refers explicitly to propositions 16, 21, 22, and 23, which would have rendered Spinoza's authorship of the text all too evident. Another passage shows how effectively the translation gave currency to Spinoza's notion that there was commonly a confusion between intellect and imagination:

Those who are ignorant of the nature of things, having no grasp of it beyond the ideas that they construct on the basis of their imagination, which they mistake for understanding, conclude that there is an order in the world, and they take this order to be whatever they imagine it to be. For men are so constituted that they believe things to be well or badly ordered according to whether they find it easy or difficult to imagine them as corresponding to the image of them that they receive through the senses. In effect, since that which least tires the imagination is the most pleasurable, it is easy to conclude that one is justified in preferring 'order' to 'confusion', as if order were anything other than a mere attribute of men's imaginations. So that to say that God has made everything with order is merely to attribute to him, as one would to a man, the faculty of imagination.[88]

I will not quote further from the translation of the appendix, for I want to turn now to how the author of *L'Esprit* transforms other sections of the *Ethics*, making them straightforwardly materialist. Thus he replies to the question: 'What is God?', with an eccentric translation of definition 6: 'He is an absolute, infinite being, one of whose attributes is to be an eternal and infinite substance.'[89] Thereby he makes being a

---

[87] *Trattato dei tre impostori*, ed. Berti, 2: 115-18; Spinoza, *Opera posthuma*, 36; Codex Towneley, fo. 21. See also letter no. 23 from Spinoza to Blyenberg (*Opera*, iv. 148).

[88] *Trattato dei tre impostori*, ed. Berti, 2: 163-76; Spinoza, *Opera posthuma*, 37-8; Codex Towneley, fo. 25.

[89] *Trattato dei tre impostori*, ed. Berti, 3: 4-6; Spinoza, *Opera posthuma*, 1; Codex Towneley, fo. 31. *Traité*, ed. Rétat, 24, remarkably, includes a passage drawn from letter no. 73 from Spinoza to Oldenburg, in which St Paul is cited (*Opera*, iv. 307).

substance an attribute, which Spinoza does not. As a consequence, in the discussion on the indivisibility of matter that
follows, he is able to maintain that, if substance is material
and infinite, then, since 'outside God there can be no
substance', God too is material.

In contrast, Spinoza's own view was that asserting the
materiality of extension did not commit one to maintaining
univocally the materiality of God. In his view, the other
attribute that is infinite by its nature and is constitutive of
substance is thought: extension does not exhaust being in all
its aspects. In *L'Esprit*, however, there is no reference to
thought as an attribute of substance: this is what makes it a
materialist text, and one with which Spinoza would certainly
not have agreed.[90]

This radical reduction of Spinoza's philosophy to a species
of materialism, based on the note to proposition 15, is of
considerable historical importance; it probably constitues the
first such presentation of Spinoza's views in French. The key
passage goes as follows: 'For if everything is in God, and if
everything necessarily follows from his essence, it follows of
necessity that he must be of the same nature as that which he
contains, for it is contradictory to claim that entirely material
beings can be contained in a being who is not material.'[91]
Here we even have a reference to Tertullian, a frequent
authority in the clandestine literature of the Enlightenment,
according to whom (at least on a Hobbesian reading of his
work) 'every substance is a body'.

From this point, what had begun as a self-conscious and
bold effort at a materialist reading of Spinoza's ontology
begins to lose strength and direction. In the last chapters of
the book it comes to be associated with an animistic and
primitive conception of the soul as material and mortal, a
conception that bears no relationship to the views of Spinoza.
The result is a crude materialism, traces of which are evident
in the chapters that discuss the Scriptures. No trace is to be

[90] In letter no. 73 he writes: 'Attamen quod quidam putant, Tractatum Theolo-
gico-Politicum eo niti, quod Deus, & Natura (per quam massam quandam, sive
materiam corpoream intelligunt), unum, & idem sint, tota errant via' (*Opera*, iv.
307: 11–14).
[91] *Trattato dei tre impostori*, ed. Berti, 3: 15–19; Codex Towneley, fo. 33.

found there of the deistic themes of Spinoza's *Tractatus*, in which the identity between the *lumen naturale* and the moral teachings of the Old Testament is upheld.

To understand the real extent of *L'Esprit*'s debt to the *Tractatus* would entail tackling the complex subject of the link in Spinoza's intellectual development between Hebrew tradition and admiration for Christ, and considering how these aspects of Spinoza's thought were received as the *Tractatus* became widely known in the eighteenth century. This cannot be done adequately here, but it is evident that the *herem* that Spinoza went through in 1656, entailing his expulsion from the Synagogue and from life in the Jewish community, did not imply an abandonment of Judaism on his part, as some have maintained. This is not simply to say, to quote Hannah Arendt, that 'one does not escape Jewishness'. Rather, I refer to the network of intellectual problems associated with his rejection of orthodoxy, his deep (although concealed) ties to the traditions of the Zohar and the Lurianic cabbalah, and his powerful notion of philosophy itself, as ontologically constructed.[92]

Spinoza's influence was important for two different traditions of thought that we encounter in the early eighteenth century (of only one of which he would have approved). One is the anti-Semitism to be found in some of the clandestine texts of the eighteenth century (including *L'Esprit*); the other is the widespread praise of primitive Christianity. This second tradition, best represented by Toland, admired the ethical teaching of the Gospels and the person of Christ, while denying his divinity. A third tradition, independent of Spinoza and more intransigent in its attitude to Christianity, also found expression in the Portuguese-Jewish community in Amsterdam. Its leading exponents were Saul Levi Mortera and Isaac Orobio de Castro, who were important sources for Enlightenment attacks upon Christianity.[93]

L'Esprit exemplifies the first aspect of Spinoza's influence but not the second, for its author is solely interested in

[92] For an extensive bibliography on Spinoza and Judaism, see Berti, ' "La Vie et L'Esprit" ', 38–9.
[93] See R. H. Popkin's chapter in this volume.

defeating the three false prophets, false legislators, authentic impostors. Here is an example at random. Having defined prophets as 'dreamers', our author continues: 'To believe such contradictions, however, one would have to be as stupid and idiotic as those who, despite Moses's wiles, believed that a calf was the God who had led them out of Egypt. But let us finish this chapter, without tarrying over the day-dreams of a people raised in slavery, and in the midst of a superstitious people.'⁹⁴ This passage is clearly inspired by a section of the second chapter of the *Tractatus*, but its significance has been completely altered, since it now reflects an absolute judgement upon the Jewish people, entirely lacking the historico-critical elements that were at the centre of Spinoza's own method: in the *Tractatus* he describes the history of the Jewish people in their infancy, still primitive and exhausted by slavery, which had made them as yet incapable of a rational comprehension of God and of the necessity of the moral law.⁹⁵

Our author was clearly well-acquainted with the *Tractatus*. For example, he refers in passing to the unreliability of the Bible: 'a patchwork of fragments sewn together at different times, and handed out to the public on the whim of the rabbis'. This itself is followed by a patchwork, joining a passage from chapter 10 of the *Tractatus*, on the rabbis' proposal to exclude Proverbs and Ecclesiastes from the sacred books, to another from chapter 2, on Ezekiel:

The Talmud relates that the rabbis debated whether they should remove the books of Proverbs and Ecclesiastes from the biblical canon. They were persuaded not to do so, because they noted several passages in them where the law of Moses is praised. They were going to do the same thing with the prophecies of Ezekiel, until a certain Chananias was successful in reconciling them with this same law.⁹⁶

⁹⁴ *Trattato dei tre impostori*, ed. Berti, 1: 193–8; *Tractatus theologico-politicus*, ch. 2 (*Opera*, iii. 40: 31–5).
⁹⁵ On this subject, see the fine discussion in L. Strauss, *Spinoza's Critique of Religion* (New York, 1965), 251–6. On Spinoza and the Scriptures, see S. Zac, *Spinoza et l'interprétation de l'écriture* (Paris, 1965).
⁹⁶ *Trattato dei tre impostori*, ed. Berti, 3: 104–9; *Tractatus theologico-politicus*, ch. 10 (*Opera*, iii. 142: 6–10), and ibid., ch. 2 (*Opera*, iii. 41: 29–35).

Elsewhere, commenting ironically on those who maintain that God is a purely spiritual being, the author again draws on the *Tractatus* to bring out the contradictions in this view: 'They say that God is a pure spirit who has nothing in common with a corporeal entity; nevertheless Micah saw him sitting down, Daniel saw him dressed in white and with the appearance of an old man, and Ezekiel saw him as a flame.'[97]

Spinoza's conception of God rendered meaningless any idea of God as creator; it is scarcely necessary to say that it was quite incompatible with any notion of the divinity of Christ. Nevertheless, one can search through the *Tractatus*, as the author of *L'Esprit* must have done, for an attack upon Christ: there is none to be found. Quite the contrary, for Spinoza implies that it is in Christ the man that God's wisdom has most fully manifested itself.[98] Spinoza's respectful treatment of the Judaeo-Christian tradition, which was probably partly influenced by Socinianism, was of no use for the attack upon Christ to which the author of *L'Esprit* devoted four chapters.[99] Levier and Rousset, who evidently knew their Spinoza well, therefore chose to insert a powerful attack on the divinity of Christ (though this does not appear in any of the manuscript copies of *L'Esprit* that I have been able to consult). They took as the basis of their text a letter from Spinoza to Oldenburg: 'But in addition, if Jesus Christ was God, it would follow, as Saint John says, that God was made flesh and took upon himself a human nature, an idea that is as grossly self-contradictory as it would be to say that a circle had acquired the nature of a square.'[100]

The final section of *L'Esprit*, which discusses the soul and

---

[97] *Trattato dei tre impostori*, ed. Berti, 1: 126–9; *Tractatus theologico-politicus*, ch. 1 (*Opera*, iii. 28: 31–5).

[98] On this subject, see the crisp discussion of Zac, *Spinoza et l'interprétation de l'écriture*, 190–9. See also A. Matheron, *Le Christ et le salut des ignorants chez Spinoza* (Paris, 1971), and R. Misrahi, 'Spinoza face au christianisme', *Revue philosophique de la France et de l'étranger*, 167 (1977), 233–68.

[99] On Spinoza and Socinianism, see H. Mechoulan, 'Morteira et Spinoza au carrefour du socinianisme', *Revue des études juives*, 135 (1976), 51–65.

[100] *Trattato dei tre impostori*, ed. Berti, 9: 55–9. Cf. the following passage in letter no. 73: 'Caeterum quod quaedam Ecclesiae his addunt, quod Deus naturam humanam assumpserit, monui expresse, me, quid dicant, nescire; imo, ut verum fatear, non minus absurde mihi loqui videntur, quam si quis mihi diceret, quod circulus naturam quadrati induerit' (*Opera*, iv. 309: 10–13).

demons, lacks vigour and originality, presenting a materialist argument that is put together from fragments drawn from various divergent sources.[101] Having failed to provide a rigorous philosophical foundation for atheism, *L'Esprit* ends up implicitly reaffirming the existence of God, although certainly not the revealed God of the Scriptures. This text is characteristic of the early Enlightenment, in that even here, where the philosophy of Spinoza has had a real impact, the author ends up turning away from Spinoza in order to present ideas that are well-worn and of little merit. How is this to be explained?

There was, I think, an underlying reason for this retreat from Spinoza. The radical Enlightenment began with attacks upon Christianity derived from Spinoza, but it also invented the modern view of politics. It could only think politically by escaping from the confines of Spinoza's concept of being, turning away from necessity in order to embrace liberty. Much of the importance of *L'Esprit de Spinosa* lies in the way in which it modified Spinoza's arguments to make them politically radical. Although parts of the text were a mere translation, the whole amounted to an adaptation of Spinoza, Hobbes, and the libertine tradition. It is this adaptation, fertile if not always intellectually coherent, that stands at the origin of the radical Enlightenment.

---

[101] Alain Niderst has already shown that the chapter 'On the soul' was almost completely lifted from the *Discours anatomiques* (1675) of Guillaume Lamy. See anon., *L'Âme matérielle*, ed. A. Niderst (Paris, 1973), 19–20.

8

'Aikenhead the Atheist': The Context and Consequences of Articulate Irreligion in the Late Seventeenth Century

MICHAEL HUNTER

Thomas Aikenhead, a student at the University of Edinburgh, was executed for blasphemy on 8 January 1697. His fate was briefly a matter of controversy in Scotland, and it also 'made a great Noise' in London, where it was widely reported in the newspapers of the day.[1] Thereafter the case attracted some attention in the late eighteenth and early nineteenth century, when the main sources concerning it were published.[2] But interest in Aikenhead was dramatically revived in 1855, when Lord Macaulay devoted a lengthy passage to the affair in the fourth volume of his *History of England*, describing the youth's execution as 'a crime such as has never since polluted the island'. Macaulay's scathing view of clerical intolerance inspired a flurry of activity in Edinburgh, as the pros and cons of the great historian's views were debated between evangelicals and others.[3] Since then, the case has

---

[*Author's Note*. For the quotation in the title of this chapter, see below, p. 238. I am greatly indebted to Tristram Clarke of the National Register of Archives (Scotland) for his unstinting assistance in the preparation of this chapter. David Berman, James K. Cameron, Roger Emerson, Trevor Pateman, George Rosie, and Paul B. Wood read a draft and made helpful suggestions for its emendation.]

[1] *Flying Post* (267), 28 Jan. 1697. Other newspaper reports of the affair are noted below, *passim*.

[2] See esp. Hugo Arnot, *A Collection and Abridgement of Celebrated Criminal Trials in Scotland* (Edinburgh, 1785), 324–7, and W. Cobbett, T. B. Howell, *et al.* (eds.), *A Complete Collection of State Trials* (34 vols.; London, 1809–28) (hereafter *State Trials*), xiii. 917–40 (no. 401).

[3] T. B. Macaulay, *The History of England* (5 vols.; London, 1849–65), iv. 781–4;

often been alluded to, usually as a means of taking the pulse
of the state of Scottish culture at the end of the seventeenth
century.[4]

In the course of this chapter I shall consider who was
responsible for Aikenhead's death, and why, adducing some
previously unknown evidence on the question, but I also
wish to devote attention to Aikenhead's apostasy in its own
right. For this episode has greater significance for the history
of early modern irreligion than has hitherto been appreciated.
In general, cases from this period where people were accused
of 'atheism' or blasphemy are highly frustrating. The charges
are often generalized and vague; even when specific individuals are denounced, the accusations against them frequently comprise unsubstantiated hearsay; and we hardly
ever have a response from those challenged to their accusers.
In the Aikenhead case, on the other hand, the materials
available are almost as rich as those deployed by Carlo
Ginzburg in his celebrated account of the Friuli sceptic,
Menocchio.[5] Not only do we have a full account of the
aggressively anti-Christian views that Aikenhead was accused
of publicly expressing, which indicate their unusual range
and ingenuity, but we also have a written account by Aikenhead of the rationale of his apostasy. This juxtaposition of
blasphemy with serious philosophizing provides a rare
opportunity to probe at the relationship between two

[anon., probably Hugh Miller], *Macaulay on Scotland: A Critique Republished from
'The Witness'* (Edinburgh, n.d.; repr. Boston, 1857), esp. 33 ff.; John Gordon,
Thomas Aikenhead: A Historical Review, 3rd edn. (London, 1856).

[4] For recent examples, see e. g. A. L. Drummond and James Bulloch, *The Scottish
Church, 1688–1743: The Triumph of the Moderates* (Edinburgh, 1973), 13–15; N.
T. Phillipson, 'Culture and Society in the Eighteenth-Century Province: The Case
of Edinburgh and the Scottish Enlightenment', in Lawrence Stone (ed.), *The
University and Society* (2 vols.; Princeton, NJ, 1973), ii. 431; G. E. Davie, *The
Scottish Enlightenment* (London, 1981), 9–10; J. K. Cameron, 'Scottish Calvinism
and the Principle of Intolerance', in B. A. Gerrish (ed.), *Reformatio perennis*
(Pittsburgh, 1981), 123–5; id., 'Theological Controversy: A Factor in the Origins of
the Scottish Enlightenment', in R. H. Campbell and A. S. Skinner (eds.), *The
Origins and Nature of the Scottish Enlightenment* (Edinburgh, 1982), 117–18. See
also L. W. Levy, *Treason against God: A History of the Offense of Blasphemy* (New
York, 1981), 325–7, and below, n. 12.

[5] Carlo Ginzburg, *The Cheese and the Worms: The Cosmos of a Sixteenth-
Century Miller* (Eng. trans., London, 1980).

phenomena that were commonly seen as integral to the phenomenon of 'atheism' that caused such anxiety at the time, but that otherwise remain frustratingly distinct in the historical record.

Thomas Aikenhead was baptized on 28 March 1676. He was the son of James Aikenhead, an Edinburgh apothecary and burgess, who in 1667 had married Helen, daughter of Thomas Ramsey, former minister of Foulden; the status and number of witnesses at the baptism is a tribute to the family's evident respectability.[6] Thereafter the Aikenheads are heard of in connection with various legal cases, one of them, in 1682, involving a love-potion sold by James that nearly poisoned someone; within a year of this, he was dead, and his wife was buried on 3 May 1685.[7] The orphaned Thomas matriculated as a student at the University of Edinburgh in 1693; he then proceeded to follow the standard curriculum of the arts course, first, for his 'bajan' or first-year class, under the regent, Alexander Cunningham, and then under William Scott for the remainder of the course.[8]

Exactly when Aikenhead achieved notoriety as a free-thinker is uncertain, though the indictment against him late in 1696 stated that the offences had been committed 'now for more than a twelvemoneth by past', while a contemporary pamphlet confirms that his views were well-known in the early months of that year.[9] What we do know is that on 10

[6] General Register Office for Scotland, OPR 685¹/8, fo. 23ʳ: Baptism Register, Parish of Edinburgh, 1675–80. I am indebted to Tristram Clarke for this reference and for his advice on the Aikenhead family. See also *Roll of Edinburgh Burgesses and Guild-Brethren, 1406–1700* (Scottish Record Society, 59; Edinburgh, 1929), 23, and Hew Scott, *Fasti ecclesiae scoticanae*, new edn. (7 vols.; Edinburgh, 1915–28), ii. 48.

[7] D. Laing (ed.), *Historical Notices of Scottish Affairs, Selected from the Manuscripts of Sir John Lauder of Fountainhall* (2 vols.; Edinburgh, 1848), i. 343, 353, 451. For James Aikenhead's will, proved 30 Mar. 1683, see Scottish Record Office (hereafter SRO) CC/8/8/77, fos. 126ᵛ–8; on Helen's burial, see Scott, *Fasti*, ii. 48.

[8] See 'Matriculation Roll of the University of Edinburgh: Arts, Law, Divinity. Transcribed by Dr Alexander Morgan, 1933–4' (typescript, Edinburgh University Library), i (1623–1774), 104; Edinburgh University Library MS Da. 1. 33, fo. 120; Christine Shepherd, 'Philosophy and Science in the Arts Curriculum of the Scottish Universities in the Seventeenth Century', Ph. D. thesis (Edinburgh, 1975), 369.

[9] *State Trials*, xiii. 919; Mungo Craig, *A Lye is No Scandal* ([Edinburgh], 1697), 8–9, 15.

November 1696 he was summoned before the Scottish Privy Council, charged with blasphemy, and remitted for prosecution in the courts. The records of the Privy Council specifically note that Aikenhead was sent 'to be tryed for his life', which shows how seriously the matter was regarded: the Privy Council could have dealt summarily with Aikenhead, but the death penalty could only be imposed through the justiciary. The reason for this may have been a defiance on his part of which we will hear more later: a newspaper report of his arrest specifically notes how Aikenhead responded to the charge by 'owning [it] in part, and maintaining his Principles'.[10]

The impious statements that Aikenhead was charged with having made are itemized in the indictment, which is evidently based on the depositions of four witnesses, most of them fellow students. These have also survived, and they display a considerable degree of unanimity, though with sufficient variation to instil faith in their essential verisimilitude.[11] Theology, Aikenhead was said to have affirmed, 'was a rapsidie of faigned and ill-invented nonsense, patched up partly of the morall doctrine of philosophers, and pairtly of poeticall fictions and extravagant chimeras'. In one of the witnesses' statements, he was reported to have condemned theology as 'worse than the fictiones of the poets, for they had some connexione, but the Scriptures had none', and this perhaps represented a conflation with the next accusation against Aikenhead, namely, that 'you scoffed at, and endeavoured to ridicule the holy scriptures', claiming them to be 'so stuffed with maddness, nonsense, and contradictions, that you admired the stupidity of the world in being soe long

[10] SRO, PC1/51: 29; PC 4/2 (unpaginated), s.v. 10 Nov. 1696; *Protestant Mercury* (109), 18 Nov. 1696. The latter states that 'the Crime against him was for being a Priest', which immediately makes sense if it is presumed that 'priest' is a misprint for 'deist'.

[11] *State Trials*, xiii. 917–20, 923–7, from SRO JC2/19: 588–90, 592–6. The originals of the latter in the High Court Minute Book, SRO JC6/14 (unfoliated), have the actual signatures of the witnesses. A handful of emendations have been introduced from the MS versions of the texts here and elsewhere. For the witnesses, see 'Matriculation Roll of the University of Edinburgh', i. 101 (Adam Mitchell, John Neilson, John Potter), 104 (Quintigernus Craig); Patrick Middleton does not appear. A further witness mentioned by Craig is Hugh Crawfaord [sic]; Craig also mentions Richard Comlie as someone who could vouch for his own innocence (*A Lye*, 5, 8).

deluded by them'. The Old Testament he was said to have
described as

Ezra's fables, by a profane allusione to Esop's fables, and saying
that Ezra was the inventer thereof, and that being a cunning man
he drew a number of Babylonian slaves to follow him, for whom
he had made up a feigned genealogie as if they had been descended
of kings and princes in the land of Canaan, and therby imposed
upon Cyrus who was a Persian and stranger, persuading him by
the devyce of a pretendit prophecy concerning himself.

The same theme continued in a lighter vein with the accusation that one day Aikenhead had felt so cold that he had
'wished to be in the place that Ezra calls Hell, to warme
yourself there': it transpires from one of the witnesses'
statements that this was in August. As for Christ and the
New Testament, he was accused of calling it 'the History of
the Impostor Christ, and affirming him to have learned
magick in Egypt, and that coming from Egypt into Judea, he
picked up a few ignorant blockish fisher fellows, whom he
knew by his skill in phisognomie, had strong imaginations,
and that by the help of exalted imaginatione he play'd his
pranks as you blashphemously terme the working of his
miracles'. Aikenhead was said to have added 'that man's
imaginatione duely exalted by airt and industry can do any
thing, even in the infinite power of God', while his view of
Moses was comparable to that of Christ. It was claimed that
he had affirmed 'Moses, if ever you say ther was such a man,
to have also learned magick in Egypt, but that he was both
the better arteist and better politician than Jesus'.

Aikenhead was also reported to have rejected the doctrine
of the Trinity, 'and say it is not worth any man's refutation';
Christ's status as both God and man he considered 'as great
a contradictione as Hircus Cervus', the mythical goat-stag,
or as squaring the circle; while 'as to the doctrine of redemp-
tione by Jesus, you say it is a proud and presumptuous
devyce, and that the inventars thereof are damned, if after
this life ther be either rewaird or punishment.' The indictment
further accused Aikenhead of claiming that the notion of a
spirit was a contradiction, and of maintaining 'that God, the
world, and nature, are but one thing, and that the world was

from eternity'. It was also alleged that 'you have lykwayes in discourse preferred Mahomet to the blessed Jesus, and you have said that you hoped to see Christianity greatly weakened, and that you are confident that in a short tyme it will be utterly extirpat'—by 1800, according to one of the statements on which the indictment was based.

The indictment against Aikenhead invoked two laws. One was an Act against blasphemy passed in 1661 by the first Scottish Parliament of Charles II, which prescribed the death penalty for anyone who 'not being distracted in his wits Shall rail upon or curse God, or any of the persones of the blessed Trinity'. A further Act passed in 1695 both confirmed this and also dealt with 'whoever hereafter shall in their writing or discourse, deny, impugn or quarrell, argue or reason, against the being of God, or any of the persons of the blessed Trinity, or the Authority of the Holy Scriptures of the old and new Testaments, or the providence of God in the Government of the World'. It was ordered that, on the first occasion, such an offender should be imprisoned and 'give publick Satisfaction in Sackcloth to the Congregation, within which the Scandal was committed'; on the second he should be fined; and on the third he should be executed 'as an obstinat Blasphemer'.[12]

Aikenhead's trial took place on 23 December 1696, when his case came before a jury composed of Edinburgh citizens; five of those summoned refused to serve, which possibly shows a degree of unease about the case on their part.[13] The witnesses were called and examined, and we learn from an account of the trial in a London paper that, though Aikenhead's counsel 'had nothing further to say in his behalf, then

[12] T. Thomson and C. Innes (eds.), *The Acts of the Parliament of Scotland* (12 vols.; Edinburgh, 1814–75), vii. 202–3, ix. 386–7. Cf. ibid. vi. 208. The Acts are also printed in R. E. Florida, 'British Law and Socinianism in the Seventeenth and Eighteenth Centuries', in Lech Szczucki (ed.), *Socinianism and its Role in the Culture of the Sixteenth to Eighteenth Centuries* (Warsaw-Łódź, 1983), 201–10 (pp. 207–8).

[13] *State Trials*, xiii. 920–3, 927, from SRO JC2/19: 591, 596, where the names and occupations of the five jurors who were 'unlawed' are given. For a petition by the Lord Advocate to the Lords of Justiciary asking that letters of diligence be granted against Aikenhead, dated 27 Nov. 1696, see SRO JC26/Box 78/1. The overlapping accounts of the trial in British Library Harleian MS 6846, fos. 398–9, and in Bodleian MS Locke b. 4, fo. 91, are slightly differently worded.

desiring Mercy. The Prisoner excepted against his Witnesses, urging, that they were *Socinians*, and guilty of the same Crimes as they would endeavour to prove against him.'[14] This, however, was to no avail, and neither was the specific objection that he made against one of the witnesses, Mungo Craig.[15] On 24 December—Christmas Eve—Aikenhead was found guilty of cursing and railing against God the Father and the Son, of denying Christ's incarnation and the Trinity, and of scoffing at the Scriptures. He was thereupon condemned to death by hanging, evidently on the grounds that his transgression came under the terms of the 1661 Act and therefore merited immediate capital punishment, rather than the milder treatment of first offences prescribed in the more recent Act.

We come now to the question of whether and when Aikenhead repented of his offence, on which point our sources are not altogether consistent. A newspaper report of his trial records how, after the sentence had been passed, he requested that its implementation be postponed, 'which occasioned the Court to ask, Whether it was in hopes to save his Life, or the better to prepare himself for Death?'[16] Earlier still, when Aikenhead was in prison but not yet convicted, he had submitted a petition (which survives) in which he protested his 'sorrow and remorse' for the words that he had uttered, claiming that he had simply repeated them from some 'most villanous and atheisticall' books that he had read, which 'ought neither to be printed nor exposed to public view'. In addition, he gloried at length in having been born and educated in a country where the Gospel was so fully preached, affirming his belief in the immortality of the soul, the doctrine of the Trinity, the divine authority of the Scriptures, and 'the whole other principles of our holy Protestant religion'. He also stressed that he was a minor: his twenty-first birthday would have fallen on 28 March 1697.

---

[14] *Protestant Mercury* (122), 1 Jan. 1697. This therefore shows that Arnot, *A Collection of Criminal Trials*, 326–7, was wrong to presume that Aikenhead had no legal representation, an error repeated by various more recent authors.

[15] Craig, *A Lye*, 11. Aikenhead's objection was partly on the grounds of the malice displayed by Craig in publishing his first pamphlet, on which, see below.

[16] *Protestant Mercury* (122), 1 Jan. 1697.

All this was reiterated in a further surviving petition, made to the Privy Council after his conviction. In this he acknowledged the justice of the sentence for his 'blasphemous and wicked expressions', which 'ought not to be so much as named', but he repeated the mitigating circumstances of his minority and of his 'extravagances' having been prompted by the reading of 'some atheistical books'. He went on to request that his execution might be delayed, 'that I may have the opportunity of conversing with godly ministers in the place, and by their assistance be more prepared for an eternal rest'.[17] In addition, the London *Protestant Mercury* records how, on the last Sunday of his life, Aikenhead made an appearance in the prison church, 'where he seem'd to be convinced of his fatal Error, and 'tis believed, he will accordingly be respited for some longer time'.[18]

The Privy Council minutes confirm that petitions by Aikenhead were submitted on 31 December and 7 January: both were said to have been 'Craveing a Repreyve', and both were 'read and refused'.[19] This was probably at least partly due to doubt as to the genuineness of his repentance, the London *Flying Post* reporting of these appeals: 'which their Lordships declared should be granted, if he would make any acknowledgement of his Errors, or repent of his Blasphemous and Wicked Tenets, which he refused to do'. This may seem at odds with the gushing profession of faith contained in Aikenhead's petitions, but it is quite possible that these were not really written by him, but were composed on his behalf by ministers or lawyers, as commentators suggested a century ago.[20] The Privy Council's scepticism about the sincerity of Aikenhead's repentance was shared by one of the witnesses against him, Mungo Craig, who thought that he gave 'but little satisfaction' to the ministers who visited him while in

---

[17] *State Trials*, xiii. 921–3 n., 927–8.

[18] *Protestant Mercury* (125), 13 Jan. 1697.

[19] SRO, PC4/2, s.v. 31 Dec. 1696, 7 Jan. 1697. The petition of 31 Dec. is reported in the *Post Boy* (262), 9 Jan. 1697, and the *Protestant Mercury* (124), 8 Jan. 1697; that of 7 Jan. in the *Post Man* (265), 19 Jan. 1697. On the latter, cf. William Lorimer, *Two Discourses* (London, 1713), pp. v–vi, and presumably also the *Protestant Mercury* (125), 13 Jan. 1697.

[20] *Flying Post* (267), 28 Jan. 1697; *Macaulay on Scotland*, 35; Gordon, *Thomas Aikenhead*, 9–10.

gaol, and that he seemed unimpressed by the apologetic reading he was given.[21]

The *Flying Post* offers the following dramatic sequel. It claimed that, although on 7 January 'particularly' Aikenhead refused to repent, 'the next Day, being that of his Execution, he did acknowledge his Errors, and Atheistical Tenets, and owned the Being of a God, and the Merits of our Blessed Saviour; but the Council not having met that Day, the Sentence was Execute upon him.'[22] This cliff-hanging story is perhaps a little improbable; it was in any case denied by another commentator.[23] What matters here is that—despite his pleas for a postponement—on Friday, 8 January 1697, Aikenhead was taken from his prison cell in the old Tolbooth to 'the Galowlee betwixt Leith and Edinburgh', where he was executed. It was reported that 'He walk'd thither on Foot between a strong Guard of Fuzileers, drawn up in two Lines', either in a deliberate display of the panoply of the state or because of genuine apprehension that popular sympathy for him might cause a disturbance. He was also accompanied to the gallows by ministers, and it was said that he died, Bible in hand, 'with all the Marks of a true Penitent'.[24]

Aikenhead left to posterity not only the memory of his execution and the events that had preceded it, but also two further documents that are certainly of his own composition: indeed, the fact that both are noticeably convoluted in style strengthens the likelihood that the more clearly written petitions were in fact penned for him. One is a letter to his friends, written on the day of his execution, in which he yet again reiterates his repentance, 'Being now wearing near the last moment of my time of living in this vain world'. The other is a 'Paper' or 'Speech'—called in one copy Aikenhead's 'Cygnea Cantio', his swan-song.[25] This is a fascinating but

[21] Craig, *A Lye*, 9, 11. [22] *Flying Post* (267), 28 Jan. 1697.
[23] Johnston to Locke, 27 Feb. 1697, in *The Correspondence of John Locke*, ed. E. S. de Beer (8 vols.; Oxford, 1976–89), vi. 18.
[24] *State Trials*, xiii. 927; *Post Man* (265), 19 Jan. 1697. Cf. Lorimer, *Two Discourses*, p. vi; Macaulay, *History of England*, iv. 784.
[25] *State Trials*, xiii. 930–4 (from Bodleian MS Locke b. 4, fos. 99–101, 103–5). It is in the copy in Harleian MS 6846, fos. 400–1, that it is described as 'Thomas Aikenhead his Cygnea Cantio'.

somewhat frustrating document, oscillating between lucidity and virtual incoherence, between repentance and an almost defiant outline of his heterodox notions, in a manner that bears witness to the tortured state that the young man's mind must have been in by this time.

In contrast to the incendiary nature of much of what was attributed to him by the indictment, here Aikenhead gave quite a profound account of how he had arrived at his sceptical opinions. He stressed his 'insatiable inclination to truth' from an early age as the reason why he challenged orthodoxy, rather in the manner of free-thinkers of the eighteenth century. Like them, he also deliberately contradicted those who presumed that free-thinkers devised their doctrines in order to justify an immorality to which they had already committed themselves (indeed, one contemporary witness vouched for the fact that Aikenhead was 'not vicious, and extreamly studious').[26] He then proceeded to make a number of quite profound points. He spoke of his suspicion 'that a great part of morality (if not all)' was of purely human derivation. On the other hand, if an absolute morality *did* exist, then he questioned its relationship to God, and accused of circular reasoning those who identified God with moral perfection and then defined such perfection in terms of the nature of God. He also rehearsed various quite ingenious arguments for the adequacy of natural as opposed to revealed religion, arguing that the doctrine of providence itself contradicted revelation; lastly, he spoke of his difficulties with the doctrine of the Trinity, which he saw as tantamount to pantheism. He proceeded: 'these things I have puzled and vexed myself in, and all that I could learn therfrom, is, that I cannot have such certainty, either in natural or supernatural things as I would have. And so I desire all men, espehially ingenious young men, to beware and take notice of these things upon which I have splitt.' He ended by voicing the hope 'that my blood may give a stop to that rageing spirit of atheism which hath taken such a footing in Brittain, both in practice and profession'.

[26] Cf. David Berman, *A History of Atheism in Britain from Hobbes to Russell* (London, 1988), esp. ch. 8, s. 1. For the comment on Aikenhead, see Anstruther to Cuningham, 26 Jan. 1697, *State Trials*, xiii. 930.

Much of our evidence about the Aikenhead case derives from official records now preserved in the Scottish Record Office, but it is a testimony to the interest aroused by the affair at the time that various copies of these survive, especially of the indictment against Aikenhead, while multiple copies also exist of Aikenhead's 'Swan-Song' or 'Paper': this was even cited by the Scottish theologian Thomas Halyburton as one of the texts that he deemed worthy of refutation alongside Lord Herbert of Cherbury and others in his treatise on the inadequacy of natural religion, posthumously published in 1714.[27] The fullest collection of material, the principal source of the early nineteenth-century published version of it, was that made by John Locke: this now survives in the Lovelace Collection in the Bodleian Library. Though Locke left no record of his opinion on the case, his interest in it is clear from the care with which he preserved and endorsed a whole series of relevant documents that he was sent with a covering letter by his friend, the Scottish politician James Johnston, Secretary of State from 1691 to 1696.[28] Apart from the legal documents and Aikenhead's letter and 'Paper', Locke also had copies of his two petitions, which do not

[27] Thomas Halyburton, *Natural Religion Insufficient; and Reveal'd Necessary to Man's Happiness in his Present State* (Edinburgh, 1714), 119–23. Halyburton cites the piece as 'Aikenhead's Speech' in his 'Index of the Authors and Books quoted in this Treatise against *Deism*' (unpaginated, unsigned), but, contrary to what is suggested in *State Trials*, xiii. 938, this does not mean that it was printed. For other MS copies, see above, n. 25. For MS copies of the indictment, see Bodleian MS Locke b. 4, fos. 88–91, and British Library Harleian MS 6846, fos. 398–9; ibid., fos. 396–7, is a further, inferior copy of this, and another copy is to be found in Edinburgh University Library, La[ing] II.89, fos. 222–3 (I am indebted to Roger Emerson for this reference). These copies derive from the version of the indictment in the process papers, SRO JC26/Box 78/1, which is slightly different from that in the Books of Adjournal, JC2/19, printed in *State Trials*, xiii. 917–20.

[28] The originals now comprise MS Locke, b. 4, fos. 86–106: on fos. 107–8, see below, n. 29. For Johnston as the source of this material, see de Beer's attribution of the covering letter in Locke, *Correspondence*, vi. 17. In *State Trials*, xiii. 928, the letter is mistakenly attributed to Locke, and as a result it has been widely but incorrectly cited as revealing his views on the case. On the Locke MSS, presented to the Bodleian in 1947, see P. Long, *A Summary Catalogue of the Lovelace Collection of the Papers of John Locke in the Bodleian Library* (Oxford, 1959), esp. p. 42. Though the Aikenhead material now forms part of a volume of miscellaneous papers on politics and current affairs, I suspect that this arrangement is recent: an early 19th-century commentator on Locke's Aikenhead material described it as being 'In a bundle of MSS. on the subject of Toleration': Francis Horner, *Memoirs and Correspondence*, ed. Leonard Horner (2 vols.; London, 1843), i. 487.

otherwise appear to have survived, together with two other letters concerning the affair, one of which has hitherto been wholly ignored.[29]

Three other sources shed light on the case, all of them contemporary publications. One is the material in the English newspapers that I have already cited. The second is a lengthy retrospective account of the affair by a divine involved in it, William Lorimer.[30] Lastly, we have two pamphlets by Mungo Craig, one of the students who gave evidence against Aikenhead at his trial, the first of which came out while Aikenhead was in prison, and the second after his death. Interpretation of these documents is complicated by the bad blood that clearly existed between Aikenhead and his erstwhile colleague, which was exacerbated by Craig's public vindication of himself in this way. Aikenhead referred to his fellow student in his 'Paper', exonerating himself from the 'abominable aspersions' of Craig, 'whom I leave to reckon with God and his own conscience, if he was not as deeply concerned in those hellish notions, (for which I am sentenced) as ever I was'. Indeed, James Johnston suspected that Craig may well have been 'the decoy' who provided Aikenhead with the atheistical books from which he was supposed to have derived his opinions, a figure who was identified in Aikenhead's first petition as one of the witnesses against him, but whose name was suppressed from the copy of the petition with which Locke was provided.[31] That Johnston was not alone in this suspicion is indicated by Craig's anxiety to vindicate himself, particularly in his second pamphlet, *A Lye is No Scandal*, dated 15 January 1697 and subtitled 'a Vindication of *Mr Mungo Craig*, From a Ridiculous Calumny cast upon him by *T. A.* who was executed for Apostacy At *Edinburgh*, the 8 of *January*, 1697'. In it, he replied both to the accusation that he had

[29] Bodleian MS Locke b. 4, fos. 107–8, endorsed 'letter Mr W. from Scotland upon burning the 7 witches'. This is a copy (lacking the postscript) of a letter from Robert Wylie to William Hamilton, 16 June 1697, now SRO GD103/2/3/17/1. On this, and the letters of Johnston and Anstruther, see further below.

[30] Lorimer, *Two Discourses*, pp. iv–vii. See further below.

[31] *State Trials*, xiii. 933, 922; Johnston to Locke, 27 Feb. 1697, in Locke, *Correspondence*, vi. 19.

corrupted Aikenhead and to the charge that it was he who had reported his fellow student to the authorities.[32] Craig's first pamphlet comprises 'A Satyr Against Atheistical Deism', composed in rhyming couplets, 'With the Genuine Character of a Deist'—which, though a specimen of a well-established genre, was obviously aimed at Aikenhead— 'To which is Prefixt, An account of Mr Aikinhead's Notions, Who is now in Prison for the same Damnable Apostacy'. Craig's satire of Aikenhead's views is heavy-handed and somewhat tasteless, while the fact that he had an axe to grind evidently explains the moralizing tone of the pamphlet, in which he poured scorn on the irreligious claims of 'scurvy *Wittlings*' before going on to assert the need for a strong line to be taken in defence of Christian orthodoxy and national honour. Indeed, if anyone called for vengeance in this affair, it was Aikenhead's fellow student, who urged the magistrates to be inspired by 'a Rational and Holy Flame' of Christian zeal, to 'attone with Blood, th'affronts of heav'n's offended throne'.[33] This itself is arguably symptomatic of the instinctive conformity of most students when placed under pressure, to which Aikenhead is so spectacular an exception. In his second pamphlet Craig went on to criticize Aikenhead's swan-song as 'very unbecoming a dying Man in his Circumstances, being so far Stuff'd with the Affectation of a Bumbast and Airy Stile', while both are also interesting for the hints they give of the intellectual milieu from which Aikenhead emanated.[34]

Two major issues arise concerning Aikenhead's heterodoxy and its context: one is how he came to express the views that he did; the other is why he was treated as severely as he was, which involves looking at who advocated that this course be adopted and who took a more lenient line. The latter may be dispatched first, since it has attracted dispro-

---

[32] Craig, *A Lye*, 9–10, 15, and *passim*.

[33] Mungo Craig, *A Satyr against Atheistical Deism* (Edinburgh, 1696), 6, 10, 12 ff., and *passim*. On atheist 'characters', see Michael Hunter, 'The Problem of "Atheism" in Early Modern England', *Transactions of the Royal Historical Society*, 5th ser., 35 (1985), 135–57, esp. p. 147.

[34] Craig, *A Lye*, 9 and *passim*.

portionate attention in the past, particularly by those hostile
to the role of the Kirk in the affair. Thus Francis Horner,
one of the founders of the *Edinburgh Review*, enjoined his
heirs to preserve the Aikenhead case along with 'similar
documents from century to century, by way of proving,
some thousand years hence, that priests are ever the same'.[35]
Many other nineteenth-century commentators were inclined
to see Aikenhead as 'this unhappy victim of priestly bigotry',
though others rightly pointed out that he was sentenced by
the justiciary, while the Privy Council was the body that
had the ultimate say in the matter through their power of
reprieve.[36] What conclusion should one draw on this vexed
question?

At least three people who were close to the affair
expressed their distaste for what happened to Aikenhead.
One was William Lorimer, a minister domiciled in London
who happened to be staying in Edinburgh at this point, who
had preached a sermon to the chief magistrates while Aikenhead's trial was pending. Lorimer paid a series of pastoral
visits to the youth while he was in gaol, during which
Aikenhead was clearly subjected to a good deal of pious
exhortation and in which Lorimer claimed that he showed
genuine evidence of repentance. In his account of the affair,
published in 1713, Lorimer was at pains to stress the force
for moderation that he and other ministers had been, referring to an attempt to gain a reprieve for Aikenhead on the
day before his execution made by himself and George Meldrum, minister of Tron Church, the scene of one of Aikenhead's blasphemous outbursts. It was Lorimer's claim that
'the Ministers could not prevail with the Civil Government

[35] Horner, *Memoirs and Correspondence*, i. 288.
[36] *Christian Reformer; or, Unitarian Magazine and Review*, NS 12 (1856), 37.
See also nn. 3–4 above, and J. H. Burton, *History of Scotland, from the Revolution
to the Extinction of the Last Jacobite Insurrection* (2 vols.; London, 1853), i. 256–7;
Robert Chambers, *Domestic Annals of Scotland from the Revolution to the Rebellion
of 1745* (Edinburgh, 1861), 163; John Cunningham, *The Church History of Scotland*,
2nd edn. (2 vols.; Edinburgh, 1882), ii. 197–8; W. L. Mathieson, *Scotland and the
Union* (Glasgow, 1905), 220–1. For contrasting views, see John Warrick, *The
Moderators of the Church of Scotland from 1690 to 1740* (Edinburgh, 1913), 100–2;
P. Hume Brown, *History of Scotland to the Present Time* (3 vols.; Cambridge,
1911), iii. 31–2.

to pardon him', a majority of the Privy Council voting for Aikenhead's execution, 'that there might be a Stop put to the spreading of that Contagion of Blasphemy'.[37]

On the other hand, Lorimer could well be accused of special pleading, since it was evidently because his conduct in the Aikenhead case had been criticized that he felt impelled to issue this defence nearly two decades later. It is worth noting that the application for a reprieve to which Lorimer refers was rather late in the day, while it may well not be coincidental that both Lorimer and Meldrum were atypical of the Edinburgh clergy of the day, the former London-based and transient, the latter an immigrant from Aberdeen. Though Lorimer vaguely asserted how 'I am sure the Ministers of the Establish'd Church us'd him with an affectionate Tenderness', this is specifically contradicted by one of our other witnesses, the privy councillor Lord William Anstruther. Anstruther claimed that he brought the matter to the vote in the Council, but was told that clemency would only be possible if the ministers interceded for the victim: they, however, 'out of a pious tho I think ignorant zeal spok and preached for cutting him off'. He added how 'our ministers generaly are of a narow sett of thoughts and confined principles and not able to bear things of this nature'.[38]

Anstruther's views are revealing. As someone who was present at the Privy Council when Aikenhead was remitted for trial, he described him as 'an anomely, and monster of nature', and he was later to publish a generalized attack on atheism in which he was conventionally disapproving of the phenomenon. He was certain that the matter was one for the Privy Council, accompanying the anticlerical sentiments already cited by adding: 'I am not for consulting the church in state affairs.' On the other hand, he considered capital punishment more appropriate for crimes against society than

---

[37] Lorimer, *Two Discourses*, pp. iv–vii; *State Trials*, xiii. 925. On Lorimer and his role, see also Gordon, *Thomas Aikenhead*, 19 ff.

[38] Lorimer, *Two Discourses*, p. v; Anstruther to Robert Cuningham, 26 Jan. 1697, *State Trials*, xiii. 929–30. Cf. Robert Mylne's note on the copy of Craig's *Satyr against Atheistical Deism* in the Advocates' Library at Edinburgh, quoted in the supplement to Gordon's *Thomas Aikenhead*, 16.

against God, and he was compassionate towards Aikenhead, whom he had visited in prison and 'found a work on his spirit', adding: 'I doe think he would have proven an eminent christian had he lived.'[39]

Another advocate of leniency was Locke's friend James Johnston, who, as Secretary of State in the early 1690s, had been an active protagonist of a comprehensive Church and an opponent of Presbyterian extremism.[40] He argued that, despite the provision for severity contained in the law of 1661, there were so many mitigating circumstances in Aikenhead's case that he should have been treated leniently, especially in the light of the milder penalties for a first offence prescribed in the more recent Act of 1695. Johnston questioned whether any of the sentiments of which Aikenhead was accused amounted to 'railing' and 'cursing' as defined in the 1661 Act; he noted the retractions in Aikenhead's petitions; he observed the youthfulness of the witnesses and the unreliability of Craig, in the light of his own involvement in the affair; and he denied that Aikenhead had seduced anyone. 'Laws long in dessuetude should be gently put in Execution', he wrote, 'and the first example made of one in circumstances that deserve no compassion, whereas here ther is youth, Levity, docility, and no designe upon others.'[41]

Johnston was out of office by this time, but confirmation that others in the Privy Council held similar views is provided by the fact that, on 7 January, Aikenhead evidently came within a single vote of being granted a reprieve.[42] The views of the majority can be gauged only by their action: but clearly—like many in the early modern period—they took it for granted that the state should take a decisive role in defending Christian orthodoxy, and this is in line with what we know of the views of men like the Lord Advocate, Sir James Stewart,

[39] *State Trials*, xiii. 930; William Anstruther, *Essays, Moral and Divine* (Edinburgh, 1701), 1–37 (this contains no reference to Aikenhead). For the attendance on 10 Nov. 1696, see SRO PC1/51: 29.

[40] P. W. J. Riley, *King William and the Scottish Politicians* (Edinburgh, 1979), 82 ff. and *passim*.

[41] Johnston to Locke, 27 Feb. 1697, in Locke, *Correspondence*, vi. 19. For comparable views, see Arnot, *A Collection of Criminal Trials*, 327; David Hume, *Commentaries on the Law of Scotland* (2 vols.; Edinburgh, 1797), ii. 518–19.

[42] *Post Man* (265), 19 Jan. 1697.

or the Chancellor, Sir Patrick Hume.[43] Indeed, it is almost
certainly not coincidental that in January 1697 the Privy
Council was responsible not only for the execution of
Aikenhead, but also for taking the initiative in the last major
witch-hunt in Scotland, the affair of the witches of Renfrew-
shire, a juxtaposition noted by Macaulay, who spoke of 'two
persecutions worthy of the tenth century'. Just as Christina
Larner has argued that witch-hunting should be seen as an act
of moral cleansing carried out jointly by Church and State, so
the execution of Aikenhead should be similarly construed.[44]

Clerical attitudes towards Aikenhead are indicated by the
fact that, although the General Assembly of the Church of
Scotland was in session at Edinburgh from 2 to 12 January,
no organized attempt appears to have been made to save the
youth. Indeed, on 6 January 1697, while Aikenhead awaited
his execution, the Assembly wrote to the king urging 'the
vigorous execution' of the 'good laws' that existed to curb
'the abounding of impiety and profanity in this land'.[45] A
more explicit commentary on the case is given in two letters,
one to, and the other from, the minister, Robert Wylie, and
it is revealing that Wylie was by no means among the most
extreme of Presbyterians of the day.[46] The first is a letter that
Alexander Findlater, a minister in Wylie's parish of Hamilton, wrote to him on the day of the execution.[47] In the course

[43] Chambers, *Domestic Annals of Scotland*, 135–6; George Brunton and David
Haigh, *An Historical Account of the Senators of the College of Justice* (Edinburgh,
1832), 451–61; see also Macaulay, *History of England*, iv. 782–3.
[44] Macaulay, *History of England*, iv. 781; Christina Larner, *Enemies of God: The
Witch-hunt in Scotland* (London, 1981).
[45] T. Pitcairn et al. (eds.), *Acts of the General Assembly of the Church of Scotland
1638–1842* (Edinburgh, 1843), 258. Cf. ibid. 261–2, 267.
[46] On Wylie, who had played an active role in the rising of the Covenanters in
1679 and who died in 1715, see *The Correspondence of the Rev. Robert Wodrow*,
ed. T. MacCrie (3 vols.; Edinburgh, 1842–3), i. 113–15, and Scott, *Fasti*, iii. 260. For
his moderate views and the way in which these were changing in the 1690s, see
Wylie to the Duke of Hamilton, 11 Dec. 1693, in *HMC Supplementary Report on
the MSS of the Duke of Hamilton* (London, 1932), 129; Wodrow to James Wallace,
8 Mar. 1701, in L. W. Sharp (ed.), *Early Letters of Robert Wodrow, 1698–1709*
(Scottish Historical Society, 3rd ser. 24; Edinburgh, 1937), 154–5.
[47] Alexander Findlater to Robert Wylie, 8 Jan. 1697, National Library of Scotland,
Wodrow MSS 4to xxx, fos. 244–5 (Letter no. 144). The letter is not signed, but the
fact that it is from Findlater is proved by the reference to 'our stipend' on fo. 244. I
am grateful to Tristram Clarke for this point, and to Trevor Pateman for initially
drawing my attention to the letter. On Findlater, see Scott, *Fasti*, iii. 262.

of reporting on the proceedings of the General Assembly, Findlater wrote: 'I did see Aikenhead this day execute for his cursing railling against our Saviour calling him a Magician & that he hade Learned it in Aegypt but he abjured all his former errors & dyed penitently & I think G[od] was glorified by such ane awful & exemplary punishment.'

Wylie himself commented on the affair in retrospect, obviously in the light of the controversy that it aroused, in a letter to William Hamilton, laird of Wishaw, dated 16 June 1697.[48] Interestingly, he juxtaposed a vindication of the correctness of the treatment of Aikenhead with a defence of the ensuing witch-hunt. Just as, on the question of witchcraft, he stood firmly by the 'Scripture Law', 'Thou shalt not suffer a witch to live', so he sought to justify the severity of Aikenhead's sentence against what might be called the 'liberal' view of the matter; he associated this especially with the London 'wits', and he would doubtless not have been surprised to find it espoused by the Anglophile James Johnston.

Wylie was openly hostile to such attitudes. 'I have heard much of the censures past upon the Government here by some pious & charitable wits at London & elsewhere upon occasion of the sentence given against Aikenhead the Atheist,' he wrote:

but when these Gentlemen understood, if they are capable of thinking or understanding any thing but a bold sparkish jest, That the Ground of that Wretches sentence was not, as I know some of them misrepresented it, a retracted errour of the Judgement, but a perverse malicious railing against the adorable object of christian worship, which simply inferrs Death without the quality and aggravation of [obstinat continuance] tho that also was in Aikenhead's case till after the sentence, and this most expresly by the first clause of Act. 21. parl. 1 Ch[arles] 2. And when these witty Criticks consider that Reason, common sense and good manners (their own Trinity) do require that no man should in the face of a people spitefully revile & insult the object of their adoration, and that a Christian could not be innocent who should rail at or curse Mahomet at Constantinople, and consequently that their pleadings against Aikenheads condemnation were most unjust & founded upon mistake of the case and matter of fact. One would think that

[48] SRO GD103/2/3/17/1. See also n. 29 above.

after all this they should be more sparing cautious, at such a distance & under such uncertainty of report in passing their little rash Judgements upon the late proceedings of this Government with reference to the witches in Renfrew.

A similar letter to Wylie's was published in the London *Flying Post*, where its author was identified only to the extent of saying that it came 'from so good a Hand, that we dare Vouch for the Truth of every Word on't'. This complained of 'false Representations' of the case—evidently also in England—and it included an epitome of the indictment against Aikenhead to illustrate how his expressions really had been

so horrid that I should not desire they were made publick, if it were not to let the World know the Justice of our Proceedings in that Matter, which it seems some are so desirous to have any occasion to find fault with; for I am not willing to believe that there are any with you that out of favour to his wicked Principles exclaim at what is done against him.[49]

The background to such views is provided by the marked anxiety about heterodoxy to be found in Scotland in the 1690s, in the context of a sustained attempt by the Kirk to achieve a truly godly society. In 1690, the newly re-established General Assembly had expressed concern about the 'dreadful atheistical boldness' of those who 'disputed the being of God and his Providence, the Divine authority of the Scriptures, the life to come, and immortality of the soul, yea, and scoffed at these things', while a further Act passed in January 1696 specifically associated such ideas with 'the Deists'.[50] Parliament's re-enactment of the 1661 law against blasphemy in 1695 is itself to be seen in the context of such concern, while 1696 saw the Privy Council ordering 'a kind of inquisition' of booksellers' shops in Edinburgh for books deemed 'Atheisticall, erronious or profane and vitious', which included the writings of the early seventeenth-century apos-

[49] *Flying Post* (267), 28 Jan. 1697. For a comparable attitude, cf. *Protestant Mercury* (122), 1 Jan. 1697.
[50] Pitcairn, *Acts of the General Assembly*, 228, 253. Cf. Lorimer, *Two Discourses*, p. v.

tate J. C. Vanini, and the deist Charles Blount, together with Thomas Burnet's *Sacred Theory of the Earth*.[51]

One clue to the likely cause of such disquiet is provided by the attitudes and activities of the doctor and intellectual Archibald Pitcairne and his circle. Pitcairne was said at the time to be 'a professed Deist, and by many alledged to be ane Atheist . . . a great mocker at religion, and ridiculer of it', who produced two openly satirical attacks on the Presbyterian Church in the 1690s.[52] In addition, it turns out that Aikenhead's was not the first but the second case of heterodoxy to come to the attention of the Scottish Privy Council in the autumn of 1696. The earlier one—which, though reported in the London papers at the time, has hitherto been almost wholly overlooked—involved a merchant's apprentice called John Frazer. Frazer was accused of arguing or reasoning against the being of a God, of denying the immortality of the soul and the existence of the Devil, and of ridiculing the divine origin of the Scriptures, 'affirming that they were only to frighten folks and keep them in order': 'And when asked what religion he could be off that held such principles he answered of no religion at all but was just ane Atheist and that was all his religion.' On being confronted with these charges, however, Frazer immediately recanted fully and acknowledged the principles of Christianity, claiming—as Aikenhead was to do—that he had merely been repeating views expressed in a book that he had heard about, in this case Blount's *Oracles of Reason*, published in London in 1693. He added that he had also referred to another book, Grotius's *Of the Truth of the Christian Religion*, 'which was able to refute what any such Atheist was able to say'. The charge was found proven none the less, and he was ordered to be imprisoned and to give public satisfaction for his

[51] SRO PC1/51: 20, 28; *Protestant Mercury* (101), 28 Oct. 1696; *Post Man* (230), 29 Oct. 1696. The newspaper reports specifically link the second instance of this with the Frazer case: see below.

[52] Robert Wodrow, *Analecta* (4 vols.; Edinburgh, 1842–3), ii. 255. See also ibid. i. 322–3, iii. 307; Douglas Duncan, *Thomas Ruddiman: A Study of Scottish Scholarship in the Early Eighteenth Century* (Edinburgh, 1965), 15 ff. It is perhaps also worth noting that John Toland had been briefly at the University of Edinburgh in 1689–90: R. E. Sullivan, *John Toland and the Deist Controversy* (Cambridge, Mass., 1982), 3.

misdemeanour in sackcloth, as prescribed for a first offence under the 1695 Act: this he did over the next few months, finally being released on 25 February 1697.[53]

The contrast between the treatment of Frazer and Aikenhead is instructive. In part, Frazer may have been dealt with as he was because he himself drew attention to the mild initial penalty for which the recent Act provided, while Aikenhead may have suffered simply because his was the second case in quick succession, suggesting that a firm line was needed to curb such dangerous tendencies. But what was almost certainly more important was that, whereas Frazer's doubts were alleged to have been divulged on one specific occasion, when in the company only of the couple with whom he lodged, Aikenhead's expression of extreme anti-Christian views was both outspoken and sustained. It was clearly this that outraged Robert Wylie, and there is more than a hint of proselytizing in Aikenhead's open and provocative expression of his ideas, despite Johnston's claim to the contrary. The indictment against Aikenhead specifically accused him of having 'made it as it were your endeavour and work in severall compainies to vent your wicked blasphemies against God and our Saviour Jesus Christ, and against the holy Scriptures, and all revealled religione', reiterating how he uttered all this 'in severall companies without the least provocatione'.[54] In addition, Mungo Craig cited 'a considerable Number of Witnesses' who had 'heard him boast of the above mentioned ridiculous Notions', while Craig himself reported Aikenhead's assertion that 'all knowing Men' shared his views, 'whatever they said to the contrary', and his claim to have converted 'a certain Minister of the Gospel' to his position.[55]

It was probably this that earned Aikenhead his severe sentence. It is symptomatic that Wylie believed that Aikenhead had been obstinate 'till after the sentence', while the

---

[53] SRO PC1/51: 22–7, 130; PC4/2, s. v. 23, 25 Oct., 26 Nov., 31 Dec. 1696, 11, 25 Feb. 1697; *Protestant Mercury* (101, 122, 124), 28 Oct. 1696, 1, 8 Jan. 1697; *Post Boy* (262), 31 Dec. 1696. See also Chambers, *Domestic Annals of Scotland*, 147.

[54] *State Trials*, xiii. 919–20 (cf. the witnesses' statements, ibid. 923–4); Locke, *Correspondence*, vi. 19.

[55] Craig, *A Satyr*, 3, *A Lye*, 9.

author of the anonymous letter to the *Flying Post* believed
that he had remained defiant till the day of his execution, and
Craig implied that he had never repented at all.[56] Even if
these commentators were mistaken about this—and in this
connection the uncertainty about the extent and date of
Aikenhead's repentance is significant—clearly, their views
and others' were affected by Aikenhead's *manner*, the way in
which he expressed his doubts, and the effect that this had on
those who heard them. The indictment was clearly intended
to stress this, emphasizing the 'reproachfull expressions' that
the youth had used towards the supreme objects of Christian
worship, while Craig's statement alleged that Aikenhead's
views about the New Testament were expressed 'in a scorning
and jeiring manner'.[57]

Taking all this into account, one could argue that, for the
authorities and, indeed, for many orthodox Christians of the
day, what was significant about Aikenhead was less the exact
nature of his statements and their intellectual coherence, than
the simple fact of his outrageous apostasy: it was essentially
an act of anti-Christian revolt rather than a piece of pure
thought. Johnston was being excessively precise in arguing
that, of the words that Aikenhead was accused of uttering,
only the accusation that Christ was an impostor (for which
the only witness was Craig in any case) really constituted
'railing' and 'cursing' (it is interesting that the eighteenth-
century historian Hugo Arnot, who took a similar line,
construed this of a different comment[58]). Rather, I think it
was for his deliberate offensiveness that Aikenhead was
convicted, the crucial factor being the affront caused to
others.

This raises the issue of what was involved in the crime of
blasphemy in this case, for the view of the offence expressed
by Robert Wylie has something in common with the modern
British legal definition, where the crucial issue is 'the manner

---

[56] *Flying Post* (267), 28 Jan. 1697; Craig, *A Lye*, 9; for Wylie, see above, p. 238.
Cf. above, pp. 227–9, and Lorimer, *Two Discourses*, p. v, where it is stated that
Aikenhead 'continued sullen and obstinate, I think for some Months'.

[57] *State Trials*, xiii. 919, 926.

[58] Locke, *Correspondence*, vi. 19; Arnot, *A Collection of Criminal Trials*, 326–7.

in which the doctrines are advocated'.[59] Wylie's attitude was not identical with the modern view that 'the substance of the doctrines themselves', however damaging to Christianity, is irrelevant so long as it is soberly expressed: that was a development that had to await the nineteenth century. But the crucial point is that, in contrast to Johnston's and others' concern with the content of anti-Christian sentiment rather than its mode of presentation, Wylie and his associates evidently saw the essence of the crime of blasphemy as having been met if—to cite a nineteenth-century judge's dictum— 'the tone and spirit is that of offence and insult and ridicule ... an appeal to the wild and improper feelings of the human mind, more particularly in the younger part of the community'.[60]

Undoubtedly, this aspect of the case is central to an understanding of why Aikenhead was treated as he was. It is also fundamental to the character of irreligion as it was perceived by contemporaries, who clearly *expected* this kind of aggressive oral assault on Christian orthodoxy.[61] The implication of this was that, for them, it did not matter very much how coherent or original Aikenhead's statements were. Indeed, it is even possible that the accusations against Aikenhead did not comprise his actual views at all, but rather the smears of people outraged by the very notion of an assault on Christianity, who embroidered the case according to their expectations of what free-thinkers were likely to say.[62] Certainly, much of what Aikenhead was accused of saying belonged to a standard repertoire of anti-Christian polemic, which recurs frequently in early modern characterizations of atheists and can be traced back to early Christian times—the

[59] Quoted from Stephen's *Digest of the Criminal Law* by Lord Scarman in connection with the famous *Whitehouse* v. *Lemon* case: Law Commission Working Paper 79, *Offences against Religion and Public Worship* (London, 1981), 3.
[60] Ibid. 7.
[61] Cf. Hunter, 'Problem of "Atheism"', 141–2; Michael Hunter, 'Science and Heterodoxy: An Early Modern Problem Reconsidered', in D. C. Lindberg and R. S. Westman (eds.), *Reappraisals of the Scientific Revolution* (Cambridge, 1990), 441–2, 445–6.
[62] For a discussion of this possibility in another, comparable case, see David Wootton, *Paolo Sarpi: Between Renaissance and Enlightenment* (Cambridge, 1983), 142–5 (where the Aikenhead case is noted).

accusation that Moses and Christ were magicians, for
instance, or that religion was the device of 'politicians', or
that the Scriptures were unreliable.[63] But it is equally likely
that he *did* say these things, since even the clichés represent
telling assaults on fundamental Christian principles, which
Aikenhead ingeniously adapted in genuinely original ways.
Moreover, it is worth noting that he did not deny making
these statements. His only specific denial (in his farewell
letter to his friends) was of having 'practised magick and
conversed with devils': his blasphemous outbursts he
acknowledged, only claiming that they were derived from
books.[64]

What, however, was the relationship between the offensive
oral outbursts that brought Aikenhead to the attention of the
authorities and the more serious streak represented especially
by the 'Paper' that he wrote while awaiting execution? The
latter contained the metaphysical speculations on the existence of an absolute morality and the like that were deemed
worthy of refutation by Thomas Halyburton, as if compris-
ing a serious anti-Christian treatise, although Halyburton
was rather disdainful of 'this inconsiderable *Trifler*, whose
undigested Notions scarce deserve the Consideration we have
given them'.[65] It is easy to presume that these sober thoughts
must represent Aikenhead's 'real' ideas, and to write off his
earlier and more outrageous outbursts as trivial and insignificant. But in fact a good case can be made for precisely the
opposite evaluatiuon, with Aikenhead's 'real' ideas being
those that he expressed at liberty among his friends. It is the
later statements of which one should surely be suspicious,
issued as they were under the heavy influence of incarcera-
tion, indoctrination, and despair, their very agenda perhaps
being set by divines like William Lorimer who ministered to
Aikenhead during his final weeks, and by the anti-atheist
tracts that he was given to read at that stage, written by
authors such as the English apologist Sir Charles Wolseley.[66]

Even Aikenhead's account of the origins of his specu-

[63] See Hunter, 'Problem of "Atheism"', 141, 145, 149.
[64] *State Trials*, xiii. 934, 922 n., 928, 933.
[65] Halyburton, *Natural Religion Insufficient*, 123 (and 119–23).
[66] Craig, *A Lye*, 11.

lations, echoed by that which Lorimer gave 'in effect from his own Mouth', may deliberately have sanitized these by placing them in a respectable setting of Christian doubt: in that context, one would hardly have expected Aikenhead to claim anything other than that his 'doubtings and inquisitions' had resulted from the fact that he had 'been ever, according to my capacity, searching good and sufficient grounds whereon I might safely build my faith'. Especially predictable is Lorimer's neat account of Aikenhead's progress from initial doubt about the Trinity to questioning the divinity of Christ: 'and from his not being God, and yet assuming so much to himself, he concluded that he must have been the greatest Impostor that ever was in the World, and that the Christian Religion is a great Cheat imposed upon the World by cunning Men', a moral tale that Lorimer included in his text for the benefit of Socinians, who might be warned by the fate of 'that poor Man'.[67]

On the other hand, even if this is a very partial view of the progress of Aikenhead's apostacy, it is worth considering it as a clue to the source of his anti-Christian ideas, the next point to which I wish to turn. One thing is clear, that the experience of doubt with regard to even the most fundamental Christian doctrines was commonplace among the highly devout in the early modern period. What is more, the kind of arguments voiced in such contexts overlapped with the opinions associated with Aikenhead—for instance, the view that the Scriptures were 'rather a Fable and cunning Story, then the holy and pure Word of God', or doubt about the existence of God, or the reality of the life to come.[68] Such notions are to be found in the spiritual autobiographies of various godly figures, and G. E. Davie has drawn a particular parallel between Aikenhead's apostacy and the experience of doubt of Thomas Halyburton, the very divine who was to take it upon himself to refute Aikenhead's ideas. Davie writes

[67] *State Trials*, xiii. 931, 934; Lorimer, *Two Discourses*, p. vii.
[68] John Bunyan, *Grace Abounding to the Chief of Sinners and The Pilgrim's Progress*, ed. Roger Sharrock (Oxford, 1966), 33 and *passim*. Cf. e.g. Richard Baxter, *Reliquiae Baxterianae*, ed. Matthew Sylvester (London, 1696), 21–4, and Sir Simonds D'Ewes, *Autobiography and Correspondence*, ed. J. O. Halliwell (2 vols.; London, 1845), i. 251–4.

how Halyburton 'in his youth, experienced a succession of similar sceptical crises, the last one (1696) contemporary with that of Aikenhead who could perhaps have been known to him personally'.[69]

Not only does Halyburton well illustrate the proclivity of the highly devout to such temptations: he also demonstrates how these might be encouraged by higher education and by reading dangerous books. Halyburton's inner doubts were exacerbated by attending university and studying theology, metaphysics, and natural philosophy, which made him 'accustomed to subtle Notions, and tickled with them'. This fostered 'the natural Atheism of my Heart', suggesting 'contrary disquieting Arguments' that would not otherwise have occurred to him. In addition, when later reading the writings of the deists in order to refute them, he found their theories unnervingly contagious.[70]

Leaving on one side the view of 'natural Atheism' that he expounds there, Halyburton's evaluation of the role of university education is certainly borne out by what we know of Aikenhead and his milieu. Aikenhead had been through most of the standard university arts course, and surviving notebooks and other sources show that the regents under whom he studied, Alexander Cunningham and William Scott, were typical of Scottish academics of their day in the way in which they cross-fertilized a basic scholastic framework with new ideas derived from philosophers like Descartes.[71] The influence of this blend on Aikenhead and his friends is well evidenced by the pamphlets of his one-time colleague Craig. The quintessential 'deist' whose character Craig sketched appears in the terminology of scholastic philosophy—'*An accidental aggregat of Contradictions actually existent*'—but Craig's familiarity with the ideas of Descartes and other modern natural philosophers is shown by his references to

[69] Davie, *Scottish Enlightenment*, 9–10.

[70] *Memoirs of the Life of the Reverend Mr Thomas Halyburton*, ed. Mrs Jane Halyburton, 2nd edn. (Edinburgh, 1715), 26–7, 41 ff., 52.

[71] Shepherd, 'Philosophy and Science', 68–70, 74–5, 99, 154, 175, 233 (on Cunningham), 126, 213, 221–2 (on Scott). On the course as a whole, see ibid., *passim*, and Christine Shepherd, 'The Arts Curriculum at Aberdeen at the Beginning of the 18th Century', in J. J. Carter and J. H. Pittock (eds.), *Aberdeen and the Enlightenment* (Aberdeen, 1987), 146–54.

such topics as vortices and the notion of a world in the moon; one of the witnesses against Aikenhead similarly claimed that he likened Christ's ascension to 'a progresse to the world in the moon'.[72]

This context undoubtedly explains much about Aikenhead's apostacy, from the point of view of both presentation and content. The disputations that traditionally comprised a significant part of the curriculum were notorious for making students 'pert and precocious', and Craig specifically remarked on Aikenhead's 'dexterity in that Art'.[73] In addition, the eclecticism typical of the late seventeenth century was commonly perceived as encouraging sceptical attitudes: indeed, in his 'Paper' Aikenhead criticized his education in terms not so dissimilar from Halyburton's for failing to produce 'really sufficient' grounds for faith, while 'with the greatest facility sufficient ground could be produced for the contrair'. More important, much of what Aikenhead dealt with in that document is easily recognizable in the context of the university curriculum—particularly of the ethics classes that he would have had in his third year (1695–6)—including such topics as the relationship of divine and natural law and the morality of human actions.[74]

Aikenhead would also have been introduced to dangerous ideas on various subjects, which were widely canvassed, largely so as to assert the superior value of orthodox ones. Thus the notions of Hobbes and, to a slightly lesser extent, Spinoza were regularly refuted in late seventeenth-century lectures, including the view that moral laws were of human rather than divine origin. It is symptomatic that Halyburton, who complained of the influence of these authors on 'our *young Gentry* and *Students*', considered Aikenhead's questioning of absolutes in morality a 'confus'd Discourse, which probably he learn'd from *Hobbs*'.[75] In addition, surviving lists of books purchased for the University of Edinburgh at this time show that some quite questionable items were

---

[72] Craig, *A Satyr*, 1, 3, 12, 14, and *passim*, *A Lye*, *passim*; *State Trials*, xiii. 926.
[73] Shepherd, 'Philosophy and Science', 30; Craig, *A Lye*, 4.
[74] Shepherd, 'Philosophy and Science', 47 and ch. 5, *passim*. Cf. *State Trials*, xiii. 930–4.
[75] Halyburton, *Natural Religion Insufficient*, 31, 119–20.

bought for the library, including Hobbes's works together with critiques of them, Charles Blount's translation of Philostratus' *Life of Apollonius of Tyaneus*, two copies of the heterodox *Letters Writ by a Turkish Spy*, Burnet's *Archaeologiae philosophiae* as well as his *Sacred Theory of the Earth*, and John Toland's *Christianity not Mysterious*.[76]

Aikenhead may have had access to private libraries too, and the full range of potentially unorthodox works with which his circle would have been familiar is illustrated by the account of the authors likely to be deployed by a quintessential 'deist' in Mungo Craig's first pamphlet. First, and most obviously, there were the ancients—Aristotle for eternalism, and Epicurus for the denial of providence and the immortality of the soul, the idea that the world comprised a fortuitous concourse of atoms, and above all the advocacy of the pursuit of pleasure as the *summum bonum*. But equally important were the moderns. Descartes's 'Dubitation' was 'a chief Pillar of his Scepticism', while he also valued the French philosopher for confirming Epicurus' theories by showing how, '*Mater and motion being granted, all cou'd fall out as they are, without the concurrance of an inteligent Over-ruling Power*.' The 'deist's' 'dearest darlings', however, were 'first the excellent Head-piece of *Malmsbury*' [i.e. Hobbes] and 'the incomparable' Spinoza, together with Blount's *Oracles of Reason*—'*Lucretius Redivivus*'— John Frazer's acquaintance with which in Edinburgh in 1696 has already been noted.[77] From this pot-pourri Aikenhead could have derived any number of the opinions attributed to him, including both the metaphysical speculations in his 'Paper' and also various of the views associated with him in the indictment: that God and nature were identical, that the world was eternal, that the notion of spirit was nonsensical, or that the afterlife was unproven. There was also his lionizing of reason as the supreme arbiter, and his stress on fraud in

---

[76] Edinburgh University Library, MSS Da. 1.32, fos. 68, 75, 82, 134, Da. 1. 33, fos. 87, 111, Da. 1. 34, fos. 1, 7, 9. On the *Letters Writ by a Turkish Spy*, see David Wootton's chapter in this book.

[77] Craig, *A Satyr*, 14 (I have read through his sarcastic emendations, e. g. of Blount's title as his '*Oracles of Nonsense*'). It is perhaps worth noting that Craig's 'deist' 'has a very ill gust of Mr *Lock's Moral way of Demonstration*, however well he may please other parts of his works'.

underwriting religion. All could be found modishly expressed in books like Blount's and Spinoza's, but they could also trace their pedigree back to antiquity.

Indeed, in view of the wide availability of such dangerous ideas and the disputatiousness induced by academic training, it is perhaps surprising that there were not more Aikenheads. Certainly, Aikenhead appears to have found a receptive audience for his ideas among his friends, who, as he argued at his trial, were as much 'Socinians' as he.[78] It is also interesting that in 1699, the parliamentary commission for the Scottish universities listed various ideas current among students that masters were to guard against, and that some of them overlap with notions voiced by Aikenhead, including excessive reliance on reason, the view that the world was eternal, and the denial of spirit.[79] But such concern apparently went no further on this or on most other occasions, and virtually the only analogous case to Aikenhead's was that of Robert Hamilton of Aberdeen, whose Hobbesian opinions lost him his post in 1668.[80] In general, students did not go very far in developing the heterodox ideas with which they came into contact, conforming instead to the orthodox framework within which these were presented to them.

Much the same may be said of the experience of religious doubt of Halyburton and others. On the face of it, this may appear to have something in common with the case of Aikenhead, whose 'Paper' could be seen as an extreme specimen of the genre to which works like Halyburton's *Memoirs* belong: a struggle with anti-Christian doubt was thus recapitulated in the context of an assertion of repentance in the hope that others would be taught the counter-arguments with which the seductive appeal of these heterodox urgings might be repelled. Yet, once again, I think that one has to take into account the context of Aikenhead's 'Paper', and to avoid laying undue stress on this as against his earlier, more aggressive remarks. For there is a fundamental difference between the way in which Aikenhead and godly auto-

[78] See above, p. 227. Cf. Lorimer, *Two Discourses*, p. v.
[79] Shepherd, 'Philosophy and Science', 305–6.
[80] Ibid. 148, 200, 262–3, 307; *The Diary of Mr John Lamont of Newton, 1649–71*, ed. J. R. Murdoch (Edinburgh, 1830), 207–8.

biographers like Halyburton handled their doubts and made use of the books at their disposal. Despite his inner struggle with anti-Christian arguments, there is no reason to believe that Halyburton would ever have contemplated a public expression of scepticism like Aikenhead's. For the godly, the experience of doubt was essentially personal and private: indeed, one of the problems that believers suffered from was a conviction that their doubts were unique, as with Elizabeth Wilkinson, who 'could not acquaint any with my condition. I did not think that it was so with any other, as it was with me.' Moreover, John Bunyan, for one, distinguished the 'atheism' suffered by a believer like himself from outright apostasy, involving open, impenitent denial of God.[81]

In Aikenhead, by contrast, what one apparently sees is an aggressive nurturing of these anti-Christian sentiments into a cogent and coherent assault on Christianity, which all the evidence suggests that he propagated in a similar manner to that alleged against Christopher Marlowe in Elizabethan England, the case with which Aikenhead's is perhaps most directly comparable.[82] Moreover, there is a clear continuum between the 'serious' doubt of Aikenhead's 'Paper' and the aggressive free-thought of his publicly expressed views. In part, he dealt with the same issues, notably the Trinity, topic of considerable concern in the 1690s: thus, while he instanced his doubts about this as a 'great point' in his 'Paper', one of the witnesses averred that he had heard Aikenhead speak about this 'oftner than any other thing'.[83] More important, however, is the ingenuity that Aikenhead deployed towards the ideas that he adopted. In the 'Paper' this is shown in various intriguing speculations—his view of the incompatibility of revelation and providence, for instance—while it is no less in evidence in the way in which he put materials to anti-Christian use in the public statement attributed to him by the indictment.

One particularly interesting theme is his stress on 'the

[81] Edmund Staunton, *A Sermon Preacht at Great Milton* (Oxford, 1659), 2; Bunyan, *Grace Abounding and Pilgrim's Progress*, 72.

[82] P. H. Kocher, *Christopher Marlowe* (Chapel Hill, NC, 1946), chs. 2–3.

[83] *State Trials*, xiii. 932–3, 924. On the debate on this issue at the time, see esp. Sullivan, *John Toland*, ch. 3.

power of the imagination' as a potential explanation of how
Christ might have executed his miracles by natural means.
This was a concept that derived from the natural magical
tradition of the sixteenth century, a very flexible explanatory
principle invoking mental forces not directly under conscious
control that could either be 'occult' or effectively psychological in rationale.[84] The idea that miracles might be
explained in these terms had been canvassed by Pietro
Pomponazzi and, following him, by J. C. Vanini, at least one
of whose works is known to have been in circulation in
Edinburgh in the 1690s.[85] That views like these were to be
expected from such men was stressed by the Cambridge
Platonist Henry More, another author whose writings were
certainly known to Aikenhead's circle, who was well aware
of, and was hostile to, the ideas of Vanini and his 'bold
Impiety and Prophaneness', and who complained of how 'the
whistling Atheists impute all to *the natural power of
Imagination*'.[86] Certainly, Aikenhead made good use of the
heterodox potential of this idea to prove how 'our Saviour
wrought no miracles but what any other man might have
wrought by ane exalted fancie', and he went further than any
of his predecessors in his cutting dismissal of Christ's miracles
as 'pranks'.[87]

A similar picture can be found in the views attributed to
Aikenhead concerning the Bible, and particularly the idea
'that Ezra was the inventor thereof'. This was a notion that
Aikenhead could have derived from Spinoza's *Tractatus*,

[84] See D. P. Walker, *Spiritual and Demonic Magic from Ficino to Campanella*
(London, 1958), esp. 76 ff., 107 ff.

[85] See W. T. Johnston (ed.), *The Best of our Owne* (Edinburgh, 1979), 21,
concerning a copy of Vanini's *De admirandis* auctioned as part of the Balfour library
in 1695. See also above, pp. 239–40. On miracles, see esp. Luigi Corvaglia (ed.), *Le
opere de Giulio Cesare Vanini* (2 vols.; Milan, 1933–4), i. 31 ff.

[86] Craig, *A Lye*, 11–12 (this also shows that Grotius was known to this group, as
well as to Fraser: see above, p. 240); Henry More, *An Explanation of the Grand
Mystery of Godliness* (London, 1660), 109, 335.

[87] *State Trials*, xiii. 924. An overlapping opinion attributed to Aikenhead by Craig
in his statement is as follows: 'baptisme was a magicall ceremony that tyed children's
imagination to that religion wherto they were baptised; and furder, if he were
banished, he would make all Christianitie tremble, and would wryte against
Christianity, and that if he or any other needed a familiar genius he could call for
it': ibid. 926–7.

chapter 8 of which specifically made this claim. Alternatively, he could have picked it up from the *Critical History of the Old Testament* by the French divine Richard Simon, published in French in 1678 and translated into English in 1682, a copy of which had been bought for Edinburgh University Library earlier in the 1690s.[88] This canvassed a milder version of a similar theory in contradistinction to Spinoza's view, arguing that Ezra had been responsible for collecting and editing what survived of earlier Hebrew writings after the Babylonian Captivity.[89] But here again Aikenhead surpassed any putative source in his aggressive taunt that the Scriptures were 'Ezra's fables', 'by a profane allusione to Esop's fables', as the indictment put it.[90]

As for the rest of Aikenhead's allegations, these could perfectly easily have been derived from an alert and cynical reading of the biblical text, together with an ingenious embroidery of the old accusation that Christ and Moses were magicians and impostors.[91] Then, further gibes must have slipped off Aikenhead's tongue on the spur of the moment, as with 'the place that Ezra calls Hell'. The same is true of items reported by witnesses but not included in the indictment—for instance, his claim that 'the Revelatione was ane alchimy book for finding out the philosophers stone', or his comparison of the Jews with the Goths and Vandals.[92] Moreover, in a slightly convoluted way, I think it may be thus that one should read the 'Catalogue of the Works promised to the World by T. Aik[enhead] Gent.' included by Mungo Craig in his *Satyr against Atheistical Deism*: for through its rather pedestrian satire comes an echo of the actual ideas that Aikenhead was claimed to have uttered that gives a real sense of their inventive bravado.[93]

[88] Edinburgh University Library, Da. 1. 33, fo. 115. Cf. MS Da. 1. 32, fo. 130.

[89] Richard Simon, *A Critical History of the Old Testament* (London, 1682), preface and bk. 1, ch. 4 *passim*.

[90] *State Trials*, xiii. 919–20.

[91] Ibid. 919–20, 923–7. See above, pp. 243–4. There could be confusion in some of these claims: thus, one of the witnesses claimed that it was of Muhammad that Aikenhead said what the indictment associated with Moses: ibid. 925, 919. Aikenhead himself appears to have confused Cyrus and Artaxerxes.

[92] Ibid. 925, 926.

[93] Craig, *A Satyr*, 3. Cf. Craig, *A Lye*, 4–5.

In short, I see no reason why the more or less serious utterances in different contexts that have come down to us should not be construed as suggesting that Aikenhead had a complete 'system' of anti-Christian ideas. These would have included weighty philosophical notions like eternalism, the belief that God might be identified with nature, or the questioning of an absolute morality. But equally important, in view of the central role of the Bible in a strongly Protestant country like Scotland, was his attack on Holy Writ and its chief protagonists in the form of Moses and Christ. Clearly, different parts of this package were appropriate in different milieux: but that is no reason for doubting its coherence. Moreover, this helps to make sense of a facet of orthodox perceptions of heterodoxy at the time that to us may seem strange, namely, why contemporaries attached such significance to a bantering approach to Christianity, usually orally expressed. Not only does a close scrutiny of the material relating to Aikenhead indicate the continuum between this and his more serious ideas; it also indicates the sheer power of his gibes at Christianity, the resonances of which echo down the centuries. The reaction of the Scottish authorities may have been excessive, but they were arguably right to see the threat posed by this youth who aggressively asserted that 'within some hundreds of years the whole world would be converted to his opinion, and the Christian religion would be wholly ruined'.[94]

[94] *State Trials*, xiii. 925: this was averred by one of the witnesses, John Neilson.

NOTE

As this book was going to press, further documents relating to the Aikenhead case came to light among the Justiciary Papers at the Scottish Record Office; these have now been added to the material in JC26/Box 78/1. They comprise the remit of the case to the Justiciary and the letters of diligence; lists of witnesses and jurors, with a petition from one of the latter who failed to serve; three executions of summons, and two records of the jury's verdict; Aikenhead's initial petition, as printed in *State Trials*, xiii. 921–3 n.; and 'Defences' for Aikenhead against the charges on which he was tried. All the items are in scribal hands, but with holograph signatures.

The new material shows that six, rather than five, jurors were 'unlawed' (cf. above, p. 226), while more witnesses are listed than those whose evidence survives, including Hugh Crafurd [*sic*] (cf. above, n. 11) and Robert Henderson, 'Keeper of the Bibliotheck of the College of Edinburgh'—an interesting point in view of the role that books from the library may have played in the case. Aikenhead's 'Defences' mainly reiterate the points made in his extant petition, but appeal is also made to the provision in the 1695 Act that only those who proved obdurate should be executed. The manuscript text of the petition differs from the printed version in that the name of Mungo Craig is clearly inserted in the place where it was suppressed in Locke's copy (see above, p. 232); at the end Aikenhead has added the following signed note in his own hand, which is absent from Locke's copy: 'And I doe hereby humbly refer my self to and bege your Lordships' mercy and compassion upon the account of the premisses'.

9

Disclaimers as Offence Mechanisms in Charles Blount and John Toland

DAVID BERMAN

> I come to bury Caesar, not to praise him.
>
> Shakespeare, *Julius Caesar*, III. ii.

In this chapter I shall be examining two influential free-thinkers—Charles Blount and John Toland—whose works were issued between 1679 and 1720. Blount was from an upper-class English family; a correspondent and follower of Hobbes, he committed suicide in 1693. Toland's background was very different: obscure, Irish, and Roman Catholic. Whereas Blount's father was a cultured free-thinker, Toland's (we are told) was either a French soldier or a popish priest. A protégé of Locke, Toland coined the word 'pantheist' in 1705. Swift called him the 'great Oracle of the Anti-Christians'.[1]

Most scholars think that Blount and Toland were deists.[2] I call them by the neutral term 'free-thinker', although I think they were atheists. Part of my aim here is to defend this view. My other aim is to explore the strategies they used to express their irreligious views. My general name for these strategies is: the art of theological lying. I speak of *lying* because I think it is the most accurate term, and that little is to be gained by

---

[1] D. Berman, 'John Toland', in G. Stein (ed.), *The Encyclopedia of Unbelief* (New York, 1985), 668–70.

[2] L. Stephen, 'Blount' and 'Toland', in *DNB*; J. M. Robertson, *A History of Free-thought*, 4th edn. (London, 1936), 649; E. Mossner, 'Deism', in P. Edwards (ed.), *Encyclopedia of Philosophy* (8 vols.; New York, 1967), ii. 328; P. Gay, *Deism: An Anthology* (Princeton, NJ, 1968), 52.

euphemisms. Given the oppressive forces of the time, the basic choice for a free-thinker was between silence or lying, between burying his gold or mixing it with lead so that it could be more safely minted—as Blount's Dutch printer nicely put it.[3] The free-thinker was in a moral dilemma: if he was silent, the truth (as he saw it) would suffer by omission; if he told the truth, he would suffer. The solution was a compromise: lying for the truth, lying so that the intelligent would know or could unravel the truth, while the authorities could not punish or victimize the writer.

That Blount was a theological liar is clear from this passage in his *Anima mundi* (published in London in 1679), where he speaks of those who:

not taking the truly wise advice of St Paul, to *beware of vain Philosophy*, have adventur'd to uphold the knowledge of Humane Souls after Death, not by Faith and the Scriptures, whose sacred Authority were the most proper support of that Belief, but out of the presumption of their own sufficiency, by the meer light of Natural Reason . . . But Divinity is too sublime a thing to be tryed by the Test of our imperfect Reason, for that were to try God by Man, and in these matters may it justly be call'd Folly before God.[4]

Now if Blount meant what he says here—in praising faith and the Scriptures, and downgrading reason and philosophy—then not only was he no atheist, but he was also no deist. For it is generally agreed that a deist magnifies reason and reasonable religion, and plays down faith, revelation, and religious authority. I take it, therefore, that all scholars would allow that Blount is not being truthful here. The disagreement is in the extent and transparency of his untruthfulness. The same can also be said of John Toland. Thus in his *Vindicius Liberius* he solemnly asserts that:

I defended my self before from the horrible Charge of *Atheism*, which is not only the Denyal of God, but also of the future

[3] 'Printer to the Reader', *Anima mundi: or An Historical Narration of the Opinions of the Ancients concerning Man's Soul after this Life: According to the Unenlightened Nature* (Amsterdam, n. d.).

[4] *Anima mundi*, in *The Miscellaneous Works of Charles Blount, Esq., containing I. The Oracles of Reason, & C. II. Anima mundi . . . III. Great is Diana of the Ephesians . . .* (n.p., 1695), 31. All quotations from these 3 works are from this 1695 edition of Blount's works.

Existence and Immortality of the Soul, of the Rewards attending the Good, and the Punishments due to the Wicked: all of which I stedfastly believe. I have no Doubts concerning the Excellence, Perfection, and Divinity of the *Christian Religion* in general as it is delivered in the holy *Scriptures*, and I willingly and heartily conform to the Doctrin and Worship of the *Church of England* in particular.[5]

If Toland is sincere in this credo, then he was a fairly orthodox Anglican Christian. But I doubt whether many critics, then or now, would take Toland at his word.

The dilemma I am posing, in short, is that *either* Blount and Toland, were orthodox, rather boring Christians, *or* they were theological liars. I do not think my critics will go for the first alternative, since it is plainly inconsistent with their deist interpretations. Instead they are likely to say that the untruths I have quoted are so transparent that they amount to irony rather than lies, and that such irony in the two writers is directed only at revealed, not natural, religion.

Against this move, it is useful to recall the well-known story (attributed to G. B. Shaw) about a woman who was asked if she would prostitute herself for a million pounds. When she said that she would, the questioner asked if she would accept one pound, to which she indignantly retorted: 'What sort of woman do you take me for?', to which the propositioner replied: 'That, madam, has already been established.' The theological untruthfulness of Blount and Toland has already been established. We must now examine the texts to determine its extent and transparency. Thus I can see nothing plainly ironical about Blount's warning or, *a fortiori*, Toland's confession of belief in the 'Christian religion' and the 'holy Scriptures', since (to take Toland's statement) it seems to be of a piece with his repudiation of atheism. There is no easy way: we need to look carefully at the texts.

In doing so, I shall be using a model that I have developed elsewhere, in a paper entitled 'Deism, Immortality and the Art of Theological Lying', where I was concerned with immortality and with a technique that Toland calls 'The

[5] *Vindicius Liberius: or, Mr Toland's Defence of Himself* (London, 1702), 105–6.

bounceing compliment . . . that saves all . . .'[6] The statement
I quoted above from Blount is an example of this technique—
in its talk of St Paul's 'truly wise advice' and the 'sacred
Authority' of faith and Scriptures. The bouncing compliment
often comes at the beginning and end of a work—at least one
finds it so in, for example, Toland's and Hume's comments
on immortality.[7] In this chapter I shall be examining a
different free-thinking technique: that of denial, which usually occurs at the beginning of a work.

There is, I think, an advantage in starting with clear—even
exaggerated—examples in order to illustrate the model. From
there we can move by degrees to deeper (and more problem-
atic) instances of theological lying. Here, then, are a few clear
examples of denial from George Ensor's *Janus on Sion*, prima
facie a biblical commentary, but really a *tour de force* of free-
thought. Ensor's first disclaimer follows his discussion of
tales similar to those in the book of Genesis: 'Let it not be
supposed, however, that I compare the ethnic tales with the
sacred relation in Genesis; for though the Jewish narrative is
as extravagant as the accounts of the origin and infancy of
other nations, it is verity itself; while they are miserable
fictions.'[8] And having mentioned the word 'orthodoxy'
somewhat later, Ensor 'scrupulously' disclaims (p. 89 n.): 'I
do not refer, I assure the reader, to the clergyman's pun,
orthodoxy is my own doxy, heterodoxy another man's doxy;
far be from me any disposition to treat matters of the last
importance with levity: I may differ from learned and pious
men, but I would comport myself with gravity.' Further on
in his book (p. 103) Ensor takes us through this odd
association of biblical ideas: 'as Eve lost mankind his happy
state by listening to the serpent, it is most fitting that the
redemption of mankind should be introduced by the sense of

---

[6] D. Berman, 'Deism, Immortality and the Art of Theological Lying', in J. A.
Leo Lemay (ed.), *Deism, Masonry and the Enlightenment: Essays Honouring Alfred
Owen Aldridge* (Newark, NJ, 1987), 61–78.

[7] Ibid. 66, 70; John Toland, *Letters to Serena* (London, 1704), 19, 56, 66; T. H.
Green and T. H. Grose (eds.), *The Philosophical Works of David Hume* (4 vols.;
London, 1875), iv. 399, 406.

[8] *Janus on Sion, or Past and to Come* (London, 1816), 17; the work is signed
'Christian Emanuel, Esq.' but is generally ascribed to George Ensor.

hearing. Yet how brought the virgin forth? Aristotle says that weazles generate by the ear . . . and Plutarch adds, they bring forth by the mouth.' Now comes Ensor's (double) denial: 'I do not say that Mary was impregnated by the ear, and became a mother by her mouth; but I say this suggestion should not be hastily rejected.' (Ibid.)

In these witty denials or disclaimers, Ensor is doing three things: (1) protecting himself; (2) signalling his true irreligious position to other knowing unbelievers; and (3) insinuating this irreligious position to open-minded and/or unwary believers. Protection, communication, and insinuation are the three essential components in what I understand as the art of theological lying. The following table may be useful:

The Art of Theological Lying

	Purpose		
	Protection (1)	Communication (2)	Insinuation (3)
Intended readers	Potential enemies; civil and legal authorities	Free-thinking friends	Unwary and/or open-minded believers

It is apparent, I think, how Ensor's denials (quoted above) could achieve all three purposes. But there are limitations; for the clearer the second purpose is, the less likely a statement will be to succeed in the first and third aims; the authorities, too, will see its purpose; and only the very naïve reader will be taken in or swayed by it. This is the case with *Janus on Sion*. As its title indicates, it is two-faced; yet its duplicity is fairly transparent and hence close to irony, as one might expect from an early nineteenth-century pamphlet.

On the other hand, the deeper the ulterior aim is, the harder it will be for everyone (including twentieth-century onlookers) to see the underlying purpose and truthful message. There is no way of avoiding this. For the art of theological lying was a serious matter that could affect a person's livelihood, liberty, and—as the case of Thomas Aikenhead shows—even life. And the dangers, on the whole, were greater in the seventeenth than in the nineteenth-century. It is useful, I suggest, to see a continuum between the more transparent techniques of later writers and the more obscure ones of earlier writers, in which theological lying merges with, but is still distinct from, irony. Yet there is also a danger in this approach, that is, of anachronistically conflating the earlier free-thought techniques with the later and more obvious ones of writers like Ensor, Hume, and Voltaire.

Bearing this caveat in mind, let us look at an early work: Blount's *Great is Diana of the Ephesians: On the Original of Idolatry*, published in London in 1680. Here Blount is, as he says, exposing the superstition of 'Heathenish' religions, and specifically their sacrifices (pp. 1–2). But more important here is what he tells us—also in the proem preceding section 1—he is not doing:

Now if any Hypocrite to glorifie his own zeal, should pretend that a discourse of this nature does through the Heathen Sacrifices, reproach those of *Moses*, which resembled them but in outward appearance, he must retrieve himself from that error, if he rightly apprehends the difference: For the one justifies his institutions as directed to the true God, and ordain'd as Typical by his appointment; whereas the other (viz. those of the Heathen) had neither of these Qualifications . . . (p. 2).

I shall argue, of course, that, despite his disclaimer, Blount is using his critique of pagan religions to reproach another closely related religion—that of Christ. (I take it that the disclaimer would have been too daringly evident had Blount written 'Christ' instead of 'Moses'.) There is a similar, implicit denial in the preface to this work, where Blount asserts that 'what I have here written concerns [Heathenish Religions] only'.

By means of these initial denials, Blount is protecting himself against criticism, but he is also putting his real purpose on the agenda. This communication would have been clear to his fellow free-thinkers (like Lord Rochester) and, no doubt, to some of his Christian enemies. But it was subtle enough in 1680 to elude many, probably the bulk, of his readers. And it would be hard to prove. After all, in the denial in the proem, he produces two pious reasons. But if we look carefully at them, we see that they are feeble, vague, and question-begging. For how do we know that the supposedly acceptable (Christian) 'Institutions [are] directed to the true God', or that he had appointed them? In *Great is Diana* Blount is writing what might be called parallel theology. By exhibiting absurdities in the heathen religion, he hopes we will see (or be led to see) the parallel absurdities of Christianity. Blount also used this technique in his *Two First Books of Philostratus, Life of Apollonius* (London, 1680), where he attacks Christianity in a dialogue (pp. 96–9) between a Jew and a Muslim. In this case, the Muslim stands surrogate for the Christian.

The technique of parallel history was widely used later in the eighteenth-century, a striking political example being Thomas Gordon's *The Conspirator; or The Case of Catiline* (8th edition, London, 1721). Here Catiline stands for the Earl of Sunderland, to whom Gordon audaciously dedicated his work. My reason for mentioning this book is that in the dedication Gordon explicitly denies that he is writing parallel history. He says (pp. x–xi):

I hope I shall stand excused by your Lordship for this Quotation, because it is the only Shadow of a *Parallel* that is pretended to be drawn as your Lordship will readily observe by the following Sheets: A *direct* and *plain* Matter of Fact is told; no one Person *obliquely* characteris'd, nor any Sarcasms *invidiously* thrown in, to make the old *Roman* Conspiracy *tally* with the Circumstances of our *domestick Villany*. But as I must be acquitted to the World of This, the Hint, perhaps, might have been spared to your Lordship.

If we convert all Gordon's denials into affirmations, then we will have an accurate picture of his work and intentions. Gordon does audaciously what Blount does more covertly and discreetly. Like Gordon, Blount denies at the beginning what he does in the work itself. He is continually attacking by association (or displacement) the Christian atonement through pagan sacrifices—as when he criticizes those who think that God 'could be no otherwise appeased for the error of the wicked, but by the sufferings of the Innocent' (p. 15);

or when he speaks of Agamemnon, 'who offer'd up his only daughter *Iphegenia*; and if he could have procured one of the Gods themselves, it is very probable he would have sacrificed him to *Jupiter* . . .' (p. 31, see also pp. 37–9).

Christianity is also Blount's real target in the following attack on pagan priests, (pp. 23–4), a discussion that Blount introduced by pointing out, in effect, the need to look below the surface if one is to understand a text on religion:

not every one . . . can hear, but only such as are well able to digest and understand what they do hear. Now this kind of reservedness and secrecy being likewise observed by the most Prudent of the Heathens . . . to fortifie themselves the better against any such Discovery, they [the Heathen Priests] ever decry'd Humane Wisdom, and magnifi'd Ignorance . . . Reason teaches, that the law of God, *viz.* that Law which is absolutely necessary to our future happiness, ought to be generally made known to all Men; which their was not.[9] Reason makes no difference betwixt their *Enthusasticks*, and our Mad-Men, Reason expects some more convincing Argument to prove the infallible Divinity of their Laws, Inspirations, and Miracles, than an *ipse dixit*.

All this, which 'Reason teaches', applies equally, or even more so, to Christianity. Blount then uses the heathen gods to attack, by sly allusion and parallels, Christ and the Virgin Mary (p. 24):

Reason would suspect the power of their *Jupiter*, who had no way to reduce the *Trojans* to himself; but was forc'd to suffer his own

[9] This sentence is used nearly verbatim in an essay, about which there has been considerable dispute. The essay, 'To Charles Blount Esq. of Natural Religion as opposed to Divine Revelation', was first printed in the *Oracles of Reason* (1693) and reprinted in Blount's *Miscellaneous Works*, 197–211. Its central argument reads (p. 198): 'That Rule which is necessary to our future Happiness, ought to be generally made known to all men. But no Rule of Revealed Religion was, or ever could be made known to all men. Therefore no Revealed Religion is necessary to future Happiness'. The essay, which is signed 'A. W.', has been attributed to Dryden, Hobbes, and Blount. The Blount attribution seems the most likely, however, given his use of the major premiss in *Great is Diana* (quoted above) and of the whole syllogism in a broadsheet he issued in 1680; *The Last Sayings, or Dying Legacy of Mr Thomas Hobbs* . . . the 27th of which reads: 'That Law which is absolutely necessary to Mankind's future Happiness, ought (if the Law-giver be just) to be generally made known unto all men: No one reveal'd Law was ever made known unto all men; *Ergo*, No one reveal'd Law is absolutely necessary to Mankind's future Happiness.' See my 'A Disputed Deistic Classic', *The Library* 6th ser., 7 (1985), 58–9.

Son *Sarpedon* to be knock'd on the Head by them. Reason would tell us that *Romulus* and *Rhemus* were Bastards, and that their Mother *Rhea's* pretence of being layn with by God *Mars*, was only a sham upon the credulous multitude, hoping thereby to save both her Credit and her Life.

Blount's initial disclaimer is crucial, in short, for seeing his irreligious purpose—as is the following denial (in the second sentence), which he may have designed as a stimulus to dullish readers (p. 28): '*Cardan* was so uncharitable as to think this Superstition [anthroporphism] (which did really sink under the ruines of Paganism) was like the River *Arethusa*, risen up again even among the Christians . . . But this impiety is so far from being practised amongst us Christians of the Reformed Church, that Atheism itself would be as soon tolerated.'

I have made much of Blount's opening denial in *Great is Diana* because I shall be using it as a pattern. I trust that I have said enough so that no one will quarrel with my interpreting it as a piece of theological lying. Given what we know of Blount, the interpretation seems conclusive: Blount was clearly and consciously writing in bad faith. We are dealing with a daring work—although it might not have seemed so subversive to unwary readers in 1680, coming upon it for the first time, unaware of the author's identity. It is the effect on this unwary audience that I should now like to explore somewhat further.

In my earlier work on the free-thinkers, I saw—partly following Toland's essay on the esoteric–exoteric—a simple, two-component strategy.[10] While I continue to believe that the free-thinkers were concerned with exoteric protection against enemies, and esoteric communication to friends, I also think that they wanted to do something more, as Richard Blackmore put it, 'the unwary to incline', or as Berkeley

<hr>

[10] D. Berman, 'Anthony Collins and the Question of Atheism in the Early Part of the Eighteenth Century', *Proceedings of the Royal Irish Academy*, 75C (1975), 85–102; John Toland, 'Clidophorus; or The Exoteric and Esoteric Philosophy', in *Tetradymus* (London, 1720).

expressed it, to 'write . . . by insinuation'.[11] For what, after all, would be the point of protecting yourself if you are only telling your fellow free-thinkers what they already know? In my view, this third, insinuative, component makes the free-thinkers' writings more profound than has hitherto been thought. My thesis, to put it simply, is that some free-thinkers were, in so far as they were writing for the unwary, trying to influence at an unconscious level. They were trying to bring about a belief without the unwary reader being aware of it.

Free-thinkers like Blount should be seen as vehicles of a subversive, threatening social unconscious. In trying to affect public opinion without the awareness of public opinion, they exploited the mechanisms of the unconscious. I have argued this thesis for the mechanisms of displacement and parapraxes elsewhere;[12] I now want to argue it for denial or negation. Here the important theoretical work is Freud's 1925 paper 'Negation', where he observes that 'the content of a repressed image or idea can make its way into consciousness, on condition that it is *negated*. Negation is a way of taking cognizance of what is repressed . . .'[13] Thus Blount is able to introduce his subversive views by negating them, and, in his reference to Cardano's view, by abusing him as 'uncharitable'. We can compare this to an analysand saying something unacceptable and then adding: 'But I could hardly believe something so foolish or immoral.' Elsewhere, Freud describes negation as a 'common type of reaction to repressed material which has become conscious: the "no" with which the fact is first denied is immediately followed by a confirmation of it, though, to begin with, only an indirect one.'[14] This is also what we have found in Blount: he does what he denies.

[11] Sir Richard Blackmore, *Creation* (London, 1712), 154; G. Berkeley, *Alciphron, or The Minute Philosopher*, 3rd edn. (London, 1752), 'Advertisement'; also see ibid. 2:23 and 6:32.
[12] 'Deliberate Parapraxes', *International Review of Psycho-Analysis*, 15 (1988), 381–4, and 'Censorship and the Displacement of Irreligion', *Journal of the History of Philosophy*, 27 (1989), 601–4.
[13] Sigmund Freud, *Standard Edition of the Complete Psychological Works* (24 vols.; London, 1986), xix. 235.
[14] 'Notes upon a Case of Obsessional Neurosis' (1909), ibid., x. 183 n. 2.

Having denied that he uses insidious parallels, he goes on to use them.

Of course, I must emphasize my adaptation of the Freudian model. Blount is *consciously* aiming to arouse, or insinuate, unwelcome ideas, although in such a way that he will be protected. For Freud, the unwelcome idea arises from the unconscious (perhaps elicited by association), and it is allowed to become conscious by being negated. Blount does all the work: he exhibits the unwelcome idea already clothed in negation. For him, negation is not a defence mechanism; it is an offence mechanism.

Another caveat is in order. I am not saying that all instances of denial should be read as I have read Blount's. Context and biographical data have to be considered. It is because scholars agree that Blount is hiding things and has covert, subversive ends, that my interpretation of his denial—as a conscious offence mechanism aimed at influencing the unwary—is likely to be accepted, or at least entertained. The same is true in psychoanalysis. Consider a patient who is known to be deeply aggressive and who says: 'I dreamt of torturing *X*, but that is *not at all* how I feel about *X*.' A free-thinking text is suitable for such analysis precisely because it is not written in a straightforward way; it is hiding something. This is generally accepted; the only disagreement (as I have pointed out above) is about how deeply the message is hidden. The main differences between the material in a work of free-thought and that coming from an analysand are that the former is *consciously* aimed at *other* minds and it comes *pre-censored*. It also uses reason not as a surface defence mechanism, not as rationalization, but as a deep offence mechanism. Yet barring these differences, the free-thought text can, I suggest, still usefully be analysed in much the same way as the utterances of an analysand.

Great is Diana is a mixture of argument and insinuation. The general argument (which is, of course, submerged) is that the weaknesses of pagan religion are paralleled in Christianity. But, on the whole, what Berkeley says of some free-thinkers is applicable to Blount here, namely, that he makes 'use of Hints and Allusions, expressing little, insinuating much . . .'.[15]

---

[15] Berkeley, *Alciphron*, 1:4.

The effect of such hinting and insinuation on the unwary would be (to quote Berkeley again) 'to undermine [his religion] by slow and insensible Degrees'.[16]

Let us move on, then, to deeper material—to what is probably Blount's most subversive work, his *Anima mundi*. Whereas *Great is Diana* is (covertly) directed against revealed religion, specifically Christianity, this work, I shall now argue, is aimed primarily at natural religion. It is, in short, a work of deep speculative atheism. Of course, Blount does not say so; indeed, he denies the charge. Where? At the very beginning of the book, of course ('To the Reader'):

Methinks I already behold some haughty Pedant, strutting and looking down from himself as from the Devils Mountain upon the Universe, where amongst several other inferiour Objects, he happens at last to cast his eye upon this Treatise; when after a quibble or two upon the Title, he falls foul upon the Book itself, damning it by the Name of an *Atheistical, Heretical* Phamphlet: And to glorifie his own Zeal, under the pretence of being a Champion for Truth, summons Ignorance and Malice for his Seconds: But such a person understands not wherein the Nature of Atheism consists, how conversant soever he may otherwise be in the Practice of it. It were Atheism to say, there is no God; and so it were (tho' less directly) to deny his Providence, or restrain it to some particulars, and exclude it in reference to others.

I do not think we should take this disclaimer lightly. Atheism has been evoked, placed on the agenda, although Blount denies the charge of atheism. But since we are agreed that he lied in his opening denials in *Great is Diana*, it is surely possible, if not likely, that he is lying here as well. If this denial is like the others, then we should expect to find atheism indirectly affirmed in the body of the work. And that, I hope to show, is what we do find, although the affirmation is more complicated and disguised. It begins with Blount's second definition or criterion of atheism (quoted above), namely, that it constitutes atheism to reject God's providence. He makes basically the same point, although more colourfully and pragmatically, in a letter to Lord Rochester printed in the *Oracles of Reason* (pp. 126–7):

[16] Ibid. 1:5.

. . . to suppose a hum-drum Deity chewing his own Nature, a droning God, sit hugging of himself, and hoarding up his Providence from his Creatures, is an Atheism no less irrational, than to deny the very Essence of a Divine Being; so . . . to believe in the immortality of the Soul without its due Rewards and Punishments, is altogether as irrational and useless . . . for what need is there of an Executor where there are no Debts to pay, nor any Estate to inherit?

In short, a non-providential God is no God, or as good as no God.

Working from Blount's definition of atheism as the denial of divine providence, then, we can find a tight, although embedded, atheistic argument in *Anima mundi*. The argument and its implications can be summarized in eight steps:

(1) '. . . men eminent for virtue . . . live and dye in misery . . . whereas others, [Blount says] notorious for vice, live and die in great prosperity' (p. 113).

(2) If there were no immortality or other-worldly retribution, then this fact—(1)—would exclude divine providence (ibid).

(3) But—thank God!—there is immortality and also other-worldly retribution.

(4) And Blount offers two reasons for (3): the one he primarily emphasizes is faith in the scriptural promise of immortality. I quoted one of his statements to this effect at the beginning of this chapter, but he also offers some non-scriptural, philosophical reasons for (3).

(5) But these non-scriptural, philosophical reasons he cleverly subverts, as I have argued in my previous essay.[17]

(6) But if there are no good non-scriptural grounds for believing in immortality, then we can only believe in God's providence on the basis of our faith in Scripture.

(7) Hence, Blount either thought that we had no reason to believe in providence, and that he was, therefore, by his own definition, an atheist; or he was not an atheist or a deist, but a fideistic scriptural Christian.

(8) But as no one thinks that Blount was a fideistic

---

[17] 'Deism, Immortality and Theological Lying', 67–8.

scriptural Christian, I hope that it will be accepted that he was really a covert atheist, despite his initial denial—or, I should say, also because of it.

Although there is much insinuation in *Anima mundi* (which I might have examined), it is really the weight of this submerged argument that is crucial for a correct interpretation of the text. Here I want to bring in the advice of Charles Gildon, once a militant free-thinker—as well as Blount's friend and editor of his works—who was reconverted to Christianity after Blount's death and published the *Deist Manual* (London, 1705), attacking the free-thought that he had formerly accepted. What Gildon (p. 195) says of Hobbes (to whom Blount sent a copy of *Anima mundi*) can, I suggest, also be applied to Blount: 'there may be some favourable Expressions of God in Mr Hobbs [says Gildon] but when the Principles he lays down are destructive of the existence of God, those who are willing to have it so, easily distinguish betwixt formal and empty words, and the force and energy of Argument.'

Similarly, the intelligent reader would not be put off if a writer plainly denies something, even if he abuses it and gets angry with it, provided that the arguments he produces for it (although repudiated) are better than the arguments he uses against it. Ignorant and shallow readers are, on the whole, impressed with flat denials (or flat affirmations), with vituperation and extravagant praise—all of which makes the work of the theological liar feasible. It is the 'force . . . of argument', although submerged, that enabled Blount's fellow free-thinkers to see that their suspicions about his initial denial were justified. The force of argument was also the way in which the open-minded but unwary reader could be insidiously led or inclined to atheism, despite Blount's surface disclaimer and vituperation against atheism. (What makes it difficult for us to see this, I suspect, is that we do not think of rational argument as a mode of deep insinuation.)

Using Blount as a basis, let us now consider John Toland and his most influential work, *Christianity not Mysterious*

(London, 1696), particularly its preface, where we have the following disclaimer (p. ix):

That the well-meaning Christian may not suspect, as it falls out very ordinarily, that I aim at more than I declare, and cunningly disguise some bad Principles under the fair Pretence of defending the true Religion; I assure him that I write with all the Sincerity and Simplicity imaginable, being as thoroughly convinc'd of what I maintain, as I can be of any thing. If any good Man should after this Protestation persist to think hard of me, it must needs proceed from violent Prepossessions . . .

Here Toland is denying that he means more than he says, that his work is more subversive than it appears. I see this as similar to the denials we have encountered in Blount, Ensor, and Gordon: Toland is alerting fellow free-thinkers to his deep subversive ends, while protecting himself. For the unwary, he is also *insinuating* his deeper aims; putting them on the agenda. Toland's denial is not, however, as obviously deceptive as Gordon's, or Ensor's, or even Blount's. But I think it would be accepted by most scholars that Toland does 'aim at more than' he declares in *Christianity not Mysterious*. Toland, in short, did not really accept that a non-mysterious Christianity was the true religion—although that is what he says. Much more is insinuated; and that is surely why the work created such a furore and is said to have started the deist controversy.

But it is not in *Christianity not Mysterious* that I am primarily interested here, for it contains little or no suggestion of atheism. I want to highlight a work called *Two Essays* (London, 1695), which Toland published at the same time as he was completing *Christianity not Mysterious*. The prefatory statement concludes as follows:

So, my lord, I will conclude this apology, which I thought necessary to premise, in order to level the way to a fair reception and interpretation of these Essays, which come from one, whom your lordship knows to be well-affected to the church of England, and not in the least tinctured with atheism; a crime unjustly charged upon many excellent men, who have a more than ordinary zeal and veneration for the surpreme, all-wise, and all-powerful Being. I have travelled many countries, yet could never meet with any atheists, who are few, if any; all the noise and clamour is against castles in the air; a sort of war, like that of Don Quixote with the windmills.[18]

Toland is denying two things: (1) that he is an atheist; and (2) that there probably are any atheists. I have a number of reasons for believing that he was theologically lying in both cases. First, given what we have already seen, we really have to be suspicious when a free-thinker denies something in a preface. There is at least a presumption of bad faith. More specifically, Toland's second denial is in conflict with *Christianity not Mysterious*, where he claims to be attacking atheists (p. vii). (Why, in short, should he attack non-existent monsters?) Again, the denial of atheism was, as I have argued elsewhere, a highly developed technique among British free-thinkers for advancing the cause of atheism.[19] The technique was used by David Hume, Charles Gildon, Lord Hervey, Thomas Gordon, Alberto Radicati, among others. It amounted to a persuasive definition, in which only the negative emotive meaning of the word 'atheism' is denied.[20]

Other reasons for reading Toland's denials as theological lies can be gathered from the *Two Essays* themselves. They are very much in the irreligious tradition of Blount's work—both in content and style—particularly the *Oracles of Reason*.[21] Also, in the *Two Essays* Toland explicitly says that there are mysteries: 'the holy scripture', he writes, 'being altogether mysterious, allegorical, and enigmatical', thereby contradicting the thesis and title of *Christianity not Myster-*

[18] *Two Essays, sent in a Letter from Oxford, to a Nobleman in London . . .* (London, 1695), by L. P., Master of Arts. For the attribution to Toland, see G. Carabelli, *Tolandiana* (Florence, 1975), 20–1. Toland's concluding remark, that arguing against atheists is a Quixotic tilting against windmills, suggests Hume's similar comment on atheists at the beginning of 'Of the Academical or Sceptical Philosophy', where he compares theologians who attack atheists to 'the knights-errant who wandered about to clear the world of dragons and of giants . . .': *An Enquiry concerning Human Understanding*, in *Essays and Treatises* (2 vols.; London, 1777), ii. 159.

[19] 'David Hume and the Suppression of Atheism', *Journal of the Theology of Philosophy*, 21 (1983), 375–87. This paper and the one referred to in n. 10 above are included (with revision) in my *History of Atheism in Britain From Hobbes to Russell* (London, 1988), chs. 3 and 4.

[20] Berman, *History of Atheism*, 103–4.

[21] Compare, in particular, the translations of chs. 7 and 8 of Burnet's *Archeologiae philosophicae*, *Oracles of Reason*, 20–76, and Blount's vindication of Burnet, ibid. 1–19.

ious.[22] Toland himself has explained how we should deal with such blatant conflicts in his 1720 essay on the eso-teric–exoteric distinction: 'That the same men do not always seem to say the same things on the same subjects . . . can only be solved by the distinction of the External [i.e. exoteric] and internal [esoteric] doctrine.'[23]

In short, I take Toland's two initial denials of atheism as theological lies, lies that offer strong evidence that he was an atheist. And this is supported by the coda of the *Two Essays*. For as Robert Sullivan has noted in his recent book on Toland: 'the coda of the essay, *Jovis omnia plena*, (Everything is full of God, who is in everything), projects Toland's mature [pantheistic] cosmology'[24]—and, we can add, is an *indirect* affirmation of what was initially denied. (I might mention that this Latin dictum is also to be found in Blount's *Anima mundi*, p. 17). Final support for my esoteric reading of the initial denial is Toland's later denial in the *Two Essays*, which runs: 'the design of this Second Part is not to diminish the authority of Moses . . .' (p. 24). Need I say that it certainly is?

To conclude this chapter, I should like to make a few comments about the form of Toland's atheism. Generally, I take his avowed pantheism, which comes out most exotically in his *Pantheisticon* (1720), to be close to the pantheistic materialism of Anthony Collins, which I have interpreted as atheistic.[25] This interpretation is borne out by another dis-claimer, this time at the end of Toland's *Letter to Serena* (London, 1704), where he denies that for him 'there seems to be no need of a presiding Intelligence' (p. 234), which I see as yet another important instance of theological lying.

---

[22] *Two Essays*, 31. Toland's cognitive theory of meaning that forms the basis of his rejection of mysteries is also contradicted in his *Letters to Serena*, where he writes (pp. 66–7) that 'what he [God] has reveal'd, though not in everything falling under our Comprehension, must yet be true and absolutely certain. And in this consists no small Advantage of Believers, that though they be equally ignorant with others about the nature of a thing, yet they may have the greatest conviction of its existence . . .'.

[23] 'Clidophorus', 85. See also David Wootton's chapter in this book.

[24] R. E. Sullivan, *John Toland and the Deist Controversy* (Cambridge, Mass., 1982), 115.

[25] Berman, *History of Atheism*, 78–88, 92, 94–5, 130.

Toland also employs negative theology in his 'Clidophorus', in the atheistic manner of free-thinkers such as Hobbes and Collins: 'In conceiving, explaining, and declaring the Divine Nature and Attributes, I readily own the Symbols and Metaphors are not only apt and useful, but the last of 'em even absolutely necessary.'[26] But if we can say nothing that is literally true about God, then have we not effectively denied such a being? This, at any rate, is the way in which Toland explicitly analyses mysteries in *Christianity not Mysterious*: to say that we can believe in X without having any idea of X, is like saying we can believe in *blictri*, nonsense. In short, the God of theism is *blictri* for Toland; only the determined, material God of pantheism exists, and he (or it) is really no God.

[26] 'Clidophorus', 88; Berman, *History of Atheism*, 66, 73, 86–7.

10

The Atheism of D'Holbach and Naigeon

ALAN CHARLES KORS

Baron d'Holbach and Jacques-André Naigeon were the two foremost proselytizers for materialistic atheism among the *philosophes* of the French Enlightenment. Their friend Denis Diderot would become the Enlightenment atheist most discussed in the twentieth century, but he cared little, in fact, if his atheistic manuscripts saw the light of day, and bequeathed most of them to Naigeon, with permission to publish only those 'that would harm neither my memory, nor anyone's peace'.[1] In 1769, as d'Holbach and Naigeon were undertaking their sustained effort to atheize Enlightenment thought, Diderot was urging Hume to abandon philosophy for history, since 'We preach wisdom to the deaf, and we are far from the century of reason.'[2] For d'Holbach and Naigeon, the world might indeed be far from 'the century of reason', but they took it as their task to bring to public consciousness the atheism that they saw as the *sine qua non* of such an age.

D'Holbach and Naigeon were not the first explicitly atheistic authors of early modern France. There was unambiguous atheism in several of the clandestine manuscripts of the early eighteenth century, most notably in the *Testament* of Jean Meslier.[3] It was, however, the published, assertive

---

[1] Denis Diderot, *Correspondance*, ed. Georges Roth *et al.* (12 vols.; Paris, 1955–70), xii. 231. See also Alan Charles Kors, *D'Holbach's Coterie* (Princeton, NJ, 1976), 46–9.

[2] Diderot, *Correspondance*, ix. 40.

[3] See the invaluable edition of Meslier's atheistic *Testament* by Jean Deprun, Roland Desné, and Albert Soboul (eds.), *Œuvres complètes de Jean Meslier* (3 vols.; Paris, 1970–2). Explicit or, in a few cases, virtual atheism also exists in the following manuscripts: Bibliothèque de l'Arsenal, MSS 2239 (2), 2257 (2), 2558 (2); Bibliothèque Mazarine, MSS 1168 (2), 1183, 1190, 1192 (6), 1194 (1), 1197 (4); Bibliothèque Nationale, MSS fonds français, 9658, 13208.

atheism of d'Holbach and Naigeon that burst upon the French reading public in the generation from 1770 to the reign of Napoleon, confirming the worst fears of the faithful about their age, dismaying deists from Voltaire to Robespierre, and capturing at least the rapt attention of the Enlightenment audience for popularized philosophy. While Diderot speculated, d'Holbach and Naigeon, in their friend's terms, 'rained bombs upon the house of the Lord'.[4]

Much of that assault was similar to that of the deistic Enlightenment: rejection of revealed theology, miracle, and original sin; anticlericalism; and a portrait of the history of Christianity as a phantasmagoria of cruelty, superstition, and socially harmful intolerance. Where it departed from the deistic Enlightenment, of course, was in its assertion of the intellectual and moral value of materialistic atheism.

D'Holbach and Naigeon were neither master and disciple nor interchangeable thinkers. None the less, they did share certain deep and interrelated convictions and conceptual schema that constituted the foundation of Enlightenment atheism. They believed not only that sensationalistic empiricism was the only epistemological system to link the human mind coherently to the world, but, more significantly, that such sensationalism entailed a thoroughly materialistic conception of all aspects of reality. They asserted that the materialist ontology entailed by sensationalism began with the conception that matter in motion from all eternity was the sole cause and agent of all phenomena, including human mental, volitional, and affective phenomena. They assumed (and argued that experience confirmed) that this matter in motion acted necessarily, according to fixed and, in theory, knowable laws. They believed that whatever the purposes to which theism and immaterialism had been put historically, these views ultimately arose from the natural desires of mankind to allay and deflect the helplessness that was felt in the presence of the awesome powers of the whole—nature—relative to the part—man. The tragedy of mankind, for them, lay not in those desires, but in the dysfunctional mode of their expression. Finally, they did *not* believe their own

---

[4] Diderot, *Correspondance*, viii. 234–5.

systems to be demonstrable philosophically, but, rather, to be preferable to other systems on two broad grounds: the fewer 'difficulties' and 'contradictions' inherent in materialist as opposed to theistic, spiritualist, or dualistic systems; and, above all else, the benefits that would accrue to humanity from adopting a materialist and atheistic world-view. Their justifications of their philosophical positions were, in the final analysis, utilitarian. Moved by the conviction that the human search for happiness and ease from pain was a self-justifying basis of all ethical judgement, they derived from that eudemonic perspective a criterion of historical assessment of philosophical systems.[5]

None of these themes was new in the Western tradition, having been held by diverse ancient or early modern thinkers, and, indeed, having been posited as the hypothetical antitheses of theistic and Christian perspectives by pious dialecticians and disputants themselves. D'Holbach and Naigeon were more than familiar with such literature. Their remarkable individual libraries were treasuries of (among other things) ancient, medieval, and early modern theology and philosophy, with great strengths in both Latin and vernacular seventeenth-century metaphysics, most of it orthodox.[6] In their atheistic works d'Holbach and Naigeon made frequent use of, and allusion to, prior thought, and their references and chosen 'interlocutors' were often systematic theistic philosophers such as Samuel Clarke or Ralph

---

[5] This synopsis of d'Holbach's and Naigeon's thought, which we shall proceed to explicate, is based on the following works in particular: Paul Henri Thiry, Baron d'Holbach, *Système de la nature ou des loix du monde physique et du monde morale* (2 vols.; London [Amsterdam], 1770); *Essai sur les préjugés, ou de l'influence des opinions sur les mœurs et sur le bonheur des hommes* (London [Amsterdam], 1770); *Le Bon-Sens, ou Idées naturelles opposées aux idées surnaturelles* (London [Amsterdam], 1772), for which there exists a critical edition by Jean Deprun (Paris, 1971); Jacques-André Naigeon, 'Discours préliminaire', in d'Holbach, *Système* (The 'Discours' remains relatively rare: see Bibliothèque Nationale, Imprimés, rés. D² 5167; *Philosophie ancienne et moderne* (3 vols.; Paris, 1791–l'an II); *Mémoires historiques et philosophiques sur la vie et les ouvrages de D. Diderot* (Paris, 1821). Many of the articles in the *Philosophie* were taken from Diderot's *Encyclopédie*, and my references to these refer only to Naigeon's indicated notes, clarifications, and additions.
[6] See *Catalogue des livres de la bibliothèque du feu M. le baron d'Holbach* (Paris, 1789) (288 pp., cataloguing almost 3,000 titles), and Gibert l'aîné (ed.), *Catalogue des livres de la bibliothèque du feu M. Naigeon* (n. p., n. d.) (cataloguing over 1,000 titles).

Cudworth, thinkers who had devised 'atheistic' syntheses with which to argue.[7] This does not diminish, however, d'Holbach's and Naigeon's historical originality: their bold and positive assertion of the atheistic implication of the epistemological, ontological, and moral positions they found in prior thought; their broad systematization of all these theses; their unflinching insistence upon ethical and historical criteria of final philosophical judgement.

The first unambivalent, published, programmatic statements of the Enlightenment atheism that diversely startled, inspired, and appalled contemporaries were passionately (and rather informally) articulated in the first chapter, 'On Nature', of d'Holbach's *Système de la nature* (1770) and in Naigeon's 'Discours préliminaire' to that *Système*, published in some editions. Most readers entered a new world. There existed, solely, a corporeal nature that was the aggregate of all real things. Human beings existed as a part of that corporeal nature, but as thinking parts who wished for diverse reasons to imagine themselves exempt from its dominion. Thought, however, was the behaviour of a physical being, arising from physical organization. We were determined in our will, behaviour, and normative judgement by an ineluctable attraction to pleasurable experience and an aversion to painful experience—determinations, however, that were based upon either true or false notions of the *causes* of well-being or suffering. The physical senses alone could be the ultimate sources of true knowledge of physical nature. For d'Holbach and Naigeon, we misunderstood all this and suffered terribly thereby. Absolute naturalism was at once our reality, the antithesis of theism, and the essential preamble to any achievement of the natural human agenda of increasing happiness and minimizing suffering.

Man, d'Holbach urged, was a product of nature and wholly subject to its laws. Seeking well-being from some imaginary and illusory reality apart from observed nature had served us ill, because nature operated inexorably around and upon and within us; either we learned about it (including, critically,

---

[7] D'Holbach, *Système*, ii. 89–190, 333–5; Naigeon, *Philosophie*, passim.

about ourselves as merely a part of it) from nature itself, empirically and experimentally, or we forfeited the possibility of that happiness and diminution of pain to which our impulses summoned us. Ignorant of the real causes of our happiness or pain, we created gods, superstitions, and myths as paths to well-being, increasing our misery in the process. Helpless and fearful, we trusted to authority that could justify itself neither by evidence, by reason, nor by moral consequence, but that based its claims of legitimate rule upon occult knowledge of, and relationships to, realms beyond experience. We could begin the reconstruction of our knowledge and the search for our well-being only in a wholly materialistic naturalism, seeing and studying physical nature as the sole cause and site—indeed, as the sum—of all that affected and concerned us.[8]

Naigeon, in support of such views, confronted his readers immediately with the sternest of his conclusions, that belief in God was the 'barrier' to all essential human progress. His 'Discours préliminaire' asserted that the natural impulses of mankind were for happiness, and, thus, that we were predisposed 'to love one another, to live in peace in this world, to think diversely', traits that he saw as features or prerequisites of that happiness. Religion was a war against those natural tendencies, and its claim to authority was that it spoke on behalf of 'a fierce God [*un Dieu farouche*] whom it presents as the Tyrant of the human race'. Religion itself was born of fear, melancholy, ignorance, and a disordered imagination; its agenda was irrational or unthinking resignation, detachment from reason, and 'hatred of pleasure', coerced by the illusory fear of eternal punishments. Political power, corrupted, intimidated, and duped by the promises of religion, also found great utility in the effects of such resignation and ignorance among its subjects, and instituted 'the monstrous alliance' of government and religion that had marked human history. Only a rethinking of the human relationship to nature and, consequently, to happiness could alter such a sad state of affairs. People would seek to understand and change the physical and social condition of mankind only after they

---

[8] D'Holbach, *Système*, i. 1–12.

understood that the 'force' governing phenomena, to which
they had attributed personality, perfection, and justice, was
merely the 'necessary laws' of an amoral physical nature, and
that their actual well-being depended upon the application of
their knowledge of that nature. Atheism, the conception of a
nature without God as source or governor, alone could lead
us to seek the satisfaction of our needs and the diminution of
our pains among their actual causes.[9]

What were the particulars of these themes, and what were
the sources of d'Holbach's and Naigeon's arguments (so
many of which already had been articulated by 1770, even if
in piecemeal fashion, different contexts, and other tones)?
This is not the place to undertake a long-term history of the
emergence of atheistic conceptualization. Suffice it to say
here that d'Holbach and Naigeon were inheritors of the
orthodox typology of hypothetical atheistic thought; that
they were indeed embodiments of longer-term tendencies of
increased naturalism, mechanism, empiricism, determinism,
and utilitarianism in Western culture; that they were well
versed in ancient and early modern epistemological, ontological, and ethical philosophy; and that they were intimate with
much of the materialist and atheist conceptualization, speculation, and polemic that had preceded them. I shall limit my
own claims of influence upon them to the obvious and the
quickly confirmable, but I do so, as the lawyers say, without
prejudice to later hearings.

The sensationalistic empiricism of d'Holbach and Naigeon
was the most common epistemological position of the
Enlightenment. Like most of their peers, they accepted the
broad outline of Locke's analysis of the origin of knowledge,
and his concomitant rejection of Cartesian notions of innate
ideas that were the only widely advanced opposition to
scholastic, Gassendist, or Lockian sensationalism in early
modern France. D'Holbach formally advanced its theses
against Cartesian theories of knowledge, but the effort was
brief and synoptic.[10] The force of d'Holbach's and Naigeon's

[9] Naigeon, 'Discours' (16 pp.).
[10] D'Holbach, *Système*, i. 103–18.

epistemological views lay not in the sensationalism, but in the claim that sensationalism entailed materialism. If our knowledge was given and bounded by our natural experience, they asked, what could we know and think consequentially about *except* a world of material phenomena capable of affecting the physical senses?

Deism was useful to them here, for its epistemological, logical, moral, and historical arguments against revelation, which d'Holbach and Naigeon helped to disseminate, eliminated one possible answer to that question. There should be no mystery, from that perspective, about why these atheists translated and published so many critical deistic works, and did so with such enthusiasm.[11] As Naigeon later explained, they 'atheized' such editions, that is (he could have specified), they removed all elements of positive deism, leaving only the critique of revealed religion.[12] Revelation, as Locke himself had argued in *The Reasonableness of Christianity*, could be seen as an empirical source of knowledge about a realm beyond the physical, whose content was not empirically confirmable but whose divine source, which would confirm content, was empirically confirmable through historical evidence of miracle and fulfilment of prophecy.[13] Deistic efforts at refutation of such a claim were more than welcome by the atheists, who shared and appropriated such work. Criticism of any natural defence of scriptural supernaturalism reduced the avenues of possible knowledge of entities not subject to direct sense-experience.

The materialistic corollary of sensationalism for d'Holbach and Naigeon, however, was that there simply was no correspondence between the units of sensory experience and any theistic, spiritualist, or dualistic language or set of conceptions. They took the simple and primary experience of nature to be one of corporeal phenomena, the physics and physiology beyond which metaphysics strove to proceed. Men mistakenly had taken 'deep' philosophy to be that which hypothesized answers to unanswerable questions about what

---

[11] See Jeroom Vercruysse, *Bibliographie descriptive des écrits du baron d'Holbach* (Paris, 1971), which incorporates and goes far beyond prior scholarship.

[12] Kors, *D'Holbach's Coterie*, 45 and n. 12.

[13] John Locke, *The Reasonableness of Christianity* (London, 1695).

preceded or underlay the bodies whose existence and behaviour we experienced. In d'Holbach's and Naigeon's sense of their positions, materialism urged a modest self-limitation of human language and thought to the superficial corporeal structure of actual experience. There was no reason from an empiricist's perspective, they insisted, to speculate hypothetically about that which was not directly sensible. If ideas arose from experience, then we had no genuine idea of that which could not affect the senses. As d'Holbach wrote in response to Newton's belief that he could infer divine existence and agency from physical phenomena:

The superficial or whatever [sort of] knowledge with which our senses furnish us is the only [knowledge] that we have. Constituted as we are, we find ourselves forced to be content with it, and we see that it is sufficient to our needs. We do not have even the most superficial idea of a God distinguished from matter or from our known substance . . .[14]

The heirs of Locke, for d'Holbach and Naigeon, had not applied their sensationalist theory of the etiology of ideas to their inherited philosophical vocabulary, which sought to represent the non-sensible. If Locke and Aristotle were correct in maintaining that all ideas entered the mind by means of the senses, then efforts to represent that which was not sensible were absurd. The foundations of theology had never related to objects accessible to the senses, and only prejudice prevented men from seeing the anti-theological, anti-spiritualist, and anti-dualist implications of their principles. Words only signified when they specifically indicated units of sense-experience, all of which occurred to us as corporeal entities and the behaviour of corporeal entities. Qualitative terms such as 'beauty' had meaning only through physical entities or experiences associated with them. Words such as 'spirituality', 'immateriality', 'incorporeality', and 'divinity', however, had no objects of sense (or memory of sense) to which one could apply them. Thus, in d'Holbach's terms: 'every time that a word or its idea does not furnish any sensible object to which one can refer it, this word or

---

[14] D'Holbach, *Système*, ii. 143–52.

this idea is derived from nothing, is void of sense; one should banish the idea from one's mind and the word from the language, since it signifies nothing.'[15]

For Naigeon, this meant that theology was literally and figuratively 'nonsense [*le non sens*]'. Language existed for the identification and communication of ideas, that is, in his view, of recorded sensory experience, but a physics and metaphysics that had accepted immaterialism of any kind 'did not have, if one can express oneself in this way, the language of their ideas'.[16] As he argued in a discussion of Anthony Collins's epistemological views, words were names agreed upon by convention to allow us to communicate about the objects of our sensory experience.[17]

The immediate source of d'Holbach's and Naigeon's equation of sensationalistic 'modesty' with a purely corporeal philosophical language seems clear enough: Hobbes's epistemological views as expressed in *De homine*, a work that d'Holbach brought back from a trip to England, that he introduced to Naigeon and Diderot, both of whom responded enthusiastically, and that he translated into French for a broader audience.[18] After reading d'Holbach's translation, the *Traité de la nature humaine*, Diderot wrote to Naigeon that Locke 'seems to me diffuse and cowardly . . . in comparison with this Thomas Hobbes . . . It is a book to read and to comment upon all of one's life.'[19] For Naigeon, Condillac was, in the light of Hobbes's *De homine*, a pure idealist, and he insisted that if Hobbes's treatise had been more widely known in France when Condillac's *Essai sur l'origine des connaissances humaines* (1746) was published, the latter would have caused no stir.[20] In his discussion of Condillac in the *Philosophie ancienne et moderne* Naigeon presented the Abbé's aversion to materialistic conclusions as the weakest link in his system.[21] In a commentary on

[15] Ibid. i. 157–86.
[16] Naigeon, *Philosophie*, i. pp. iii–v, xiv–xv.
[17] Ibid. i. 752 n. 1.
[18] Thomas Hobbes, *Traité de la nature humaine*, trans. d'Holbach (London [Amsterdam], 1772).
[19] Diderot, *Correspondance*, xii. 45–7.
[20] Naigeon, *Mémoires sur Diderot* 294–5, 301–6.
[21] Id., *Philosophie*, ii. 1–7, 10 n. 1

Diderot's article on Hobbes in the *Encyclopédie*, Naigeon noted that it had been written before Diderot had read the *Traité de la nature humaine* in 1772, terming the latter 'one of the most beautiful works ever issued from the human mind', and he explicated the text at length.[22]

In *De homine* Hobbes had insisted that all conceptions proceeded from the senses, and that all significant knowledge arose from such conceptions and was ultimately 'remembrance' of sense-experience. Given the nature of the senses, corporeal entities affected by corporeal phenomena, such experience could be conceived of only in corporeal fashion. Words that referred to 'beings' unperceived by the senses were mere sounds without signification. From such principles, Hobbes concluded, a consistent natural philosophy could understand the object of its enquiry solely and wholly as corporeal, for 'substance without dimension', that is, spirit, would be a contradiction in terms, and 'incorporeal' could have no meaning at all.[23] This was the school at which d'Holbach and Naigeon studied.

It was more than possible, however, to be a 'materialistic' naturalist without being an atheist, as revealed by several clandestine manuscripts or by the formal (if insincere) claims of La Mettrie.[24] As an epistemological sceptic, one could claim no *natural* knowledge of immaterial substance, but one could accept from revelation and faith an incomprehensible God. Nominally, at least, Hobbes formally espoused this position.[25] Much of d'Holbach's and Naigeon's dissemination of deistic criticisms of all but natural theology was directed against such a position. One could believe matter capable of producing all manifest phenomena, including thought, but deem it incapable of self-existence and thus created by an

[22] Ibid. ii. 704–16.

[23] Hobbes, *Traité*, 5–54, 128–32.

[24] For two examples of materialistic but theistic naturalism among the clandestine manuscripts of the early 18th cent., both available in published critical editions, see Alain Niderst (ed.), *L'Âme matérielle (ouvrage anonyme)* (Paris, 1973), and Roland Mortier (ed.), *Difficultés sur la religion proposées au père Malebranche* (Bruxelles, 1970); see also J. O. de La Mettrie, *L'Homme machine*, ed. Aram Vartanian (Princeton, NJ, 1960), 175–6.

[25] Hobbes, *Traité*, 125–8, 140–2.

immaterial being, God. Locke's *Essay concerning Human Understanding*, to use the best-known example, had pronounced it as being as rash to conclude that God could not endow matter with the power of thought as to conclude that matter had that power, but he argued for God as 'first cause'.[26] Finally, of course, as all early modern students familiar with accounts of pre-Socratic, Stoic, and, indeed, peripatetic philosophy knew full well, one could believe matter eternal, but incapable of producing the order of the world or incapable of spontaneous motion, and thus arranged or set in motion (or both) by an intelligent God. There was no *atheism* entailed by an operational materialistic 'naturalism' not linked to further ontological claims.

Locke, of course, had urged that his empiricism concluded in ideas of nominal, not real, essences, and from such a perspective no empiricist ought to have sounded like an ontological realist, let alone an assertive materialistic monist. D'Holbach and Naigeon, however, whatever their epistemological scepticisms, certainly wrote in the manner of such ontological realism, and, indeed, made those further claims. They were materialists in several seemingly dogmatic senses of the term. Having denied any significance to the language of immateriality and divinity, they further asserted that the material substance equated with the cause of all experience and knowledge was eternal, that motion was essential to its nature, and that *all* phenomena were the result of its operations.

For d'Holbach, we 'knew' matter in some way from sensation, but imagined it necessary to add a God to explain diverse aspects of material phenomena. In his *Bon-Sens* he described such a procedure as saying that 'in order to explain what you hardly understand, you have need of a cause that you do not understand at all'.[27] That alleged need, he believed, arose from an error of the highest consequence: man had made the mistake of viewing nature as an 'effect'.

---

[26] John Locke, *An Essay Concerning Human Understanding* (London, 1690), bk. IV, ch. 3, s. 6, and ch. 10.

[27] D'Holbach, *Le Bon-Sens* (this and all subsequent references are to the Deprun critical edition), 27.

Sensation revealed to us 'the vast assemblage of beings, diverse materials, infinite combinations and various movements to which our eyes are witness'. This is what we properly termed 'the universe'. Instead of hypothesizing beyond experience that it was the effect of some cause of which we could have no empirical knowledge, we could eliminate a host of useless questions and contentions with one commonsensical reformulation: 'The universe is not an effect; it is the cause of all effects.'[28]

In d'Holbach's view, questions about the 'first cause' and the origin of motion presupposed the universe as effect rather than cause, but this was contrary to experience, for it was the combinations and recombinations of the matter before us that constituted all 'cause' as we knew it. We experienced not the creation or destruction of matter, but the inextinguishability and recombination of matter. Why hypothesize beyond that? From our experience—that is, our observations of nature—the assumption that matter existed eternally was far more compelling than the incomprehensible hypothesis of its creation from nothing. Thus, if someone asked: 'Whence came matter?', the proper response would be: 'We shall say that it had always existed.'[29]

Similarly, despite our constant observation of a universe of activity and motion, we had hypothesized a matter essentially inert and passive, receiving its motion from some 'immaterial' entity beyond it. Nature, in our experience, however, was everything, '*le grand tout*', and there was no 'outside' of which anyone could speak knowingly. Motion, once conceived as a force inherent in nature, would cease to be a problem soluble by metaphysical appeal, but would be understood as a property of mass, no more mysterious or unmysterious than extension. Whatever knowledge we could have of cause and effect, then, must be in terms of the action and reaction of matter in motion, or of the combination and separation of the parts of the material world. These were the 'natural causes' of which we actually knew.[30] 'Theology', by explaining what we did not know by 'immaterial' and 'super-

---

[28] Ibid. 28–9, 33–4.   [29] D'Holbach, *Système*, i. 1–40.
[30] Ibid. 13–55.

natural' means, was 'the ignorance of natural causes reduced to a system'.[31] Nature was an endless cycle of bodies as causes and effects, of the generation and destruction of new forms and particular entities, without beginning or end. Individuals came and went, all returning to and emerging from 'the universal storehouse' of nature, from which there came the vast variety of the beings that constitute the world. Death or extinction of an individual entity was merely a change of form, and the elements of a body that decomposed became the stuff of a new combination.[32]

For d'Holbach, experience taught that the laws of cause and effect were 'invariable': where circumstances and agents were identical, consequences were identical. Therefore, 'each being of nature, in the circumstances and according to the properties given, can act in no other way than it does'. The more knowledge, then, the more prevision. All phenomena must be understood as the determined effects of physical causes, including the mental life of mankind.[33] An understanding of human thought and behaviour would arise from the study of brain, the nervous system, the sensory apparatus, and the effects of formal and, in the broadest sense, informal social education, not from metaphysical speculation and hypothesis detached from sensible experience. It indeed was surprising that we existed as we did, but that should be an invitation to empirical enquiry, not an argument for its cessation.[34]

All of these themes were reiterated by Naigeon. The 'commonly received distinction' between a material and immaterial world, Naigeon wrote, was 'chimerical and contrary to sound philosophy: there are not two worlds; there is only one, and it is the WHOLE [*il n'y a pas deux mondes; il n'y en a qu'un, et c'est le TOUT*]'.[35] All that we knew and could know of the structure of nature, after observation, experiment, and calculation, was that all phenomena, including thought and will, were aspects of matter in motion

[31] D'Holbach, *Le Bon-Sens*, 'Préface' and 8–9.
[32] D'Holbach, *Système*, i. 1–70.
[33] Ibid. 41–55.
[34] Ibid. ii. 71–118.
[35] Naigeon, *Philosophie*, i. 441.

according to 'eternal and necessary laws'. The world 'could
not be other than what it is'. Given material necessity, 'Let
us leave nature what it is, and not speak of its perfection, nor
its wisdom, nor its goodness.' All such attributions of moral
qualities to a reality of blind matter necessarily acting according to its nature were 'expressions . . . devoid of meaning . . .
very out of place in the mouth of a philosopher in whose
eyes the universe, considered as a whole and in its details,
offers nothing that can be praised or condemned'. Nature as
we experienced it was 'the fortuitous combination of productions', and, both as a whole and in 'the infinite variety of its
phenomena' was solely 'matter and movement'. This matter
is 'eternal, necessary [and] endowed with an infinity of
attributes or properties, some known and some unknown',
and this motion is 'inherent, essential to this matter'. Indeed,
since phenomena are perceived only by means of motion, a
motionless matter is literally 'inconceivable'.[36] As d'Holbach
wrote, Descartes had believed that matter *and* motion were
necessary to the formation of the universe; matter, entailing
motion, sufficed.[37]

Two things in particular appear to have struck contemporaries in such a conceptualization: the assertion that motion
was essential to matter; and the belief that matter in motion
without intelligence and design sufficed in our conceptualization of the causality of natural phenomena. The influential
Catholic critic of both Enlightenment deism and atheism,
Nicolas Sylvestre Bergier, understood that these claims challenged deism. 'There are only two sides that the deists can
choose,' he wrote: 'either to make common cause with the
theologians', or to accept a triumph of atheism. He predicted
that they would choose the latter course, but he profoundly
misunderstood the deists here.[38] The issue posed was whether
we found ourselves in a universe whose activity and structure
led us to knowledge of an intelligent being beyond the
properties of amoral matter. Deists did indeed have deep
beliefs about that, reflecting more than a century of a natural

[36] Ibid. ii. 397–411.
[37] D'Holbach, *Système*, i. 26–8.
[38] Nicolas Sylvestre Bergier, *Examen du matérialisme, ou Réfutation du Système
de la nature* (2 vols.; Paris, 1771), i. 489–91.

theology shared with important strata of more orthodox culture.

In *Émile*, thinking back to discussions with atheists at d'Holbach's salon, Rousseau offered his most formally philosophical response to them: Newton had demonstrated that matter was inert and indifferent to both rest and motion, entailing an immaterial source of its activity; the adaptive design of nature, inconceivable as a product of chance, entailed an intelligent cause. Atheism, for Rousseau, was immoral and arrogant, but it was also philosophically untenable because of the problem of motion and the evidence of intelligent design of the universe.[39] Voltaire, as sceptical as he could be on matters of deistic theodicy, and as willing as he was to argue the purely social dangers of atheism, also found d'Holbach's *Système* to be philosophically invalid. Five of the six arguments of the *Système* that he formally controverted in his addition to the article on 'Dieu' in his *Dictionnaire philosophique* addressed issues of a materialist conception of our world (the sixth, not unrelated, sought to refute the notion that 'virtue' and 'vice' referred only to the organism's experience of self-interest): that sensationalism entailed the inability to posit the existence of a God inaccessible to the senses; that 'order' and 'disorder' were not inherent in the universe apart from our relational judgements; that matter sufficed as a first cause; that human mental phenomena did not prove the existence of a supreme intelligence; that motion was inherent in matter.[40]

These were generally consistent themes of Voltairean deistic philosophy, preparing him intellectually for a rejection of d'Holbach's atheism on substantive grounds of knowledge and conceptual coherence. In his *Traité de métaphysique* (1734) he had considered 'the order that is in the universe' and 'the end to which each thing seems to relate itself', and concluded 'that it is probable that an intelligent and superior being had prepared and fashioned matter with artfulness'. Voltaire saw the voluntary production of spontaneous

[39] Jean-Jacques Rousseau, *Collection complète des œuvres de J.-J. Rousseau* (33 vols.; Geneva, 1790), iv. 9–54.
[40] Voltaire, F.-M. Arouet, *Œuvres complètes*, ed. L. Moland (52 vols.; Paris, 1877–85), xviii. 369–76.

motion as sufficient proof of matter's essential indifference to motion, arguing that if a human being could produce a movement, then the motion did not exist before: 'thus motion is not essential to matter . . . matter receives it from elsewhere . . . there is a God who gave movement to it'. The existence (though not the nature) of the divinity was demonstrable.[41] A generation later, in his *Le Philosophe ignorant* (1766), Voltaire argued that even if matter could be understood as eternal, 'the order, the prodigious artifice, the mechanical and geometric laws that rule the universe, the means, the innumerable ends of things', all prove the existence of a 'Supreme Eternal Intelligence'. 'Nothing', he wrote, 'can weaken in me this axiom: "Every work reveals a worker!"'[42] Atheism, he wrote to Mme de Saint-Julien in that same year, was 'the greatest aberration of reason' because it denied that the order of the world proved 'a supreme artisan', which was as absurd as saying that 'a clock does not prove a clockmaker'.[43] Thus, in his poem 'Les Cabales', directed specifically against d'Holbach, Naigeon, and their partisans, he stressed the order of nature: 'I cannot dream that this clock exists and has not a clock-maker.' He could not be an atheist, he concluded, because he was one of those 'who admire the wisdom of an eternal motor'.[44]

The Benedictine Louis-Mayeul Chaudon, whose *Anti-Dictionnaire philosophique* of 1775 included an examination of atheistic materialism, may have written against Voltaire, but they agreed on the proper grounds of the refutation of atheism. Nature announced a God, Chaudon concluded, in the same way that a watch proved the existence of a watchmaker, for it was impossible to explain 'order, organization and thought . . . without a God'. The best antidote to atheism, the Benedictine averred, was knowledge of matter and its motions: 'The study of physics is quite properly the cure of the two extremes, Atheism and Superstition . . . It proves that there is an intelligent first cause, and it makes

[41] Ibid. xxii. 193–202.
[42] Ibid. xxvi. 58–65.
[43] Voltaire, *Correspondance*, ed. T. Besterman, (107 vols.; Geneva, 1953–65) lxiii. 182–3.
[44] Voltaire, *Œuvres*, x. 184.

known the particular mechanical causes of this and that effect. Physics augments admiration and diminishes astonishment.'[45]

Chaudon announced his own limits as an apologist against atheism, however, and referred his readers to what he promoted as two more systematic refutations of d'Holbach's materialism: Jean de Castillon's *Observations sur le . . . Système de la nature* (1771) and Nicolas Sylvestre Bergier's *Examen du matérialisme, ou Réfutation du Système de la nature* (1771).[46]

Castillon, in full agreement (on this) with Rousseau and Voltaire as well as with Chaudon, saw the 'physical' issues of materialistic naturalism as the critical questions dividing theist from atheist. 'In order to accord the non-existence of God with the actual state of things,' he wrote, 'these are necessary: (1) that matter exists by itself; (2) that movement is essential to it; (3) that all that exists is either matter or a mode of matter.' Unless the atheists could demonstrate these three propositions, he insisted, then 'The existence of immaterial beings is very possible.' The issue, he maintained, was one of inductive logic, not one of the heart. Indeed, he instructed, the atheists erred above all because they tended to follow their emotions instead of their minds. True religion, however, 'teaches . . . that man must repress the movements of his heart when they are not in accord with the precepts of reason'.[47]

The noted Catholic apologist Bergier, whom the Assemblée du Clergé commissioned to refute the materialism of the *Système de la nature* on its behalf, felt so confident about these 'physical' issues that he specified them as the heart of his refutation.[48] D'Holbach's fatal error, for Bergier, was to have assumed that matter was active, that it contained within itself the cause of its movement, and that it was capable of

---

[45] Louis-Mayeul Chaudon, OSB, *Anti-Dictionnaire philosophique* (2 vols.; Paris, 1775), i. 66–70.

[46] Ibid. ii. 125–9.

[47] Jean de Castillon [Salvemini de Castiglione], *Observations sur le livre intitulé Système de la nature* (Berlin, 1771), 70–2, 500–1, 529–36, 548.

[48] *Collection des procès-verbaux des Assemblées-générales du clergé de France*, vii/2, 1817–20.

spontaneous activity. These claims, he believed, were demonstrably false as matters of fact: all observed motion was acquired, communicated from a body already in motion; thus, matter as the aggregate of bodies in motion and at rest was known to be essentially inert and passive, and must have acquired initial motion from an immaterial source. 'It is a demonstrated point', he insisted; 'matter is essentially inert and passive; spirit alone is active'.[49] Where d'Holbach and Naigeon, as we shall see, required the issue of atheism and theism to be resolved ultimately on moral grounds, the official spokesman of French Catholicism insisted that the issues were empirical. Bergier envisaged the triumph of belief in God on such terms:

As soon as it is evidently proven that motion is not essential to matter, that the latter is purely passive by its nature and without any activity, we are forced to believe that there is in the universe a substance of a different nature, an active being to which movement must be attributed as it is the first cause, a Motor that is not itself matter.[50]

In brief, for Bergier, the decision hinged on which perspective, materialism or dualistic theism, made the most sense of observed phenomena. If the conception of the materialists was 'less unclear than our own', if it presented 'fewer difficulties', then 'we must not hesitate to prefer it'. It was not the atheists who insisted on such criteria.[51]

D'Holbach and Naigeon were heirs to a long and complex history of speculation about a material universe conceived without reference to God, spirit, or design. They were, their libraries and texts show, intimately familiar with seventeenth-century metaphysical debate, so much of which had consisted of the mutual polemical reduction to atheism and materialism of competing philosophical systems. For example, they both revealed detailed knowledge of Ralph Cudworth's *True Intellectual System*, which had sought to show that only an ontology including 'plastic natures', immaterial but not

---

[49] Bergier, *Examen du matérialisme*, i. 127–41, 159–63; ii. 135.
[50] Ibid. i. 154.
[51] Ibid. 155, 174–6.

divine, could rescue Aristotelian or Cartesian philosophies and their derivatives from pure atheistic materialism.[52] Seventeenth-century Cartesians and Malebranchists had argued that peripatetic 'substantial forms' allowed the agency of motion and activity to be understood as essential to material beings, and they reminded readers that Aristotle had deemed the matter of the universe to be eternal.[53] Aristotelians had argued that without 'substantial forms', Cartesian dualism had no place for 'motion', and that given the Cartesians' definitions of the essence of matter and of spirit, they logically should see motion as an essential attribute of extended substance.[54]

Further, d'Holbach and Naigeon were each students of the history of philosophy, and knew both the near consensus among the ancients on the eternity of matter and the scholarship that had explicated this theme in the seventeenth and earlier eighteenth centuries.[55] They also were heirs to the seventeenth century's great interest in Epicurean thought. While Gassendi and Bernier had (at least nominally)

[52] While d'Holbach and Naigeon both knew Cudworth's work at first hand—Naigeon in the Latin edition of 1733—the *True Intellectual System* was best known in France through Jean le Clerc's lengthy excerpts and summaries in his *Bibliothèque choisie*, published in 26 volumes from 1703 to 1713 and in a second edition from 1712 to 1718. When d'Holbach (*Système*, ii. 333–5) appealed to Cudworth in favour of ancient 'atheists' (atheists by implication for Cudworth, in fact), he did so with reference to le Clerc's synopses.

[53] See e.g. Dom François Lamy, OSB, *L'Incrédule amené à la religion par la raison* . . . (Paris, 1710), 78–118; Valerien Magnus, OFM Cap., *Principia et specimen philosophiae axiomata . . . atheismus Aristotelis . . .* (Cologne, 1652).

[54] Given the wide appeal of Cartesian philosophy in the late 17th and early 18th cents., the reduction to materialism of Cartesian ontology by scholastic critics was not an unimportant source of arguments often wrongly attributed to the Cartesians themselves. See e. g. Jean-Baptiste de la Grange, Oratory, *Les Principes de la philosophie, contre les nouveaux philosophes* . . . (Paris, 1675), 7–19, 30–6, 51–176; Gabriel Daniel, SJ, *Voiage au monde de Descartes*, 2nd edn. (Paris, 1691), 144–53; Jean du Hamel, *Réflexions critiques sur le système cartésien de la philosophie de Mr Régis* (Paris, 1692), *passim*, espec. pp. 220–5 and 330–44; J. Galimard, *La Philosophie du prince, ou La Véritable Idée de la nouvelle et de l'ancienne philosophie* (Paris, 1689), 53–216; Rodolphe du Tertre, SJ, *Réfutation d'un nouveau système de métaphysique* (3 vols.; Paris, 1715), i and ii, *passim*.

[55] See my discussion of this in 'The Preamble of Atheism in Early-Modern France', in Alan Charles Kors and Paul J. Korshin (eds.), *Anticipations of the Enlightenment in England, France and Germany* (Philadelphia, 1987), 52–3, and Alan Charles Kors, *Atheism in France, 1650–1729*, i. *The Orthodox Sources of Disbelief* (Princeton, NJ, 1990).

Christianized and sought to maintain a system of creation and providence in their atomism, they were not the sole guardians of an Epicurean tradition.[56] Then, of course, there was Lucretius himself: d'Holbach and Naigeon owned diverse editions of, and commentaries on him, and, indeed, the tutor of d'Holbach's children published a new translation of Lucretius' materialist and anti-finalist poem.[57]

More immediately, however, d'Holbach had been smitten by the later materialism of John Toland (leaving aside the issue of *its* provenance), specifically the *Letters to Serena*, which the Baron translated and published.[58] Toland had argued in 1704 that 'Motion is essential to Matter no less than Extension.' In his criticism of Spinoza Toland had rejected what he took to be the pantheist's limitation of the essential attributes of the one being in general to 'extension' and 'cogitation', and his failure to see that motion was prior to thought. As Toland explained it, thinking could occur where, and only where, matter was organized into 'a Brain'. There was a perfect correlation between the presence of physical brain and the actions we associate with thought, and 'we observe no sign of Thought in any things that want a Brain'. Motion, however, was essential to all phenomena, for it was the *sine qua non* of all activity whatsoever. Philosophers who used motion to refer only to 'local motion', the acquired motion of particular beings from which we derived the science of mechanics, might well see matter as 'inert', but they failed to acknowledge the presupposition of their concept of motion: 'the moving Force'. Matter had 'Action' as an essential attribute, as necessary to conceiving of both local motion and rest as extension was to conceiving of dimension

[56] See e.g. the influential Guillaume Lamy, *De principiis rerum: libri tres. In quorum primo proponuntur & refelluntur principia peripateticorum. In secundo Cartesiana philosophandi methodus atque de rerum principiis opinio rejiciuntur. In tertio Epicuri principia paululum emendata nova methodo stabiliuntur* . . . (Paris, 1669).

[57] See above, n. 6. Lagrange's translation of Lucretius appeared in 1768. Some scholars have seen d'Holbach's and Naigeon's hands in this edition, but see Vercruysse, *Bibliographie descriptive*, 40.

[58] D'Holbach had translated, and Naigeon had provided the notes, of John Toland, *Lettres philosophiques sur l'origine des préjugés, du dogme de l'immortalité de l'âme, de l'idolâtrie, et de la superstition; sur le système de Spinosa & sur l'origine du mouvement dans la matière* (London [Amsterdam], 1768).

and shape. It required force to produce or maintain both 'local motion' and 'rest', and that force was the 'motion' essential to matter, the understanding of which should be as much a part of the enquiries of physics as the description of laws of local motion. Local motion was an 'effect' whose cause was the motive force of matter. Rest itself was an 'activity', 'a real Action of Resistance between equal Motions'. Those who attributed this force to 'God' were faced with the absurdity of attempting to explain all local motion in terms of an original communication of impetus, and had fallen into the perennial trap of attributing to God natural causes of which one happened to be ignorant. Conceive of motion as essential to matter, and one could engage in serious enquiry, avoiding the ontological separation of cause and effect and all the conceptual and explanatory difficulties attendant on such a separation. From experience, for Toland, we knew matter as essentially active, all sensible qualities depending on motion, and the very 'divisibility' that was part of all concepts of corporeal being presupposing it. There was the material whole and its activity: that was the ontology our experience disclosed. To label that activity a substance, 'soul', or 'immaterial being', was to create an imaginary world beyond experience that was conceptually incoherent, unproductive of further knowledge, and unamenable to experience.[59]

D'Holbach embraced Toland's conception wholeheartedly, and tended to believe it confirmed by what he took to be the Newtonian 'discovery' of gravity as a force affecting all mass. Only prejudice and inconsistency, he thought, prevented Newton from positing gravity as an essential attribute of matter.[60] Naigeon found Toland clearer than earlier philosophers in his conception of motion, but, in the final analysis, too metaphysical and speculative. The issue, for Naigeon, was not how to conceive of motion, but what followed from

[59] John Toland, *Letters to Serena, containing . . . the Origin and Force of Prejudices . . . The History of the Soul's Immortality among the Heathens . . . The Origin of Idolatry . . . A Letter . . . showing* SPINOSA's *System of Philosophy to be without any Principle or Foundation . . . Motion Essential to Matter . . .* (London, 1704), 131–239.
[60] D'Holbach, *Système*, i. 41–55; see also 43–152.

observation. Since mechanics did indeed describe acquired motion for Naigeon, most arguments for Toland's position (including Toland's) 'shed only shadowy light'. Rather, 'the clear and decisive proofs of his opinion are drawn directly from chemistry'. In the 'laboratories' of the chemists, where combinations and recombinations reveal the motive force of matter in new, spontaneous motions, we saw that the evidence refuted the hypothesis of passive, inert matter.[61] In his commentaries on Diderot Naigeon argued that physiology and the life sciences provided the same evidence.[62] A materialist ontology was not only entailed by a sensationalist epistemology, but, in some real sense, it was confirmed by empirical evidence.

For most of their contemporaries, the world, whatever its substance, bespoke intelligent providential design, and foremost among the evidence for this was the adaptedness of living beings, and, in particular, humans, to their environments. To deny the premiss of a design known from experience and to account for adaptedness, d'Holbach and Naigeon turned to a diversity of commonplace theoretical motifs in the Western tradition. As the proponents of disbelief always have done, they utilized the arguments of a pious but philosophically sceptical fideism that denied our ability to discern, without faith, God's will or providence in the midst of such confusion and suffering. More formally, they called upon Cartesian anti-finalism, upon diverse strains of anti-Galenism, and upon the standard Epicurean 'explanation' of adaptation by means of the survival of a few fit forms of life from among a random diversity generated by nature. The latter account, available in countless synopses and presentations of Epicurean thought by orthodox historians of classical thought and, of course, by Lucretius himself, always had been there in the Western tradition, but it had simply seemed too speculative and far-fetched to medieval and early modern minds. A thousand Christian apologists before the *Système de la nature* had experienced no difficulty in finding such an exclusively materialistic naturalism with which to argue. The

---

[61] Naigeon, *Philosophie*, iii. 653–725.
[62] Id., *Mémoires sur Diderot*, 207–307.

force of these arguments in d'Holbach and Naigeon lay not in their originality (they simply were not original), but in their place in a systematic presentation of a convergent set of reasons to conclude in favour of materialism.

For d'Holbach, all we meant by 'order' was a moment of natural configuration conducive to our human survival and happiness; by 'disorder', a natural configuration conducive to our destruction or suffering. The imposition of such relational notions on essential nature in and of herself was risible and pitiable. We were but a moment in the eternal flux, but the narrowness of our time-frame and our illusory self-flattery about our place in the cosmos led us to believe that eternal change and natural structure existed in order to make us possible. For example, every living entity known to us existed for a while, and then, as conditions changed, decomposed, providing materials for new entities. That was an appropriate model of nature writ large. While our experience was inadequate to answer precise questions about our origins and our seeming adaptability, what we did know suggested that our planet had detached itself from some other celestial body, that plant and animal (including human) life were the particular productions of matter on this particular globe in its particular circumstances, that terrestrial diversity was due to environmental and climactic differences, and that if essential physical relationships changed, which they must, then forms of life unable 'to co-ordinate' with their surroundings would die out, and only varieties capable of that co-ordination would survive. We believed ourselves to be the king of nature, but let one atom displace itself in the universe, and it could begin a sequence that would lead to our destruction and the reign of new forms of life on earth.[63]

For Naigeon, experience should lead us to pronounce not on behalf of providence and design, but of the fragile, exposed situation of the species. Against Bacon's use of the argument from design, Naigeon replied that there was nothing inherently 'beautiful' or 'horrible' in nature. For human beings who 'coexist' successfully with nature, the universe will appear a lovely example of art and design; for those who

---

[63] D'Holbach, *Système*, i. 32–40, 56–89.

'coexist' painfully with the universe, the very same sequence of eternal causes and effects will appear dark and imperfect indeed. We wanted so desperately to believe ourselves part of a universal and eternal 'coexistence', Naigeon wrote, but the spectacle of nature revealed only the permanence of matter *per se* and the impermanence of any of its particular forms, of which man as a species was one. The beings who coexist today will pass away as conditions change, Naigeon concluded, and no one 'can foresee and determine with any appearance of certainty or even of probability what will become of these diverse aggregates and what will be their organization'.[64]

These notions of 'co-ordination' and 'coexistence' with nature were the keystones of d'Holbach's and Naigeon's argument with their contemporaries. If we limited our framework and claims of knowledge to our experience, they urged, we found ourselves part of a natural order that was indifferent to us and that overwhelmed each of us in the end, in which we were constrained by our particular natures to seek our survival, our well-being, and the diminution of our suffering. All things, including philosophical systems, ultimately must be judged from that perspective. Men had devised gods and religions to seek to propitiate forces of nature beyond their control. Theism had not worked as a system of such control; it had not worked as a system of knowledge leading to expansion of such mastery; it had not made us happy; it had contributed to our suffering, adding a superstitious tyranny, beyond natural eudemonic judgement and appeal, to the circumstances of our misery. Materialism linked us to natural causes; it provided a potentially progressive, cumulative mode of knowledge; it restricted claims upon our will to issues of natural human happiness and suffering; it removed the irrational support for forms of social and political life that did not satisfy the heart's demand for life, well-being, and ease from unnecessary pain.

In the final analysis, they staked their claims there. Historians of atheism too often have missed the profound scepticism

[64] Naigeon, *Philosophie*, i. 368–9.

that they revealed about the status of their own philosophical propositions. When the issues were drawn, they conceded that they could not know the 'real' nature of the agencies that underlay phenomena, that from a formally philosophical point of view, materialistic atheism was more a moral choice than a philosophical choice, a will towards the pursuit of happiness. Man suffered; theism deepened that suffering and, at its best, could not affect it; materialistic atheism put human beings in a relationship to natural phenomena and the quest for well-being that offered our only hope of amelioration. There was no reason to be resigned to suffering. From our human perspective, whatever moved the universe was amoral and indifferent, and we were our only source of moral concern. How absurd to prostrate ourselves before the amoral.[65] What if I am wrong, d'Holbach once asked himself, and God punishes me for having followed my compassion and reason? I should congratulate myself, he answered, for having been free, for a while, of his tyrannical yoke.[66]

D'Holbach believed that he understood the limitations of his systematic philosophy: 'It is not given to man to know everything; he cannot know of his origin; he cannot penetrate unto the essence of things, nor can he ascend to first principles.'[67] He proposed, in effect, that, in the interests of happiness, the species chooses to limit itself to 'the feeble rays of truth with which our senses furnish us'.[68] He himself, for all his seeming determinism, had translated faithfully Hobbes's argument that the whole notion of cause and effect was a mere presumption, that 'we make Remembrance to be the Prevision of things to come, or Expectation, or Presumption of the future', and that, thus based, nothing properly could be called true or false from experience, but only probable: 'Experience concludeth nothing universally.'[69] It

---

[65] See e.g. d'Holbach, *Système*, i. 1–12, 31, 54–5 n., 90–102, 224–56; ii. 56–88, 261–338; *Le Bon-Sens*, 40–4, 67–9, 84–96, 115–17, 229–36; Naigeon, 'Discours préliminaire', 11–16; *Philosophie*, i. 368–9, 441; ii. 397–411, 876–7, 897–8.
[66] D'Holbach, *Système*, ii. 299–305.
[67] Ibid. i. 88–9.
[68] Ibid. ii. 188–90.
[69] Hobbes, *Traité*, 33–8 (d'Holbach's translation: 'Nul homme ne peut avoir dans l'esprit la conception de l'avenir, l'avenir étant ce qui n'existe point encore; c'est de nos conceptions du passé que nous formons le futur, ou plutôt nous donnons au

was a constant of Naigeon's philosophy that a purely speculative atheistic materialism could be resisted by ingenious
hypotheses, and that only an empirical, 'experimental' atheism had compelling philosophical force, but he too withheld
certainty from empirical knowledge, explicitly affirming and
explicating Hobbes's argument that experience could not
conclude beyond probability.[70] He explicitly agreed with
Berkeley that fallibility began with any judgement beyond
the mere recording of the immediate objects of perception in
ideas, and he accepted—indeed, insisted—that we reasoned
from appearances, not from knowledge of real qualities.[71] He
declared himself disappointed by Hume's willingness to
remain in a state of scepticism about theism, but, exception-
ally, he did not propose a single philosophical argument
against the *Dialogues*, except to complain that they contained
nothing concrete that could be drawn from them.[72]

They offered their atheism, thus, as an attitude towards
knowledge, towards our experience of nature, towards being
human, towards seeking happiness, not as a demonstrable
system. It was a human strategy, to be employed in the wake
of the failure of the system of theism that had been tried for
millennia. This sense of belief systems as strategies, and, in
particular, of religion as a human strategy against the pains of
nature, was derived above all from the work of Nicolas-
Antoine Boulanger, the *Antiquité dévoilée par ses usages* and
the *Recherches sur l'origine du despotisme oriental*. Boulan-

---

passé relativement le nom de futur. Ainsi quand un homme a été accoutumé à voir
les mêmes causes suivies des mêmes effets, lorsqui'il voit arriver les mêmes choses
qu'il a vues auparavant, il s'attend aux mêmes conséquences ... Voilà comme le
souvenir devient une prévoyance des choses à venir, c'est-à-dire, nous donne l'attente
ou la présomption de ce qui doit arriver ... [Un homme] dit que l'antécédent et le
conséquent sont des 'signes' l'un de l'autre ... C'est dans la connoissance de ces
signes, acquise par l'expérience, que l'on fait consister ordinairement la différence
entre un homme & un autre homme relativement à la "sagesse", ... mais c'est une
erreur, car les signes ne sont que des conjectures; leur certitude augmente & diminue
suivant qu'ils ont plus ou moins souvent manqué; ils ne sont jamais pleinement
évidens. Quoiqu'un homme ait vu constamment jusqu'ici le jour & la nuit se
succéder, cependant il n'est pas pour cela en droit de conclure qu'ils se succéderont
toujours de même ... L'expérience ne fournit aucune conclusion universelle.')

[70] Naigeon, *Mémoires sur Diderot*, 207–307; *Philosophie*, ii. 704–16.
[71] Naigeon, *Philosophie*, ii. 510 n. 1; 512 nn. 1 and 3; 513 n. 1; 514 n. 1.
[72] Ibid. ii. 748–56.

ger's enquiries into comparative mythology and sacred traditions convinced him that belief in God and the phenomena
of religion had arisen as the response of a terrified human
species to awesome natural catastrophes, primarily climactic,
that had devastated the distantly ancient world. The effect of
such trauma had been a helplessness that led the species to
respond in desperate ways, projecting a punishing being, an
angry and vengeful father of nature, upon the destructive
operations of that nature. Theism and religion had been
nothing more and nothing less than efforts to reduce terror,
to appease nature's 'anger', to propitiate the source of the
floods and earthquakes that had altered the human condition.[73] D'Holbach not only disseminated Boulanger's
works *per se*, but incorporated his sense of the etiology of
belief in God into his own work.[74] Naigeon published and
explicated him also, calling him a 'philosopher' beyond
philosophy in effect, who had opened for mankind the most
important routes of enquiry and understanding.[75]

Given their view of the origin of theism in a human fear
of, and helplessness before, nature, however, neither d'Holbach nor Naigeon saw much hope for obviating the need for
it. What men regarded as essential to happiness and ease from
pain, d'Holbach reasoned, could not be taken from them.
Man was, in fact, 'a weak being, filled with needs, [who]
requires at each moment aid that he cannot give to himself'.[76]
Man makes it a crime to dissipate his fears, and 'He who
combats religion . . . resembles a man who uses a sword to
kill fruit-flies: as soon as the blow is struck, the fruit-flies . . .
return . . . and take again, in people's minds, the place from
which one believed to have banished them.'[77] Naigeon also

[73] Nicolas-Antoine Boulanger, *Recherches sur l'origine du despotisme oriental*, ed.
d'Holbach (n. p. 1761) (with many reprintings and editions from 1762 to 1794);
*L'Antiquité dévoilée par ses usages, ou Examen critique des principales opinions,
cérémonies & institutions religieuses & politiques des différens peuples de la terre*, ed.
d'Holbach (3 vols.; Amsterdam, 1766) (with many reprintings and editions from
1767 to 1794).

[74] D'Holbach, *Système*, i. 1–55, 232–60.

[75] Naigeon, *Philosophie*, i, pp. xxiii, 533–73.

[76] Paul Henri Thiry, Baron, d'Holbach, *Système social* (3 vols.; London [Amster-
dam], 1773), i. 210.

[77] D'Holbach, *Le Bon-Sens*, 106.

saw the need for religious belief as 'inherent in human nature', and predicted that this would 'submit the weak human race, in all times and in all countries, to the yoke that fanatics want to impose upon them'. He only could envisage 'occasional epochs' when, from 'particular and momentary causes', life could be less 'painful' and less 'disastrous'.[78] They both hoped, perhaps, that the Enlightenment might initiate such an epoch, but, to say the least, they did not insist on such a view. The belief that humanity could be improved in any fundamental way, Naigeon had written to Diderot in 1766, was a 'sweet error' and 'beautiful chimera'. It was also, he urged, indispensable to all those who cared for mankind but would not choose knowingly to be Sisyphus.[79]

[78] Naigeon, *Mémoires sur Diderot*, 307–8.
[79] Naigeon to Diderot, 6 Apr. 1766, in Diderot, *Correspondance*, vi. 169–72.

INDEX OF NAMES

DATE DUE

HIGHSMITH 45-220